In Search of the Argonauts

Also available from Bloomsbury

Magic in Ancient Greece and Rome, Lindsay C. Watson
Mythical Monsters in Classical Literature, Paul Murgatroyd
Tracking Classical Monsters in Popular Culture, Liz Gloyn

In Search of the Argonauts

The Remarkable History of Jason and the Golden Fleece

Helen Lovatt

BLOOMSBURY ACADEMIC
LONDON • NEW YORK • OXFORD • NEW DELHI • SYDNEY

BLOOMSBURY ACADEMIC
Bloomsbury Publishing Plc
50 Bedford Square, London, WC1B 3DP, UK
1385 Broadway, New York, NY 10018, USA
29 Earlsfort Terrace, Dublin 2, Ireland

BLOOMSBURY, BLOOMSBURY ACADEMIC and the Diana logo are trademarks of
Bloomsbury Publishing Plc

First published in Great Britain 2021
Reprinted 2021

For legal purposes the Acknowledgements on p. x constitute an extension
of this copyright page.

Cover design: Terry Woodley
Cover image © AlgolOnline / Alamy Stock Photo

A catalogue record for this book is available from the British Library.

Library of Congress Cataloging-in-Publication Data
Names: Lovatt, Helen, 1974- author.
Title: In search of the Argonauts : the remarkable history of Jason and the Golden Fleece /
Helen Lovatt.
Other titles: Remarkable history of Jason and the Golden Fleece
Description: London : Bloomsbury Academic, 2021. | Includes bibliographical
references and index.
Identifiers: LCCN 2021004219 (print) | LCCN 2021004220 (ebook) | ISBN
9781350115125 (paperback) | ISBN 9781848857148 (hardback)
| ISBN 9781350115149 (ebook) | ISBN 9781350115132 (epub)
Subjects: LCSH: Jason (Mythological character) | Jason (Mythological
character)—In literature. | Jason (Mythological character)—In motion pictures. |
Argonauts (Greek mythology) | Argonauts (Greek mythology) in literature. |
Mythology, Greek, in literature. | Mythology, Classical, in motion pictures.
Classification: LCC BL820.A8 L59 2021 (print) | LCC BL820.A8 (ebook) |
DDC 398.22—dc23
LC record available at https://lccn.loc.gov/2021004219
LC ebook record available at https://lccn.loc.gov/2021004220

ISBN: HB: 978-1-8488-5714-8
       PB: 978-1-3501-1512-5
       ePDF: 978-1-3501-1514-9
       eBook: 978-1-3501-1513-2

Typeset by RefineCatch Limited, Bungay, Suffolk
Printed and bound in Great Britain

To find out more about our authors and books visit www.bloomsbury.com
and sign up for our newsletters.

To Andrew: Argos, Tiphys and Mopsus combined

Contents

Illustrations

Acknowledgements

This search began in 2006, when I first taught the module 'Jason and the Argonauts', to help students think about the workings of myth (repeated in 2008, 2010, 2012, 2017 and 2020). Thank you to all the students who participated, particularly for their excellent research projects. Alex Wright, formerly of I. B. Tauris, sent me off, and Alice Wright took over the helm for Bloomsbury. Lily Mac Mahon has patiently steered its course. Thank you to Richard Hunter and Cambridge University Press for permission to use the map of Apollonius' Argonaut journey.

I have taken my Argonauts to many locations: Reading with Dunstan Lowe and Kim Shahabudin; Lampeter with Owen Hodkinson; Warsaw with Katarzyna Marciniak; Bradford with Steve Green; Eton College with Christopher Smart; the *Orphic Argonautica* reading group at Nottingham, organized by Oliver Thomas; Durham with Rachel Bryant Davies and Barbara Gribling.

Any expedition relies on the special talents of others: Heike Bartel participated in the Jason module; Helen Van Noorden and Christos Tsirogiannis found me a photograph of the Volos Argonaut monument; Nick Lowe helped me access *Young Hercules*; Emily Hauser discussed her work; Lynn Fotheringham and Matt Brooker found more Argonauts; Liz Gloyn shared her forthcoming book. Marie Millwood and Millen Lam were excellent research assistants. The Facebook group *Writing Buddies*, organized by Lily Panoussi, provided advice and inspiration as of the Oak of Dodona, especially Lucy Grig and Helen Morales. Friends and colleagues have read parts or all of the book and helped to improve it: Peter Hulse, Oliver Thomas, Heike Bartel, Helen Van Noorden. The two referees for Bloomsbury helped to direct it. All remaining wanderings are, of course, my own. In short, my friends have had my back as I faced this monstrous project.

Nottingham colleagues have supported and given time and space: I especially thank Mark Pearce and Jeremy Gregory for an extra semester of research leave in 2018–19. Eversden Band and Royston Town Band have kept me sane. Jonathan and Caroline have put up with endless Argonaut references and comparisons, read books with and to me, and watched films, operas and TV shows with me.

This book is for Andrew, who has kept me company on many quests, made sure I've not abandoned any crew members, and never given up on me.

Versions, Texts and Abbreviations

Abbreviation	Date	Edition or translation
Pindar *Pyth.* 4	462 BCE	Pindar *Pythian* 4 Nisetich, F. J. (1980), *Pindar's Victory Songs*, Baltimore: Johns Hopkins University Press.
Eur. *Med.*	431 BCE	Euripides *Medea* Mossman, J. M. (2011), *Euripides. Medea. Introduction, translation and commentary*, Oxford: Aris and Phillips.
AR *Arg.*	270–240 BCE	Apollonius Rhodius *Argonautica* Seaton, R. C. (1912), *Apollonius Rhodius: The Argonautica*, Cambridge, MA: Harvard University Press. Hunter, R. (1993), *Jason and the Golden Fleece*, Oxford: Oxford University Press. Green, P. (1997), *The Argonautika*, Berkeley: University of California Press.
VF *Arg.*	79–96 CE	Valerius Flaccus *Argonautica* Barich, M. (2009), *Valerius Flaccus Argonautica*, Gambier, OH: XOXOX press. Mozley, J. H. (1934), *Valerius Flaccus Argonautica*, Cambridge, MA: Loeb Classical Library.
OA	Fourth to fifth century CE	*Orphic Argonautica, Orphica* Vian, F. (1987), *Les Argonautiques Orphiques*, Paris: Budé.
VA	1431	Maffeo Vegio, *Vellus Aureum* Putnam, M. C. J. (ed.) (2004), *Maffeo Vegio: Short Epics*, Cambridge, MA: Harvard University Press.
Lefèvre	1477	Raoul Lefèvre, trans. William Caxton *History of Jason* Munro, J. (1913), *The History of Jason*, London: Kegan Paul.
Giasone	1649	Cavalli, *Il Giasone* (2012), [opera DVD] Cond. Federico Maria Sardelli, Dir. Mariame Clément, Austria: Dynamic SRL.

Abbreviation	Date	Edition or translation
Grillparzer	1821	Franz Grillparzer, *The Golden Fleece* Grillparzer, F. (1995), *Das goldene Vliess*, Stuttgart: Reclam. Solomon, S. (1969), *Franz Grillparzer: Plays on Classic Themes*, New York: Random House.
Hawthorne	1853	Hawthorne, N. (1950), *Tanglewood Tales*, London: Dent.
Kingsley	1855	Kingsley, C. (1912), *The Heroes or Greek Fairy Tales for my Children*, London: Riccardi Press.
Morris	1867	Morris, W. (n.d.) 'The Life and Death of Jason', in *The William Morris Archive*, ed. Florence Boos. Available online: http://morrisedition.lib.uiowa.edu/jason-w-images.html (accessed 17 August 2019). This text collates the draft, 1867, 1882 and 1895 editions.
Du Bois	1911	Du Bois, W. E. B. (1911), *The Quest of the Silver Fleece: A Novel*, Chicago: A. C. McClurg.
Colum	1921	Colum, P. (1921), *The Golden Fleece and the Heroes who Lived Before Achilles*, New York: Palgrave Macmillan.
Golden Fleece, GF	1944	Graves, R. (1944), *The Golden Fleece*, London: Hutchinson.
Graves's *Greek Myths*	1955	Graves, R. (1955), *The Greek Myths*, Vol. 2, London: Penguin.
Lancelyn Green	1958	Lancelyn Green, R. (1958), *Tales of the Greek Heroes*, London: Penguin.
Le Fatiche di Ercole	1958	*Le Fatiche di Ercole* (1958), [Film] Dir. Pietro Francisci, Italy: Lux Film.
I Giganti della Tessaglia	1960	*I Giganti della Tessaglia* (1960), [Film] Dir. Riccardo Freda, Italy and France: Alexandra and Lyre.
Treece	1961	Treece, H. (1961), *Jason*, London: Sphere.
Harryhausen	1963	*Jason and the Argonauts* (1963), [Film] Dir. Don Chaffey, USA: Columbia Pictures. Visual effects by Ray Harryhausen.
Seraillier	1963	Seraillier, I. (1963), *The Clashing Rocks*, Oxford: Oxford University Press.
Pasolini	1969	*Medea* (1969), [Film] Dir. Pier Paolo Pasolini, Italy: San Marco.

Gardner	1973	Gardner, J. (1973), *Jason and Medeia*, New York: Alfred A. Knopf.
Naden	1981	Naden, C. J. (1981), *Jason and the Golden Fleece*, Mahwah, NJ: Troll Associates. Illustrated by Robert Baxter.
Zeff	1982	Zeff, C. ([1982] 2003), *Jason and the Golden Fleece*, London: Usborne. Illustrated by Stephen Cartwright.
Severin	1985	Severin, T. (1985), *The Jason Voyage: The Quest for the Golden Fleece*, London: Hutchinson.
Evslin	1986	Evslin, B. (1986), *Jason and the Argonauts*, New York: Morrow. Illustrated by Bert Dodson.
Sawyer	1990	Sawyer, R. ([1990] 2016), *Golden Fleece*, Mississauga: SFwriter.com.
Zarabouka	1993	Zarabouka, S. ([1993] 2004), *Jason and the Golden Fleece*, Los Angeles: Getty.
Brooks	1997	Brooks, F. (1997), *Jason and the Argonauts*, London: Usborne. Illustrated by Graham Humphreys.
Wolf	1996	Wolf, C. ([1996] trans. 1998), *Medea*, London: Virago. Trans. John Cullen.
Young Hercules	1998–9	*Young Hercules* (1998–9), [TV series] Creators: Andrew Dettmann, Rob Tapert, Daniel Truly. USA, NZ: MCA Television, Renaissance Pictures.
2000 mini-series	2000	*Jason and the Argonauts* (2000), [Mini-series] Dir. Nick Willing. USA: Hallmark.
Catran	2000	Catran, K. (2000), *Voyage with Jason*, Melbourne: Lothian.
Riordan/Cockroft	2003	Riordan, J. and Cockcroft, J. (2003), *Jason and the Golden Fleece*, London: Frances Lincoln. Text: Riordan; illustrations: Cockcroft.
Bradman/Ross	2004	Bradman, T. and Ross, T. (2004), *Jason and the Voyage to the Edge of the World*, Orchard Books: London. Text: Bradman; illustrations: Ross.
Yolen/Harris	2004	Yolen, J. and Harris, R. J. (2004), *Jason and the Gorgon's Blood*, New York: HarperCollins.
Malam/Antram	2005	Malam, J. and Antram, D. (2005), *Jason and the Argonauts*, Brighton: Book House.

Abbreviation	Date	Edition or translation
West	2005	West, C. (2005), *Jason!*, Bristol: Eagle House Press.
Wood	2005	Wood, M. (2005), *In Search of Myths and Heroes*, London: BBC Books. Book to accompany TV series: *In Search of Myths and Heroes* (2005), [TV Mini-series] BBC2, last broadcast 9 May 2007.
Holdstock	2001–6	Holdstock, R. (2001), *Celtika*, London: Simon and Schuster. Holdstock, R. (2002), *The Iron Grail*, London: Simon and Schuster. Holdstock, R. (2006), *The Broken Kings*, London: Gollancz.
Rise of the Argonauts	2007	*Rise of the Argonauts* (2007), [Computer game] UK: Codemasters.
Pirotta/Lewis	2008	Pirotta, S. and Lewis, J. (2008), *First Greek Myths: Jason and the Golden Fleece*, London: Orchard Books. Text: Saviour Pirotta; illustrations: Jan Lewis.
Yomtov/Sandoval	2009	Yomtov, N. and Sandoval, G. (2009), [Comic] *Jason and the Golden Fleece*, Minneapolis: Stone Arch Books. Text: Yomtov; illustrations: Sandoval.
Whitehead/Banerjee	2011	Whitehead, D. and Banerjee, S. (2011), [Comic] *Jason and the Argonauts*, New Delhi: Campfire. Text: Whitehead; illustrations: Banerjee.
Gunderson/Takvorian	2012	Gunderson, J. and Takvorian, N. (2012), *Jason and the Argonauts*, London: Raintree. Text: Gunderson; illustrations: Takvorian.
Atlantis	2013–15	*Atlantis* (2013–15), [TV series] Creators: Johnny Capps, Julian Murphy, Howard Overman. UK: Urban Myth Films, BBC Cymru Wales, BBC America.
Jeffrey/Verma	2013	Jeffrey, G. and Verma, D. (2013), [Comic] *Jason and the Argonauts*, New York: Gareth Stevens Publishing. Text: Jeffrey; illustrations: Verma.
Zimmerman	2013	Zimmerman, M. (2013), *Argonautika: The Voyage of Jason and the Argonauts*, [Script] Evanston, IL: Northwestern University Press.

Argonauts board game	2014	*Argonauts* (2014), [Board game] Creators: Lefteris Iroglidis, Konstantinos Iovis and Ioannis Stammatis. Athens: AF Games.
Spence	2014	Spence, S. (2014), *Jason and the Golden Fleece*, Itunes: Early Myth.
Hoena/Estudio Haus	2015	Hoena, B. and Estudio Haus (2015), [Comic] *Jason and the Argonauts*, Minnesota: Capstone. Text: Hoena; illustrations: Estudio Haus.
Byrd	2016	Byrd, R. (2016), *Jason and the Argonauts*, New York: Dial Books.
Kneupper	2016	Kneupper, K. (2016), *Argonauts*, CreateSpace: Kevin Kneupper.
Hauser	2017	Hauser, E. ([2017] 2018), *For the Winner*, London: Black Swan.
Hoena/Takvorian	2017	Hoena, B., Takvorian, N. and Nathan, J. (2017), [Choose your own adventure book] *Jason, the Argonauts and the Golden Fleece*, Minnesota: Capstone. Text: Hoena; illustrations: Takvorian and Nathan.

1

Back-stories and Beginnings

The Argonaut myth is a tale of searching: Jason and his crew of demi-gods and heroes seek the Golden Fleece. Often, they know only its location and not how to get there. Once they have found Colchis, they still need Medea's help to find the Fleece itself. Even then, they must search for a way home, through the frozen north or the desert wastes of North Africa. This book tells the story of the Argonauts and of those who search for them. It shows how the myth acquires new meanings: the Fleece could represent gold itself, a guarantee of fertility or royal power, wealth and success in the Californian Gold Rush, even, recently, a database of genetic information.

Jason is famous for teaming up with the greatest heroes of Greece, sailing the *Argo* through the Clashing Rocks to Colchis on the Black Sea, fighting the bulls and Earthborn men with the help of Medea, witch and princess, stealing the Golden Fleece from its guardian dragon and absconding with princess and fleece back home to Greece. Jason is also famous for betrayal: he abandons Medea for a more convenient princess, and becomes the victim of her unspeakable revenge when she kills their sons. Perhaps the most influential text on the tradition of Jason is Euripides' *Medea*. In this tragedy, first performed in 431 BCE at Athens, Jason is a cowardly rhetorician, untrustworthy and despicable. When the play begins, Medea's nurse laments her terrible situation: Jason is preparing for his new marriage and Medea is about to be exiled along with her children by Creon, king of Corinth. Jason is the object of Medea's irrational desire, the man for whom she gave up family, homeland, reputation, by helping him steal the fleece. When he finally comes on stage in person, his first speech at 446–64 does not present him in a sympathetic light. He blames Medea's situation not on his own abandonment of her, but on her anger and dissenting speech. Medea replies by listing all her services to him: her help with the fire-breathing bulls; her personal slaughter of the guardian dragon; her abandonment of father and home; her murder of her brother, and later of his uncle, Pelias. Jason's reply casts her speech as a storm to be battled (himself as the valiant sailor, 522–5) and attributes his success to Aphrodite and Eros, who made Medea help him. He claims that his marriage to a different woman is in her best interests. Medea is a rhetorician too, but most of what she claims is accepted as true by characters in the play, while Jason's arguments induce incredulity. Characters other than Medea blame Jason for breaking his promises. Euripides' Argonaut story is filtered through Medea's outrage: the voyage is transgressive and destructive, and leads inevitably to murder and filicide.

Euripides' *Medea* has so dominated the tradition of Jason and Medea that Jason remains in Medea's shadow. There are excellent studies of the reception of Euripides' *Medea* but few focusing on Jason.[1] This book redresses the balance: Jason's masculinity needs critiquing as much as Medea's subjugation and alienation. We may feel that heroes get all the attention, but in this case Medea has overshadowed Jason. The different Jasons with their reinterpretations of heroism and masculinity also hold valuable lessons about ways of being a man. One study that prioritized Jason is Colavito (2014), which gathers interesting material, but focuses primarily on the origins of the Argonaut myth and symbolic interpretations.[2] Here I foreground themes of gender, sexuality, Otherness, heroism and the supernatural, all of which are particularly susceptible to variation in different contexts.

This book takes as its focus the Argonautic expedition, not the events in Corinth afterwards, broadly beginning at the departure of the *Argo* and ending at its arrival back in Iolchos, using the framework of Apollonius' third-century BCE epic poem, *Argonautica*, but not assuming it is the 'standard version'. A key question for this book is how much Apollonius' epic is central to this tradition. We will see the variety and complexity of the tradition in extant versions, both ancient and modern. Myth is polymorphous, and processes of reception and transmission only serve to increase its thousand shapes.

Previous academic study of the Argonaut myth has focused on ancient versions, such as Dräger (1993) and Moreau (1994), both important but granted a mixed scholarly reception.[3] More useful is Gantz (1993) on evidence for the early myth and Fowler (2000) on mythography. On later material, the afterlife of the myth in more recent cultures, secondary literature is patchy to non-existent: Zissos has studied the reception of Valerius Flaccus and Dominguez's *The Medieval Argonautica*.[4] Versions which had literary or artistic prestige, such as Lefèvre and Grillparzer, Pasolini or Waterhouse, Robert Graves or Christa Wolf gain some attention, especially if mainly about Medea.[5] Children's literature is a growth area in Classical Reception scholarship, but there is very little specifically on children's Argonauts.[6] Greek myth in film and television attracts scholars, but less to the Argonaut films, even the best known.[7] In our search, we will often explore uncharted territory.

This book focuses primarily on complete, stand-alone versions of the Argonaut story. In recent years loose adaptations, prequels, sequels, paraquels and mash-ups have predominated, reflecting the ways that popular culture tropes itself as myth and interacts with myth.[8] This material will form the basis of a separate, future project, so will receive less attention here. The Argonaut story also features frequently in collections or anthologies of Greek myth, but as they are not the main focus, I will refer to them only when necessary to understand the patterns of the tradition. In the twentieth and twenty-first centuries, I have mainly prioritized Anglophone versions, for reasons of space and practicality, and because they are often widely disseminated elsewhere (as with the 1963 film).[9] A much bigger project would be to study the myth in different national and linguistic traditions. The broad scope of this project inevitably means that this is a 'big picture' analysis: this first journey scopes the landscape and explores future possibilities for trade and settlement. There is much room for future research into individual versions or groups of versions, but this search charts the routes for later voyages. Without a sense of how the wider tradition fits together, it is hard to contextualize individual versions. Within these limitations, this book outlines the development of the Argonaut myth from its beginnings to the present day.[10]

In this introduction, I give a brief overview, set up definitions of myth and reception and their interactions, introduce the eight landmark versions which we revisit throughout the search, discuss how they each begin the story, and introduce the *dramatis personae*, as the Argonauts assemble. First, I summarize early literary evidence for the myth.

The shape of the Argonaut tradition

The *Argo* was already famous by the time of the Homeric *Odyssey*.[11] When Circe advises Odysseus to avoid the Planctae ('wandering rocks') in favour of Scylla and Charybdis, she mentions the *Argo*:

> One sea-borne ship alone has sailed through there,
> *Argo* well-known among all (*pasi melousa*), sailing from Aeetes;
> even her the swift wave would have thrown against the great rocks,
> if Hera had not sent her through, since Jason was dear to her.

Od. 12.69–72

The *Argo* is 'well-known': to a Homeric audience the Argonaut tale is old. Scholars have long felt that the Argonaut story was a source for the *Odyssey*, an oral epic tradition lying behind myriads of later journey tales.[12] Martin West (2005: 39) calls this 'one of the most certain results of Homeric scholarship', and suggests that the Clashing Rocks, Circe, the Sirens, and the Laestrygonians (based on the Earthborn giants at Cyzicus) all derive from the Argonautic tradition. In Homer, the *Argo* myth already involves a journey to Aeetes' country and back, the hero Jason and Hera's sponsorship. Other early sources include Hesiod's *Theogony* 992–1002, which summarizes the story: Pelias sends Jason to the court of Aeetes; he returns with Medea to Iolchos, where their son was educated by Chiron. Other early evidence is preserved by the first-century BCE geographer Strabo, such as a few lines of the seventh-century BCE poet Mimnermos: 'Mimnermos says: "Never would Jason himself have brought back the great fleece from Aea, accomplishing his mind-racking journey and fulfilling the difficult task for insolent Pelias, nor would they have come even to the fair stream of Oceanus..." and further on he says: "To the city of Aeëtes, where the rays of the swift Sun lie in a chamber of gold beside the lips of Oceanus, where glorious Jason went."' (1.2.40) These fragments show Jason's reliance on unspecified help and suggest that the story already held its familiar shape well before the Homeric poems took their current form.

Early Argonaut epic poems included the mid-sixth-century *Corinthiaca* of Eumelos, which introduced Corinthian material, and the *Carmen Naupactium*, or *Naupactia*, possibly by Carcinus, also probably Corinthian, and a 6,500 line poem on the building of the *Argo* and the journey to Colchis, ascribed to a poet called Epimenides, mentioned by the ancient commentators (*scholia*) on Apollonius. None of these early poems survives. Our first continuous and complete narrative of the Argonautic expedition dates from the Hellenistic period, centuries later: Apollonius Rhodius' *Argonautica*, a four-book epic poem from about the mid-third century BCE.[13] Since Apollonius comes after Euripides, and engages closely with his *Medea*, later traditions are irrevocably Euripidean.[14] Apollonius' Jason, like Euripides' Jason, is not a wholly sympathetic character, combining a tendency towards indecision and panic with a manipulative attitude to others.

Jason may not always have been this problematic. Another early version is Pindar: in *Pythian* 4, a choral lyric poem, from 462 BCE, thirty years before Euripides. Pindar celebrates Arcesilaus' victory in the Pythian chariot race. Arcesilaus was king of Cyrene in North Africa, a city founded by the Argonaut Euphemus; Pindar tells a 300 line miniature version of the Argonaut story.[15] It contains the tyrannical figures of Pelias and Aeetes, the powerful prophetic or semi-divine Medea, and her love for Jason. Pindar's Jason is a 'spearman' (*Pythian* 4.12), emphasizing his military effectiveness, and the feats are Jason's, not Medea's. When Jason fights the fire-breathing bulls (232–8), he is active ('he toiled through his allotted measure'), and Medea's spells only fireproof him. Pindar's elliptical narrative emphasizes the dragon's size and ferocity: '[the] dragon loomed above [the Fleece], foam dripping from its cruel jaws, huger than a fifty-oared, iron-bolted ship' (245–6, trans. Nisetich). But he then steps aside from narrating: 'time presses. I know a certain shortcut ... Medea's wiles helped him past the green-eyed, speckle-backed serpent; and she took part in her own abduction ...' Frustratingly, we do not know how Pindar's Jason defeated the dragon, or how he escaped from Colchis. Pindar's poem of praise for Arcesilaus was commissioned by a certain Demophilus, exiled from Cyrene and angling for a pardon. Jason, as a figure that stands up to tyrants, could exemplify Demophilus; as a successful leader, he could inspire Arcesilaus. In either case, Pindar chooses (or creates) a positive version of Jason. At the end of this Argonaut miniature, Pindar turns away from the story, perhaps indicating that his version is tendentious.[16]

Jason has many different faces, even in the earliest stages of the extant material. There is much we do not know about early Argonaut traditions, especially before Apollonius and Euripides. Ancient visual art shows the story's complexity and variety in its early stages. For instance, an Attic red-figure kylix attributed to the painter Douris and dating from about 500–450 BCE, about the same time as Pindar, portrays a striking image Jason and the fleece's serpent guardian (see Fig. 6.3). A muscular Jason (helpfully labelled), watched by Athena, hangs, apparently without agency, half-out of the dragon's mouth. Jason seems to be alive and conscious, because his eyes are open, but the limpness of his arms does not suggest that he has single-handedly fought his way out. There is no Medea here – perhaps Athena instead provided the crucial help. This image suggests that the oral tradition of the Jason story was varied. We need to be careful in making speculative assumptions about early versions.

There is no canonical Argonautica, despite a stable cluster of key recurring elements (fleece, *Argo*, Jason, Colchis, Medea). This might seem a big claim to make, since Apollonius and the mythographers (especially Apollodorus) are very important. However, this myth in particular is characterized by variety as much as repetition, and data from the lists of Argonauts (discussed below) show a lack of consensus about the details. This book, therefore, is not a history of the reception of Apollonius. Reception of Apollonius is only one aspect of the complex development of the tradition over time. Rather, the myth consists of its versions, which vary in importance depending on the context. If the history of the Argonautic myth is seen as a journey, there are landmark versions and other much less important, even if memorable, ports of call.

Euripides and Apollonius are the two most important surviving ancient versions, but there was a phase during the late antique and medieval periods when Greek literature was not much read in the Western empire, and the first-century CE Latin epic of Valerius Flaccus had not yet been rediscovered. In this period Latin mythographers, such as Hyginus, poets, like Ovid, and late-antique romances such as Dares Phrygius, shaped the tradition and creative engagements with it.[17] Ovid features the stories of Hypsipyle and Medea in his *Heroides* (6 and 12), and a condensed version of Jason and Medea at the beginning of book seven of his *Metamorphoses*. Most important in the late-medieval period was the prose romance by Raoul Lefèvre (1460), translated into English, printed and disseminated by Caxton as *The History of Jason* (1477). After this, the Medea tradition is strong in drama, opera and music, and occasionally Jason comes to the forefront, such as in Cavalli's very popular 1649 opera *Giasone*. In the nineteenth century, the well-known Austrian playwright Franz Grillparzer contextualized his *Medea* in a trilogy of plays, which told the episodes of Phrixus and the Argonauts in Colchis. But three nineteenth-century texts established the Argonauts as a canonical part of Greek mythology: Nathaniel Hawthorne's *Tanglewood Tales* (1853), which included the Argonauts as the final story of the twelve included in *Wonder-book* (1851) and its sequel, Kingsley's *The Heroes* (1855) and Morris's *Life and Death of Jason* (1867). Hawthorne's 'myth as entertainment' model stimulated Kingsley, who strove for authenticity and emphasized his own Classical learning. These two children's versions, along with Grillparzer's tragedy, and a strong awareness of the medieval tradition, seem to lie behind Morris's book-length poem, which established his literary reputation. This version, in turn, was particularly influential on visual art, and key versions of the early twentieth century, such as Padraic Colum's children's book *The Golden Fleece and the Heroes who lived before Achilles* (1921). In this text, the Argonauts were not just a canonical part of Greek mythology, especially the tales of heroes and heroism, but a framing narrative through which the whole of Greek mythology could be retold. Crucially, it was through the Argonauts that Robert Graves, author of the most influential twentieth-century work of mythography, *The Greek Myths* (1955), seems to have first become interested in the area. His novel *The Golden Fleece* (1944), published in the US as *Hercules, My Shipmate* (1945), also included a wide variety of inset stories. The other landmark version of the mid-twentieth century is the successful film, with groundbreaking special effects by Ray Harryhausen, *Jason and the Argonauts* (1963), directed by Don Chaffey. Later writers and artists may claim to be going back to the originals, but Harryhausen or Graves often lurk unsung. This brief summary gives a rough itinerary for our journey in search of the Argonauts.

Sometimes there are surprises: for instance, a Greek hexameter poem, purporting to be the first-person narrative by the mythical poet Orpheus, known as the *Orphic Argonautica*, which probably dates from the fifth century CE, is surprisingly influential. This text still does not have an authoritative translation into English. However, when Kingsley wrote *The Heroes*, he followed the *Orphic Argonautica* closely. Kingsley was an excellent Hellenist, capable of reading the untranslated Greek. Kingsley's version was influential on later children's versions, so Chiron's education of Jason arguably starts the 'school for heroes' genre, resulting in the Chiron of Rick Riordan's *Percy Jackson* series and TV series such as *Young Hercules* (1998–9). Orpheus features prominently in the 2000 TV mini-series *Jason and the Argonauts*. The *Orphic Argonautica*, far from being irrelevant, has a lasting legacy. A single champion can change a text's fortune and the shape of a tradition.

Children's literature is often underestimated as a cultural force.[18] The Argonaut myth is popular, along with other Greek myths, from the Victorian period onwards. Kingsley and Hawthorne made Jason part of the canon of Greek heroism. The most recent children's versions show the current state of the myth.[19] Two that stand out are the Usborne chapter-book by Felicity Brooks (first published 1995, illustrated by Graham Humphreys 1997), and the graphic novel, text by Dan Whitehead and art by Sankha Banerjee, published in New Delhi by Campfire in 2011. Brooks seems to have become the standard for many picture books that follow, while Whitehead and Banerjee create a rich and powerful visual reading for the twenty-first century. The play *Argonautika* by Mary Zimmerman, script published in 2013, is another interesting recent intervention, which has been widely performed, especially in schools. This 'adaptation' mixes Apollonius and Euripides with significant new interest in Valerius Flaccus.

Mythography, the collecting of myths as an educational aid, producing a reference work not itself considered literary, is also influential.[20] Most important is the *Library* of Ps. Apollodorus, probably written in the first century BCE, drawing on earlier sources. William Morris's daughter, May, emphasizes the importance of both children's literature and mythography on William Morris's *Life and Death of Jason*: 'Morris used no other authorities ... than nursery tales and works of reference, such as Lemprière's *Dictionary* with occasional hints from Ovid and Apollonius.'[21] Once we can outline the interplay of texts and ideas in shaping different versions, we can appreciate their uniqueness and their relationship to their own times and contexts: the intertextuality of the Argonaut tradition is a recurring focus.

Myth and reception

This book asks how myth relates to reception. How do traditions change over time? Does 'living tradition' become a series of repetitions and adaptations? Is ancient reception any different from later interactions? Is reception of myth different from reception of particular versions? To approach these questions, we need to define both myth and reception. Definitions of myth can be controversial. Bob Fowler, renowned scholar of mythography, for instance, recently defined myth as 'a story that explains something.'[22] A more orthodox definition is that of Burkert (1979: 23): 'myth is a traditional tale with secondary, partial reference to something of collective importance.' Janet Bacon (1925: 1–11), Argonaut mythographer, attempted to unpick layers of myth, legend and folk-tale from the Argonaut stories: for her, 'myth is explanatory' (4), while legend 'is true tradition founded on the fortunes of real people or on adventures at real places' (4), and folk-tale is 'wholly the product of the imagination', whose 'only aim is entertainment' (5).[23] Explanatory force is an element of some myths, but not by any means all, although many stories can be used to explain things (and the Argonaut story is used by Herodotus as part of the sequence of rapes and revenges leading to the Persian wars, *Hist.* 1.2.2). Myth is more than simply a story, because it is multiple (repeated in different contexts) and part of a system of beliefs and ideas, as well as having importance for communities. It is hard to attribute explanatory force to the Argonaut myth, but people give it significance differently in different contexts.

Scholars of myth and scholars of Classical Reception studies often operate separately, with the notable exception of Zajko and Hoyle (2017). There seems to be an assumption that after a certain date, versions 'cannot tell us anything about the myth'. So Dowden (1996) regrets the space Moreau (1994) spends on Dracontius' *Medea*, for instance. This perhaps equates 'myth' with oral culture,[24] perhaps reflects nineteenth-century models of Greek culture as 'original'.[25] Reception studies, which as a term has mostly replaced 'Classical tradition' amongst Classicists, valorizes the study of later readings of and engagements with earlier material:[26] it rebalances the power between author, text and reader, to empower the act of receiving. A weak model of reception argues that later readings are important in their own right as cultural products, and can also stimulate new readings of ancient material. A strong model argues that traditions of reception influence us to such a degree that we must understand our own reliance on them and how it shapes interpretations. Myth, in its ancient Greek form, is perceived as alive, variable, multi-media, socially important. Receptions on the other hand can be perceived as lesser, derivative, female (receptivity rather than creativity), marginalized and less valuable. I see both phenomena, myth and reception, as aspects of the same processes, part of cultural history: neither one is less complex or less important. This book explores the ways that myth and reception interact and complement each other, form webs of intertextuality, dances of creators, displays of variation and ingenuity. The Argonaut tradition acts as a case study of the complexity and vibrancy of traditional stories.

Eight landmark versions

This book takes eight important versions, which exemplify their times, cultures, genres and media, and returns to them frequently. The first is Apollonius' *Argonautica*, the earliest surviving full account of the journey of the Argonauts from beginning to end. Apollonius' poem was studied by ancient scholars and commentators (*scholia*) who give us much of our information about lost ancient material (especially fragments of Greek tragedy and mythography). His poem was influential on the subsequent Latin epic tradition (Virgil's *Aeneid*, Ovid's *Metamorphoses*, Valerius' *Argonautica*). The peculiar nature of the Argonautic story, in particular, the ambivalence of its central characters, Jason and Medea, results partly from Apollonius' combination of epic and tragedy. Alexandrian poets, writing in the Hellenistic period between Alexander and Augustus, drew on previous literature with complex, learned engagement: Apollonius was a scholar-poet. He enjoyed nothing more than playing with Homeric ideas, words and structures, as well as ideas of heroism, the epic storyworld, gender, cosmology and geography.[27] With Apollonius, we have to expect the unexpected. Apollonius also engages with developments in political power and its representation, religion and philosophy of the Hellenistic period. He represents an idiosyncratic but rich entrance point into a fascinating period of Greek culture.

The transmission and translation of Apollonius affects his availability to later versions: we have noted that Greek texts became prominent again during the fifteenth-century humanist revival. For Apollonius in particular, a first

edition was produced in Florence by Janus Lascaris in 1496; a Latin translation
by Hartung in 1550; and an Oxford Classical Text by Seaton in 1900. A reliable
translation into English was not available until that of Coleridge in 1889, shortly
followed by the Loeb translation of Seaton in 1912.[28] This brief summary of
Apollonius' transmission shows one of the reasons why this book cannot be
simply a history of the reception of Apollonius' *Argonautica*.

The Argonaut tradition has two other surviving ancient epics, the Roman
poem of Valerius Flaccus, and the *Orphic Argonautica*, introduced above.[29]
Valerius' Latin epic was probably written between 79 and 96 CE, although the
orthodox position puts it earlier rather than later.[30] This poem is equally rich and
complex, showing detailed knowledge of Apollonius, the mythographic tradition
and tragedy, including Seneca. Valerius is a successor of Rome's most famous
epic, Virgil's *Aeneid*, re-using and re-working elements in an Argonautic
context.[31] Valerius incorporates the rationalizing account of the first century
BCE Greek historian Diodorus Siculus in surprising detail: a number of elements,
such as the deaths of Jason's family, the storm, the prominence of Hercules and
the Hesione episode, match Diodorus' narrative. Valerius' text seems to have
disappeared from circulation for a long period, and was rediscovered in 1416
by the Italian humanist Poggio Bracciolini, at the monastery of St Gall in
Switzerland.[32] The first edition was published in Bologna in 1474, before that
of Apollonius.[33] The first widely available English translation was the Loeb, by
Mozley (1934), followed eventually by the loose translation of David Slavitt
(1998) and the independently published but good translation by Michael Barich
(2009). I showcase both ancient epics to see the ancient reception of Apollonius
and a Roman perspective on the myth and its significance, especially given the
importance of Latin for later readers. The imperial context of Rome shapes
Valerius' poem, both in its reflections on emperors, journeys and the edges of
empire.

Representing the medieval tradition, I have chosen Caxton's 1477 translation
of the 1460 French prose romance by Raoul Lefèvre. This translation was in the
possession of William Morris and may well have influenced him (and through
him later versions).[34] Lefèvre was writing for his patron, Duke Philip the Good
of Burgundy, who had created a chivalric Order of the Golden Fleece in 1430.
Churchmen were not pleased with his choice of Jason as model, and Lefèvre
represented one of several attempts to rehabilitate Jason.[35] His *Histoire de Jason*
was widely read, translated into English and into Dutch in 1485. The medieval
Jason tradition was influenced by Dares and Dictys (prose accounts of the Trojan
War), and seems to show awareness neither of Apollonius nor Valerius. The

chivalrous Jason is idiosyncratic, but traces of the medieval traditions remain in many later contexts. As a prose romance, it shows a different genre, and explores issues of patronage, power and religion.

The nineteenth century was key in re-popularizing the myth, and so I have chosen two versions from this period: the drama *Die Argonauten* ('The Argonauts') by Franz Grillparzer (1791–1872), with the translation by Samuel Solomon (New York, Random House: 1969), and Charles Kingsley's *The Heroes* (1855). Franz Grillparzer's trilogy (*The Golden Fleece*), first performed in 1821, had considerable influence. It is still widely read and performed in the German-speaking world. Grillparzer's Medea is both sympathetic and alien, part of a culture characterized by exoticism: his Jason is impetuous, emotional, daring and adventurous, a very different character from those of both Euripides and Apollonius. The trilogy creates a strong trajectory from the death of Phrixus to Medea's revenge on Jason, with Aeetes' greed for the fleece the central driving force of the plot. *Die Argonauten* shows how the epic Argonaut story can be re-incorporated into a dramatic structure, with a minimal cast, and episodes tightly focused on the events at Colchis. In this, it exemplifies dramatizations that meld the Argonaut story with Euripidean tragedy, such as Pasolini's film *Medea* (1969). The sympathetic portrayal of Medea comes to a climax in the German tradition through Christa Wolf's 1996 novel *Medea*.

The other nineteenth-century text represents children's mythologies: Charles Kingsley's *The Heroes* (1855). We have seen above how his reliance on the *Orphic Argonautica* changed the shape of the tradition.[36] *The Heroes* was Kingsley's first book for children, before *The Water Babies* (1863) granted him lasting canonical status. Both books are still widely read and are not yet out of print. Kingsley seems to respond to Hawthorne's *Tanglewood Tales*, writing in 'a somewhat more Classical fashion'.[37] He displays his learning, and his choice of the *Orphic Argonautica* creates authenticity: the text presents itself as a first-person account from the mythical poet Orpheus who travelled on the *Argo* and witnessed the adventures himself. Kingsley draws extensively on this Orphic version, and frequently urges his young readers to find out about the ancient world themselves. Where the *OA* omits material (most of the events in Colchis), Kingsley abridges Apollonius' account. His Argonauts feature as the central story of three chosen for *The Heroes* (Perseus, Jason and Theseus), a triptych of quest stories, which focus on initiation, kingship and challenged paternity. Kingsley represents a nineteenth-century British approach to the myth, and draws in Hawthorne by comparison: these two authors created the modern category of myth as entertainment.

In the twentieth century, Robert Graves's novel *The Golden Fleece* (1944) stands out for its influence on later versions, particularly the novels of the British poet and writer Henry Treece, *Jason* (1961), and the New Zealand television script-writer and novelist for young adults, Ken Catran (*Voyage with Jason*, 2000). Graves (1895–1985) was both a maverick and an establishment figure: he fought and almost died in the First World War as a young man, when he wrote his first published poetry. His obsession with the poet Laura Riding once led to him jumping out of a window after her when she attempted suicide.[38] He later became Professor of Poetry at the University of Oxford.[39] Graves is probably best known for *I, Claudius* (1934), and its sequel, later a very successful BBC television series. *The Golden Fleece* (1944) is another of his well-known novels, nearly 500 pages of densely printed prose, complete with maps, epigraph from Diodorus Siculus in Greek and historical appendix. The epigraph shows his fundamentally rationalizing approach: Diodorus uses the inconsistency of ancient myth to claim licence in re-inventing it himself, and Graves is his successor. Graves combines rationalization with a fascination for mythical variants (often late and obscure). In contrast, the 'Invocation' emphasizes Graves's sense of mystical connection to the myth, through his physical location on Majorca, imagined as site of goddess worship and grave of the Argonaut Ancaeus. This novel is important for understanding Graves as both mystic and mythographer, closely connected to both *The White Goddess* (1948) and *The Greek Myths* (1955). All of these works are still widely read, and scriptwriters as well as novelists and children's authors will have referred to Graves's idiosyncratic version.

The two major Anglophone film versions are also central texts: first, the 1963 *Jason and the Argonauts*, produced, inspired and with visual effects by the legendary Ray Harryhausen, directed by Don Chaffey, with a screenplay by Jan Read and Beverley Cross, himself a well-respected playwright. This film is revered for its ground-breaking special effects, especially the battle between Jason and the skeleton Earthborns that forms the climactic action sequence. The score by Bernard Hermann is also a classic. This version significantly re-shapes the story to suppress Medea's agency, creating a stronger Jason (played by the American actor Todd Armstrong), who purposefully organizes his crew in a successful expedition against an orientalized enemy, and finishes with the happy couple sailing into the sunset. The 1963 film was a showcase for Ray Harryhausen's monsters, especially the tragic Talos and the multi-headed hydra which guards the fleece. The script has an ambivalent relationship with the supernatural, making the gods a central part of the action, but presenting Jason as a sceptic, challenging their power. The influence of its imagery can be clearly seen, especially in the prevalence of the name Phineas and the change of Earthborn men into skeletons, throughout the later twentieth and twenty-first century.

The much less well-known and studied TV mini-series from 2000, also entitled *Jason and the Argonauts*, adds a twenty-first century element. Although not well-received by fans, (felt to be 'not as good as' the 1963 'classic'), it won several awards at the time (for production design, visual effects, sound and make-up). It starred Jason London as an earnest, youthful and often hapless Jason. The two episodes were directed by Nick Willing, in the wake of a successful Hallmark *Odyssey*, and co-written by Matthew Faulk and Mark Skeet. The longer format covers more mythological episodes, aimed more squarely at an adult audience. The Lemnian women episode, for instance, is prominent, and the return to Iolchos allows Medea more agency than in the 1963 film. The plot shows similarities with Morris's epic poem, although this under-rated version has its own distinctive vision for the twenty-first century. As well as a sub-plot focusing on Atalanta, it features a black Orpheus. This version, too, influences subsequent television (such as the 2013–15 series *Atlantis*), graphic novels and children's literature, showing that despite the mixed critical reception it has clear cultural importance.

Beginnings

A goatherd sleeps: suddenly he wakes to see armed men running towards him. He runs past a busy sea-shore scene, shouting warnings. We follow the violently charging troops through the gates as they cut people down and break through defences. A temple: where a woman prays for help to a statue of a goddess. A young boy looks around in confusion. The conquering invader enters, removes his helmet: he is the king's brother, and embraces him, only to stab him in the back. He takes the boy, but, before he can kill him, a wounded soldier jumps up, grabs him and races out. Jason wakes up.

This is how the 2000 TV mini-series begins, closely shadowing the opening of the 1963 Harryhausen film, with its nearly identical shot of the usurped king's daughter praying to Hera. King Pelias of Iolchos is this usurper, who orders the Argonaut expedition to remove Jason and his challenge for the throne; many versions begin from Pelias and his back-story. This dramatic opening, with its strong hook, and polarization between the innocent baby Jason and his murderous uncle, is especially filmic. Pelias as evil usurper of his brother Aeson is surprisingly uniform in later versions from Lefèvre (where he is called Peleus) to Zimmerman.[40] This contrasts with early myth, where he was variously portrayed as killer of his mother's tormentor in Hera's temple,[41] regent, or even king of Thessaly in his own right, simply envious of Jason's success.[42] Pindar *Pythian* 4 popularizes Pelias the usurper, followed influentially by both key nineteenth-century children's versions. By looking at the beginnings of all our landmark versions, starting from the earliest back-story and moving into the different initial scenes of the *Argonautica* itself, I draw out recurring themes and ideas, and further introduce the eight versions.

In both the 1963 and 2000 films, Pelias commits sacrilege against Hera, earning her hatred: the beginnings focus on prophecy, temples and divine statues, emphasizing the role of the gods in the narrative. Robert Graves's *Golden Fleece* also begins from the gods: the elderly Argonaut Ancaeus seeks refuge with the Nymph of the Orange Grove, tells her of the abandonment of Mother Goddess worship by the Greeks, and is executed as a dangerous heretic. This frame of matriarchal theocracy versus patriarchal Olympians dominates Graves's interpretation, which presents the Argonaut myth as part of a long sweep of human development.

The other element of back-story which is often prominent at the beginnings of versions is that of the Golden Fleece itself. The Fleece belonged to the golden ram which rescued two young children, Phrixus and Helle, from being sacrificed by their father. King Athamas of Thessaly had married again and Ino, his second wife, wanted to destroy her young stepchildren. She fabricates a famine and an oracle demanding their sacrifice. At the last minute their mother Nephele, a cloud goddess, sends down a miraculous golden ram to whisk them away. They fly to Colchis, but Helle falls into the sea, later known as the 'Hellespont' (Helle's sea).[43] Graves creates a new version in which Ino (later to become Leukothea, the White Goddess) is a hero, resisting Athamas' destruction of traditional rites. She herself both condemns and rescues Phrixus and Helle, showing the double nature of female power in Graves's imagination, both destructive and protective.

Phrixus forms the beginning for Grillparzer's *The Golden Fleece* (1821). In both Apollodorus and Hyginus, ancient mythographers, Phrixus arrives in Colchis, sacrifices the ram and marries Aeetes' daughter Chalciope. This version probably summarizes the plot of an ancient tragic play, which no longer survives. Phrixus later stars in Grillparzer's one-act play *The Guest*, first play in his tragic trilogy. A proud Amazon-huntress, Medea must help her father kill Phrixus, so he can steal the fleece, which Phrixus himself took from a statue of the Colchian Zeus, Peronto, at Delphi. In Grillparzer's trilogy, Phrixus and Jason double and resemble each other, fast-talking, flirtatious, acquisitive. Later children's versions tend to begin with Phrixus, including Kingsley, Brooks, Riordan, the graphic novel of Yomtov. Several others have Pelias tell the story at his feast for Jason (Seraillier, Zarabouka, Whitehead).

Other versions use the figure of Jason as their central organizing principle. Lefèvre's Medieval *History of Jason*, for instance, begins with Jason's birth, his parents' childlessness, his father's old age and his mother's death in childbirth. Lefèvre focuses on Jason's life, and recuperates him as hero: the miraculous child born late in life is familiar from the Old Testament (Isaac, Jacob and Esau, Samuel), associating Jason with respectable religious heroes. William Morris begins his *Life and Death of Jason* similarly, with Jason's miraculous birth to elderly parents. Treece's 1961 novel *Jason* starts with his conception: Perimede, his priestess mother, frustrated by Aeson's infertility, seduces a Cretan slave. Treece throughout is fascinated by female sexuality and deceptiveness.

Jason's education is also a prominent starting point, particularly in children's literature. The first sentence of Hawthorne's chapter on 'The Golden Fleece' in *Tanglewood Tales* is: 'When Jason, the son of the dethroned King of Iolchos, was a little boy, he was sent away from his parents, and placed under the queerest schoolmaster that you ever heard of' (201). Chiron has been part of the myth of Jason from its earliest origins. The centaur is both teacher and healer in the *Iliad*, where he teaches healing to Atreus and Achilles (4.217–19; 11.830–2). In Hesiod (fr. 40 Merkelbach/West) and Pindar (*Nemean* 3.53–4; *Pythian* 4.102–3) he is the teacher of Jason.[44] In Kingsley's *The Heroes*, our key version, Aeson takes Jason to Chiron's cave. Aeson himself holds back, while the boy listens to Chiron's singing, and is welcomed into his school for heroes. The other pupils include Aeneas, Herakles, Peleus, Coeneus and Asclepius, each praised for heroic achievements. In the next chapter, Jason has grown up and insists on leaving Chiron to take back his kingdom. This moment, illustrated most famously by William Russell Flint, depicts Chiron and Jason looking out together over the Greek seascape, evoking Kingsley's emphasis on heroism as exploration and conquest. In the fascination with Chiron and education, children's literature and film (Pasolini's *Medea*, 2000 TV mini-series) follow Kingsley. The Argonaut myth from Pindar onwards always had a significant concern with education and personal growth, reflecting interest in young people's entry into society ('initiation').

As Jason travels to Iolchos to claim his usurped kingdom, he encounters Hera at the flooded river Anauros and carries her across. Hawthorne and Kingsley and both films also give this scene prominence, and it remains part of the canonical version in current children's literature. The first scene of Zimmerman's 2013 play is the crossing of Anauros, introducing both Hera and Athena as Jason's patrons, who stay on stage throughout. Athena pins down Jason's sandal and Hera insists that he leave it behind; stage directions indicate that he remains one-sandalled throughout.

The prophecy of the 'one-sandalled man' (*oiopedilon*, AR 1.7) was early: Apollonius mentions it (5–7), as he kicks off the narrative after a brief four line invocation to Apollo, god of poetry. Both Pindar and Pherecydes include it. In this motif, Pelias is terrified by a prophecy that says a one-sandalled man will either kill or depose him. The 'one-sandalled man' is distinctive enough to the Argonaut myth that scholars use it to identify Jason in ancient visual art. This motif evokes anthropological interpretation: scholars associate wearing one sandal with initiation rites.[45] A well-preserved wall-painting from Pompeii shows the confrontation between Pelias and Jason with his one sandal, in the House of Jason (Fig. 1.1).[46] Jason, on the right, approaches a table where an

Fig. 1.1 Fresco from Pompeii of Pelias and Jason with his one sandal. House of Jason, Pompeii (IX, 5, 18–21, triclinio f), first century CE. Naples National Archaeological Museum. Photo by Marie-Lan Nguyen. Available at: https://commons.wikimedia.org/wiki/File:Pelias_meets_Jason_MAN_Napoli_Inv111436.jpg (accessed 22 August 2019).

attendant places a vessel, staring at him. Jason wears only one sandal. At the top of stairs, in front of architectural detail, suggesting an imposing palace, stands Pelias, with a daughter on either side, all shocked by Jason's arrival. Pelias is bearded and elderly, in Greek dress. Another attendant brings a bull, presumably for sacrifice.

There are two main versions of the confrontation scene: that of Pindar and that of Pherecydes, an Athenian mythographer probably writing at around 465 BCE. In Pindar (*Pythian* 4.78–169), Jason encounters Pelias in the marketplace of Iolchos. He declares he is the son of Aeson, come to take the throne back from 'lawless Pelias' (101). His family welcome and feast him, and take him to Pelias' palace where he demands the kingship. Both men remain calm, but Pelias claims that Phrixus came to him in a dream, and ordered the Golden Fleece returned from Colchis. If Jason returns with the fleece, he will hand over the throne, and Jason agrees to this bargain.

Pherecydes preserves an older version (or possibly combines more than one, since this was his practice) in which Pelias is legitimate king of Iolchos and Jason (simply?) a keen farmer. Pelias is sacrificing to Poseidon, when he sees Jason, who lost a sandal ploughing near Anauros. Pelias asks him what he would do with a citizen prophesied to kill him. Jason replies that he would send him to fetch the Golden Fleece, an idea put into his mind by Hera, Pherecydes says, who wanted to bring Medea back to Iolchos for vengeance on Pelias. Jason, then, is not always a prince returning to claim his throne, and this makes more sense of the return to Iolchos. Even after achieving the mission and killing Pelias, Jason often still does not become king of Iolchos, instead exiled in Corinth. If Jason was never legitimate heir, but rather a potential usurper, the story becomes darker and more complex.

The Pompeian wall-painting matches Pherecydes' version, with sacrifice at the palace, in contrast to Pindar's marketplace meeting, surrounded by friends and family. The wall-painting is set in a room with two other mythological scenes, moments of confrontation and potential violence: Achilles falling in love with Polyxena, causing her sacrifice on his tomb; a third, badly damaged, painting may show Pentheus rejecting Dionysus, leading to Pentheus' dismemberment by his own mother (the subject of Euripides' *Bacchae*). This combination of paintings suggests a focus on Pelias' disrespect for Hera, and his destruction by Medea: her orchestration of Pelias' dismemberment and boiling by his daughters, who hope to rejuvenate him, tying the departure of the *Argo* to its return, the beginning to the Iolchan end.

The Argonauts Assemble

To seek the Golden Fleece, Jason needs a crew and a ship. Both *Argo* and Argonauts are defining elements of this myth: the heroic sailors (*nautai*) are named after the miraculous ship in which they sail (*Argo*). None of the surviving ancient epics are called after Jason: the poems of Apollonius, Valerius and 'Orpheus' are all called *Argonautica* ('Argonaut stories'); the fragmentary poem of Varro from Augustan Rome is *Argonautae*.[47] This is Apollonius' beginning: a catalogue of the Argonauts. What makes this story special, as with *Avengers Assemble* (2012), is the gathering together of many greatest heroes in a storyworld in a single awe-inspiring endeavour.

There is enormous variation in the number and composition of the Argonauts. This section introduces the Argonauts, their gathering and membership. It sets up the *dramatis personae* for the story, and gives a different overview of the tradition. Which Argonauts join the tradition when? Which are the most popular, where versions select only a few? What do selections of Argonauts tell us about the position of various versions in the tradition?

In the *Orphic Argonautica*, the extended description of Jason's recruitment of Orpheus suggests a non-extant version in which Jason travelled to recruit former students of Chiron and guest-friends. Orpheus is the first Argonaut in Apollonius' catalogue, joining at the request of Chiron, and is also in one of the earliest images of the *Argo*, a sculptural relief on a *metope* from the Sikyonian treasury at Delphi (around mid-sixth century BCE, fragmentary). It shows two figures standing on the deck holding lyres, next to another figure, now missing, and two figures on horseback below the ship. Inscriptions identify one horseman as Polydeuces and one lyre player as Orpheus, so the other horseman is probably Castor. The other lyre player might be Philammon, mentioned by Pherecydes, but not present in later traditions. Orpheus, Castor and Pollux, then, were key Argonauts at this very early stage.

The overall number of Argonauts varies among ancient sources: Apollonius includes 53 (presumably Tiphys as helmsman, Orpheus as musician and either Argos or Jason did not row, since fifty-oared ships were one standard size), while his contemporary Theocritus, who wrote two Argonautic miniatures, implies 30 (*Idyll* 13.75). Among ancient mythographers, Apollodorus has 44, and Hyginus seems to combine multiple traditions with 67. I have found 112 different names in the tradition (not counting variant spellings of the same name). Catalogues are a feature of ancient (particularly epic) poetry, one that ancient audiences seemed to particularly enjoy and value. Complete crew lists exist in Apollonius,

Valerius and the *Orphic Argonautica*. Ancient marginal comments attest to complete lists in two lost tragedies, Aeschylus' *Kabeiroi* and Sophocles' *Lemnian Women*. Pindar gives a selection, as do most modern accounts, and indeed Lefèvre, who only mentions Jason, Hercules, Theseus, Argus and Mopsius (*sic*). Morris positions himself as an epic poet with a complete list in book 3.[48] Mythography also loves lists, and Graves in both novel and *The Greek Myths* gives two different catalogues.

There may never have been a canonical list. Even Apollonius and Apollodorus have significant variation, though these texts are elsewhere similar in many details. Ancient Greek cities included their own legendary characters; families added in their forebears. Eumelos, for instance, writing in the Corinthian sphere of influence, probably in the seventh or sixth century BCE, would have included Corinthians. There is a significant Athenian contingent: if not Theseus and Pirithous, then nearly always Phalerus and Butes.

Valerius Flaccus places his catalogue later, as the Argonauts board, allocating them spatially to rowing positions. As a Roman poet looking back on Greek epic tradition, he is more interested in literary ancestry than literal ancestors. He idiosyncratically includes forebears of characters associated with the Trojan War: Nestor (in the *Iliad* as an old man); Philoctetes (whose bow, in Sophocles, was essential to the fall of Troy); Tydeus (the father of Diomedes); and well-established crew members with Iliadic pedigrees, such as Menoetius (elderly companion of Achilles); Peleus (father of Achilles); Telamon (father of Ajax) and Oileus (father of the other Ajax).

Gantz points out that Argonauts come in pairs: many catalogues contain several pairs of brothers, such as Idas and Lynceus, Castor and Pollux, Echion and Erytus. Some have other family relationships: Laertes and Ulysses, father and son, in *Le Fatiche di Ercole* (the 1958 Italian film which popularized the 'sword and sandal' genre); or Meleager and his uncle Iphiclus, in several versions. More recently, there is a list engraved on the monument to the Argonauts in the town of Volos, near the site of ancient Iolchos, which focuses primarily on names well-known from myth and literature.

In the 1963 film, Jason refuses Zeus' help in gathering a crew, instead using 'the hearts of men', by organizing games: 'no greater games shall ever be held'. The brief montage of events introducing different heroes displays Polydeuces as boxer, Castor as wrestler, Acastus, throwing the hammer, Phalerus as champion archer, Euphemus as swimmer and the otherwise unattested Spyros of Syracuse, throwing the javelin. One pattern is that versions follow the famous characters, but assert their originality or their connection to the 'history behind the myth' by adding one new character of their own: for instance, Morris adds the unique Ephebus; Graves in *The Golden Fleece* uniquely mentions Cytissorus, in Apollonius as a son of Phrixus (2.1155); Zimmerman adds Hesperre and Kekyra to her resonant-sounding roll-call.

In one of the most famous scenes of the 1963 film, Hercules arrives and is immediately accepted, and the obviously unathletic, rather camp, Hylas challenges him to a discus throw towards a rock. Hercules surpasses expectations by hitting the rock, and Hylas sends it beyond the rock by skimming it across the waves. This scene delicately alludes to Hercules' relationship with Hylas in ancient versions. Games suggest ancient epic heroism as athleticism, as well as film stars as body builders and athletes. Steve Reeves, Hercules in the 1958 film, was a professional body-builder, and Roland Carey, Jason in the 1960 Italian Argonaut film *I Giganti della Tessaglia*, was a keen sportsman.[49] Hercules' extraordinary discus throw shows the clear relationship between the 1958 and 1963 films: in *Le Fatiche di Ercole*, Hercules shows his divine powers, while teaching a lesson to the arrogant Iphitus (here son and heir of Pelias), by throwing a discus so far it never even returns to earth. Both films use similar sound effects for the miraculous throw, but the 1963 film trumps Hercules' achievement with Hylas' wiliness.

The 2000 TV movie subverts the tradition differently: Jason is young, poor and naïve. Pelias gives Jason the ship, and forces the ship-builder Argos to sail with him. Argos is the experienced sailor, disgusted at his new recruits. Jason wanders into a bar intending to appeal, like his predecessor, to 'the hearts of men'. He is about to be knifed when Mopsus hits him over the head. These criminals and alcoholics are not interested in glory or honour. Instead, Jason recruits from farm boys and workers: Laertes is a shepherd and expert bull-leaper; Castor and Pollux are quarrymen; Zetes (who has the miraculous eyesight normally attributed to Lynceus) is the map-maker's apprentice; the thief who tries to steal the map, Actor, joins the crew to escape the guards. But it is not wholly a rationalizing and de-bunking of the epic mode: the arrival of Hercules and his miraculous strength, as he pushes the boat single-handedly into the water, inspires the boat-builders to join. Orpheus and Atalanta, one black, one female, arrive late, and stay marginalized: Orpheus volunteers, and Atalanta insists on going with her friend Jason, even though Argos is anxious about a woman on the ship. They stay behind together on Lemnos, for instance. In short, the gathering is not one of great men, but of ordinary mortals (and one woman). This version rationalizes in a different way from Graves, or Emily Hauser, whose Argonauts are powerful princes, accompanied by retinues of slaves, instead bringing out the potential of ordinary men to become heroes. This gives the 2000 mini-series a surprisingly Alexandrian flavour: Callimachus, Apollonius' elder contemporary, for instance, was famous for focusing on Theseus' encounter with a humble old woman who gives him supper, rather than his battle with the Marathonian bull.

Most genres avoid catalogues and create selections, which stand in for the whole. Zimmerman's 2013 script has a 'Roll-call' scene. The company introduce themselves in rhyming boasts, while everyone else chants and affirms them. Hercules stands out by breaking the rhythm, and the frame, as Hera responds with disgust and Athena with pragmatism. Zimmerman ends by thematizing the process of 'casting', with Meleager's uncle, who boasts that he plays 'others too', leading into the company performing a complete list, mostly inspired by Apollonius. Selections are the rule in children's literature: many picture books for younger children, such as Naden, Bradman, Malam and Gunderson, simply let the word 'Argonauts' stand on its own.

Pindar's selection uses the criterion of divine birth, presented according to the importance of the divine fathers: first Hercules, then Castor and Pollux, sons of Zeus; Euphemus and Periclymenos, sons of Poseidon; Orpheus, son of Apollo; Echion and Erytus, sons of Hermes; Zetes and Calais, sons of Boreas, the North Wind; and finally the seer Mopsus. This list is close to defining the most well-known Argonauts: the only exceptions are Tiphys, the helmsman, and Argos, the ship-builder, structurally required by the narrative. Mopsus, who knows the language of birds, is the most frequently attested of the seers. The next most popular Argonauts are Peleus, creating a connection with Chiron and Achilles; Acastus, son of Pelias, traitor in the 1963 film, who arrives last in Apollonius. Lynceus, with his miraculous eyesight, is more popular than his irascible brother, Idas.

There are variations across different periods: Atalanta is frequently included in recent versions, starting with Hawthorne, Graves and Treece. Of the ancient versions, she only appears in Apollodorus. Some are frequent in the ancient world, but disappear in recent versions, such as Menoetius, Achilles' companion, who is in all ancient versions plus Morris, and then not at all; and Oileus, father of the lesser Ajax, in all but one of the ancient versions, Kingsley, Morris and Graves's *Greek Myths*, but then absent. We can see changing fashions in Argonauts, moving from genealogical to literary significance to diversity in identity. Special abilities appeal, so that abilities sometimes remain even when names change: one that can run over water; one that can see through solid materials; one that can fly; one that can see into the future.

Analysis of overlaps and variations in the different lists strengthens the suggestion that there never was a canonical list. Apollonius only shares 26 names with Apollodorus, while between them they muster 41 names that are different from each other. In contrast Hyginus includes 49 of Apollonius' 53 Argonauts, but adds another 16 new ones. Valerius has clear overlaps with both Apollonius (40 the same) and Hyginus (42 the same), but adds two unique to him in the ancient world: Nestor and Tydeus. Tydeus does not catch on, and remains unique, while Nestor also occurs in Colum's *Heroes before Achilles,* Riordan's 2003 picture book and Hauser's *For the Winner,* an odd collection of texts suggesting coincidence rather than influence. The *Orphic Argonautica* is substantially Apollonian (45 the same), although Aithalides appears in both the *OA* and Valerius Flaccus, but not in Apollonius. Hyginus seems to avoid following Apollodorus (47 different Argonauts), even though Hyginus has the largest number in his catalogue (67). Graves mainly follows Apollodorus: Peneleos, Poeas and Staphylos only occur in Apollodorus and either Graves's *Golden Fleece* or his *Greek Myths* (and the Volos monument), while Phanos appears in Apollodorus, Graves and the 2000 TV movie. The Volos monument includes 59 Argonauts, among them Nestor and Theseus, and has more in common with Apollonius than Apollodorus or Graves, but matches none of them.

From comparing these lists, it seems that Pindar is most central to the tradition, followed by Apollonius, then Apollodorus. But Apollonius has not chosen well-known names (for instance, Amphidamas (Hyginus and *OA*), Areius (only *OA*), Clytius (Hyginus and Morris), Laocoon (only Hyginus and the Volos monument), Talaus (Valerius and *OA*)). Laocoon may have ceased to be attractive after the name is used in Virgil's *Aeneid* for the Trojan priest who is killed by snakes when he denigrates the Trojan horse. Clytius may be an ironic choice, given that his name means 'famous', but he really is not. Apollonius also excluded some of those who were commonly involved, and included three pairs with identical, repeated names (two each of Ancaeus, Iphiclus and Iphitus), which gives the impression of realism, but also puts off later authors from following him exactly.

Versions aimed at mass culture are relatively idiosyncratic: in particular, the 1958 film includes Eurystheus from the Hercules tradition; the computer game *Rise of the Argonauts* includes Daedalus, Lycomedes (normally king of Scyros), the god Pan, and Medusa, presumably to increase the number of female participants. Their intended audiences were wide, and may not have had much previous interest in Greek mythology, so they include as many well-known names as possible. Catalogues of Argonauts make relatively dry reading for modern audiences (the ancient equivalent of football scores?). But they give concrete data about the variability of the tradition and its complexity, and indicate some of the different ways cultural products use Greek myth.

Itinerary

We have seen the story's beginnings and met the Argonauts. Now we will follow the *Argo* from launch to return. The chapters combine episodes in roughly the order of Apollonius, with themes arising from them. Each chapter begins with key episodes and expands its focus to bring in other material relevant to the themes under consideration. This mixture of episodes and themes has a number of advantages: we can see the separate reception histories of different episodes, where selective or excerpted versions can change the dynamic of the tradition, while still gaining an overview of important ideas and concepts. We can follow the story, and see its changing significance in different contexts.

Chapter 2 focuses on femininity and sexuality, beginning with the Argonaut last to arrive in the 2000 TV mini-series, who recently inspired Emily Hauser's novel *For the Winner*, Atalanta: the only female Argonaut. It moves onto the first major episode in Apollonius, the Lemnian women and their all-female society. The next major episode in many versions is the loss of Hylas and Hercules. This chapter features versions created by women, and explores the varying treatment of women and erotic adventures in contexts where attitudes vary widely to both. Hylas as beautiful boy is the object of both predatory nymphs and Hercules himself, and problematizes gender roles at the same time as exemplifying approaches to Greek pederastic relationships. The final section focuses on Medea, the inescapable love interest, helper, hero and threat of the second half, giving a flavour of her importance for the Argonaut quest.

In Chapter 3, we rejoin the Argonauts with the loss of Hercules, exploring the relationship between Hercules and Jason, their complementary and contrasting masculinity, their rivalry and differing modes of leadership and heroism. We see Jason's anxieties in the build-up to departure, and the election scene at Iolchos, where the crew choose Hercules, not Jason, as their leader. The abandonment of Hercules is Jason's biggest challenge in managing his crew, and we trace the tradition of mutiny among the Argonauts. The chapter finishes with the consequences of the loss of Hercules: the Argonauts must face the man-slaughtering boxer Amycus, antagonist and monstrous violator of guest-friendship. As the other Argonauts come into their own, this section explores antagonists as foils for Argonautic heroism.

The next big episode after Amycus is the Argonauts' encounter with the prophet Phineus, crucial for finding their way to Colchis and getting through the Clashing Rocks. Chapter 4 explores these central episodes through themes of entertainment and the supernatural: prophecy and Phineus; the Clashing Rocks, themselves often presented as sentient landscape, with the episode's crucial divine intervention. After the Argonauts successfully cross into the Black Sea, Apollonius presents an insight into the minds of the gods: Hera and Athena, who decide to make Medea fall in love with Jason. After the gods, the chapter concludes with the non-human antagonists, central to the myth's entertainment value: its monsters. The section focuses on different types of monsters: the feminine-monstrous Harpies, the Earthborns of Cyzicus and mechanical Talos, giving an overview of Argonautic monstrosity.

In Chapter 5, we return to the story with the Argonauts' arrival in Colchis, and their meeting with the Colchian king, Aeetes. As they journey past the edges of normal Greek society, we explore themes of ethnicity and Otherness: Aeetes as tyrant; the Colchians, sometimes represented as black; ethnography (writing about different peoples or tribes), Black Sea peoples and peoples encountered on the widely varying return journeys. The chapter showcases versions that explore race and identity, especially those produced by creators of colour.

The events at Colchis form Chapter 6, and the themes of heroism and betrayal: Jason's feats of the bulls and Earthborns rely on Medea's assistance, itself an act of betrayal; Medea also betrays the dragon and the fleece becomes an icon of deception; the escape from Colchis, and the death (often itself a murder) of Medea's brother Apsyrtus. This chapter explores the relationship between moral tensions and mythic complexity, and the *Argonautica*'s complex questioning of masculinity and heroism, with its dramatic, monstrous antagonists defeated by the agency of a woman, and our hero's ultimate compromise and betrayal in the episode of the death of Apsyrtus. Finally, in Chapter 7, the whole comes together: I lay out rationalizing and symbolic interpretations of the Argonaut voyage as a whole and the Golden Fleece itself. The book concludes with findings and endings, drawing together the significance of what we have discovered and surveying the way different versions handle their final moments.

Names are a challenge in Greek myth and many characters in the Argonautic myth have names spelt differently in different versions. I generally follow Robert Graves's *Golden Fleece* as the most accessible version that contains the vast majority of names: this means Jason, not *Iason*, Hercules, not *Herakles*, Medea, not *Medeia*, and Aeetes, not *Aietes*, except for Chiron not *Cheiron*, and Iolchos, not *Iolchus*, which are more recognizable. For dates of films, I have followed IMDb in using date of release in country of origin, rather than production date.

2

Femininity and Sexuality

After Apollonius' Argonauts depart from Iolchos, their first adventure is at the island of Lemnos, where they encounter a society of women. Jason enters a mutual seduction with their young queen, Hypsipyle, until Hercules insists on leaving to follow their heroic destiny. This chapter puts the Lemnian women in dialogue with themes of gender and erotics. Jason's relationships with women dominate the plot; many versions question gender roles and reveal changing attitudes to sexuality, from the silent, contained women of ancient Greece, to chivalry and various responses to feminism. Medea has always inspired and discomfited audiences, both male and female. After Lemnos, the beautiful boy Hylas is stolen by predatory nymphs, again highlighting both femininity and sexuality. Hylas is feminized as an object of desire, while Hercules' excessive emotion removes him from the expedition.

This chapter explores representations of women and sexuality: it begins with one crucial absence from Apollonius' catalogue of Argonauts, an absence playfully evoked in the Lemnian episode, during Jason's erotic arming before meeting Hypsipyle: Atalanta, the only female Argonaut mentioned in an ancient source. The first section examines her in the context of female-authored versions of the story. Next we face the Lemnian women, who function as both helpers, obstacles and threats, as well as modelling a society turned inside out, gendered Otherness. We then move to the eroticized boy, Hylas, and what this myth reveals about changing attitudes to homosexual desire. The Hylas episode also shows how individual episodes can be excerpted and have very different traditions from the rest of the myth. The chapter finishes with Medea, inevitably the most important woman in the story, focusing on her agency and power in the *Argonautica* and outlining the relationship between Argonaut myth and the later Corinth story.

Atalanta the Argonaut

Atalanta has a life of her own in ancient myth: her appearance as an Argonaut, as with that of Hercules, or Theseus, would only be a cameo in her rich mythological story. Most famously, Ovid tells of her refusal to marry, and the fatal footrace she set up to avoid marriage (10.560–707). Any suitor had to beat her in a race or die. Only when Hippomenes distracted her with a golden apple did she finally lose the race. She is a descendant of Minyas by her mother Clymene (Apollodorus 3.9.2), so one of the Minyans. She also participates in the Calydonian boar hunt, another set piece in Ovid's *Metamorphoses* (8.260–546), along with other Argonauts.[1] During this, the hero Meleager falls in love with her, honours her for taking first blood, to which his uncles object; Meleager ends up killing his uncles, at which his own mother kills him, by burning the log on which his life depends. Aeschylus may have written a tragedy about this (the title *Atalanta* survives).[2]

There were almost certainly two Atalantas, the daughter of Schoeneus (of footrace fame) and the daughter of Iasius (associated with the boar hunt), but they often become one in both ancient and modern versions. There is early evidence of Atalanta participating in the funeral games for Pelias, where she wrestled Peleus for a boar's hide: a Chalcidian *hydra, c.* 540 BCE, now in Munich (596), supplemented by details in Apollodorus. Her presence along with other Argonauts at these events in early versions makes a cumulative case that Apollonius deliberately wrote her out of the myth, rather than Apollodorus writing her in.

Atalanta is in Apollodorus' Argonaut catalogue, but Apollonius pointedly excludes her. He keeps this information back until the Argonauts arrive at Lemnos, obscuring her further. To approach the Lemnian queen, Jason adorns himself with his famous cloak and a spear: 'which Atalanta had once given to him as a mark of friendship when she greeted him in kindness on Mainalos. Great was her desire to join the expedition, but he refused to accept her, as he feared the terrible conflicts which love causes' (AR 1.769–73). Atalanta becomes a canonical Argonaut in the twentieth century, but her inclusion is not always straightforwardly a feminist gesture. This section explores the different ways versions handle Atalanta, whether as token woman, or central character, and shows how strong female action heroes are frequently eroticized and marginalized, even while arousing fascination. Does Atalanta shake up the Argonauts? What happens when you add a single woman to a group of men bonding on an adventurous expedition?

The conflicts of love dominate Henry Treece's 1961 novel, *Jason*. His versions shows us how Atalanta can be both important and problematic. Treece's Jason describes her as 'a most notorious whore' (84); 'her only running was from bed to bed' (85). Treece does create some distance from his first-person narrator: Jason admits 'how afraid I was of women' (85), and readers may be intended to dislike and disapprove of him. But Jason's attitudes and emphases disturbingly suggest the fantasies of a 1960s male readership. The narrative frequently showcases his sexual exploits, for instance with Pelias' daughters. He continually presents women as sexual objects. Atalanta has primal power from the Mother Goddess, both through withholding sex (as a devotee of 'the Mother in her virgin form as Diana') and using sex to destroy men. She drinks heavily (outlasting the priestesses of Samothrace, 86) and is humiliated by being pierced by an arrow during sex with Meleager (224–5).

Treece's Atalanta can show positive facets despite Jason's narration. For instance, her prophecy of dark futures for both Jason and Achilles aligns her with external reader knowledge: Jason asks if baby Achilles will eclipse his own glory, and might have had him 'dealt with'. Atalanta replies, 'Jason will gain a queen, Achilles a dead friend' (108). For an audience knowledgeable in Greek myth, this shows her correct understanding of the future and endorses her acid de-bunking of heroism. Jason is equally negative and aggressive towards his own mother, also a priestess, and also a 'strumpet'. However, much of his condemnation is reflected in Atalanta's actions, suggesting the author shares his negativity and fascination. Atalanta and Meleager attempt to assassinate Jason after a swimming race (ironic, as in Graves and the 1958 movie Jason cannot swim) (108–11). Atalanta takes vengeance against Hercules by arranging the death of Hylas and excluding Hercules from the expedition (137–50). She does have medical and ritual efficacy: she heals Acastus (113–14) and delivers a slave-girl's baby (225). She becomes Medea's *alter ego* and accomplice, despite their lack of affection; she helps to sacrifice and dismember Apsyrtus (240–1) and kill Pelias (254–6). However, Atalanta is also an object of uneasy desire for Jason, and attempts to seduce him (or perhaps makes a genuine declaration of love) at 172–3. Medea claims Jason called out for Atalanta during his first night with her (199). Treece's Atalanta is deceptive and unreliable: she betrays Jason to Aeetes (190–1) and conspires with Aeetes' minister (204). Jason, in his last words, an old man, ignored by all, sums up his story as a futile battle of the sexes: 'A man can never win. Not against the goddesses, the women ... that dark love-grave whose inner secrets a man can never know, never share' (335–6). Treece's version is ultimately misogynistic. The women are powerful, but rapacious, ruthless and relentlessly sexualized.

Treece draws on Graves's novel, in which Atalanta and Meleager are key characters. Treece's framing mythological rationale for the story, the conflict between 'Mother Goddess' and Poseidon, is lightly adapted from Graves's own of the Triple Goddess versus the Olympians. The frank sexuality is also in Graves, who does not shy away from Hercules and Hylas any more than Atalanta and Meleager. Graves introduces Atalanta as Meleager's love and hero of the Calydonian boar hunt, presenting an Ovidian version. When she arrives, Meleager is excited, but Great Ancaeus resists her inclusion: 'No ship is lucky with a woman aboard' (107). Meleager counters by reminding him that Atalanta saved his life in the boar hunt. Atalanta ensures her inclusion by proclaiming herself a representative of Artemis, here an aspect of the 'Triple Goddess'. Thus Graves's overarching personal mythology trumps Apollonius' refusal to include Atalanta, and legitimizes her inclusion in later versions. Atalanta refuses, as a representative of Artemis, to sleep with Meleager, and because he is married to someone whose family she does not want to offend. However, Graves implies that she is nevertheless working to attract him: 'Atalanta did not by any means wish Meleager to forget her' (107). Atalanta is defined primarily by her relationship with a man, although active and an effective fighter. She shot and scalped two centaurs, who were planning to rape her, which 'horrified Jason' (109). Graves gives a full rendition of Atalanta's birth, development and the Calydonian boar hunt (110–12). He makes Atalanta clearly the best hunter, ridicules the men for ignoring her advice: 'Thus the prejudice against hunting with a woman was confirmed, for five men had died that day; and yet one might say with equal truth that it was the prejudice itself that had killed them' (112). Later, he focuses on how attitudes of men around her affect her: for instance, in the funeral games for Cyzicus, the foot race is not held because the Doliones will not race against Atalanta (181) but Jason does not want to offend her. Graves plays around with Apollonius' refusal to include Atalanta: he keeps the spear she gave Jason (134), but also includes Atalanta in the crew, and brings out the problems caused by her presence, especially her relationship with Meleager. Later in the story she collaborates with Melanion (here the son of Phrixus, elsewhere in myth a lover of Atalanta) to rescue Butes from Colchis (300–2) and subsequently Meleager is jealous (366, 391). The afterword (432–3) makes these relationships her main story, as in Ovid.

Graves's Atalanta, however, does have agency and uses her special abilities as archer, hunter and runner: she and Meleager hunt gazelles (236); in the process of rescuing Butes, she kills Aeetes (301), and continues to fight even though wounded. She also acts as Medea's double and assistant on occasion, less than in

Treece, helping to heal the Argonauts (315–16). Graves's Atalanta, then, is influential on Treece, and we will see this recur in the 2000 TV mini-series, and perhaps unconsciously in Emily Hauser's 2017 novel, *For the Winner*. Graves is certainly ahead of his time in granting a female character other than Medea agency without evil, but throughout Atalanta is evaluated by her relationships with men.

Graves's Atalanta goes well beyond previous incarnations in Hawthorne, Morris and Colum. Atalanta is briefly mentioned in Hawthorne's *Tanglewood Tales*, but has no action.[3] In Morris she is golden-haired, grey-eyed and fearless, given a name in return for virginity (3.131–45), and hunts effectively during the return journey (10.241–9, 11.137–42, 456–7). Colum allows her to narrate her own story, and to back up Hercules on leaving Lemnos. Of the more recent children's books, only two include her: Riordan/Cockcroft (2003) and Felicity Brooks, who creates an active and battle-hungry Atalanta. She comes first in the catalogue; in the Lemnian episode, Atalanta, along with Hercules, is keen to attack the women (28). Together, they scornfully demand departure, both driven by desire for glory. Atalanta speaks frequently: she mocks Hercules (32), congratulates Pollux (47), and remembers Phineus' prophecy (51). When Jason, Medea and Orpheus run for their lives with the fleece, Atalanta shoots Jason's attacker. This Atalanta is a warrior, bloodthirsty, reliable, intelligent. This is a female-authored Atalanta, notably non-sexualized.

The 2000 TV movie shows similarities with both Brooks and Treece. Their Atalanta is the first Argonaut introduced, helping Jason with his archery. In the Lemnian episode, she and Orpheus stay to guard the ship. But her suspicions go much further than in Brooks: she follows the Lemnians and finds the remains of the previous 'sacrifice of men'. This Atalanta, however, is still defined by romantic involvements, primarily love for Jason, and jealousy of his relationships with Hypsipyle and Medea. Atalanta confronts Jason in the middle of the drugged Lemnian feast and insists they are about to be killed. Jason is initially reluctant, but does believe her, and the Argonauts flee ignominiously. In Colchis, Atalanta plays a key role in the debate about abandoning Jason, where she argues passionately for staying. She is suspicious of Medea: when Medea goes to kill Pelias in Iolchos, Atalanta believes she has betrayed Jason. Atalanta's version of Medea, dangerous sorceress and not to be trusted, is the Medea from elsewhere in the tradition. Atalanta resists the optimistic innovations of the 2000 movie's script. When Jason brings Medea onto the ship, Atalanta cannot believe he is really in love with her, and in many versions, of course, he is not. Nevertheless, she is made to participate in the romanticization of Jason: she declares her love for him, he replies that he loves her 'like a brother', and she remains distressed and sulky. She, in turn, settles for the love of the cringing but resourceful thief, Actor. In sum, Atalanta shows the complexity of the 2000 mini-series' relationship to the Argonautic tradition. She is suspicious of the romanticization of both Lemnian women and Medea, but is still herself defined by her relationships with men. In this, she resembles Graves's Atalanta more than that of Brooks, although she does participate in various battles on equal terms.

In the children's picture book by James Riordan (illustrated by Cockcroft) Atalanta is less prominent in the text than the illustrations, which visually recall the 2000 mini-series. The assembled Argonauts include both Atalanta and a black Orpheus. The text describing the monsters on Cyzicus presents Hercules killing them, but the image shows Atalanta. When the Argonauts shelter from the Stymphalian birds Atalanta and Orpheus are prominent among the crew. This feels like a conscious attempt to be more inclusive.

Emily Hauser's novel *For the Winner* (2017) gives a contemporary take on Atalanta and the Argonaut myth. This novel, aimed at least partly at young women, makes Atalanta the central character. She sets out to prove herself a true hero, and the true daughter of King Iasius, by joining the quest for the Golden Fleece, disguised as the Argonaut Telamon. The Argonaut expedition is the central movement of the story. Her disguise as a man means she is both included and not included, creating complications for thinking about gender: she is not treated as a woman, and can only be accepted if maintaining a masculine persona. When her deception is revealed, she is immediately thrown off the ship. This may be for reasons of plausibility, to make ancient Greek misogyny clearer, or a reaction against the easy inclusion of Atalanta in the 2000 mini-series. Further, 'Telamon' is still treated as an object of desire, but as a desirable boy. Meleager tries to rape 'Telamon', while Hippomenes is the long-suffering friend who accepts her true identity, rescues her, helps her reach home, and ultimately marries her. She chooses to let him win the fatal race, by chasing the golden apple, for the sake of her kingdom: so the Argonautic coming of age story also becomes a romance. There are similarities to Graves, including the trip back over land. However, Hauser told me that she had decided not to read Graves to avoid undue influence, although she had seen the 2000 TV movie. This is a feminist *Argonautica* in a number of ways: Atalanta does not reach the Golden Fleece, which decentres the quest and its goal. Ultimately, she acknowledges that proving oneself can be destructive. However, the story is resolved through the marriage plot and Atalanta is never truly self-sufficient.

Hauser is a woman writing mainly for a female audience, and displaces Jason with Atalanta, perhaps showing how the quest itself is a masculine concern. Few female-authored versions of the *Argonautica* exist. There are at least three aimed at children (Brooks, Zeff, Gunderson) and many focusing on Medea, but mainly on events in Corinth, most notably Christa Wolf's *Medea*. The Polish author Eliza Orzeszkowa (1841–1910) wrote a novel *Argonauci* (*The Argonauts*, 1900, trans. Curtin, 1901) which uses the myth as a frame for a domestic story of the destructiveness of wealth, in which the businessman Aloysius Darvid first alienates his entire family, indirectly causes the death of his young daughter, and then commits suicide.[4] The female characters play important roles, not easily mapped onto the Argonaut myth, although his older daughter Irene evokes Medea in her power and fieriness. It is the men who are compared to Argonauts, though: first Kranitski, Darvid's wife's lover, when he leaves his rural home as a young man, then Darvid himself, travelling the world as a ruthless capitalist, then his son Maryan, leaving for America to make his fortune.

Female artists also interpreted episodes, such as Henrietta Rae's painting *Hylas and the Nymphs*, and women are involved in the collaborative projects of film, music and opera (for instance, the 2012 DVD of Cavalli's opera *Giasone* is of a 2010 production by Vlaamse Opera, Antwerp, directed by Mariame Clément). The only adult retelling of the Argonauts by a woman is Mary Zimmerman's play. Zimmerman includes Atalanta reluctantly: in the catalogue, Atalanta asks, 'Do you think I'm out of place?' To which Hercules responds, 'Yes!' Her only action is to run back to the ship to fetch Zetes during the Harpies episode, on Jason's orders. Zimmerman makes her deliberately and ironically tokenistic.

Male authors who include Atalanta, such as Hawthorne, Morris and Graves, are often broadly or paradoxically progressive in their approach to gender and sexuality, from evidence both inside and outside their Argonaut interpretations. In the twenty-first century it becomes an exception to leave her out. Another recent example shows a different way of handling her: the TV series *Atlantis* (2013). This mash-up features as protagonists Jason, Hercules and Pythagoras, and they are being chased by Scythians who hunt strangers for sport, when Atalanta rescues them. She has agency, but operates through mystique as a priestess of Artemis, self-sufficient and a powerful warrior. Atalanta is a clear example of how attitudes to women have shifted, and how that is reflected in myth: she is now regularly prominent, and a part of the action, much less sexualized, but she remains exotic, problematic, marginalized and almost always defined by her relationship to men.

Lemnian horror

The Lemnos episode in Apollonius foreshadows and doubles events to come at Colchis.[5] Both Hypsipyle and Medea look back to the women of Homer's *Odyssey*, especially Nausicaa, but also Calypso and Circe, as powerful figures that offer potential benefits but also potential harms. Lemnos stands between Greek culture and the Otherness of Colchis: although close by and integrated into Greek systems of hospitality, the Lemnian women have created their own Otherness. The largely positive encounter in Apollonius, in which the women welcome the Argonauts into their homes and beds, to repopulate the island, always lies in the shadow of the violence, which brought this female society into existence. Apollonius' Argonauts never discover that the apparently idyllic island of Lemnos harbours a horrifying secret: the women are on their own, because they murdered all their male family members. While the Lemnian women bid a fond farewell to the Argonauts, there is always the possibility that, like Virgil's Dido, they might ultimately refuse to let them go. The episode of the Lemnian women divides the tradition: prominent, even dominating in some versions, it is excluded from many others. The Argonauts encounter Otherness in many forms: this episode combines feminine sexuality with underlying threat.

The myth of the Lemnian women was well-known by the time of Apollonius. The *Iliad* mentions Jason's son by Hypsipyle (Euneus, *Il.* 7.467–71). Titles of plays by Aeschylus cited in later sources include a *Hypsipyle* and a *Lemnian Women* (or *Lemnian Men*), probably part of an *Argo* tetralogy.[6] Pindar places the Argonauts' encounter with the Lemnians after their return from Colchis, to create a link with the founding of Cyrene from Lemnos (*Pythian* 4.251–4); however, other aspects match later versions. By the mid-fifth century BCE the Lemnian women are already 'man-slaying' (252) in Pindar, and Aeschylus refers to the proverbial 'Lemnian horror' (*Libation Bearers* 631–6). The Lemnian women were associated with the Argonauts from the earliest references; it is clearly a canonical episode in the ancient *Argonautica*.

Apollonius' Lemnian episode (1.609–909) gives a sympathetic portrayal of the Lemnian women but puts emphasis on deception. We see the Argonauts' arrival through the eyes of the Lemnian women (630–9), who initially think the Argonauts are invading Thracians. First contact leads to a council of the Lemnians (653–707), which the reader sees but the Argonauts do not, where Hypsipyle worries that the secret of their crime will escape, but the older Polyxo argues that they need to repopulate.[7] Hypsipyle then gives Jason a twist on the truth by claiming the men abandoned them for Thracian slaves, and were forced into exile in Thrace, taking the male children with them (793–833). Apollonius' Argonauts never find out the secret, but leave at Hercules' insistence (861–74). Gantz speculates that tragic versions might have focused on a revelation of the truth, leading to the Argonauts departing in anger and disgust, or even a plot by the women to kill their new lovers after conceiving children.[8]

Apollonius gives no hint of the version in which the Lemnians' failure to propitiate Aphrodite caused them to smell, as in Apollodorus (1.9.17). There is no representation of the murders, just a short statement of what happened (609–19); instead, he highlights the difficulties of maintaining an all-female society and the distress felt when the Argonauts leave. Hypsipyle's deceptive speech is a plausible rationalization of the myth. At 1.627–30 Apollonius even says that the women find the men's duties easier than their own. Far from being a *femme fatale*, Hypsipyle is a young, vulnerable ruler, overwhelmed by Jason's erotic appeal. As he approaches the palace he is like the dazzling sun (725–6) and a star that charms the eyes of love-sick girls (774–81). The Lemnian women greet the Argonauts with help, gifts and rejoicing, not unlike the Phaeacians with Odysseus, or Dido with Aeneas. But while Dido curses Aeneas on his departure, Hypsipyle wishes Jason every success, accepts that he will return to Iolchos, even though she offers him the kingship of Lemnos (888–98). The women gather round the departing heroes like bees around lilies (879–82), an image which presents them as hard-working and attractive rather than threatening.

The Roman versions of the Lemnian episode are darker: Ovid's Hypsipyle in *Heroides* 6 is juxtaposed with the suicidal Dido, and re-frames herself as a new version of both Dido and Medea, cursing Medea and apparently causing her future violence. Both Valerius Flaccus and his late-first-century CE contemporary Statius give graphic descriptions of the murder of the Lemnian men. Valerius massively expands (and visualizes) Apollonius' account of the murder and contracts the council and departure scenes.[9] This is the only episode of the *Argonautica* which Statius incorporates into his epic *Thebaid* (the story of the Seven against Thebes), an inset story told by Hypsipyle. Banqueting, sex and death are vividly intermingled: for instance, Gorge kills her husband in his post-banquet sleep, while he thinks she is embracing him. Although both Flavian Hypsipyles are supposedly innocent themselves, Statius throws some uncertainty onto Hypsipyle's reliability as narrator.[10] Did she really save her father Thoas? Statius' version, along with Ovid's *Heroides*, is mentioned by Boccaccio as his source for the Lemnian episode, later influential on Lefèvre/Caxton, which shows how a one-off intervention can affect traditions of particular episodes.

This may be why the Lemnian episode is remarkably prominent in Lefèvre.[11] In recuperating Jason, the medieval romance multiplies and complicates his love life: Jason first hones his seductive skills on Queen Mirro of Olliferne, who he defends from the king of Esclavoniya, so that when he encounters Hypsipyle (Ysiphyle) he is already betrothed. There is strong influence from Classical sources, including Virgil, Ovid and Statius. When Jason returns with the fleece, Ysiphyle sees his ship passing and commits suicide by throwing herself into the sea, performing the part of Catullus' Aegeus in Theseus' abandonment of Ariadne. Her corpse is washed onto his ship, complete with a love letter (*Heroides* 6, one presumes).[12] These alterations are partly generic, following the priorities of romance. The Lemnian episode is one of only two episodes narrated on the voyage out, along with Hercules' Laomedon encounter. This reference to Laomedon, plus Jason's substantial battle scenes watched by Mirro, might suggest knowledge of Valerius Flaccus: but it is hard to prove direct influence, rather than a combination of invention and awareness of medieval mythography, including Pompeius Trogus and Boccaccio.[13]

The structure of Lefèvre's Lemnian episode is surprisingly Apollonian, and perhaps (mediated?) knowledge of the Greek tradition may have existed. It begins with the murder of the Lemnian men (58–60), lightly adapted: King Thoas and his men, obsessed with war, stayed away too long and, despite the women's entreaties, refused to return. The women killed their boy children, and swore to kill their husbands and fathers on their return. All except Hypsipyle did so. Further, they swore never to allow any men on the island, and only admit the Argonauts because of their dire need after storm and shipwreck. Despite Caxton's reference to Statius, in his brief epilogue (148–9), Lefèvre does not include violent scenes, and gives Hypsipyle one son, not two (65). There is no hint that the Lemnians intend to murder the Argonauts; Hypsipyle and the other women are reluctant to let them leave, again more like Virgil's Dido than Apollonius' Lemnians. Hercules leaves briefly (62), but returns to demand they pursue the quest (65–6). Jason initially resists Hypsipyle's charms; only when Hypsipyle creeps naked into his bed does he let her seduce him (65). Despite his emphasis on the island of murderous, seductive women, Lefèvre does not explore the functioning of this all-female society; instead the female warriors terrify through numbers (at least fifty thousand). Lefèvre creates sympathetic versions of Jason and Hypsipyle, whose suicide atones for her immoral seduction. These Lemnian women are far from *femmes fatales*. Lefèvre's Hypsipyle is the heroine of a different tragedy, and the importance of women and erotic motifs reflects the ideology of courtly love.

Cavalli's opera *Giasone* (1649) also develops the Lemnian episode, following Ovid's *Heroides*. Cavalli was arguably the inventor of opera as we know it, and *Giasone* was his most popular opera, performed widely throughout Italy by travelling companies.[14] Cavalli's Giasone is primarily an erotic hero: he has been detained on the island of 'Colchos' for some time by his love for Medea. Hypsipyle (Isifile) has come to find him. The plot revolves around his attempts to keep both Medea and Hypsipyle happy, while each intrigues against the other. This Medea is the wife of Aegeus, and she is eventually reconciled with him, while Giasone ends up with Hypsipyle. The opera skirts tragedy, with Giasone attempting to kill Hypsipyle, but accidentally almost killing Medea instead (his captain throws her off a cliff, perhaps evoking Hypsipyle's end in Lefèvre). This version is primarily about the love relationships of the two heroines, not Giasone's heroism or coming of age. The Lemnian and Colchian episodes are merged physically, with Medea and Hypsipyle meeting and competing for Jason's love. There is little emphasis on Lemnos or on either Medea or Hypsipyle as violent figures: rather Giasone's feats are the backdrop against which the complexities of his emotional relationships play out. This erotic drama appealed to Venetian audiences, and playfully rewrote Classical epic as romantic comedy.

Nineteenth-century versions find various ways of avoiding the Lemnian episode: Grillparzer does not mention it, Hawthorne and Kingsley both simply sail past. Morris takes a more interesting tactic: he retains the story, but keeps the Argonauts away. A male survivor of the Lemnian massacre hails the ship from the shore and tells the story of the massacre. This repeats the way Virgil and Ovid refuse to embroil Aeneas in a repeat of Odysseus' Cyclops episode. In *Aeneid* 3, the Trojans pick up one of Odysseus' abandoned sailors, Achaemenides, from the shore and he warns them away from Polyphemus. The Cyclops story was so famous that it could not be ignored, but could not be bettered. In Morris's inset tale of the Lemnian women, violence is extreme, and the survivor only escapes by throwing himself off a cliff (again evoking Lefèvre's Hypsipyle?), and hiding in a cave. The Argonauts avoid the moral danger of sexual temptation and the literal danger of murderous Lemnian women, while Morris includes the sensational story. Jason, too, can display his honour and kindness (and be like Aeneas) by rescuing the survivor. This configures the Lemnian women as almost wholly Other and monstrous, like the Cyclops, and tells the story wholly from a male viewpoint. This is arguably more misogynistic than simply ignoring or bypassing the episode.

Twentieth-century versions vary considerably by genre. Children's literature, for instance, tends to avoid or purify the story. After omission by nineteenth-century versions, the episode is re-integrated by Colum's *Heroes before Achilles*, in line with his reliance on Morris, but carefully sanitized: the Lemnians have banished rather than killing their menfolk, thus making Hypsipyle's narrative in Apollonius the true version. The Lemnian banquet is the setting for stories: Orpheus on Persephone, Atalanta on her own race, and Castor and Pollux on Pandora. This latter is used as the reason for the Argonauts' departure: the 'golden maid' causes evil and destruction to enter the world, and the Lemnians have become the 'golden maids' for the Argonauts, a version of the Homeric lotus eaters. Colum avoids explicit sexuality: the Argonauts gather flowers with their special friends; Jason is fascinated by Hypsipyle's voice like birdsong and the feeling of her small hand in his. Colum changes the order, placing this episode after the Phineus episode, with further elements evoking the male–male hospitality of the Cyzicus episode, so the Argonauts do not land on Lemnos willingly, but instead are blown back there in a storm (as in Lefèvre). In this way Colum both bypasses the island, like Kingsley, going past, and includes the episode, by coming back, with both men and women rehabilitated, in comparison to Morris's demonization of the Lemnians.

Subsequent children's literature mostly avoids the episode: the only versions that include it are those by Brooks, Catran, Riordan, West, Malam and Antram, and Whitehead and Banerjee's graphic novel, almost all for older readers. Malam and Antram's comic-style picture book segregates the episode, in a text-box. Riordan/Cockcroft has the Argonauts go to Lemnos to escape a storm, adding a hint of the Sirens, as the boat is drawn there by 'snatches of song'. Atalanta and Hercules are the only Argonauts to resist the women's 'charms'. The Argonauts enjoy 'love' and father children, and Hypsipyle's honest tale allows the Argonauts knowledge. Brooks incorporates the 'disgusting smell' from Apollodorus to explain the men's abandonment of the women and does not pull punches on the murders. The Argonauts find out after they have left, only staying four days.

The tradition of the Lemnians as *femmes fatales* is strong in the twentieth century, particularly evident in both novels and films. While Graves balances sympathy and threat like Apollonius, later versions such as Treece, Catran and the 2000 TV movie foreground threat. For Graves, the men are killed for worship of Hephaestus against the will of the Triple Goddess. The men use the 'foul smell' to justify their abandonment of their difficult wives for more willing Thracian slave-girls. The Argonauts already know about the killing because they encountered Thoas, Hypsipyle's rescued father. Nevertheless, Hypsipyle's account differs from the narrator's in making their murder more of a pitched battle, and blaming the men, not the women's crazed pseudo-Maenadic ritual (as Thoas tells it). Jason claims to believe her, and volunteers sex as an act of piety, to make their harvest fertile. Jason and Hypsipyle are a matched pair: both tall, one dark, one blonde, both equally interested in each other. The Argonauts stay only for three days, until Hercules explodes with rage about the delay, but then himself ends up drunk, and Orpheus brings the Argonauts back to the ship with his song. Graves preserves both the independence of the women and the power of the men, who knowingly but piously take their pleasure and leave without shame.

Treece adapts and intensifies Graves. He combines the Lemnian episode with the Hylas episode: the six chapters form an important section of his novel. His goddess-worshipping women are both sexually desirable and terrifying: Hypsipyle confesses that they slaughtered the men at the instigation of the Black Ones, the priestesses of the Mother, from Samothrace, and they take Hylas as a sacrifice at a festival of Dionysus, in place of Jason, drowning him in a pool while they physically restrain Hercules. The idea of a Maenadic element to the Lemnian killing, which surfaced in Graves, is amplified here. Lemnos is a land of Otherness: 'we were suspended between heaven and earth; we were in dreamland where men desired only to eat and drink and laugh' (125).

This Otherness also strongly characterizes the episode in film and TV. While the 1963 film avoids this episode, to maintain its family rating, the Lemnians of the 1958 *Fatiche di Ercole* become Amazon witches. At first the Argonauts are excited by this paradise of willing women, and Giasone falls in love with their queen Antea. But Odysseus realizes that the Amazons are planning to kill the Argonauts, warns Hercules and the men remaining on the ship, who use drugs provided by Asclepius to send both women and comrades to sleep, before carrying them away. This melding of Amazons and Lemnians, along with Odysseus' use of drugs, which evokes the Homeric Circe, turns the female antagonists into composite versions of threatening women in Greek mythology.

The strong emphasis on the women as erotic objects and the importance of drugs are motifs re-used in the 2000 mini-series: here too Jason is drugged and confused, as well as erotically obsessed with Hypsipyle. This Lemnos is both paradise and potentially fatal: not just one but all of them will be killed. As the Argonauts wallow in the baths, befuddled by alcohol and drugs, Atalanta discovers the imminent 'sacrifice of men' and persuades Jason to drag them away. Atalanta's agency is set against the highly negative representation of the sexual power and drugged orgies of the Lemnians. Hypsipyle in her garden is both powerful and threatening, made more evil while Medea becomes more sympathetic. Film and TV sensationalize and sexualize the Lemnian women, but allow the men knowledge, even if their escapes are somewhat lacking in masculine vigour: drugged and carried out in the 1958 film; running terrified and unarmed, pursued by armed women in the 2000 mini-series.

We might expect to see feminist readings of the Lemnians, but they are less apparent than reactions against feminism. For instance, John Gardner's narrative poem *Jason and Medeia* (1973) reveals contemporary distrust and dislike of feminism. Jason's first-person narrative archly presents the Lemnian women as proto-feminists, who grew tired of men's demands, wore men's clothes and cut their hair short, to be supplanted by willing and subservient Thracian slave-girls. Jason talks of the women's tendency to 'cackle and cavil at each least hint of tyranny', their obsession with 'traducing' phallus-shaped objects, although he also laughs at the Thracian slave-girls as 'soft concubines who'd not yet seen their reasonable rights' (96). The anachronistic references suggest Gardner's unease with modes of feminist discourse. Gardner's Jason presents the murder of the men as a continuation of feminist ideology and instead of showing their capability in running a female-only society (as Apollonius does), Gardner's Lemnians are a panicked rabble.

We can see how attitudes to women in different contexts change the representation of the Lemnian story, although genre and audience also have important effects. A society of women moved from being so unthinkable as to be ridiculous and yet still sensational (in the ancient world),[15] to being so disturbing that they must be left out or avoided altogether (in the nineteenth century), to being both an enjoyable fantasy in the age of sexual liberation and a serious threat, as gender relations changed. It is perhaps more surprising that the episode has changed so little into the 2000s, and that Graves's version of it remains the most progressive. The Lemnian women are not developed as feminist icons, as Medea is, perhaps because of their greater ambiguity, both Greek and not-Greek, both feminine and not-feminine, sexually available but also potential predators.

Abducting Hylas

The Lemnian women episode has an idiosyncratic tradition because of the intervention of Ovid's *Heroides* and Statius' *Thebaid* and its controversial violence combined with sexuality, the influence of these Latin versions on medieval versions, which echo on in later imagery. The Hylas episode exemplifies the excerptibility of episodes in the Argonaut myth. Stand-alone poems by the Hellenistic poet Theocritus and the Roman elegist Propertius shape a tradition rich in lyric poetry and visual art, focused on the powerful moment. I will discuss the abandonment of Hercules in the next chapter: this section focuses on Hylas.

In the Hylas episode, *femmes fatales* meet homoerotic desire. Hercules' young companion (or lover) Hylas goes searching for water. The local nymph (or nymphs) fall for him and pull him into their pool. Hercules is distraught, goes mad with sorrow, and cannot be dragged away from searching, so the Argonauts leave without him. The Hylas story was popular in the ancient world: Virgil uses Hylas as example of the clichéd stories he will not repeat: 'Who has not told of the boy Hylas?' (*Georgics* 3.6). Apollonius' version focuses on the loss of Hercules: the Argonauts stop in Mysia after Hercules breaks his oar in a rowing competition; a single nymph pulls Hylas down; Hercules wanders the landscape searching for him, bellowing like an ox.

The iconic image of Hylas is the painting by J. W. Waterhouse, *Hylas and the Nymphs* (1896), 'thanks to thousands of posters on student walls' (Goldhill 2007: 167). In it, the beautiful, calm figure of Hylas, dark-haired, adult, with well-defined muscles, refuses to be distracted from his task of fetching water. Seven nearly identical auburn-haired nymphs gaze at him mournfully, while the boldest draws him down by his arm. The painting encapsulates the myth as an erotic fantasy, and is closely based on Theocritus *Idyll* 13, in which multiple nymphs pull the young boy into the black water (43–50). Hercules is absent from Waterhouse's picture, and while Theocritus goes on to imagine the nymphs consoling the child-like Hylas, the opaque expressions of Waterhouse's nymphs create a sinister mood.[16] The moment of Hylas being pulled down is often visualized in ancient art: both Waterhouse and the ancient artists suspend the narrative at the moment of the viewer's desire, emphasizing the potential for erotic viewing of both Hylas and nymphs.[17]

The main surviving ancient versions, visual and literary, are Hellenistic and Roman, suggesting that the story became popular at the time of (and through?) Apollonius and Theocritus.[18] Hylas may have featured in a lost epic about Hercules; the *scholia* to Apollonius mention a poem by Kinaithon, probably from the eighth century BCE.[19] The story relates to a ritual from Kios, to which Apollonius alludes, described by the ancient geographer Strabo.[20] This ritual probably consisted of a search, by men, repeatedly calling Hylas' name, a lament for the dead boy, and a sacrifice, culminating in a ritual invocation and echo: three times the priest called Hylas' name, and three times it echoed back. The relationship between myth and ritual is complex, and this ritual is not straightforwardly 'the story behind' Hylas, especially given that much of the evidence for reconstructing the ritual relies on the story preserved in ancient literary texts.[21] The package of myth, ritual, story and art suggests ways an ancient audience might interpret this episode.

Apollonius dominates mythography, meaning any early versions are hidden from us: Apollodorus' account (1.9.19) follows him closely, as does that of Hyginus (*Fabulae* 14) and, later, Robert Graves (227–9). Rationalizing interpretations existed but only traces survive: for instance, the ancient or medieval commentators on Virgil's *Eclogues* 6.43 state that Hylas fell off the *Argo* while sailing, or fell in a pool and drowned.[22] Our two main Hellenistic versions, Apollonius and Theocritus, are roughly contemporary and we do not know which came first.[23] Theocritus presents Hercules' love for Hylas as sexual: *Idyll* 13 begins with Eros, when Theocritus shows his addressee Nicias that immortals too experience desire (Theocritus *Idyll* 13.1–9).[24] But is Hercules' love for Hylas wholly erotic or also parental?[25] Hylas' beauty is both physical ('curly locks') and moral ('good man'). Hercules' awe-inspiring heroism, encapsulated in his conquest of the Nemean lion, is overcome by the power of *Eros*, but he is also presented as teaching Hylas 'as a father teaches his son'. In Theocritus at least, the distinction does not necessarily make sense: Greek ideals of pederastic love placed much emphasis on the educational value of a close relationship between the older lover and the young boy.[26] For many later cultures, this blurring of the parental and the erotic is problematic, and influences later omissions and adaptations of this episode. In Apollonius, Hercules' desire for Hylas is not so explicit, but his response to the boy's loss uses clear imagery of erotic suffering:[27]

> When Hercules heard this, sweat poured forth in abundance from his forehead and the dark blood seethed deep in his gut.... As when, stung by a gadfly, a bull charges forth ...
>
> AR 1.1261–2, 1265–6

The importance of search and the echo in texts and rituals suggests that the myth may have been erotic from its outset. Both evoke longing and desire. However, responses to bereavement also often involve yearning and searching, the desire to make the absent present.[28]

In Latin literature, both interpretations (the parental and the erotic) continue to be powerful. Propertius, writing love elegy in Augustan Rome, dedicates the last full-length poem of his first book to Hylas (1.20). As in Theocritus, Propertius gives advice to a lover in the context of the poetry of desire: look after your beloved, or they will be stolen. He ends the poem with: 'Warned by this, Gallus, you will keep your loves (*tuos amores*) safe, if you do not want to lose your handsome Hylas again' (Propertius 1.20.51–2). While Roman love poets usually take a woman as primary love object, Catullus and Tibullus also address love poetry to boys, and there is a broad equivalence in ancient love poets' treatment of boys and women.[29] Propertius' Hylas is the most clearly eroticized Hylas in the tradition: *amor* features in both first and last couplet, and the emphatic final position of lines 1, 3 and 51. Propertius focuses on the appearance of Hylas (5) and describes Gallus' boy as his desire (literally, burning). Hylas is harassed by Calais and Zetes, who kiss him in flight ('kisses' is the first word of lines 27 and 28). The apples over the spring also symbolize erotic readiness.[30] The desire of the nymphs is emphasized with *accensae* ('set on fire', 45). The poem ends at the moment of snatching and alludes to the echoing cries of Hercules (48–50). Propertius reduces the epic quest of the Argonauts to the backdrop for a warning to a lover. He replaces desire for glory with desire, as part of the love elegist's resistance to epic values and ancient generic hierarchies, which put epic on top.

Our key Latin epic, Valerius Flaccus, re-epicizes the episode.[31] He re-works the story, echoing Virgil's *Aeneid*: Juno causes Hercules' removal, as she does Aeneas' troubles; Hylas is tempted away from Hercules by chasing a deer, just as Juno tempts Ascanius into starting war in Italy by hunting a deer. Juno offers Hylas to the nymph just as Juno in *Aeneid* 1 offers a nymph to Aeolus to shipwreck the Trojans. Desire is there, but it is Hylas' desire to hunt the deer (*ardore*, VF 3.549). At first, Hercules' relationship with Hylas is presented as parental rather than erotic: as he leaves the ship, Hylas accompanies Hercules with unequal steps (VF 3.456), just as Virgil's Ascanius walks beside his father, Aeneas, as they escape Troy (*Aen.* 2.724). In book 1, Hylas carries Hercules' heroic accoutrements, but cannot bear the weight of the club. However, as Heerink points out, the hunting motif is also erotic, and the unequal steps of Hylas evoke the unequal metrical lines of elegiac couplets, a hexameter followed by a pentameter, which fundamentally evoke love.[32] Hercules' ultimate response to Hylas' loss is just as anguished and eroticized as in Apollonius and Theocritus (575–91). He is compared to an imminent storm (577–80), a bull stung by a gadfly (581–4) and a wounded lion (587–91), epic hero and subject of violent emotion. In ancient literature, then, Hylas is both erotic object and potential epic hero. He crosses genres and is excerpted, a beautiful boy and symbol of poetic repetition.

Hylas emerges frequently in later cultural products, but tends to stand alone. Many Argonaut retellings do not include Hylas, and many versions of the Hylas episode stand outside the Argonautic tradition, single poems in collections, single paintings or scenes. Hylas' fate in the tradition mirrors his fate in the story: he exists to be removed. The prominence of the myth in small lyric poems, painting and sculpture shows its excerptibility. Hylas' lyric afterlife is exemplified in the poem 'Hylas' from the Canadian poet Bliss Carman's 1906 collection *From the Book of Myths* (91–3). Hylas features in the collection along with other famous figures from Greek myth, including Pan, Daphne and Marsyas. These figures allow reflection on poetry itself. The eight four-line stanzas each end with the name Hylas, recreating ancient echo effects. The poem begins with the pastoral setting: 'Cool were the grey-mottled beeches …' The second stanza begins: 'Whistling a song of the rowers', evoking his Argonautic role, and 'Dipping his jar' recalls the visual tradition. Multiple nymphs gaze and desire him. But the main focus is on the loss of the Argonauts, his adventuring and their longing for him. The final stanza finishes on the power of music to convey loss:

> With a great star on the hill-crest
> In purple evening a flute-note
> Pierces the dusk and a voice calls,
>   'Hylas, Hylas!'

Carman uses the myth to convey his poetic virtuosity; he focuses on loss of innocence and fellowship, along with a connection to mystical nature and the mythical past. The desiring gaze is explicitly female: there is no Hercules here. A homoerotic version is avoided, and Hylas himself is a rower among the Argonauts not a sexually desirable child.

The sculpture *Hylas* by Henry Alfred Pegram (1922), which stands in St John's Lodge Gardens, Regent's Park, London, presents Hylas in the midst of a pool, being pulled down by a single nymph who embraces his legs (Fig. 2.1). The idealized male beauty of the boy is the main focus of the sculpture, as with H. W. Bissen's 1846 sculpture *Hylas*, in the Ny Carlsberg Glyptotek, Copenhagen. This shows a confident, naked Hylas, stick nonchalantly over the left shoulder, the only sign of his imminent fate the water jug in his right hand, which recalls ancient visual representations. This is the ultimate excerption of Hylas, now a body almost entirely separate from his narrative, no nymphs even, no pool, object of the viewers' gaze alone.

In contrast, many later narrative versions de-eroticize the episode (almost) entirely. The *Orphic Argonautica* presents a miniature version: as Hercules hunts, Hylas loses his way and the nymphs find him: 'They caught sight of him coming, still a boy with the looks of a god, and detained him so that he could be immortal among them and unageing for all his days' (*OA* 643–8). Even Hercules' rage is omitted. When Kingsley adapts, he adds back a little both of the nymphs' desire and Hercules' emotion. However, he counterbalances by calling Hylas the nymphs' 'playfellow, forever happy and young' (78), as in Theocritus. The 1963

Fig. 2.1 Hylas and his pool made part of the London landscape. *Hylas* (1922) by Henry Alfred Pegram. St John's Lodge Garden, Regent's Park London. Photo by Ham. Available at: https://commons.wikimedia.org/wiki/File:Hylas_by_Henry_Alfred_Pegram,_St_John%27s_Lodge_Garden.JPG (accessed 22 August 2019).

film does include Hylas, but de-eroticized: this Hylas is a grown man, whose close relationship to Hercules is portrayed in terms of hero worship rather than desire; his camp persona allows an implicit reading of a love relationship, but there is no hint that Hercules reciprocates. Hylas still dies, and more explicitly for the sake of Hercules: bringing Hercules the 'hair-pin of the gods' that he rashly stole. In the 2000 mini-series, Hylas is excised entirely in favour of the expanded Lemnian episode, avoiding any attempt to go beyond heteronormative romance.

Where Hylas does appear in children's literature, he is almost always de-eroticized.[33] In Catran's young-adult novel (2000), Pylos sees the Argonauts' growing resentment of Hercules, coming to a climax with the rowing competition. Catran's Hylas is Hercules' comic sidekick who sings songs praising him and denigrating the Argonauts. It is implied that the Argonauts drowned Hylas deliberately to rid themselves of Hercules, while the narrator interprets his death as an accident, and their need to escape the angry and violent Hercules as terror of his madness in his grief.

A surprising number of children's versions do include Hylas, perhaps due to the fame of Hercules, or the fact that Hylas can be presented as a child in an otherwise adult myth. This is a striking contrast with the Lemnian episode, and perhaps indicates the fact that the Hylas myth is held to be 'high culture'. Many even present the nymphs as *femmes fatales*: the images frequently tell a darker story than the text. Zarabouka's illustration of Hylas pulled down into the moonlit pool, with the dark Hercules attacking the landscape in the background, sits uneasily with her text, where Hylas 'was bewitched and captured by the nymph ... he was so awfully handsome that she wanted to keep him' (n.p.). Similarly, Riordan/Cockcroft, which closely follows Apollonius and devotes a chapter to the episode, describes Hylas as Hercules' 'young friend', 'the darling of the crew, a boy of tender years' (31–3). His abduction is briefly related by Glaucus, emphasizing his new life as an immortal. However, Cockcroft's illustration shows the boy pulled through the water, screaming, by four inhuman-looking, naked, green women. In contrast, Seraillier's 1963 *The Clashing Rocks* (a chapter-book for older readers) has darker text: a graceful illustration, by William Stobbs, shows an adult Hylas kneeling by the pool while a nymph opens her arms invitingly. The text emphasizes depth, silence and stillness: 'Silently the water closed above them, and the pool was still' (26). The 2009 graphic novel by Yomtov/Sandoval/Fuentes includes an adult, bearded Hylas violently drowned by two seductive nymphs. The *femme fatale* image is so compelling that authors include it even when it seems to go against their instincts on how to treat their target audience, or illustrators bring it back in, even in conflict with the text.

One exception, which does give Hercules his prominent role as Hylas' lover, is Robert Graves's novel. He blends Apollonius and Theocritus with his own rationalizing fiction. His Hercules is both humorous and terrifying, and had, as in Apollonius, killed Hylas' father in a quarrel over an ox. The involvement of the nymph Dryope also follows Apollonius, as does Polyphemus' founding of Cios; while Hercules' onwards travel to Colchis on foot at the very end of the chapter evokes the last lines of Theocritus 13. In Graves's version, Hylas is both child and beloved: Hercules keeps him fiercely away from romantic entanglements with both Jason and the Lemnian women, but treats him like a small child, hugging him, kissing him, continually addressing him as 'my sweet' or 'my darling', and treating him as both slave and lover. Hylas, though, has fallen in love with one of the Lemnian women, and deliberately engineers his own apparent death, with the help of the nymph Dryope. Graves acknowledges the homoeroticism of the

Hylas episode in Theocritus and elsewhere, but is not wholly comfortable with it. Sexual 'deviance' is segregated in the extreme figure of Hercules, and Graves creates normative heterosexual relationships to restore Hylas his own agency and power. The nymph here is no longer a *femme fatale*, but instead a helpful, motherly figure, part of Graves's fantasy of a matriarchal society.

Many versions since antiquity obscure or reduce the element of sexual love between Hercules and Hylas, even if they keep the violence and predatory sexuality of the nymphs. This is clearly a deliberate choice: a reference in Christopher Marlowe's *Edward II* (1594) demonstrates that Hylas and Hercules were still icons of gay desire at that point. When Gaveston, Edward's favourite, returns from exile, Edward expresses his joy by invoking the Hylas myth:

> Not Hilas was more mourned of Hercules,
> Then thou hast beene of me since thy exile.

Scene 1.1

The varying receptions of Hylas show that different episodes in the Argonaut myth have different cultural histories. The generic tension between erotic and epic Hylas in ancient poetry is replaced by tensions between eroticized and de-eroticized, heterosexual and homosexual, adult and child Hylas in later receptions.

Redeeming Medea

Medea often overwhelms the Argonautic tradition. She has been invented and re-invented innumerable times. In this section, I briefly trace how Medea affects and fits into the Argonaut tradition. How do the two Medeas (those of Apollonius and Euripides, Colchis and Corinth) relate? How does the representation of Medea in the Argonaut versions change with attitudes to women and sexuality? How do women adapt Medea? Can a sympathetic Medea retain her disruptive power? The section moves from positive to negative versions.

In the ancient world, Medea is already a complex figure, who disrupts gender norms. As both royal and semi-divine (the granddaughter of the sun god), her exceptional status resembles that of Hellenistic royal women.[34] In Pindar *Pythian* 4, she is a prophet who speaks at length, explaining and interpreting the plans of the gods. In Euripides, she successfully takes vengeance on Jason for his oath-breaking and ultimately escapes from Corinth in a chariot drawn by flying snakes. Her witchcraft is left implicit in the text, but can be added by performers, an interpretive choice. She is powerful, violent, rhetorically effective and destroys gendered expectations (obedience to her husband, maternal love, acceptance of female roles). Although she can be seen as a terrifying monster, she is allowed to be ultimately successful, a semi-divine exception to the rules.

Apollonius' Medea is a prequel to that of Euripides, a young, frightened, sometimes suicidal girl, who, while a powerful priestess already, is manipulated and controlled by the gods (also arguably representing her own desires and decisions). In Latin poetry, too, Medea remains complicated: Ovid's monologue of self-division in *Metamorphoses* 7 shows her fighting against herself as she decides whether or not to help Jason, while Seneca's Medea is a character aware of her own literary heritage and able to step outside her fictional universe to watch herself. The cosmopolitan contexts of Hellenistic Alexandria and early imperial Rome offered possibilities for female power and self-sufficiency, at least for wealthy women. The complexity of these ancient texts, and the shock of Euripides' child-killing, portrayed frequently in ancient visual art, too, stimulates a multitude of different adaptations and interpretations in later traditions. Medea becomes both a feminist icon and a monster to be tamed.

Christa Wolf's *Medea: Voices* (1998) is an influential modern retelling of Euripides' *Medea* by a feminist author, which looks back in detail on the Argonautic back-story. It is set in Corinth and told in the voices of six narrators, of which Medea herself is the most important. This Medea tells her own story. For Wolf, Medea has been framed, both in Colchis and Corinth, and, instead of child murderer, becomes healer and detective, unearthing secrets in both places. She escapes Colchis not because of love for Jason (that only happens later) but because she is horrified at her father's sacrifice of her brother Apsyrtus. She is then accused of his death in Corinth, an accusation designed to silence her when she finds out about their own human sacrifice, of the young princess Iphinoe. The motif of human sacrifice is prominent in earlier versions, such as Pasolini, where Medea takes charge of established ritual sacrifice, then perverts it with her own killings of brother and children. Wolf's Medea in contrast rebels against the primitive horror of human sacrifice, but is also part of a conspiracy to overthrow Aeetes and return to an ideal Colchian society of equal distribution, and feminine power. Both Colchis and Corinth, it seems, in Wolf's version, originally privileged the female side, evoking the matriarchal society so mesmerizing for Graves and Treece: 'Tradition has it that in earlier times there were Queens in Colchis' (73), the conspirators against Aeetes remember. Similarly the Corinthian astronomer's account of the reasons for sacrificing Iphinoe focus on a conflict between Queen Merope and those aiming to re-establish old ways, and King Creon, champion of new developments: 'the King would receive the crown on loan from the Queen' (94). As an East German, Wolf had been part of a society with a strong emphasis on equality of the sexes, changed when it reunited with West Germany. Gender roles function differently in Colchis and Corinth for both Pasolini and Wolf: in Pasolini, Medea has equal power in Colchis, but is subjugated and required to be obedient in Greece. She is stripped of her Colchian finery and re-dressed as a Greek chattel.[35] In Wolf, Medea is an unruly refugee, who brings with her a refusal to comply with Corinthian expectations. She uses her medical skill, her charisma and persuasiveness to disrupt Corinthian society: 'according to the Corinthians I'm still wild ... Corinthian women seem like thoroughly tamed house pets to me' (9). The supposed 'primitiveness' of Colchis is set against Corinthian magnificence, but the latter hides violence and oppression. Ideas of both Corinth and Colchis are contested by different characters, who respond differently to Medea's independence and determination. Medea portrays herself as a hero, but Agameda, her enemy and another Colchian refugee, sees her as an entitled princess, assuming she is above the law: 'I could rely on Medea's fancying herself untouchable .... Medea, the king's daughter, Medea, Hekate's priestess' (65). In this, there are similarities with Franz Grillparzer's Medea, who begins as an entitled huntress, complaining that her freedom has been interrupted by the arrival of Phrixus. Aeetes uses her skills with potions to subjugate and kill Phrixus. Grillparzer's Medea is horrified at her father's treachery and her own complicity, and overwhelmed by an irrational passion for Jason. She loses her entitlement and becomes a refugee in Corinth, stripped of her power and privilege.

Wolf's Medea dominates the voices and forms the main perspective, beginning and ending the novel, with four chapters, compared to Jason's two. Wolf also removes irrational passion from the story: Medea's relationship with Jason is almost incidental. This is no longer a story about a man helped by a woman and then abandoning her, but about a woman discovering unbearable secrets and suffering the consequences. Wolf's Medea seeks the origins of stories, but they are used against her by others. Myth becomes a tool of patriarchal oppression. Medea's Colchian experiences drive what happens in Corinth. In her own tale, instead of murdering her brother, she rescues his bones and scatters them on the water in retaliation against her father. She helps Jason to obtain the fleece on one condition: that he takes her with him. In this, Wolf reverses the normal order of events and instead follows the rationalizing story of Diodorus, where Medea leaves Colchis as a rejection of Colchian sacrifice of strangers. In Wolf's version, Medea travels with several shiploads of other Colchians, who form a community in Corinth. She is leader of refugees in search of a new life, not a desperate lover wholly dependent on her man. Wolf creates a new version of the myth, using less well-known and almost forgotten early variants, in which Medea represents a strong woman, turned into a monster by the words of others. Jason remembers listening to the songs: 'At the end she said, They've made what they need out of each of us. Out of you, the Hero. Out of me, the Wicked Witch. They've driven us apart like that' (40). Myth itself destroys their relationship, and the children. Wolf incorporates variants as rumours and legends, accounts for all the ways the story is told, but creates her own truth, intended to overcome and replace previous versions, just as Euripides (perhaps inadvertently) wiped out the Pindaric, prophetic Medea. But in exonerating Medea, Wolf compromises her power to shock and disrupt, the power that makes her compelling in the first place.

Mary Zimmerman's play, another female-authored version, ends with an uneasy tension between Medea as murderess and Medea as semi-divine. She is the last of the Argonauts to be turned into a star, and is cleansed of killing her children, when Hera and Athena re-dress her in the original pure white dress she was wearing when Eros shot her. Zimmerman re-dresses the Medea of dramatic tradition and offers her a happy ending, a: 'second marriage ... [HERA] The happy one. To Achilles' ghost in the underworld. [ATHENA] Yes, she is a queen there. She never dies. Her realms are the Elysian fields.'

Medea's ascent to the sky in her dragon-drawn chariot at the end of Euripides' play emphasizes her divine Otherness, bringing out her strong divine connections from the earliest traditions: Hesiod, *Theogony* 992–1002 presents Medea herself as Jason's prize. Although she is not specifically called divine in this passage, Aeetes is called *diotrepheos* ('Zeus-nurtured', 992), and she is set amongst a list of goddesses who had children with mortal men. Pindar, in *Pythian* 4, emphasizes her wisdom and role as prophetess of the foundation of Cyrene 'speaking from her immortal mouth' (9–12). She is neither monstrous nor a witch in Pindar's text, not even demonized as much as the Odyssean Circe.

Zimmerman's Medea is also Apollonian, a young girl, a promising sorceress, but innocent in her white dress. While Aeetes blusters and threatens, she sits silently in the corner, until Eros intervenes. Hera appears to her, disguised as her aunt Circe (like Venus in Valerius, 7.210–390) and Medea shows her innocence by failing to understand the symptoms of her love: 'Something has gone wrong with me' (109). She girlishly dislikes her official fiancé Styrus (also in Valerius, 3.497). She does not resist as much as in Valerius, where Medea endures an entire book of watching Jason's heroics, and the intervention of Venus, literally dragging her to the temple to meet him. In Zimmerman, Athena and Hera, visible on stage, physically push Medea and Jason into each other's arms. As in Apollonius, Medea considers suicide rather than disgracing herself and her family, but recollects the sweetness of life (narrated by Athena at 113; Apollonius 3.802–19). In both ancient epics and Zimmerman's play, we watch Jason from Medea's perspective, with Valerius and Zimmerman adding the gods, constantly present and driving her. Zimmerman fuses epic and dramatic traditions of Medea, using Apollonius and Valerius to overwrite the Euripidean heroine.

Some versions tell only the Colchian episode, with Medea as focus. For instance, Maffeo Vegio's 1431 *Vellus Aureum* (*Golden Fleece*) tells the story of Medea in Colchis in four short books of Latin hexameters. Vegio, best known for his thirteenth book of the *Aeneid*, was writing in Milan, before either Apollonius or Valerius were well-known, at the height of Renaissance humanism. His main influences were Virgil, Ovid and Seneca and he may have seen himself as writing a prequel to Seneca's *Medea*.[36] Vegio's Medea enters during Aeetes' banquet for the noble Argonauts. Vegio emphasizes Medea's intelligence and power: Aeetes' hope and glory (1.202), she wears a gleaming necklace, gold in her hair and a golden dress, displaying her descent from the sun (203–5). She is not just witch, but also inventor: she herself created the fire-breathing bulls, the dragon's teeth and even the dragon. Vegio's complex divine apparatus emphasizes the characters' close family connections with the gods and can be allegorized as a battle of psychological traits. Vegio multiplies divine intervention to make Medea fall in love, outdoing Valerius: Sol (the Roman sun god) asks Athena, Medea's patron, to save her. Medea is transformed from protégée of Hecate, goddess of witchcraft, in Apollonius, to Athena's craftswoman in Vegio. Vegio's Medea shifts between playing Virgil's Dido, like a doe wounded by a poisoned arrow (*VA* 2.43–7; cf. *Aen.* 4.69–73), and Virgil's Aeneas. She recognizes divine intervention and complains that she can never embrace Athena, like Aeneas, encountering Venus in *Aeneid* 1. This Medea is both hero and victim. Athena personifies Medea's good sense, rescuing her, as when Athena prevented Achilles from killing Agamemnon in *Iliad* 1. But Medea falls again the moment she sees Jason at another banquet. The doubling of banquet scenes emphasizes the complexity of Vegio's plot: his literary belatedness is matched by Medea's resistance. The tussle between Venus and Pallas embodies Medea's divided self in Ovid's *Metamorphoses* where 'a new force drags me unwillingly: desire persuades me one way and reason the other' (Ovid *Met.* 7.19–20). In Ovid, too, she persuades herself out of love, but when she sees Jason, the flame relights (77). Vegio, Valerius and Ovid all emphasize Jason's oath of faithfulness (and in Zimmerman a Fury even appears on stage to note it down). Medea's resistance is an index of her power for both good and evil, intensifying her ultimate capitulation.

Vegio's Medea is similar to another sympathetic version, by the influential female author, Christine de Pizan, writing in the early 1400s, to support her family. Her most famous book rehabilitates women (*Book of the City of Ladies*, 1405). Shortly beforehand (1403) she produced a universal history, *Book of Changing Fortune*, which included the Argonauts and the Laomedon episode. De Pizan has a disproportionately long section on Medea, and her Medea, like Vegio's, is primarily a woman of knowledge, not magic.[37] Love competes with Science for Medea's attention, just as Venus competes with Athena in Vegio. De Pizan's Medea is seduced by a deceptive Jason and meets her tragic end, but is not demonized or presented as witch. Similarly, Lefèvre in our key medieval version separates Medea from magic: in the long sequence where she falls in love with Jason and cannot persuade him to betray Mirro, her old nurse perceives her desperation. This lady uses sorceries on Jason's bed to make him obsessed with Medea. Medea's power to help Jason lies in the knowledge, bequeathed to her by her dying mother, of how to gain the Fleece. Lefèvre's Medea has long soliloquies and, like Vegio's, resists her love lengthily, so while de Pizan rehabilitates Medea at the expense of Jason, Lefèvre succeeds in protecting both.

Several children's versions present wholly or mostly positive Medeas. One is by a woman: *Jason and the Golden Fleece* by Claudia Zeff for Usborne Young Reading (1982). The afterword identifies her main source as Apollonius. In Zeff's version the perspective shifts from Jason to Medea after Jason accepts Aeetes' task. Medea asks Hecate for help, and gives Jason a potion to protect him. Cartwright's illustration evokes the scene of Medea praying to Hecate in the 1963 film. The chapter of Jason's tasks ends with Medea's anxiety as she realizes how angry her father is. She warns Jason of Aeetes' plan to kill them, sings the dragon to sleep and has the idea of deceiving and killing Apsyrtus to escape pursuit. However, Circe successfully absolves her, and the story ends happily. This version targets readers beginning to read chapter-books independently, about age six to eight, and retains some complexity in its short scope. Cartwright's illustrations do not exoticize or demonize Medea: she has dark, neatly arranged hair and a slightly ornate costume, evoking Greekness. The images focus on her emotions, mostly fear, worry and anxiety. Saviour Pirotta, writing for a similar or younger age group, gives an even more positive representation, told from Medea's point of view, though Jason takes precedence in the title (*Jason and the Golden Fleece*). The first and last illustrations feature Medea; the frame is Medea's longing to leave Colchis, and it tells only the Colchian episodes. Medea shows determination and agency: she takes Jason to the king, tells him how to defeat the Earthborns, gives him a magic flower to subdue the serpent, and prevents her father's pursuit: 'Medea whipped up a fog and hid the *Argo*. At last the powerful princess was free.' Medea has done no wrong and her epithet changes from 'beautiful' to 'powerful'. Jeffrey's graphic novel only develops the Colchis episode: this Medea is much more adult, and instructs Jason throughout his feats. She is dignified, neither sexualized nor resembling a witch. They fall in love after the death of Aeetes, as in the 2000 movie. This graphic novel contains none of Medea's traditional crimes, except the betrayal of her father. The afterword mentions her killing of Pelias, and hints at her Euripidean child-killing in a footnote. These children's versions from the 2000s present Medea as active heroine, and sympathetic young girl.

In nineteenth-century Britain, Medea was frequently painted, and she is still popular amongst visual artists today. One female painter, Evelyn de Morgan, produced a well-known Pre-Raphaelite *Medea* in 1889 (Fig. 2.2). Her Medea is strikingly different from those of her male contemporaries, presented primarily as a lover rather than a witch, and as sympathetic and romanticized, rather than exotic and potentially monstrous. De Morgan's painting was hung with a quotation from William Morris, showing the influence of his poem on the visual arts:

> Day by day she saw the happy time fade fast away
> And as she fell from out that happiness
> Again she grew to be the sorceress
> Worker of fearful things as once she was.
>
> Morris *Life and Death of Jason*, 17.439–42

This is the moment when Medea realizes that Jason has fallen out of love with her because of his passion for Glauce, the Corinthian princess. Without epigraph, the painting does not clearly reveal its setting as Colchis or Corinth, and the quotation itself shows the doubling of Medea's situation. She has been driven by love to one act of betrayal (and murder), which inevitably leads to another ('Again . . . as once she was').

In De Morgan's painting, Medea walks towards the viewer, framed by heavy square pillars in multi-coloured marble. Her blonde hair is elaborately piled around her head. She looks down and to the right, with an abstracted and sorrowful expression.[38] She wears a long, dark pink robe, from which one bare foot escapes. In her right hand, she carries a vial. Around her flutter doves, and in the foreground on the floor are two roses. The scene evokes both Colchis and

Fig. 2.2 The softened and feminized Medea of Evelyn de Morgan, in a luxurious marble setting that evokes Morris. Note doves and roses to symbolize love and phial to evoke Medea's magic. *Medea* (1889) by Evelyn de Morgan (1855–1919). Williamson Art Gallery, Birkenhead. Photo by Alonso de Mendoza. Available at: https://commons.wikimedia.org/wiki/File:De_Morgan_Medea.jpg (accessed 22 August 2019).

Corinth, showing the strong relationship between the two halves of the Medea story. The vial could be the potion to make Jason invulnerable or the poison to kill Creon's daughter. The location could be the luxurious palace of Creon, or the imposing temple where she meets Jason. Her distress could relate to her suicidal impulses in Colchis or her murderous intentions in Corinth. The roses and doves indicate the importance of love, key in both episodes. Her bare foot evokes two ventures into the woods in search of magical ingredients in Morris's accounts of her witchcraft, both barefoot (7.279–80; 17.461–4). Morris's eight-fold repetition of 'once more' in the Corinth scene (461–70) emphasizes the repetition of her previous suffering, magic and betrayal. What is more, Morris's Jason meets Glauce in the temple of Venus, surrounded by doves and roses; Jason is intoxicated by the scent of the roses. Morris's Medea, like De Morgan's, has a calm wisdom: 'in her face and calm grey eyes divine / He read his own destruction' (17.391–2). The emphasis in De Morgan's representation is on Medea's point of view, her sadness caused by love. Apart from the vial, there is nothing too uncanny, monstrous or evoking witchcraft. She is both object and subject of desire. Elise Lawton Smith suggests that framing her in the powerful and luxurious architecture presents her as a trapped woman.[39]

In comparison, three paintings of Medea from this period by men, all with Pre-Raphaelite connections, present her primarily as a witch: Frederick Sandys' *Medea* from 1868 (Fig. 2.3), probably conceived and produced earlier, during the

Fig. 2.3 The strange pallor and angst of Sandys' Medea. The backdrop that illustrates the Argonaut story may be a wall-painting in her Corinthian home. *Medea* (1866–8), Frederick Sandys (1829–1904). Birmingham Museums and Art Gallery, 1925P105. Photo by Crisco 1492. Available at: https://commons.wikimedia.org/wiki/File:Medea_-_Frederick_Sandys_-_Google_Cultural_Institute.jpg (accessed 4 January 2021).

same period that Morris was writing his *Jason*; Valentine Prinsep's *Medea the Sorceress* (1880) and John William Waterhouse's *Jason and Medea* from 1907. Sandys' *Medea* was well-received and attracted much critical attention.[40] Contemporary critics were fascinated by Medea's pallor and the painting's eerie lighting. Morris also emphasizes baleful light while Medea petitions Hecate and makes her potion for Jason: 'their bale-fire flamed up bright' (7.247); 'with new light Medea's wearied eyes / gleamed in the fireshine o'er those mysteries' (7.250–1). Sandys' Medea was perceived as both noble and exotic. She was based on the model Keomi Grey, who seems to have been of Romany heritage. Critics mostly ignored the 'goldback' in which *Argo*, the dragon and the fleece are represented (as her previous feats or as what currently obsesses her?), and assumed that this was Corinthian Medea. So the reception of this painting again blurs the two halves of the story. Medea is both object of desire and terror, and subject in love, self and Other, lover and witch; De Morgan's female perspective gives a more sympathetic approach to Medea in comparison to Sandys.

Morris himself is sympathetic: Jason and Medea fall in love mutually on sight. Aeetes makes Medea herself announce Jason's tasks and it is at this moment that 'Love ... cast his golden yoke about them both' (7.87–8). Morris's narrative takes pains to look through Medea's eyes as well as at her: he frequently describes her clothes and the colour and light in which she moves, but also the feel of the ground beneath her bare feet, and her terror that others might wake and see her. His Medea has agency and is respected by the Argonauts. This calm and purposeful Medea contrasts strongly with that of Apollonius, who Richard Buxton has shown is restless, always moving, darting her gaze around, except when she is moving threateningly in a situation of magical control.[41] Apollonius' Medea cannot face Circe's gaze (AR 4.697–750) and her spirit whirls like a spindle (AR 4.1061).

The theme of movement and travel is important in other texts: Ovid's Medea in *Metamorphoses* 7 is characterized by her powerful ability to travel; her magical flights in search of outlandish ingredients replace the *Argonautica* itself as a fantastic voyage (7.179–237).[42] Ovid frequently miniaturizes and displaces the major epic narratives of his predecessors as he transforms them. Morris seems to have had Ovid's account in mind: Ovid's Medea too goes barefoot into the night forest. Unlike most epic heroines, Medea moves successfully through the landscape.[43] This mobility and urge for freedom frequently appears later in the tradition: Saviour Pirotta presents a Medea who longs for freedom; Christa Wolf's Medea frequently roams the city and transgresses social norms by attending Corinthian rites, going amongst plague victims, and joining Colchian rituals. Medea's mobility assimilates her to an epic hero and underlines her transgressive nature and Otherness. Where epic women usually remain in place and seek to make men settle (the Homeric Penelope, Nausicaa and Calypso, the Virgilian Dido), Medea controls her life by undertaking journeys and herself becomes the one memorable for her achievements.[44]

In the 1963 film, Medea is much less important and active: she enters the film passive, rescued after a shipwreck. As priestess of Hecate, she is essentially a dancer; the long, indulgent dance routine in Colchis features Medea as star, and Jason as audience, reversing the erotic viewing of the Latin epic tradition. This Medea is ship-wrecked in full make-up, resembling Elizabeth Burton's Cleopatra, and the dance scene exoticizes and sexualizes her further: she wears gold body make-up and a tightly clinging silver dress, and is ritually dressed in a red, jewelled over-robe. The subsequent banquet evokes an orgy, particularly resembling the Amazon scene in the 1958 film. Later, Medea prays to Hecate, but has no ointment to give Jason, since there are no bulls. Instead, she takes him to the fleece, but can only watch as he fights. Rather than healing others, she takes an arrow in the back, and is herself healed by the fleece. She is even removed from watching the skeleton fight: Jason tells Argos to take her back to the ship. This Medea is prize, love interest, damsel in distress and exotic helper, sympathetic but lacking power.

The Medea of the 2000 mini-series has much more agency: she is a prophetess, who watches Jason's progress from Colchis, a mediating internal audience. Medea, the king's daughter again, must stay with the fleece for ritual reasons, and does not fall in love with Jason until later in the journey. On the *Argo*, she heals Acastus, and the loss of her father brings Jason and Medea together. Zeus propositions her, and removes Cupid's arrow, but she protests that she genuinely loves Jason and Zeus allows her to refuse him.[45] We wonder in Iolchos whether Medea will revert to her traditional murderous persona, by betraying Jason or murdering Pelias, but Jason and his crew break into the throne room before she can do it. This Medea is threatening and potentially powerful, but her actions are carefully curated so she remains sympathetic, a romantic heroine, like that of Morris, with a touch of moral cleansing as in Wolf. In both Wolf and the 2000 film, Medea's power with drugs and ritual effectiveness remains, but she uses it for good, not evil.

Medea's witchcraft in Morris, Wolf and the 2000 film coexists with royal status and domesticated femininity. The stereotype of the witch can be used to empower women or to exclude powerful women from society as monsters. While Circe in the *Odyssey* is terrifying, she is also an independent woman, at least semi-divine, beautiful and deserving of respect.[46] In the poetry of Augustan Rome (Horace's *Epodes* and the love elegy of Propertius and Ovid), witches arouse disgust and horror: an old woman consumed by desire, a sexual predator, who perverts religious rituals, an alcoholic, hideously ugly.[47] We have seen Sandys' painting of a threatening and exoticized Medea, represented primarily as witch. Medea's witchcraft interacts in complex ways with her gender elsewhere. Felicity Brooks' retelling for older children presents Medea as exotic and demonic, in contrast to Brooks' positive representation of Atalanta as 'one of the lads'. In Medea's room, Jason sees 'a big bronze cauldron full of bubbling black liquid. "You're a . . . witch!"' Brooks lists labels on jars: 'Toads' Eyes (Medium strength); Powdered Unicorn Horn (apply sparingly)' (62) to evoke fairy tale witchcraft. Medea first flirts with Jason ('I prefer "sorceress" myself – it sounds a little more glamorous'), then directly demands marriage. Jason is 'rooted to the spot, too surprised to speak'. The tone is light-hearted but Medea is outrageous and manipulative. Jason is the victim here, overwhelmed by perfume; all he can see is 'alluring green eyes, appealing lips and lustrous, long hair'. Humphreys' illustrations show Medea bathed in green light, wearing a dramatic peacock-feather headdress, large gold earrings and a purple robe embroidered with magical signs. Next to her is a jar of eyes (63). Apsyrtus (here a young boy) calls Medea 'old witch' (72), while the illustration represents her as tall, powerful, robed and dragging him along with her, bearing a distinct resemblance to Jadis, the witch-queen in C. S. Lewis's *The Magician's Nephew* (as famously illustrated by Pauline Baynes). Most dramatic of all is Medea over the cauldron, framed by flames, devising Pelias' death. In the final full-colour double page image 'she laughed a maniacal laugh . . . as she soared up through the smoke', after killing Glauce, Creon and her own children. This Medea is exotic, powerful and evil, with no hint of her as anxious, distraught, innocent young girl, even in Colchis.

In this wholehearted demonization of Medea as powerful witch, Brooks draws on the tradition of children's literature, embodied by Kingsley, who throughout refers to Medea as 'witch-maiden' (86, 92, 97). Nevertheless, Kingsley's Jason does seduce her consciously into helping him: 'he looked at Medeia cunningly, and held her with his glittering eye, till she blushed and trembled' (88). In these versions for children, Medea acts as scapegoat, taking the blame for the negative aspects of the expedition, protecting the heroism and virtue of the Argonauts. In adult and young adult films and texts, Medea is often a powerful religious figure, strongly ambivalent, inscrutable, for instance in Pasolini, Graves, Treece and Catran, but not demonized.

Elsewhere she acts as an antagonist: for instance, she has a love–hate relationship with the narrator in Holdstock's *Merlin* Codex. The most negative Medea, however, is that of Bernard Evslin's retelling for young adults. During Jason's extended stay in Colchis, he is seduced by the water nymph Lethe, and Medea finds out. She plots to kill Lethe and arranges for her to be abducted and murdered by Boreas, the North Wind, who she wants to marry. Boreas suggests that killing Jason would not be sufficient revenge, so Medea creates her daughter in the image of Lethe and then kills her too, by throwing her off a cliff, and leaves Jason to mourn forever. This Medea is characterized by animal features (bird claws), dehumanized and powerfully Other.

The Medea of the *Argonautica* is closely related to the *Medea* of Euripides: only hints remain of a possible earlier Medea, divine and heroic, less clearly demonized. Apollonius' mixture of anguished young girl and terrifying witch has tended in the later traditions to separate: the Argonautic Medea is either sympathetic or monstrous, but rarely both. Many versions attempt to segregate the Apollonian and Euripidean parts of the story, but often with little success. Colchis and Corinth mirror and blur into each other. Medea will always become herself, as she does famously in Seneca's tragedy, declaring *Medea nunc sum!* ('Now I really am Medea!' Sen. *Med.* 910) She activates a fascination with powerful and destructive women, a fantasy that functions in different ways for male and female audiences and creators, but persists through time with no clear change or development.

Conclusions

Representations of women and sexuality are significant areas of variation in the Argonaut tradition. Desire drives the Argonaut story: Medea's love for Jason is almost always central to the narrative trajectory, and Hercules' loss of Hylas prevents him from taking over the expedition. While reasonably consistent in ancient myth, the Lemnian episode and the loss of Hylas have distinctive and varied afterlives. Often more popular than the myth as a whole, they provoke anxiety in some contexts. Nineteenth-century and children's versions tend to avoid erotic adventures. In contrast, mid-twentieth-century adult versions, especially Graves and Treece, are highly sexualized and treat women primarily as sexual objects. More recently, children's versions dominate: Lamb's adventures of Ulysses laid the foundations for Greek journey myths to be domesticated as children's adventure stories.[48] However, adult versions persist: William Morris,

John Gardner, Robert Holdstock and the 2000 mini-series all enjoy the myth's sexualities. *Femmes fatales* are much more acceptable than boy lovers. While Propertius clearly treats Hylas as a gay icon, it is often hard to be sure whether Hercules' relationship with Hylas is sexual or simply emotional, and more repressive versions ignore Hercules' relationship with Hylas entirely. This shows how deeply ingrained homophobia remains.

The Argonaut myth also challenges gender roles and subverts gender stereotypes. The presence of Atalanta, the Lemnian women, Amazons (in some versions) and Medea all give opportunities to engage with femininity. The Argonaut myth is a product of the misogynistic cultures of Archaic Greece and before, but Hellenistic Alexandria preserves more complex, nuanced attitudes to women, even if women were still largely expected to remain unseen and silent. The reversal of gender roles on Lemnos and among the Amazons is both marvel and threat. The Argonauts venture into a shocking world of Otherness and surprise, and gender is one aspect of that Otherness. Later versions refashion the myth though their own gendered expectations (and their rupture), keeping a balance between alienation and domestication of the ancient world and portraying marvellous adventures. This chapter has explored the complex representations of mortal women, but later chapters will look at female monsters and goddesses. Femininity, however, is only one side of the coin: the *Argonautica* contains equally complex portrayals of masculinity, already touched upon through Hylas. The importance of women in this story creates compromised men, especially Jason.

Masculinity and Leadership

Jason is a problematic hero. There is much scholarship on this, even just in Apollonius: is Apollonius 'redefining heroism'?[1] Is Jason a 'new type of hero'?[2] Is he a love hero?[3] A healer?[4] An anti-hero?[5] A human amongst demi-gods?[6] Other Argonauticas, from those of Pindar, Euripides and Valerius, to the 2000 TV movie, or the recent novels by Holdstock and Kneupper, create different solutions to the representation of Jason.

But is the problem Jason, or the concept of 'heroism'? Many similar questions arise in scholarship on Aeneas, or even Odysseus. I find several interlocking issues here: first, a hero should 'always be the best' (*aien aristeuein*, Homer *Iliad* 6.208, motto of the University of St Andrews, among other places).[7] The *Iliad*, code model of ancient epic, revolves around Achilles' conflict with Agamemnon about what 'best' means: most powerful and important, or most successful warrior? Secondly, the word 'hero' has varied implications in different times and places.[8] Modern English substitutes the word for 'protagonist': 'the hero of the story'. This can cause difficulties: not just the protagonist is 'heroic' in ancient epic, and protagonists may not be heroes. Even more confusing is the assumption of a moral element to heroism. Modern heroes are often expected to be virtuous. Current English also uses the term ('my hero', NHS heroes) to refer to someone who sacrifices their own well-being to save others. The idea of hero as saviour is less prominent in ancient texts. Moral heroism is particularly expected in the nineteenth century, where Hawthorne, Kingsley and Morris all find elements of the Argonaut story difficult, and seek ways of exonerating characters. Ancient heroism, on the other hand, is closely related to religion and the gods: heroes receive cult, are sponsored by gods, and maintain appropriate relationships with the gods.[9] By separating out these different facets of heroism, we can analyse receptions and transformations of ancient heroes more easily.

First, an ancient hero should be an impressive warrior: even Odysseus, well-known for cunning, also needs to fight (and kill). Second, there is a strong association between Greek heroism and leadership or aristocracy: Thersites, as a common soldier, cannot be heroic. In the modern world, heroes from disadvantaged backgrounds are often more admired, although they often become rich and powerful. Occasionally, a hero is a lone warrior, but mostly ancient heroes lead and influence others. Heroism is strongly gendered: women can be heroic, but they often do this by taking on masculine characteristics. Modern Anglophone culture tends to think of heroes as self-sufficient and self-reliant, but in the ancient world, heroes are more impressive if they have divine sponsorship and help.

Apollonius' Jason, and those influenced by him, often does not meet expectations of heroism, in many cultures.[10] We can see this in online responses to the Jason of the 2000 mini-series, who is too confused and not strong enough to meet the expectations of a twenty-first-century TV audience. As with Medea, who is represented on a spectrum from sympathetic to monstrous, so Jason goes from admirable to despicable, either as victim, monster or both. Jason and the cultural history of the *Argonautica* show clearly how ideas about heroism and masculinity radically change.

I will explore heroism in two separate chapters, this one and Chapter 6. This first chapter focuses on the journey out and themes of masculinity and leadership; the second on moral readings. In the first, I examine the election scene and Jason's actions as leader in Iolchos and the character of Hercules as foil to Jason. How are the two characters different, what is their relationship and what effect does the comparison have on evaluations of their masculinity? I tackle the loss of Hercules, which forms a major challenge for Jason as leader, causing unrest and dissent amongst his crew. How does Jason handle this? The chapter finishes with Amycus and antagonists: what do opponents tell us about ideals of masculinity and leadership? To what extent is Jason an ideal man? How effective is he as a leader? How impressive is he as warrior (and athlete)? How does Jason relate to the gods? How effective is he as a religious leader?

Chapter 6, on heroism and betrayal, comes as the Argonauts reach Colchis and Jason performs his major feats and survives serious threats, but only at the cost of betraying others. This addresses the question of excessive help and heroic (im)morality. The book tackles these different aspects following the order of episodes, focusing first in the current chapter on Iolchos, then Hercules after losing Hylas, and then the Argonauts' first major challenge without him, the contest with Amycus. Jason's preparations and journey prepare him for the complex denouement in Colchis.

There are as many different Jasons as there are Medeas: for Nathaniel Hawthorne, Jason has long, blonde hair, is glamourous and glib; for Robert

Holdstock, he is dark, ruthless, untrustworthy and brooding. In the 1958 *Le Fatiche di Ercole*, Jason is a side character, not even commander of the *Argo*. He is young, friendly, and reliant on Hercules. In the 1963 film, Todd Armstrong plays him as older, bearded, sceptical and organized. In the 2000 TV mini-series, Jason is young, naïve and confused. He has long, flowing mousey-brown hair and is cocooned in layers of clothing. This particular Jason (played by Jason London) alienates many viewers. A selection of comments from the influential website IMDb demonstrates this: according to chathaf on 2 March 2002 'it was very difficult to get past Jason London's poor acting ... he never seemed regal, charismatic (a leader), or powerful'; the characterization of Jason is seen as the fault of the actor. EdgarST on 1 March 2001 complained of a 'Psychology 101' approach to characterization: 'in the case of Jason, being an action hero, his uncertainty and doubts tend to diminish the empathy with the viewer.' Many viewers compare the 2000 Jason unfavourably with Armstrong in the 1963 Harryhausen film, which they refer to as 'the original'. Most damningly, Nilsson-5 (6 April 2008) concludes that Jason 'has the charisma of a bowl of soggy cornflakes. He always has the same "I just woke up and don't know what's going on yet" expression.' One could imagine readers of Pindar making similar complaints about Apollonius.

Pindar's Jason is strong and active: he negotiates effectively with Pelias and himself takes charge of the preparations for the voyage (169–70), praises and chooses his crew (189). There are no hints of self-doubt, uncertainty or immorality. He is a strong hero, favoured by the gods, with the cunning, soft, speech of an Odysseus. Apollonius' Jason, in contrast, is not allowed a grand, dramatic arrival in the marketplace or a bold, subtle encounter with Pelias. Instead, the catalogue presents the Argonauts as the group protagonist, and the crowd, who watch Jason, worry for his parents. His first action is to comfort his grieving mother; his second to ignore the priestess Iphias, as the young leave the old behind.[11] His beauty is conveyed by a comparison to Apollo (AR 1.307–10). Throughout the poem, he has a tendency to 'resourcelessness': while Odysseus is *polumetis* ('the man of many plans'), Jason is frequently *amechanos* ('lacking resources', 'at a loss'). For instance, as the heroes feast before departure, Jason 'all helpless (*amechanos*) was brooding over each event in his mind, like one oppressed with thought' (AR 1.460–1). Idas accuses him of being afraid, causing a quarrel with Idmon, until Orpheus uses his music to restore harmony. Similarly, when Aeetes sets his challenges, Jason responds with despair: 'and he, silently fixing his eyes on his feet, sat there, voiceless, resourceless (*amechaneon*) in the face of his evils' (AR 3.422–3).

Most revealingly, the poem's first scene of Jason interacting with his Argonauts puts into question his leadership. He asks the crew to select a leader, specifically the best man (*ariston*, 338), but he defines 'best': at organizing, keeping the peace and negotiating with strangers. Despite this attempt to redefine leadership, the crew immediately choose Hercules, in what feels like a Macedonian ritual of acclamation.[12] However, Hercules refuses and forbids anyone else to stand, saying 'Let him who gathered us also lead us' (347). Just as Agamemnon's attempt to raise morale in *Iliad* 2 backfires, when the Greek army are only too happy to head for home, and only Odysseus manages to stop them, this seems like a failed tactic to strengthen Jason's position, which ends up with Jason relying on Hercules for authority.

This election scene may be Apollonius' invention: Pindar does not hint at it and no other sources on possible previous versions mention it. Apollonius may be combining two incompatible traditions, one in which Jason is unquestioned leader and another in which Hercules is leader. The mythographical tradition has both: Apollodorus presents Jason as commander without question, while Diodorus (41.1) says the Argonauts chose Hercules. Valerius plays with the election scene, first omitting it and then referring back to it (3.699–702).[13] This suggests he acknowledges the scene's tendentiousness, while making Jason at first appear stronger, but later more like Apollonius' Jason. The *Orphic Argonautica* includes and intensifies it: Jason himself expresses feelings of inferiority, not just to Hercules but to the many famous heroes of divine descent (280–302). Jason himself suggests Hercules as ideal leader, which gives him a self-deprecatory agency and a self-awareness less negative than the embarrassing miscalculation in Apollonius, although it also weakens him in comparison to the narrator, Orpheus. The *OA* gives Hercules a good reason for insisting on Jason's leadership: the favour of Hera.

The election scene only appears sometimes in later versions. Given that Apollonius and the *OA* include it, but Valerius and Apollodorus do not, this is unsurprising. Lefèvre has a very brief gathering and departure scene, and builds up Jason as a character, so omits it. Neither Hawthorne nor Morris include it, and Graves does not mention it in his *Greek Myths*. Genres that require a strong Jason avoid it, including all the film versions, the looser adaptations (Holdstock, Kneupper, Hauser), and most children's versions. Where Pelias authorizes and controls the expedition, such as in Treece's novel and the 2000 movie, where he pays for the boat, Jason is designated leader by Pelias and there are no democratic processes.

However, Kingsley does include the scene, reducing it in comparison to the *OA*: the heroes 'chose themselves a captain from their crew: and . . . all called for

Hercules, because he was the strongest and most huge but Hercules refused, and called for Jason, because he was the wisest' (72). Kingsley softens the scene by giving agency to the crew and emphasizing Jason's wisdom. Of the children's versions that include it, Seraillier minimizes it still further (15). Colum (25–6) briefly reiterates Apollonius' version, but softens it with some Argonauts choosing Jason and some Hercules. Brooks (1995) subtly adjusts the scene to strengthen Jason: her Jason literally steps down amongst the crew, creating 'a moment's surprised hush'. Rather than acclaiming Hercules, the crew turn to him for advice. Hercules insists on Jason, the crew applaud and Jason returns to the prow 'grinning from ear to ear' (23–4). The scene could have been pre-orchestrated, and acts as the morale booster it completely fails to be in Apollonius. Similarly, in the graphic novel by Whitehead and Banerjee: when Hercules arrives, Orpheus suggests he should 'lead the quest', but Hercules replies 'This is not my quest to lead . . . I will gladly follow him' (17). This scene needs some adaptation to work as Mori suggests Apollonius' should, presenting the Argonauts as a miniature society, with Jason taking charge and cleverly acting as a democratic leader, supported by the impressive power and reputation of Hercules.[14]

Other versions bring out the scene's incongruity. Graves's *Golden Fleece* intensifies the scene, creating a more negative portrayal of Jason even than that of Apollonius. Argus initiates the discussion of leadership. Hercules casually knocks down a seabird with a meat-bone and refuses the role of leader, claiming he is 'too often made insensible by drink' (100), but does not acclaim Jason instead. The crew suggest Admetus, Ancaeus, Castor and Pollux 'But nobody cried, "Jason"' (101). Hercules intervenes again with a recommendation on the authority of Chiron, which he presents himself as doubting ('Can you really mean Jason, the son of Aeson?'). Chiron's choice of Jason is based on the fact that 'most men either envy or despise him, but most women fall in love with him at first sight' and 'women everywhere . . . hold the secret reins of power' (101). Jason himself makes no contribution, and Hercules finishes enigmatically with 'But whether I despise or envy Jason, let no man impudently enquire.' It is not until the next chapter that Jason thanks Hercules 'humbly' and takes control of proceedings; but the scene of his depression is also included, along with Idas' challenge. Graves presents women as powerful but nevertheless despises their power, and seems to despise Jason's masculinity along with his attractiveness.

The departure sequence effectively reveals attitudes to leadership and masculinity. Apollonius' Jason defines leadership as taking care of details, creating collaborative harmony and negotiating effectively. Nevertheless the Argonauts choose Hercules as leader, because he is the most famous, the strongest and the best in battle, illustrating a clash between different models of effective leadership.

Elsewhere in Apollonius' departure sequence, we see Jason's religious competence and emotional intelligence: he interprets the significance of prophecies, performs or organizes sacrifices, soothes his mother's grief, chooses his crew and allocates roles. But throughout the tradition others often help with these tasks too: in Apollonius, Argos masterminds the launch, Orpheus calms the quarrel between Idas and Idmon. In the *OA*, Orpheus takes charge of religious activities. Tiphys handles navigation, Echion performs negotiations, as herald (for instance in Graves and Evslin). In the 2000 movie, Atalanta hunts for food; Castor and Pollux cook, while Laertes the bull-leaper teaches Jason to do somersaults. He crashes to the floor and all laugh, but later these are the skills he uses to defeat the bronze bull. The tradition puts great emphasis on the Argonauts as a team that work together and need each other. The election scene and departure sequence make Apollonius by no means overwhelmingly central to the tradition. His Jason is more hapless than most, younger, less competent, less effective as a leader, at one end of the spectrum. The tradition explores many different types of heroism, and one alternative as hero and potential leader is Hercules.

Hercules and the Argonauts

In Apollonius, and often elsewhere, Hercules and Jason are contrasting models of both masculinity and leadership: Hercules relies on physical strength and extreme violence; Jason persuades and seduces. Hercules is often excessive, while Jason is sometimes weak and often untrustworthy. They have become a canonical duo in recent popular culture (in TV series such as *Young Hercules* and *Atlantis*), building on the 1958 film, which combines the two myths. Hercules is often a problem for the Argonauts, usually abandoned along the way. In the evidence for the early myth, mostly taken from fragmentary mythography, there are many variants: Herodorus (31F41) excludes Hercules, who is the slave of Queen Omphale, cross-dressing, at that time. Apollodorus at 1.9.19 lists various versions, including Pherecydes, who, along with Hesiod (Fr 263MW) and Herodotus (7.193), put him ashore around the corner from Iolchos, at Aphetae. Theocritus *Idyll* 13 and Apollonius both lose him in Mysia, searching for Hylas, but Theocritus mentions that he reaches Colchis on foot on his own, where he presumably re-joins the Argonauts. Other early mythographers, Demaratos and

Dionysios (of Mytilene or Miletus, also mentioned at Apollodorus 1.9.19) keep him on board all the way to Colchis. Apollodorus prioritizes the Apollonian version but lists these other versions, making them all available to the later tradition.

Both the Hercules myth and the Argonaut myth are varied and early. Both take place chronologically in the generation before the Trojan wars. The two traditions often meet and combine uneasily. It is impossible to imagine a gathering of the greatest heroes of Greece that did not include Hercules. But it is equally hard to see how the story could take its familiar form with Hercules present. Hercules is a *deus ex machina* figure who transforms any story he enters. The way versions handle this tension shows attitudes to myth, heroism, leadership and masculinity. The tension between the two traditions matches a tense relationship between the two heroes, Hercules and Jason. Who is really the best? Who is really the protagonist? Who is really in charge? This section will explore the Argonautic Hercules thematically, looking at excessiveness; competitiveness in the rowing contest; following after Hercules in Apollonius; Hesione and Prometheus, especially in Valerius; madness and violence, especially in Graves and Treece; masculinity and didactic heroism in film and children's literature.

Some versions pass over, exclude or substitute him: Pindar mentions Hercules, but does not represent his actions; this reinforces the self-sufficiency of Pindar's Jason. Of the films, three put great emphasis on Hercules, while *I Giganti* (1960) and Pasolini's *Medea* exclude him. Famous and easily recognizable, Hercules is popular in children's versions. Versions that exclude Hercules either have a reduced cast of Argonauts (Grillparzer, for instance, names only one: 'Milo', Jason's confidant), or replace Hercules as foil with another character (Ekion in Evslin, Atalanta in Hauser). Kneupper's science-fiction romance hero Jason is the only 'real' Argonaut, set against Idas and Antaeus, both defined by size and strength, but with their physique created by genomancy and their heroism created through staged battles and 'vids'.

There is one version which excludes Hercules polemically and makes Jason the central hero and unproblematic protagonist. In the 1960 peplum *I Giganti della Tessaglia*, which responds to the 1958 *Fatiche di Ercole*, Giasone himself takes on the Herculean role, and is also legitimate king of Iolco, an Odysseus figure trying to return to his kingdom, while a treacherous regent tries to marry his wife. This Giasone carries out his major feats solo. He is not even reliant on Medea, because the love interest is outsourced to a lesser character, Euristeo. This version creates a wholly positive Giasone as cinematic spectacle and hero.

Apollonius plays with the tensions between Argonaut myth and Hercules myth, Jason and Hercules, in a typically Hellenistic fashion: Alexandrian poets delighted in setting mythical traditions and generic models against each other. As Richard Hunter well demonstrates, Apollonius' Hercules is a foil for Jason, but not his polar opposite.[15] The figure of Hercules in Greek myth is complex and multivalent.[16] He is overwhelmingly masculine, yet often loses control of himself and on occasions crosses gender boundaries, for instance, by dressing up as a woman. He saves the world from evils, founds endless cities, fathers countless children, but also kills his own family, becomes an exile and mostly acts alone. In Apollonius, he is in the middle of his labours, and 'not a young man'.[17]

In Apollonius, too, Hercules is a figure of excess. When he sits down on the *Argo*, the ship sinks deep beneath him (1.532–3). This alludes to the tradition of Hercules as too heavy for the ship, a play on his epic seriousness. Apollodorus reports that Pherecydes evicts Hercules from the *Argo* at Aphetae when the boat itself complains about his weight. Hercules is more epic even than Achilles; he eventually becomes a god; he takes part in the battle of the giants and the gods, the gigantomachy, most epic of epic subjects.[18] Like epic, though, Hercules is generically omnivorous, taking in and being part of many different types of literature: lyric (Pindar *Olympian* 2, 3, 6 and 10 as founder of the Olympic games), tragedy (Sophocles' *Trachiniae* and Seneca *Hercules Furens*), and comedy (Aristophanes' *Frogs*, where Dionysus dresses as Hercules). Hercules is too epic for epic and too tonally complex to be contained in any one genre.

Hercules' excessiveness dominates the rowing contest before the loss of Hylas. At 1.1153–71, Apollonius' Argonauts compete to see who can row longest and Hercules is left rowing the boat on his own: 'But Hercules ... pulled the weary rowers along all together and made the strong-knit timbers of the ship quiver' (1161–3). He threatens the integrity of the *Argo*, let alone the crew. Different receptions of this episode show how Hercules varies across the tradition. In Valerius' Roman *Argonautica*, the contest is started by Eurytus and Idas; Hercules is exhilarated and frames it as a contest against the waves themselves, but breaks his oar before a winner emerges. This shows Valerius' cosmic interests, but erases Jason and does not even allow Hercules victory. The rowing contest next resurfaces in Graves's novel, where Hercules sets up the contest and offers a formal prize, as a way of speeding progress. He challenges Jason, who then keeps going the longest, after even Castor and Pollux. Graves intensifies the competition between them. The D'Aulaires, children's mythographers, feature the rowing contest; the loss of Hylas and Hercules, along with the Phineus episode, are the only events on the outward journey. They present the same version of the rowing contest as Graves, followed by the recent, gorgeously illustrated, version by Byrd. Seraillier also follows Graves, but has his Hercules revive the exhausted Jason with a helmet of water, in a gesture of reconciliation. Similarly, Seraillier's Pollux later revives Amycus after the boxing match, instead of killing him. Brooks also lightens the tone: after the rowing contest, 'Jason lay sprawling on the deck, laughing and gasping for breath' (40). Catran emphasizes the unity of the crew in opposition to Hercules: 'It was the crew pitting themselves against Hercules' (68). James Riordan closely follows Graves's version, as do Malam and Antram. Zimmerman's comic Hercules excessively harangues the resigned Argonauts as he insists on competing with them: when his oar breaks he explodes into obscenity and rage in capital letters, while Jason attempts to mollify him. In Whitehead and Banerjee's version, it is Jason who challenges Hercules, showing this version's determination to recuperate Jason. In this episode, at least, later versions view Apollonius through Graves, more interested in the rivalry and tensions between Jason and Hercules even than Apollonius, although versions for younger audiences often make the competition more jocular. Athletic contests appeal to children's culture and spectacular feats to visual versions. Physical strength remains an important part of heroism, along with endurance, and this scene emphasizes Hercules' extraordinary strength.

Often, even after his abandonment, Hercules remains an important figure in the story. In Apollonius, after offering him leadership, and being shamed by him into leaving Lemnos, the crew are devastated by his loss and long for him throughout the poem. After Pollux defeats Amycus, an anonymous Argonaut reflects (2.145–50) that Hercules would quickly have destroyed Amycus. When they visit Lycus, the king tells at length of Hercules' feats (2.774–95). When Aeetes arms himself at 3.1232–4, his armour evokes the gigantomachy: he used it to fight 'Phlegraean Mimas' (Phlegra was the battlefield and Mimas a giant). The narrator claims only Hercules could have faced Aeetes in single combat.

The Argonauts follow Hercules around the Mediterranean: to Lycus, the Amazons and later to North Africa, where they encounter the Hesperides, and the corpse of the dragon Ladon, guardian of the golden apples. Hercules saves them retrospectively in their extreme thirst, since he had created a spring (4.1393–1484). They rush off to search for him, suggesting versions where they succeed in reconnecting; and Lynceus with his marvellous eyesight sees, or thinks he sees, Hercules in the distance. He reports that no searcher will find Hercules on his journey, read as an intimation of his apotheosis: by the end of the poem, Apollonius' Hercules has been definitively separated from the Argonauts and may already be a god.[19]

In Apollonius, and more so in Valerius, the Argonauts try to make up for the loss of Hercules and follow his lead geographically, morally and heroically.[20] Hercules' refusal of Lemnian hospitality suggests philosophical self-control. But elsewhere in myth he is a keen connoisseur of women, and in Apollonius his reasons for leaving Lemnos emphasize not morality but the quest itself and the prospect of glory. Although Apollonius' Hercules is a saviour, he is not a moral paradigm. The Hesperides comment on his brutality and bestial nature; he took Hylas when he killed his father in an argument over an ox. He is godlike in his Otherness, his extremity and his self-sufficiency, and an extreme example of ancient heroism.

Nevertheless, as Hunter demonstrates, the Argonauts also double, repeat and match Hercules' achievements.[21] Pollux defeats Amycus; Lycus emphasizes his similarity to Hercules' own boxing prowess. Jason's battle against the Earthborns at Colchis echoes Hercules' killing of the six-armed giants in Cyzicus. Jason's theft of the Golden Fleece and defeat of its dragon guardian matches Hercules' acquisition of the golden apples and his dispatch of Ladon. While all these repetitions are marked by difference (Medea drugs the dragon, while Hercules kills his), it is not straightforwardly the case that the Argonauts fail to live up to Hercules: the Argonauts cause Rhea to create a spring on Mount Dindymum (1.1145–8), named after Jason, just as Hercules creates the spring in North Africa. At 2.1052–7, Amphidamas deals with the birds of Ares by remembering Hercules' plan to scare the Stymphalian birds with noise. The Argonauts successfully repeat the trick. Pollux too will become a god. But what Hercules can do largely on his own, the Argonauts only attain as a group. Apollonius creates a group that is more than the sum of its parts, that achieves through co-operation and collaboration; he gestures towards overlap with Hercules, but keeps his heroes' successes separate. The Argonautic voyage is like a palimpsest, a manuscript which has been turned inside out and re-used to write another text: the story both repeats and precedes the *Odyssey* and both follows and includes Hercules. This is one of its main attractions for Apollonius and others (Colum and Graves, for instance, who use the story as a microcosm or frame for wider systems of Greek myth). But it contributes to the complexity of Argonautic heroism, which feels like it never quite reaches Herculean heights.

An alternative tradition subordinates the Argonauts explicitly to the Hercules myth. Its Greek roots are visible in Diodorus Siculus. His account of the Argonauts occurs during his section on Hercules, and may be drawing from a Hercules-centred narrative, perhaps Dionysios Scytobrachion's prose *Argonautica* or a lost Hercules epic.[22] Diodorus includes a sea storm and Hercules' rescue of Hesione from a sea monster at Troy as part of the Argonautic journey. The Hesione episode resembles Perseus and Andromeda, most famously told in Ovid *Metamorphoses* 4: the Trojans were attacked by a sea monster; an oracle told King Laomedon to sacrifice his daughter Hesione to it. Hercules breaks her chains and offers to defeat the monster in return for Laomedon's miraculous horses. He successfully rescues Hesione, but Laomedon refuses him the horses. In Diodorus, Hercules stays with the Argonauts all the way to Colchis, and they then help him fight the oath-breaking Laomedon for his prizes, replace Laomedon with Priam, and eventually hold games to celebrate their mutual assistance. Diodorus' Argonautic story keeps Hercules present (and central) throughout and makes the Argonauts the companions of Hercules, as in the 1958 movie. This version also features briefly in late antique texts by 'Dares' and 'Dictys', Latin accounts of the Trojan War, which influenced medieval historiography.

Lefèvre includes Hercules as one of Jason's few named companions and relates the conflict with Laomedon. He rationalizes the Hesione episode through the Trojans' terror at the marvellous ship, as if it were a sea monster 'in the sea, a great monster, lifting himself, marvellously swimming' (72) and bigger than the 'monster also great as a whale', that Hercules killed on another occasion. Laomedon refuses permission for the Argonauts to stop at Troy and take on supplies, thinking them spies sent by Hercules; Hercules is angry and predicts Troy's complete destruction by Greeks. After leaving, a storm drives them to Lemnos: two elements of the Diodoran narrative are re-purposed to explain why they had to stop at Lemnos, while accounting for the stories about the Argonauts and Hercules at Troy that were current in history-writing.

Valerius includes the rescue of Hesione along with other Diodoran elements. Valerius' Hesione episode (2.451–78) again showcases the cosmic nature of Hercules' heroism, and outdoes Ovid's Perseus episode. The Roman Jason and Hercules compete in an arms race of intensifying epic heroism. However, Valerius' Hesione also has agency: she herself tells her story and persuades Hercules to rescue her. The monster is a cosmic phenomenon: the whole bay 'roars' (498); the water 'piles up' (499); the monster's eyes are 'starry' (499) and its mouth produces a 'thunderous crash' (501). Hercules initially attacks it with arrows, but changes his tactics, and tears off crags to crush it. Hershkowitz argues that Hercules here demonstrates both intelligence and strength, combining different types of heroism.[23] He exceeds Ovid's Perseus and kills the monster without the help of Medusa's head.

In the later tradition, only Zimmerman, explicitly following Valerius, and Zarabouka, include the Hesione episode. Zimmerman makes much of Hesione's persuasiveness, flattery and determination in the face of the reluctance and indifference of her unintelligent and self-obsessed rescuer. Zimmerman's Hercules (shouting 'Hercules!') is showing off to Hylas and telling stories to his friends, and not keen on acquiring some girl, or even inconvenient horses ('We … can provide for no horses on board.' 53). Zarabouka devotes a full-page illustration to the monster, portraying Hercules, recognizable by his lion skin, held naked in the claws of an iguana-like dragon, both victim and hero. In this version, he takes Hesione's place, substituted for the statue-like heroine of Ovid and Valerius. Both Valerius and Zarabouka emphasize the consequences of this episode: Laomedon's betrayal of Hercules will lead to Priam's rule at Troy, the Trojan War, and eventually the founding of Rome. The cosmic impact of Hercules' battle fits with the historical significance of its outcome, which in Valerius is part of Jupiter's world-plan, for power to move from East to West.[24] Hercules expands the Argonauts' epic significance. Hercules' over-sized achievements encapsulate cosmic epic heroism, shaping history but ignoring or disrupting other people's lives. Unlike Jason with Medea, there is never a sense that Hercules has a relationship with Hesione.

Valerius also augments Apollonius' reference to Prometheus in the Caucasus, creating a full-blown rescue scene with Hercules again intervening as cosmic power.[25] Apollo asks Jupiter to send Hercules to release Prometheus at 4.60–81. As the Argonauts arrive at Colchis, Hercules is freeing Prometheus, but they do not recognize what is happening (5.154–76). This expands Apollonius' brief reference at 2.1246–59, where the Argonauts see the eagle and hear the agonized cries of Prometheus as it eats his liver, without understanding. In Valerius, they retain their ignorance, but Hercules releases Prometheus, violently destroying the landscape. As he pulls out the chains, the mountain crashes and trees collapse along with the rocks, while rivers flow backwards (160–2). A simile compares his violence to Jupiter's thunder or Neptune's earthquakes (163–4). The Argonauts' ignorance highlights Valerius' innovative insertion of this story into the outward journey ('who would believe it', 171). For Colum, in his 1921 children's version, this moment allows him to tell the story of Prometheus. His Hercules is an exemplar of sublime heroism: as the Argonauts go to sleep before facing Aeetes, they think of 'the look in the eyes of Hercules as he raised his face to the high, black peak of Caucasus', and this finishes part I of the book. However, Colum does not narrate the actual release of Prometheus: it remains a mysterious possibility. Hercules as cosmic and philosophical hero serves as a forerunner of the mystical dimensions of later versions, such as Pasolini's Chiron educating Jason on the nature of reality, or Gardner's Jason's visions of an apocalyptic future.

Robert Graves's Argonaut novel had the title *Hercules, My Shipmate* in the United States, showing Hercules' value in selling Greek myth. When Hercules joins the crew, Melampus adapts the Athenian saying 'Nothing without Theseus' (Plutarch, *Life of Theseus* 29) to refer to Hercules: 'You have all heard the saying "Nothing without Hercules," and it is true that he has been absent from no great military exploit for the last thirty years' (78). This speech shows Graves at his ironic and tendentious best: he thematizes his use of Hercules to sell the Argonaut story, while alluding to his exclusion of Theseus, and creating a sense of immersion in the Argonautic present.[26] Graves's Hercules is more excessive than Apollonius', and his relationship with Jason more tense, as in the election and rowing race scenes. Hercules has an odd habit of throwing bones at birds, killing them and chuckling: 'I hit her every time' (79, 100). Pelias encourages Jason to propitiate Hercules in the hope that Hercules will destroy him, or the ship, in his occasional fits of madness (79). Jason behaves obsequiously towards Hercules and the two obviously dislike each other. Graves several times alludes to Hercules' weightiness. For instance, Pelias says: 'I doubt whether your ship ... will long sustain the weight of a champion as massive as Hercules' (79). Graves highlights the story of Theiodamas, with Hercules himself boasting about killing him and taking Hylas. 'They say his mother died of grief at her double loss. If so she was a silly woman' (83). At Pagasae, waiting to depart, Hercules goes carousing with the Centaurs and accidentally kills Chiron. Despite his own grief, Jason has to placate him, saying it is better to die by the hand of Hercules than anyone else (109–10). At Lemnos, Graves's Hercules indulges his legendary appetites for food, drink and women. He often tends towards the comic, as when he throws a mud pie at Hypsipyle to stop her talking, then gets drunk and 'offered her his sincere condolence on her union with Jason. "He is a worthless wretch."' (145) Graves's Cyzicus insists on treating Hercules as the real leader, and serves him wine in a cup that portrays him, reflecting metapoetically his status as mythical celebrity (169), and Graves's own learning. Graves emphasizes his exceptionality and self-sufficiency: during battle with the Doliones, Hercules fights separately, while the other Argonauts operate as a military unit. Graves, however, avoids the 'following Hercules' motif. In North Africa, instead of searching for Hercules, the Argonauts makes jokes about his crudeness with the native 'Tritonians', who remember him bellowing, bashing and shouting 'Holy serpents!' (402–3) Graves gives Hercules tonal complexity, as well as intensifying the rivalry with Jason and reducing Hercules' divine connections. Graves circles around redefining masculinity, while committing to nothing, endorsing neither Hercules' violence nor Jason's manipulativeness.

Henry Treece intensifies Hercules' role still further, while retaining his complexity. Hercules enters the novel wearing women's clothes (60), and is Jason's 'twin' throughout. He is violent and sexually rapacious, but Jason is devastated to lose him in Mysia. After Colchis, he re-joins the expedition. He has put Priam on the throne of Troy and now has Trojan warships. He becomes entangled with Medea and conspires against Jason. In the end, it is Hercules who fires the temple in Corinth that contains Jason's beloved sons. When Jason is travelling the world as an old one-eyed beggar, he sees Hercules in Tiryns, 'fat and pink as a swine' (330), having sex with a woman who looks like Medea. Treece more drastically deconstructs the heroic masculinity of both Jason and Hercules.

The 1958 Italian 'peplum' film *Le Fatiche di Ercole* (dir. Francisci, released as *Hercules* in the US in 1959) was the beginning of a long tradition of 'sword and sandal' films. The overarching plot-line is substantially that of Jason and the Argonauts and Apollonius is mentioned in the credits. Hercules is its protagonist: first he rescues and falls in love with Pelias' daughter Iole, then establishes his heroism by killing the Nemean lion and the Cretan bull, then undertakes the Argonautic quest to restore Jason to the throne and prove that Pelias really killed Aeson. Blanshard and Shahabudin point out the importance of this film in making the male body a starring feature: Steve Reeves was well-known as a body builder and the film 'relishes Reeves' body' (70).[27] Jason in contrast is slight and pretty. This Hercules is awkward and uncompromising, but far from the often mad and terrifying figure in Graves and Treece. In a motif that recurs frequently in superhero films, he gives up his immortality and invincibility to feel mortal emotions and experience true love.[28] There is no hint of Hylas, bisexuality or cross-dressing to this Hercules.[29] He is a virtuous, didactic hero, misunderstood and envied, but clearly a 'good guy'. His powers are miraculous, and Jason takes a subordinate role throughout, so there is no tension.

Harryhausen consciously reacted against this 'sword and sandal' Hercules.[30] The substitution of the 'Isle of Bronze' for three key Argonautic episodes (Lemnos, the loss of Hylas and Talos) still highlights the 'choice of Hercules'. Hercules' desire for spoils, along with his refusal to obey Jason's command and the gods, causes the death of Hylas and Hercules' exclusion from the expedition. Since this Hercules is de-emphasized and de-idealized, Jason has more room to play the strong, effective military leader. In the 2000 mini-series, Hercules becomes more important again: he arrives like a helping god just as Jason's precious map has been stolen, to rescue Jason and punish the thief. His boastful bonhomie follows the 1963 Hercules: he frequently details his own labours (as also in Graves), such as when lounging with Lemnian women in their hot pool. But there is no Hylas: instead Hercules remains with the expedition until Colchis. Here he single-handedly holds off the Colchian pursuit, as the Argonauts escape using Jason's improvised zip-wire. This Hercules sacrifices himself for his friends, fighting one against the multitude and then throwing himself off the cliff into the river below, where Jason finds his body. As Jason desperately laments, it vanishes, conveying the apotheosis suggested at the end of Apollonius. The cliff-top leap suggests the 1963 Jason, as if his own more conventional cinematic past is lending support to this fallible, less violent but more ingenious Jason.

Mostly, Hercules is de-emphasized in the children's literature, to avoid tensions and complications. Hawthorne makes an ironic reference to his strength at the *Argo*'s launch ('Hercules, I suppose, had not grown to his full strength', 220) but gives him no action. Kingsley reinstates Hylas and allows Hercules to kill Cyzicus and be abandoned, but narrates these episodes briefly, and Seraillier treats him similarly, with emphasis on his affection for Hylas as paternal: he is 'frantic with anxiety, for he loved him like a son' (27). Zeff only includes him in the catalogue. Brooks does give him a prominent role, following Graves and Apollonius, but avoids presenting him as mad or terrifying. He performs a double-act with Atalanta rather than Hylas. When they leave him, Hercules says he must find Hylas' body because 'I owe his mother that much' (41). This reacts strongly against Graves's Hercules and his denigration of Hylas' mother. Catran's Hercules is very like that of Graves and Treece, and reflects the darker tone and violence of his version.

Comics are more interested in Hercules: Sandoval draws him to contrast with Jason, short dark hair, a red bandana, heavily muscled; Jason in contrast is blonde with long hair, but with a determined expression, dynamic poses and impressive muscles. Hoena and Estudio Haus make Hercules prominent in the catalogue, carrying the Erymanthian boar (as in Graves), but only include him in one further page, encompassing both Cyzicus and Hylas. Whitehead and Banerjee bring out the tensions between the Jason and Hercules: Hercules' dramatic arrival, and a half-page panel of him standing two heads taller than everyone else, with his enormous lion skin raising him still higher, his effective rebuke at Lemnos, and tensions over leadership.[31] Hercules' increased stature leaves room for Jason as strong hero beside him. There is a move towards authenticity (Hoena, for instance, includes an academic 'content consultant'), but Jason's heroism is protected and strong masculinity seems if anything more important.

There are important differences of genre, audience and time period in the treatment of Hercules' masculinity and his heroic rivalry with Jason. Epic is attracted to him, more modern versions are torn between using him to generate recognition and refusing to allow him to overshadow the Argonauts. Children's versions find many aspects of Hercules problematic, while the novels, especially those of Graves and Treece, revel in his complexity. His heroism is epic, cosmic and excessive, bringing out the subtler, more collaborative and often deceptive masculinity of Jason. Hercules also sells and augments the tradition, tying the Argonauts into wider movements in world history and cosmic significance.

Mutiny and leadership

After Hylas' loss, many versions leave Hercules behind. The mentor and great hero the Argonauts relied on to succeed in their quest is gone: as in many subsequent quest narratives, such as with Gandalf in *Lord of the Rings*, Hercules moves to another level and the remaining heroes must achieve the quest themselves. This loss causes dissent and anger amongst the Argonauts, and tests Jason's leadership. In Apollonius, the Argonauts abandon Hercules by mistake: the wind comes up at dawn, while they are still asleep. They only realize they have left Hercules, Hylas and Polyphemus of Eilatus behind when they are far out at sea. It would cost considerable effort to return, exhausted after the previous day's rowing contest, struggling against the wind.[32] Jason is engulfed by misery: 'The son of Aeson was so struck by helplessness that he could not speak in favour of any proposal, but sat gnawing at his heart' (AR 1.1286–9). Telamon angrily accuses Jason of deliberately engineering the loss of Hercules, through jealousy (1290–95), and goes on to attack Tiphys, presumably to turn the ship around. Zetes and Calais prevent him, and Apollonius drops an authorial aside (1302–9) that Hercules will later kill them.[33] But the sea god Glaucus appears and explains that the three were not fated to continue (1315–25). Jason does belatedly display leadership, when Telamon apologizes, and he replies graciously, forgiving Telamon, since he was angry on behalf of his friend. But the decision to leave and to continue sailing are removed from Jason: Apollonius presents both Argonauts and Jason as passive victims of events and divine plans.

Valerius' Roman Argonauts are more aware and responsible: they wait for Hercules despite the winds changing the night before. They are upset and demand him back with tears and sad prayers (VF 3.601); Jason himself 'stands and weeps' (606), and goes through the group, counting again and again. The Argonauts actively shout for Hercules and keep fires alight (602–3). Juno arranges the favourable wind, and Tiphys actively demands that they leave.

Jason's speech (617–27) gives the choice to the crew: go now or delay and search. Valerius presents the Argonauts as vainglorious and over-confident: 'puffed with windy pride, [they] swell up their hearts with empty talk' (631–2). Valerius even makes his Argonauts continue without divine reassurance: the consoling vision appears to Hercules instead, a dream of Hylas sent by Jupiter. Valerius' Jason democratically allows his crew to make their own decision, shows intense emotion, but neither comforts nor reconciles. There is no mutiny, but no divine ratification either. The crew come together in shared grief, shared ignorance and vanity.

Dissent, discussion, challenge, even democracy in the Argonautic crew is not present in every version. Kingsley simply states: 'Hercules was left behind and never saw the noble Phasian stream' (78). In William Morris's poem, Juno actively forces the Argonauts to leave, blowing them out of harbour against their wishes; a figure with golden wings (evoking angels) explains that the loss of Hercules is fated. All three nineteenth-century accounts (Hawthorne too) remove the opportunity for dissent and mutiny.

Graves, using his rationalization, in which Hylas has deliberately escaped, plays with levels of knowledge: he allows the Argonauts to deduce what has happened to Hylas, while Hercules remains ignorant and stomps around shouting. Yet they wake at dawn and stumble aboard ship without noticing that they have left Hercules behind. Meleager accidentally sits in his seat and it is not until they had sailed well out from land that Admetus notices Hercules' absence. So Graves has his cake and eats it, by including his own rationalization in addition to haplessness and passivity. Admetus accuses Tiphys and Jason, but in a long sequence, Graves's Jason refuses to engage with the crew: 'Jason sat and glowered, unwilling to say a word' (194); . . . 'Jason you are as silent as a fishmonger in the market of Athens' . . . 'Jason, Argus, Tiphys and the rest seem caught in a divine trance' (195). The prophecy scene is reduced to Mopsus listening to creaking in the prow. Graves intensifies Jason's resourcelessness but de-emphasizes dissent. Seraillier also allows the *Argo* to leave without noticing Hercules' absence, and the chapter ends with Jason hearing the echoing cries of 'Hylas! Hylas!', and thinking it a bird. At the beginning of the next chapter, a messenger of Nereus confirms Tiphys' decision, without the crew quarrelling. Also drawing on Graves's rationalization, but to the opposite extreme, is Catran, in whose version the Argonauts deliberately kill Hylas as vengeance on Hercules for belittling them, and flee from his justified anger, although they do leave Polyphemus by mistake, and refuse to go back for him. The narrator Pylos is the only one to speak out, horrified at what has happened, but as ship's boy, he is unable to change anything, and not wholly sure of his interpretation of events. This lack of dissent does not necessarily improve the presentation of Jason's leadership: in some cases, it avoids challenging or compromising him (such as Kingsley), but in others it results from intensified helplessness (Graves) or even sinister scheming (Catran).

Colum's version is the first where the Argonauts consult Hercules before deciding to leave: 'They called to Hercules . . . Hercules would not go on board. "I will not leave . . . until I find young Hylas or learn what has happened to him."' Jason commands the Argonauts to leave and Telamon responds accusingly, as in Apollonius. The message from Nereus (as in Morris), however, is much more of a surprise. He tells them about Hylas' death, with Hercules there too, and ultimately commands Hercules back on board. The rescue of Prometheus awaits him and *Argo* is his transport. Later, Colum follows the adventures of Hercules as his main narrative, and reconnects with the *Argo*. The book shifts from a central focus on the Argonauts with cameos from Hercules, to a central focus on Hercules, interwoven with fates of the Argonauts. For Colum, the two traditions interconnect usefully, bringing together different strands of Greek mythology, but he suppresses conflict, focusing rather on complementarity.

Films love a mutiny. Despite (or because of) the genre's investment in strong leadership, it seems impossible for a film set on a ship not to have a (threatened?) mutiny. In the 1958 movie, Eurystheus foments dissent and sabotages the ship, the Argonauts have run out of wine, and a storm strikes. They survive, but afterwards there is growing mutiny. Angry men surround the captain, who tries to calm them, while Eurystheus primes them with arguments. Hercules intervenes and threatens to throw the mutineers overboard, at which point they meekly return to rowing. Hercules is strong and effective, Jason nowhere to be seen. A mutiny scene is the first on board ship in the 1960 *Giganti della Tessaglia*. After a long expository sequence in Iolchos, we finally meet Jason on the *Argo* during an impressive storm, given added drama by Rustichelli's score. Jason plays the role of Hercules by using his strength to push back a hole in the prow as the water rushes in. After the storm, the men are disconsolate, hungry and thirsty, and Jason makes a stirring speech to inspire them. Storm and mutiny establish Jason as an effective leader, just as Hercules acted as true leader in the 1958 film.

The 1963 Harryhausen movie already has the men thirsty and starving in the first scene on board; Jason deals with his men's distress by seeking the help of Hera through the figurehead. Hera guides them to 'The Isle of Bronze', where Hercules causes the bronze giant Talos to wake and wreck the ship. The figurehead tells Jason it was Hercules' fault. After destroying Talos, the Argonauts search for Hylas (crushed under Talos) and Jason tells them to search until nightfall. Hercules, however, is determined to keep searching: 'Sail when you please, Jason. I cannot leave this island until I've found Hylas.' This gives Jason the consent of Hercules to leave, but still the Argonauts refuse. Jason has to call upon Hera and the figurehead to directly address the crew, telling them that Hylas is dead. Acastus, the son of Pelias, plays the role of Eurystheus in fomenting mutiny and challenging Jason, at the Clashing Rocks and when they arrive in Colchis, and ultimately betrays them. Although Todd Armstrong's Jason is perceived by viewers as a strong and successful hero, he fails to persuade Hercules not to take spoils and repeatedly relies on Hera's help to make decisions and control his men.

Despite his failures, however, this Jason shows no signs of depression and indecision, as in Apollonius: the Jason of the 2000 TV mini-series does. As in both Graves and Treece, he falls into negativity and resourcelessness after escaping the Lemnian women. When Mopsus asks him what to do, he gloomily, even sulkily, says 'You decide', and Mopsus replies: 'Damn well do your duty.' The Argonauts row without purpose and direction, desperately hungry. Castor and Pollux fantasize about roast boar with fried onions; Actor the thief threatens to eat Orpheus' dove, and challenges Jason, with a scornful 'Sir'. Mopsus and Hercules defend Jason, but he is distant and empty. He lost both map and protective amulet during his romance with Hypsipyle, along with his self-confidence. Suddenly he remembers the map and Zetes' miraculous eyesight: in the broad daylight Zetes looks at the stars and draws a chalk map on the deck. The resumption of *Argo*'s theme in the soundtrack signals a renewal of narrative momentum: they regain purpose and find Phineus' island. Later in Colchis, in a twist to the normal abandonment of Hercules scene, the Argonauts (including Hercules) decide whether or not to abandon Jason. After the crew argue, the audience are left in suspense, until the moment they all arrive to help him. Although this Jason is seen as less strong and impressive, he uses his own resources and persuades his crew more effectively than the 1963 Jason. The 2000 Hercules and Jason double each other and swap roles, and Jason is both like and unlike his Apollonian forebear.

The 1963 film's influence on later versions is clear from the motif of consulting Hercules and the figurehead. Brooks includes a discussion with Hercules and an intensified mutiny. Jason tries to console Hercules 'gently' and Hercules' 'eyes filled with tears' (41). But anonymous younger Argonauts accuse Jason: 'Everybody started running around shouting and the *Argo* began drifting aimlessly, pitching from side to side' (41). Brooks also intensifies the divine epiphany: an enormous figure of Poseidon (not the lesser sea god Glaucus) sucks the boat into a whirlpool then spits it out, shooting them, passive and terrified, into the next episode. James Riordan doubles the prophecy, giving both consultation with Hera's prow and the appearance of Glaucus. This version appears also in Yomtov and Sandoval, where Jason first receives instructions to leave from Hera, then a messenger (with an angelic silhouette, as in Morris) appears to ratify. Whitehead and Banerjee keep other aspects of the 1963 film: Hercules acknowledges to himself that he has abandoned the crew, but Jason makes the decision to leave, and Acastus spreads dissent, accusing him of envy. This Jason, tough, dark and gloomy, acknowledges his own inexperience, but inspires the Argonauts with talk of destiny. The 1963 film has particular influence on children's literature and graphic novels, but often lurks unacknowledged behind versions that consciously follow ancient material.

Even this relatively simple scene is subject to massive variation. The ancient versions offer significant differences and no one version is inevitably at the centre. Narrative choices change with time period, genre and audience: none of the nineteenth-century versions put dissent in the foreground, while mutiny is a key theme in the films, and novels for young adult and adult audiences bring out negativity, darkness and complexity. Each version gives the scene different nuances: shared motifs do not lead to shared presentations of masculinity, heroism or leadership. While Apollonius, Graves and the 1963 film are all influential, later versions rarely follow their predecessors in every single detail or even the thrust of characterization. Nevertheless, Jason rarely displays positive leadership: either dissent is omitted, the gods intervene or he is negative: passive, overwhelmed, indecisive or actively malevolent, he remains a problematic figure.

Amycus and antagonists

After they lose Hercules in Apollonius, they face King Amycus of the Bebrycians, who makes strangers fight him in a boxing match. Script-writing lore holds that every good story needs a powerful antagonist, an opponent that inspires hatred and fear, even more effective if they also have a tragic back-story.[34] Antagonists are often defined by visions of masculinity and leadership that conflict with and problematize the protagonist's identity. An article entitled *The Greatest Villains of all Time* in Empire magazine (Willow Green, 30 July 2019) ranks movie antagonists by public vote, and gives an idea of how influential antagonists function. The top five are Hannibal Lecter, Hans Gruber, Loki, The Joker and Darth Vader. Hannibal Lecter's seductive power mesmerizes Clarice Starling; Hans Gruber in his suit, with his urbane ruthlessness, contrasts strongly with John McClane's barefoot desperado; Loki is the foil of Thor, competing for rule of Earth and Asgard; Darth Vader is ruthless imperialist, yet Luke's father; The Joker embodies chaos and anarchy. Villains, like heroes and monsters, are culturally constructed: they respond to fears and desires of their own times and places. The Argonaut tradition is rich in antagonists: Pelias, Aeetes, Acastus, Apsyrtus, many of those encountered during the journey, of which Amycus is one of the most obviously villainous. The ancient epics show particular concern with dysfunctional political power, but hospitality remains a significant anxiety too, as in the *Odyssey*.

Apollonius' Amycus is an arrogant son of Poseidon (AR 2.2). His boxing challenge appeals immediately to Pollux, the Olympic boxing champion: he overturns conventions of rule-bound contest and Olympic truce. As the two face each other, Amycus is compared to a monstrous Giant about to attack Olympus (38–40), suggesting his disrespect for prevailing social and religious order, while Pollux, son of Zeus, is like the evening star (40–2). Amycus is bestial, like a lion (26–9), but Pollux also has the strength of a wild beast (44–5). Apollonius contrasts the raw force of Amycus with the well-honed skills of Pollux: Amycus is like a wave (70–75), but Pollux returns blow for blow. Their fighting sounds like shipwrights hammering (79–87). Amycus goes in for the killer blow, rising to destroy Pollux like a man sacrificing an ox (90–2) but Pollux bobs aside, taking the blow on his shoulder and smashing Amycus' head above the ear, killing him instantly. The angry Bebrycians attack, but the Argonauts fight them off. The rich imagery emphasizes epic heroism: even without Hercules, the Argonauts are demi-gods and superb warriors. Pollux is the star here, and Jason's only involvement is to join in the battle. The Argonauts exemplify successful, Greek masculinity, while Amycus embodies the barbaric Other, refusing to respect Mediterranean traditions of hospitality. Later, King Lycus of the Mariandyni praises Pollux for ridding the world of a tyrannical and predatory leader (2.752–8, 792–5). Amycus embodies tyranny, excessive violence and the breakdown of hospitality.

This episode is popular in the ancient world, in both art and literature, and significant variations exist. As Hylas features in Theocritus 13, so Amycus forms the first half of Theocritus *Idyll* 22, his hymn to the *Dioscuri* (Castor and Pollux). In Theocritus' version, the Argonauts fight for access to a spring, and instead of killing Amycus, Pollux beats him until he surrenders and makes him promise never to attack strangers again. Valerius Flaccus (4.99–343), Apollodorus (1.9.20) and Hyginus (*Fabulae* 17) all follow Apollonius' epic version, although the Hellenistic mythographer Peisandros (16FS) follows Theocritus. The Theocritean version probably evokes dramatic tradition, which was also popular in art: Sophocles wrote a satyr play called the *Amycus*, and Epicharmos composed a comedy. A fragment of Epicharmos tells us that Pollux bound Amycus (frr. 6 and 7, Kaibel), and Amycus tied to a tree or a rock, with a water-carrier (*hydria*) nearby, features notably on a Lucanian *hydria* (water jar) of about 420 BCE (Fig. 3.1).

One fascinating ancient image featuring Amycus is the Ficoroni Cista. This Etruscan metal cylindrical box was discovered in the seventeenth century by Francesco di Ficoroni. It dates from fourth-century BCE Praeneste and a dedicatory inscription states: 'Novius Plutius made me in Rome; Dindia Macolnia gave me to her daughter'. It was probably used to store make-up. The main decorative feature is a very detailed image of the Argonauts watching Pollux tie Amycus to a tree. This may illustrate a satyr play, possibly Sophocles' *Amycus*. The Argonauts become a group of young men in search of a drink. The feet of the cask exemplify its mixture of heroic and humorous: lion's claws standing on

Fig. 3.1 This vase shows the tragic and visual tradition of the binding of Amycus. Red-figure Lucanian *hydria* by the Amykos painter, *c.* 425–400 BCE. Cabinet des Medailles. Photo by Bibi Saint-Pol. Available at: https://commons.wikimedia.org/wiki/File:Amykos_Argonautes_Cdm_Paris_442.jpg (accessed 22 August 2019).

squashed frogs. The beautiful bodies of naked Argonauts take up much of the space: but it is hard to identify who is who. The winged figure behind Pollux could be Zetes or Calais, or as Wiseman argues, Mopsus, since Etruscan art represented prophets as winged, and he seems to be listening to a disembodied head at the bottom of the tree where Amycus is being tied.[35] The motif of prophecy might link the myth to an Italian or Roman context: a foundation myth or the establishment of cult to Castor and Pollux. To the right are two watching figures, perhaps Jason and Hercules. The first is young and beautiful and the second is heavily built and bearded. However he is not wearing a lion skin, which may have been stolen by Silenus, who is wearing one as he sits next to the spring. This lion skin might not have belonged to Hercules, but to Amycus, who wears one in Theocritus (52), functioning as an anti-Hercules figure. A cloaked Argonaut drinks from a decorated *crater*, presenting art within art, while another carries the *hydria* (water jar), and two others, one wearing a cap, an arm draped around his friend's neck, chat affectionately. The energy, physicality and social complexity of these figures and their interactions emphasize the spectacular and collaborative nature of the Argonautic expedition. The presence of gods throughout (Minerva, Victoria, Silenus, and Liber/Dionysus himself) brings out the divine sponsorship of the expedition. However, the Argonauts are not acting, but resting, not killing but training, not fighting but drinking. Generically, this is an un-epic representation, although Apollonius' poem, too, often emphasizes avoidance of fighting and killing. Argonautic masculinity is complex here too.

As in the Hylas episode, Theocritus is influential on later versions, and Theocritean motifs recur. In Theocritus, Amycus is a terrifying sight, with pulped ears (45), flesh like a hammered statue (47), and muscles like boulders in a winter torrent (48–50). Theocritus' dialogue between Pollux and Amycus focuses first on guest-friendship and then on rules. The two fight for position, to avoid having the sun in their eyes (83–6). In the fight, Amycus' face is violently disfigured (99–101). Finally, smashed to a pulp, Amycus is down, but not dead, and Pollux makes him swear not to fight strangers again.

Valerius Flaccus, with a Roman interest in violent spectacle, increases the monstrosity of Amycus, compared both to the giant Typhoeus (236–8), and the Cyclops (104–9), both as son of Neptune/Poseidon, and destroyer of strangers. When the Argonauts arrive at Bebrycia, a survivor of Amycus' violence, Dymas, warns them away, just as Virgil's Achaemenides warned Aeneas' Trojans away from the Cyclops. Valerius uses this tactic to increase their bravery and awareness, since his Argonauts still face Amycus. Valerius also brings out familial enmity:

Pollux is son of Jupiter and Amycus is son of Neptune, so they are cousins.[36] Matthew Leigh shows the intensification of the sacrifice imagery, and how Amycus' practice of throwing victims off his cliff as sacrifices to Neptune links him to monstrous sons of Neptune civilized by Theseus and Hercules, such as Cercyon and Eryx.[37] Although Pollux is the main enthusiast for battle, Valerius' Jason also volunteers. Valerius manages to put him first in the list of volunteers, but then adds that everyone else volunteered before him (222–5), both re-epicizing and undermining his hero. He also intensifies the Argonauts' terror and longing for Hercules, by mentioning it at the beginning of the episode, in contrast to Apollonius' reflection afterwards (246–8). Amycus is even more unthinking in Valerius ('Amycus rages helpless with no strategy', 296; 'lacking reason', 303). He falls like a mountain, Athos or Eryx, embodying monstrous size, solidity and destruction (320–2).

Two epic versions: Evslin's young-adult novel makes Amycus the main episode on the outward journey, evoking epic, particularly Valerius. His Amycus episode comes after the Clashing Rocks (as in Theocritus) and his narrator Ekion encounters a girl who needs rescuing, evoking the Hesione episode. In Graves's novel, Echion is also first to go ashore, speaking suavely. Evslin's Amycus insists on killing all suitors for his wife's sisters in the boxing ring, adding story motifs from the myths of Atalanta and Hippodamia. Ekion is planning a rescue, when Jason and Pollux arrive. Pollux is only too excited to fight and Jason to allow him. As in Valerius, they have had advance warning, and further they see Amycus, a giant with an enormous, polished head that looks like brass, pulling a cart, and then killing an ox with a single head-butt (recalling the image in Apollonius). The image of metalwork evokes similar craftsman imagery in Theocritus and Apollonius. Castor and Pollux plan to fight next to the cliff, also recalling Graves, whose battle takes place in a flowery dell like that of Theocritus, next to a cliff, which Amycus likes to keep at his back. Evslin's Argonauts have already filled their water barrels, so fight Amycus purely for the joy of success. Pollux cleverly manoeuvres Amycus first into exhaustion and irritation and then into desperate determination to smash him against the cliff. But Pollux's head 'slid away' (91) so that Amycus instead bashes a crater in the cliff and stuns himself. Pollux completes with a killer blow to the windpipe (92). Valerian elements include the crying girl (Valerius' Echion finds Dymas crying secretly in a secluded valley, 133–6) and the emphasis on the Argonauts' enthusiasm in contrast to Dymas' fear (174–6), which is reflected in Ekion's worry about his own cowardice. This richly intertextual retelling dehumanizes Amycus with his outlandish headbutts, and creates a gendered story of rescue to intensify the polarization. Zimmerman's play also follows Valerius: the Argonauts react strongly against Dymas' fear, which they see as cowardice. Pollux threatens Dymas and Jason tries to restrain him, when the 'slow-witted' Amycus arrives, spouting xenophobic catch-phrases ('keep these waters free of trash', 77). After Pollux kills Amycus, Jason gathers information from Dymas, which he cannily keeps from the crew. We can here see Zimmerman's leaderly, careful Jason in action, against a politicized caricature of mindless violence.

Graves's version passes Theocritus on to some later versions, especially through the motif of fighting with the sun in his eyes.[38] Graves's Amycus likes to fight with the cliff behind him and Pollux repeatedly manoeuvres him into the sun (201, 202). Zeff also makes this a feature (15), along with an illustration of Amycus shading his eyes with his arm. Riordan and Cockcroft also emphasize this motif, with a full-page illustration of the sun blazing down behind Pollux' fists onto the dazzled Amycus (34–5). The fight with the Bebrycians and the sacrifice of cattle to Poseidon, which follow, also draw on Graves, and are not in Theocritus.

The *Orphic Argonautica* shapes the versions of Kingsley (and Lancelyn Green), with its brief summary of Pollux' killing. Seraillier obviously did not find this version satisfactory, so here follows Theocritus, perhaps through Graves ('maoeuvred him round till the sun was in his eyes', 30), including the non-epic ending by introducing the oath ('made him swear never to bully strangers again'). The motif of throwing the spiked boxing gloves (Roman *caestus*) into the sea, in an undoing of Amycus' sacrificial practice, suggests Valerius, however.

Whitehead and Banerjee also follow the Theocritean version, calling Amycus both a 'bully' (according to his people) and a 'blustering oaf' (28). Pollux politely asks Jason for permission to take him on, and Jason replies 'Be my guest', suggesting he would have been perfectly happy to do it himself. Three panels show Pollux hammering Amycus, until he is a heap on the ground, and Pollux says 'Perhaps now you will learn some manners', implying he is not dead. Theocritus is both more and less violent than Apollonius, with more emphasis on disfigurement, but a less severe outcome, and this duality attracts children's versions.

Brooks softens the epic version. She allows Pollux to kill Amycus, but offers him many chances to surrender: nevertheless 'some primitive, animal force took over and kept the big man on his feet' (47). The antagonist is bestialized to valorize his destruction. When Brooks' Argonauts arrive, she focuses on Jason, who sees Amycus' rowdy men, thinks 'Oh no!' (44) and instinctively wants to flee. Jason wishes for Hercules and responds to Amycus' taunt with an 'involuntary sigh'. Jason is relieved when Pollux volunteers: his apparent cowardice turns out to be willingness to fight himself. The brief dialogue between Pollux and Amycus about rules may evoke Theocritus, as might the pounding of Amycus' face into an 'unrecognizable mess' (47). But the boxing gloves 'studded with bronze spikes' (45) and Pollux' fear at them (his 'knees weaken') evoke Valerius, probably via Graves, who also begins the fight with a 'bull-like rush' (201); Brooks has 'bull-like charge' (45). Brooks' Pollux is considerably more sporting than Graves's, who continues to hit Amycus when he is down. 'In a public contest, a boxer is considered a fool who does not follow up his blow', comments Graves (202), explicitly contrasting his version of Greek boxing to British 'sportsmanship'.

Different episodes have different traditions, and as with Hylas, the tradition of the Amycus episode is shaped partly by Theocritus.[39] Sophocles' satyr play and its associated visual tradition, Valerius' innovations, and the episode's affinities with epic and athletic games, are all important, as is Graves's colourful account, especially in more recent versions, given the episode's absence from all the films. Amycus is not essential to the quest plot, and can be omitted for narrative economy, but the episode allows an Argonaut to use his special talent. It develops themes of Otherness, monstrosity, the treatment of strangers and (in)appropriate use of force. Ancient versions portray different levels of violence, so it remains available to products aimed at children. Children's versions often prefer the clean, quick death of Apollonius to the more complicated (and graphic) pulping and binding of Theocritus. In contrast to his relationship with Hercules, Jason collaborates easily with Pollux. In most versions, he takes charge and deploys him like a weapon, or acts as friend and equal. The representations of both Amycus and Pollux vary wildly, from young and beautiful to grotesque and monstrous, although the majority follow Apollonius by making Amycus monstrous and Pollux beautiful. The physical application of bodily violence is essential to successful masculinity in this episode, but violence is tempered by technical skill, and excess leads to monstrosity, from which the Argonauts themselves are not exempt. Amycus as antagonist is tyrannous, uncivilized, lacking humanity, demonized and sometimes racialized.[40] In Greek and Roman culture, where violent spectacles were common, Amycus is less transgressive, but the use of a rule-bound activity to deliberately go beyond hospitality expectations is as problematic for Greek athletics as for modern boxing. Amycus' divine parentage, like that of Aeetes, the ultimate antagonist, makes him less bound by expectations of humanity, but this motif does not transfer to later cultures, where moral polarization is usually intensified.

Conclusion

A distinctive feature of the Argonaut myth is the variety and complexity of masculinity on display, both in the character of Jason and others. The importance of the Argonauts as a group and of teamwork and collaboration is also unusual in the ancient epic tradition. The fact that the *Argonauts* board game (see below, pp. 182–3) is a solely collaborative one shows good understanding of the myth. These two inter-related phenomena (complex masculinity and collaboration) make this myth and its tradition particularly rich in explorations of leadership, balances of power, dissent and negotiation. Persuasiveness, charisma and attractiveness all play a part, along with duplicity, untrustworthiness and manipulation. Sometimes, and in some versions, often, Jason barely leads at all, functioning as a focal point of emptiness, a pawn pushed about by others (literally in the 1963 film). The character Bles Alwyn, who plays the Jason role in black activist and academic W. E. B. Du Bois' *Quest of the Silver Fleece* (1911), is often represented in this way. He is used by others as a token of black involvement or appeasement of Southern interests. Ultimately his greatest agency lies in his refusal to be used, while real leadership lies with Zora, the female protagonist, who builds up a community and holds it together. This model of resistance and collaboration outside existing power structures is available through the Argonaut myth. Jason comes from outside to challenge a ruler, gathers an informal group of friends and supporters, and disrupts existing power structures. The Bebrycians are a good example of this: the Argonauts arrive, destroy Amycus, violently shake up the situation, but often leave chaos behind them (Laomedon and Phineus are other examples). On the other hand, they can be co-opted to reinforce power structures, as when Valerius' Aeetes uses them to oppose his brother Perses' challenge to the throne. As often in Hercules stories, the Argonauts swoop in and cause change. A strong association with the gods, too, is an important aspect of ancient heroism and leadership. Jason's religious competence brings group cohesion, not just in Apollonius, but also in the 1963 film. But representations of the supernatural, like those of masculinity and heroism, vary enormously. Sometimes they create a powerful sense of ancient Greek Otherness for later cultures. We move next to the relationship between the supernatural or the marvellous and ideas of entertainment, starting from an episode which connects prophecy with transgression, political power, gendered violence and monstrosity: Phineus and the Harpies.

4

Entertainment and the Marvellous

The demi-gods and godlike heroes of the *Argo* have already defeated monstrous antagonists; prophecies have shaped Jason's confrontation with Pelias. After laying Amycus low, the Argonauts visit the prophet Phineus, who features in all ancient versions, but represented very differently, either as helpless victim, or evil villain. The Argonauts then face the most iconic barrier of their journey: the Clashing Rocks, which they often navigate with divine assistance. As they arrive at Colchis, Apollonius presents his only major scene set in Olympus: Hera and Athena scheming to make Medea fall in love with Jason. This chapter focuses on the supernatural elements of the Argonaut story: prophecy and monstrosity in Phineus and the Harpies, the gods and marvellous landscape through the Clashing Rocks and Hera and Athena episodes, and monsters in the wider Argonaut tradition. How do more modern realist narratives handle the discomfort of the supernatural? What is considered monstrous and why? What is the role of the marvellous in the Argonaut myth?

The Argonauts are often 'entertainment': Ray Harryhausen and Tony Dalton certainly discussed the 1963 film in these terms.[1] This chapter explores and deepens understanding of 'entertainment' as a capacious category.[2] The phrase 'it's just entertainment' can be used to resist analysis of cultural products. But that move only defers the questions: why are Argonautic gods and monsters 'entertaining'? What does it mean to be 'entertaining'? The word implies enjoyment and pleasure, and a broad, perhaps non-elite audience.[3] What is it about Greek myth that appeals to a mass audience?[4] Escapism may be one element: various escapist fantasies shape narratives that feature quests, heroes, gods and monsters. These features come together in the story of the Argonauts with particular effectiveness: first, the fantasy of an ordinary protagonist who discovers they are extraordinary. So Jason discovers that he is not just a boy, but a king's son, heir to the throne of Iolchos. More than that, the quest for the Golden Fleece gives him glory and ensures that his memory survives. Both Jason and Medea can function as proxies for the reader, allowing them to participate in this glory, both allocating and experiencing the pleasure of success, especially in versions that finish before their relationship deteriorates, as those considered entertainment often do.

Secondly, the quest object, which magically solves problems and creates meaning, is itself a sort of fantasy: we do not know why Pelias needs the Golden Fleece, we only know that he forces Jason to seek it. This fits with both hunter-gatherer and capitalist drives for acquisition: one can argue that the Golden Fleece, like many of the objects of Hercules' labours, functions as a McGuffin, an object that exists solely for the plot.[5] It gives meaning to the lives of the Argonauts, their abilities, efforts and journey. While readers accompany the quest, they too have meaning and a clear goal. The third element is the fantasy of clear-cut moral boundaries: the existence of black-and-white characters, hideous monsters, noble heroes, evil villains, allows readers the pleasure of certainty in alignments and identifications. Many versions of the Argonaut myth which function as entertainment tend to polarize characters.

Fourth comes the idea of divine providence, a supernatural figure who provides guidance and oversees the progress of the protagonists, to whom they can turn in difficulties. The gods watching from above and orchestrating events can be both disturbing and reassuring; various versions play with the complexities of these emotional reactions, but ultimately divine machinery offers further layers of meaning to the actions of mortal characters. Fifth, escapism: the quest narrative takes audiences far away from current concerns and troubles to a different world, exotic and unfamiliar, in which success is achievable and after which disaster can be left behind. 'Entertainment' does not have to reassure, reinforce and provide escape, and many versions of the Argonaut story complicate, make things difficult and resist definition. There is pleasure too in complexity, games of intertextuality, paradoxical stimulation of contradictory emotions. But this might rather be thought of as 'art' not 'entertainment' – although I would argue that 'art' is 'entertainment' with added social and cultural prestige.

The supernatural is particularly significant for the pleasure of the text and in the importance of Greek myth for both children's literature and popular media. Prophecy, divine intervention and monsters all function to buttress providence, destiny, narrative control and moral certainty, as well as raising the stakes, intensifying significance. However, Apollonius, ironically, thrives on the complexity and uncertainty generated by the multiplicity of myth and resists easy categorization or interpretation of his supernatural elements. Most artful of all are texts like Virgil's *Aeneid* or Valerius Flaccus' *Argonautica* that can be read in both ways, as reassurance or destabilization, depending on the politics of the reader.[6]

Phineus and the Harpies

A villainous Phineus occurs in Rick Riordan's successful *Heroes of Olympus* series: in *Son of Neptune*, which features Percy Jackson, protagonist of the previous series, the child-heroes encounter 'Phineas' in Portland, Oregon. This resurrected Phineus torments the Harpies who used to torment him: he prevents them from eating food using a 'weed whacker' (strimmer). He bargains with Percy, to give them information for capturing a Harpy, but Percy refuses, pitying the 'poor bird ladies'. The children make friends with Ella the Harpy, who acts like an autistic child, making prophecies from all the books she has memorized. This version makes Phineas (whose name recalls the 1963 film) the monster: squalid and uncanny, in his bathrobe splattered with food and 'fuzzy pink bunny slippers', he is fat and bald, as well as old and blind. The pleasure of the text comes partly from his oversharing of characters' secrets, and partly from Percy's rebellion against the overarching antagonist, Gaia, relying on her own plot to defeat her protégé. Riordan enjoys reversing both Apollonius and the 1963 film, refusing to demonize or cage his Harpy.

Apollonius' Phineus (2.178–536) in contrast inspires sympathy: he was given the power of prophecy by Apollo but blinded by Zeus for revealing his plans too fully, and further punished by Harpies that snatch his food or foul it before he can eat it. He hears the Argonauts arrive and details of his state encourage empathy: he 'crept to the door on his withered feet, feeling the walls; ... his parched skin was caked with dirt and only the skin held his bones together' (2.198–201). His prophecies closely mirror later narrator-text, creating affinity between this punished prophet and the poet-narrator.[7] His friends and neighbours look after him since he helps them: 'To all alike, however poor ... the aged man gave his oracles with good will and freed many from their sorrows by his prophetic art; so they visited and tended him' (2.453–5).

This sympathetic Phineus is almost wholly dominant in later traditions, especially film and children's literature, but signs remain in Apollonius of negative traditions. Gantz calls Phineus 'an atrociously complicated figure' (350). In Hesiod's *Catalogue of Women*, Phineus is blinded for showing Phrixus the way, possibly to Colchis (Hes. fr. 254 MW). Asclepiades of Tragilus, who wrote about the subjects of tragedy in the fourth century BCE, presents Zeus punishing

Phineus for his treatment of his sons, allowing him to choose either death or blindness. In this version, Helios is offended by his choice not to see the sun, and sends the Harpies as further punishment. Phineus was a popular subject for tragedy, although the plays survive only in fragments or references: Aeschylus wrote a *Phineus*, about the Harpies; Sophocles probably wrote three plays on Phineus' family, in which he takes a second wife, and he or his wife blinds or kills his sons from his first marriage.[8] An ancient commentator on Sophocles' *Antigone* tells a version in which Phineus put aside his first wife, Cleopatra, to marry Idaea, and Cleopatra blinded the children in revenge. In an epigram (*AP* 3.4) the sons kill their stepmother as their mother rejoices. Apollonius plays with this troubled family myth-history: when Phineus comments on his family relationship to Zetes and Calais, Cleopatra's brothers, and asserts his own ancestry (son of Agenor) and location (ruling in Thrace) as guarantees of truth (AR 2.234–40). There are two mythical problems here: Agenor is based in Egypt, but Phineus is king in Thrace. How does this often contested element guarantee his relationship to the sons of Boreas? Why should they help the man who abandoned their sister and blinded their nephews? Apollonius also alludes to the complicated relationship between the different choices and punishments of Phineus when Zetes and Calais question whether the gift of prophecy really caused his punishments (245–6). Their expressions of horror and disbelief draw attention to Apollonius' choice of version. The Boreads demand a guarantee for their own safety, evoking an alternative storyworld in which they are punished for helping him. Similarly, Iris' intervention to stop them killing the Harpies assumes this intention from previous versions. Evidence of Harpy-killing exists: an ancient commentator on Apollonius (*scholia* on AR 2.296a) mentions it; Philodemus implies that Harpies were killed in Ibycus, Aeschylus and Telestes (see Gantz 1993: 353). Apollodorus preserves a version in which the Boreads either kill the Harpies or themselves die if they fail to catch them (Ap. *Bib.* 1.9.21), and later mentions the Boreads dying in the chase (3.15.2). A black-figure kylix (Fig. 4.1) from about 550 BCE shows a Boread, wings on his ankle, grabbing a Harpy, or perhaps both Harpies, by the neck, with his sword drawn ready to kill them. But this image is compatible with both versions, set as it is in the moment before either killing or prevention of killing.

The Harpies in this vase are women with wings on their shoulders, dressed and human in appearance, as in other ancient art. Apollonius does not describe them clearly: they snatch food with their 'jaws' or 'claws' (*gamfelesin* (188) is used of both lions and horses in Homer and birds in Euripides).[9] Instead, Apollonius suggests a rationalizing interpretation by comparing them to 'sudden storms or

Fig. 4.1 Laconian black-figure kylix, showing the Boreads about to kill the Harpies, *c.* 550 BCE, National Etruscan Museum, Rome. Author's drawing.

flashes of lightning' (267) as they swoop down on Phineus' banquet. They fly faster than the West Wind as they flee (276–7), recalling their rationalization as destructive winds. Apollonius puns on their name by using the word *harpazo*, 'snatch', to describe their actions (189; 223). The description of their movements, noise and smell emphasizes their bestial nature, and they seem more monstrous than in the visual representations.

The Phineus episode is frequent in ancient art, from a now lost krater by the Nessos painter, from the last decades of the seventh century BCE, which showed the Boreads pursuing the Harpies over the sea, to a red-figure hydria of the Kleophrades painter, showing winged, robed, Harpies stealing food from Phineus. Most interestingly, the fragments of a Corinthian column krater, now in the Archaeological Museum of Thessaloniki, show Jason laying his hands on the eyes of Phineus (both named).[10] This suggests a variant, otherwise unattested, in which Jason heals Phineus' blindness.[11] Mackie has used this evidence to redeem Jason as a serious, important hero by giving him a special talent in healing.[12] Perhaps he did have some healing talent in early stories, but Jason as a healer is not prominent in surviving versions. Apollonius may play with this variant too, when Jason wishes a god would heal Phineus ('if he should bring sight to your eyes, indeed I would rejoice', 441–2).

While Apollonius presents his version as the only and authoritative one, and alludes without explicit signals to other variants, the mythographic tradition highlights them. Diodorus Siculus here discusses the complex nature of myth: 'ancient myths do not give us a simple and consistent story; so it would not surprise if we find, when we put ancient accounts together, that in some details they do not agree with those given by every poet and historian' (4.44.4–6). Diodorus' own version follows the tragedians, with Hercules added, who kills Phineus, and puts Cleopatra and her sons in his place as rulers. Apollodorus also emphasizes the variants: the parentage of Phineus, the causes of his blinding, and the outcome of the Boreads' chase. Robert Graves, too, outlines variant versions in his *Greek Myths*, but prioritizes Apollonius' account by putting it first.

Apollonius is central to later traditions in this episode: Valerius, Morris, the 1963 and 2000 films, and almost all children's literature follow him. Valerius builds suspense by withholding explanation at the beginning of the episode, giving details of Phineus' punishment, but no explanation (4.430–1), leaving open the possibility that he will follow Diodorus, as elsewhere. The ambiguity is resolved with a knowing allusion: 'Don't believe that I am paying for the fault of savagery or crimes of wickedness' (4.477–8). Valerius' Harpies seem to be humans with wings, since they have both hands (495) and jaws (504).[13] His inclusion of Celaeno, as chief Harpy, evokes Virgil's *Aeneid*, which presents the Harpies as winged creatures with women's faces, themselves prophetic: 'Virginal faces of winged creatures, foulest filth from their stomachs and clawed hands' (*Aen.* 3.216–7). The 'taloned feet' (233) equivocates between bird and human.

Morris describes the Harpies, and creates a new motif: Phineus living in a palace in royal luxury. Morris's Harpies arrive like a storm, with darkness and magical opening of all doors and windows. They are described as:

The dreadful Snatchers, who like women were
Down to the breast, with scanty coarse black hair
About their heads, and dim eyes ringed with red,
And bestial mouths set round with lips of lead,
But from their gnarled necks there began to spring
Half hair, half feathers, and a sweeping wing
Grew out instead of arm on either side,
And thick plumes underneath the breast did hide
The place where joined the fearful natures twain.

5.231–39

Morris emphasizes monstrosity through ugliness, animal features, metallic imagery, but above all by a focus on their hybridity and the join between different parts. The coarse hair and red-rimmed eyes recur later in the tradition. Despite their bestial appearance, Morris's Harpies have voices and speak frequently, making prophecies as in Virgil. Most strikingly, Morris sexualizes their interaction with Phineus. Celaeno threatens to kiss him and the Harpies hide him from view and 'fawn over him', taking delight in his pain (5.268–72). From behind their wings, Phineus offers Zetes and Calais treasure to free him. Neptune acts to stop the killing of the Harpies, hinting at their allegorization as storm winds.

The Harryhausen film makes Phineus more sympathetic: the Argonauts arrive mid-attack. His Harpies have bat-like wings and human bodies, blue, with breasts but no other obviously feminine features. They steal Phineus' stick and clothes as well as his food, physically attacking him as he lies prone in his ruined temple. Phineus himself claims the gods decreed he should help the Argonauts, but he resists them and demands the Argonauts help neutralize the Harpies. 'Zeus, I defy you!' he shouts, and thunder rumbles in response. But the Argonauts sympathize; Jason too showed scepticism towards the divine. Nevertheless they trap the Harpies rather than killing them. Acting as an organized military force, they put a net over the ruined temple, and drive the Harpies into the net. The scene finishes with the screaming Harpies desperately trying to escape their cage (Fig. 4.2). Jason observes the reversal: 'From now on, they'll witness a banquet every night, and eat the scraps you leave.' We can see how influential this version is from later Harpies with bat wings and the spelling of the name 'Phineas'.[14]

The 2000 mini-series ties the Harpies to the location rather than to Phineus: his punishment, along with blindness, is exile where the only food comes from a magical table in what looks like a Mycenean *tholos* tomb, dark, contained, with a dome. The Harpies kill anyone who touches the food. The Argonauts arrive both starving and looking for information. The Harpies kill and eat two of them. The Argonauts encounter Phineus and agree to help him. Jason acts as bait and steals an apple, evoking biblical imagery of the price of knowledge; he hides under the table and darts around the tomb while the Harpies pursue him, and the Argonauts, led by Hercules, push in blocks of stone from the dome above to crush them. Jason again avoids fighting, characterized by speed and agility, while Hercules organizes and kills. The Harpies are straightforwardly demonized: dark-skinned, with monkey-like faces, bat-like wings instead of arms, bird-like legs and reptilian tails. Called demons by the Argonauts, they are racialized and bestialized as much as feminized. Neither film gives the Harpies words or names.

Fig. 4.2 Jason (Todd Armstrong) confronts the caged Harpies, with their bat wings and blue skin. Foot on fallen stone represents successful conquest as he taunts them with the reversal of their situation. Screenshot from *Jason and the Argonauts* (1963), [Film] Dir. Don Chaffey. Visual effects by Ray Harryhausen. Screenshot by author.

The 2000 film corrects the anachronistic setting of the 1963 movie, where the temple is ruined, while keeping the atmosphere of sacrality.

Various children's versions follow this essentially epic version: Hawthorne focuses on the Harpies, who have 'the faces of women but the wings, bodies and claws of vultures' (224). Colum follows Morris in portraying Phineus as king in his palace, but corrects him by removing the prophecies of the Harpies and their sexualized tormenting of Phineus. Seraillier emphasizes the Harpies' monstrosity, calling them 'foul creatures', with 'wicked wings' (32). He suggests awareness of the healing myth, when Phineus says 'I knew you by your hands, Jason' (31); later Jason wishes that the gods 'could have given you back your sight' (34). His Phineus is an ideal king: 'both the leader and the servant of his people, selfless and devoted as every king should be' (35). Naden is idiosyncratic, with a battle between the Argonauts and the Harpies (also in Bradman). Brooks' Phineus is king in a flourishing city, and attributes his punishment to Helios, showing independence from her immediate predecessors. As with many (Morris, James Riordan, Malam, Zarabouka) she plays on the word 'snatch' as an etymology of their name. Brooks also corrects Harryhausen by specifying that the Harpies can neither be trapped nor poisoned. Whitehead and Banerjee show Phineus entering a prophetic frenzy, with his eyes turning black. Harryhausen's influence is clear in the frequency of Harpies with bat wings (Brooks, Malam and Antram, 2000 film). Twenty-first-century Harpies are either more monstrous and less human, or return to being winged women: Hoena/Estudio Haus show them as birds with red eyes and mask-like faces and no resemblance to women.[15] The 2000 movie shapes the illustration in Hoena/Takvorian, where there is a hole in the roof and Phineus cowers under a table (24–5).

Despite the dominance of the Apollonian Phineus, a significant minority follow the tragic version, primarily the rationalizing tradition, especially novels. The *Orphic Argonautica* is unique: Phineus has blinded and exposed his sons, 'because of a woman's love potions'. The sons of Boreas heal their nephews and blind Phineus; Boreas himself whirls Phineus away into the wilderness to die. This Phineus is straightforwardly a villain to be defeated, and instead of Harpies the *OA* has the North Wind. Kingsley combines many different versions, but gives some prominence to the idea of Phineus as a negative character: when the Argonauts arrive, he feasts them and the Harpies arrive with 'the faces and hair of fair maidens but the wings and claws of hawks'. Phineus allegorizes them: 'they haunt me, and my people, and the Bosporus, with fearful storms; and sweep away the food from off our tables so that we starve', but does not explain his punishment. When Zetes and Calais reveal themselves, he 'hid his face in terror' (79). The sons of Boreas use words very similar to the *OA* to describe his crimes, and only when Phineus swears to 'right our sister and cast out that wicked woman' do they agree to help him. Jason cures the sons, while Zetes and Calais chase the Harpies as in Apollodorus, leaving the expedition for 'the battle of the winds', in which both join a never-ending chase. Kingsley gives alternative endings for the lives of Zetes and Calais but asserts that 'the heroes never saw them again' (81). His final description of the graves of Zetes and Calais, marked by a pillar rocked by the winds at Tenos, is straight from Apollonius (1.1298–1308). Kingsley's is the version summarized by Roger Lancelyn Green in *Tales of the Greek Heroes* (206). Kingsley supplements his primary version with elements from many other sources, creating a complex and unresolved mixture.

Robert Graves rationalizes Phineus in his novel, primarily following Diodorus. Calais and Zetes are here the older sons of Phineus, exiled for challenging the schemes of his second wife, Idaea. The Argonauts find the blinded Phineus by himself in his palace, surrounded by kites and other birds of prey attracted by rotting food and filth, deliberately placed around him by Idaea's servants. The monstrous Harpies are entirely imaginary, and the Argonauts prove that by giving him edible food. They chase away the birds and clean up the mess, rescue the younger sons, ambush Idaea, and as in Diodorus, send her back to her

Scythian father. Graves accounts for the existence of the Harpies through Phineus' blind paranoia, but self-consciously acknowledges that this is an unlikely deceptive contrivance: 'why did Idaea not murder Phineus outright?' (218) Treece and Catran follow Graves's bird rationalization. Treece presents a Phineus who is not a prophet but is kept in subjugation by priestesses of the Mother (154–7), led by his wife Yaga Mash, more obviously Othered than Graves's Idaea. His Atalanta tells Jason that Phineus has an eye condition caused by the winds and dust, which she could heal with a salve, but she refuses to do so. Zetes and Calais set up scarecrows and light fires to chase the Harpy birds away. The released sons subsequently go mad and have to be imprisoned again. Similarly, they send Yaga Mash away, but Jason points out that she will return when they go. Catran's Phineus (80–3) is an old man ruling a village, whose wife has conned the villagers out of their ornaments. Phineus himself caused the plague of hawks and kites by leaving rotten meat around after frequent sacrifices. As in Treece, Phineus has 'eyes inflamed and half-blind by the bad dust-winds'. The episode ends with his partial information, which Pylos treats sceptically: 'If he told us more, the Gods would punish him dreadfully. Meaning that he did not know, the old fraud' (83). The tragic family conflicts are minimized in Catran's version for younger readers. Severin also points to the bird rationalization: his reconstructed voyage includes the small natural harbour of Garipce, thought locally to have been the location for the Phineus episode, which had been known as Gyropolis, the place of the vultures (142). He imagines Phineus as a local wise man, whose advice brought gifts of food and hence scavenging birds.

There are clear differences across genre, medium and audience. The certainties of impressive prophecies and divine intervention appeal more to epic, film and children's literature, while complex rationalizations and tragic family relationships attract novelists, historiographers and documentary makers. We can see the influence of Harryhausen peaking and waning again in representations of the Harpies. Ultimately, the version in Apollonius is more pervasive and where usually influential authors, like Kingsley, Morris and Graves have chosen idiosyncratic approaches, later versions do not always follow, even when they normally would do.

In epic and film, the Phineus episode gives the Argonauts control over both the divine and monstrous Harpies (who they subdue either using their own marvellous abilities, or their ingenuity and teamwork) and over the quest itself (finding their way to Colchis). These versions tend to polarize, and demonize the Harpies as extreme, bestial, even sexualized, monsters. The tragic and novelistic versions, in contrast, minimize the marvellous and instead emphasize the horrors of old age, blindness, poverty and abuse. Yet in all these versions the unsettling nature of both Phineus and the Harpies remains. The Argonauts, like the readers and viewers, are driven by desire for knowledge, while Phineus and the Harpies compete in their desire for food. Phineus' punishment imposes starvation as the result of revealing inappropriate knowledge, linking the two elements. In both versions of the episode, epic and tragic, the conflict is over control: the rationalizing traditions displace anxiety about relationships with immortals onto anxiety about family power structures, sometimes transforming divine capriciousness into the arbitrary destructiveness of the natural world. In both versions, the Argonauts intervene to restore order and bring plenty and healing. The marvellous elements serve to distance suffering and its relief from mortal responsibility.

The Clashing Rocks

To reach Colchis, the *Argo* must pass through the Clashing Rocks (*Symplegades*) also known as the Cyanean (or Dark Blue) Rocks. This iconic episode often stands in for the whole myth. Apollonius mentions them (and their location at the mouth of the Black Sea) first in his proem (line 1–4). In this, he echoes the first lines of Euripides' *Medea*, which begins with the *Argo*, Colchis and the Cyanean Symplegades (1–2). Nearly all versions include them, and Ian Seraillier names his *The Clashing Rocks*. Diodorus does not include them, but the historical novels, which often follow him, do. The earlier film versions also omit them: *Le Fatiche di Ercole* and *I Giganti di Tessaglia* go straight to Colchis, stopping only for Amazons, presumably because the special effects required were too challenging. Pasolini, too, avoids the episode. For Harryhausen, this moment formed one of his concept drawings, and along with Talos and the Hydra featured on posters. The drama and spectacle of the Clashing Rocks episode, the marvellous nature of both the rocks and the divine interventions that so often assist the Argonauts, make this episode key to understanding the relationship between entertainment and the marvellous in the Argonaut myth.

The first mention of the *Argo* is in connection with the Wandering Rocks, or Planctae, in the *Odyssey* (12.59–72). In Apollonius, the two sets of rocks are distinct: the Clashing Rocks are at the entrance to the Black Sea, guarding the Bosphorus, and the Argonauts go through them with the help of Athena (2.317–40; 549–610); the Wandering Rocks are between the Ionian gulf and the Ceraunian sea, after their visit to Circe, before the Phaeacians in Drepane

(4.753–884; 922–81), where they are helped by Thetis and carried through by sea nymphs. These two sets of rocks are not always distinct, nor is it always clear what is special about them. A scholiast on Eur. *Med.* 1–2 reports that the Greek lyric poet Simonides of Ceos called the Clashing Rocks the *Synormades*, the 'rushing together' rocks. Herodotus describes the Persian emperor Darius visiting them in the Black Sea, and refers to them as Cyanean but also *Planctae* (4.85), suggesting some traditions held them to be identical. Pindar describes the Argonauts' encounter:

> they called on the Lord of Ships
> to save them from the crash of boulders
> rolling with a roar together:
> two of them, rocks
> > instinct with life,
> quicker than the winds' rumbling cohorts –
> > now they are still,
> > > stopped when the heroes sailed between
>
> Pind. *Pyth.* 4.207–11, trans. Nisetich

Poseidon presumably answered their prayer. In Apollonius (2.537–648), the rocks are part of a long narrow passage, full of high winds and powerful currents (549–52). The Argonauts hear the thunderous sound before they turn the corner and see them (553–60). Euphemus sends out a dove, which Phineus told them to bring, and they watch in high anxiety as the dove flies between the moving rocks (561–5). She escapes, her tail feathers clipped, and Tiphys urges them to row as hard as they can (571–5). He steers them expertly over the waves, which push them both backwards and forwards, while Euphemus exhorts them (579–93). When it seems they will inevitably be crushed, Athena intervenes, holding one rock back and pushing the ship through, although the rocks shear off the tip of the stern (598–603). As they recover, Tiphys credits their survival to Athena, but for making the ship, not literally pushing them through (610–14). Jason, however, is still gloomy: but when they respond enthusiastically to his despairing speech, the narrator reveals he was testing morale (619–47). Apollonius' version cleverly combines rationalizing (the waves, currents, timing, effort) with supernatural explanations (the dove as omen, Athena). Note also his continuing portrayal of Jason's ambivalent leadership.

In this episode, the main variance is not between different ancient versions, but between ancient and modern. Other ancient versions are broadly similar to Apollonius: Apollodorus suggests that the clashing of the rocks is caused by winds, but narrates divine assistance rather than timing: Hera helps them through, the dove showing they can make it. Valerius emphasizes the cosmic enormity of the Clashing Rocks, comparing them to thunder and lightning, and the ultimate historical consequences of their stilling, which opens the Black Sea to trade. Valerius' Jason takes a more active role than in Apollonius, encouraging the crew (4.647–53), and taking an oar himself (653–5). Phineus' prophecy focuses on the timing of their approach (572–6), and the dove does not feature in this version, although the stern of the ship is clipped (691–3); Valerius, as often, refers back to a narrative element from other versions, but missing in his own. Valerius' gods play a prominent role: first Athena sends a sign (670–4), then Juno and Athena collaborate to hold the rocks back, and are compared to two men wrestling with bulls (682–5), anticipating Jason's labours. As they depart the rocks, the crew are compared to Hercules and Theseus leaving the underworld (699–702), reversing the idea of the journey to Colchis as a journey to the underworld.[16] The *Orphic Argonautica* presents the rocks as driven by winds, and gives Orpheus a more prominent role: first he warns Tiphys, then his singing holds the rocks apart. The *OA* combines divine intervention with timing: Hera asks Athena to send a bird (a heron) which activates the rocks, and Tiphys then urges the heroes to row through. Physical divine action is replaced by Orpheus' singing.

Later receptions fall broadly into two groups, based on their different interpretations of the bird motif, both interpretations already present in Apollonius. The bird either shows whether the gods favour their enterprise, becoming an omen, or is a device for timing their approach to have the best chance of passing through. The former prioritizes gods and religion; the latter evokes action films and computer games. For instance, the graphic novel by Hoena and Estudio Haus uses the dove for timing: 'As soon as the rocks clash together, row as if your lives depended on it.' Brooks suggests this, when they row with 'the boulders on the rebound' (52). Others emphasize the bird as omen but do not explicitly portray divine intervention: Colum closely follows Morris and Apollonius, but uses the 'Lemnian pigeon' to show where they should go; in Seraillier, when the Argonauts see the dove successfully go through, they shout in triumph, and Tiphys says 'Let the dove be our pilot, let us follow her!' (37) Hints of the *OA* remain: when the noise of the rocks is stilled, they realize 'All this time Orpheus had been singing, unheard' (40).[17] Seraillier also rationalizes Athena's help: 'the power of the gods was in their arms and guiding the helmsman's hand' (37). Broadly speaking, prevalence of rationalization increases and explicit divine intervention decreases as the tradition develops, although with outliers at both ends. The timing motif is prevalent in more recent children's literature, and patterns of imitation emerge: the phrase 'Row for you lives!', for instance, is prominent in Riordan, and then used by both Yomtov and Whitehead.[18] The timing motif may well show the effect of new media, namely computer game models of engaging with obstacles, based on timing and agility, here changing the interpretation of the story.

Rationalization may lurk beneath, however: Apollonius and the *Orphic Argonautica* show traces of it. Athena's intervention can be read as reflecting the power of the highly variable currents, as highlighted by Severin in his description of actually rowing a small boat through the Bosphorus. Kingsley uses the striking rationalization of the clashing rocks as icebergs: he describes them as 'the blue rocks shining like spires and castles of grey glass, while an ice-cold wind blew from them and chilled all the heroes' hearts' (81–2). Janet Bacon acknowledges this rationalization, along with the idea that the rocks were connected by a spur only visible at low tide, and gives a parallel story from 'Eskimo' traditions (79–80).[19] The idea resurfaces in Graves's *Greek Myths*: 'The Clashing, Wandering, or Blue Rocks, shrouded in sea mist, seem to have been ice-floes from the Russian rivers adrift in the Black Sea' (235). This interpretation is adopted by Treece and subsequently denied by Catran, here correcting Treece. Pylos narrates: 'I had heard stories about floating mountains of ice. But these were not' (85). Brooks explicitly rejects rationalizations relating to the powerful currents of the Bosphorus: 'Even today the Bosphorus is known for its fierce, erratic currents ... but ... modern sailors do not have to face the Symplegades' (51). Severin is not convinced by either the submerged rock or the icefloe rationalization: instead he focuses on Apollonius' realistic depiction of the eddies and currents, throwing the boat around, apparently keeping her at a standstill and then suddenly pushing her forward, and the powerful waters of the Black Sea: 'the spray being flung high by the storm-driven swells surging into the constricting funnel of the Bosphorus' northern mouth, and the booming crash of the waves as they strike the headlands on either side and rebound in a tossing backwash' (147). Locals and ancient accounts identify 'two large chunks of rock' a little off the northern headland at Rumeli Fener as the remains of the Clashing Rocks: he concludes that the story was 'pure myth, an invented symbol to explain the real difficulties of passing through the straits of the Bosphorus' (148). The intellectual exercise of coming up with plausible rationalizations of the marvellous is itself a form of entertainment, as can be seen in documentaries and books such as Severin's. The inevitable remaining uncertainty and layers of possible interpretation, symbolic and rationalizing, bring together the intellectual and emotional aspects of engaging with a story in satisfying complexity.

The 1963 film and the 2000 TV mini-series exemplify the different approaches to the Clashing Rocks. For Harryhausen, it is all about the gods; for the 2000 film, all about timing and human ingenuity. In both films, the *Argo* approaches the rocks without knowledge of them and finds out from the fate of another ship: in the 1963 film, Medea's ship is crushed by rocks falling, while in the 2000 film they retrieve the sole survivor, Apsyrtus ('Aspyrtes'), who narrates his own ship's crushing. In the 1963 film, Jason has no plan but decides to power on anyway. He is urged to pray, and the scene cuts to Zeus and Hera watching as they play their board game. Jason seems cynically aware: 'The gods want their entertainment.' Hera plays the piece Triton on the board, echoing the amulet of Triton which Phineus gave Jason. Triton himself appears, flashing a giant fishtail, as he wordlessly holds back the rocks, and the Argonauts row through beneath his arm (Fig. 4.3). When urged to pray, Jason replies 'The gods of Greece are cruel. In time, all men shall learn to do without them.' As the Argonauts rest, Zeus and Hera discuss the gods' decline and reconcile with each other: does Zeus consider her weak for staying with him? 'Not weak,' he replies, 'Almost human.' Jason's scepticism and divine intervention are paradoxically connected: at the moment Jason refuses to honour the gods, the gods help him most. Entertainment is generated by advances in special effects, allowing film to go further beyond accepted reality. The script reflects on the paradox of the marvellous, simultaneously unbelievable and thematizing belief, creating a spectacular story,

Fig. 4.3 The miniature *Argo* approaches the model rocks, while Triton and his fish tail hold them apart. Note the outsize splashes and the rocks falling from above. Screenshot from *Jason and the Argonauts* (1963), [Film] Dir. Don Chaffey. Visual effects by Ray Harryhausen. Screenshot by author.

with plausible characters and motivations. Entertainment is paired with philosophical reflection, allowing Christian or secular audiences to feel comfortably superior to ancient Greeks, while maintaining a fantasy of divine providence.

The 2000 mini-series replaces watching gods with watching seers and tyrants, both of which mistakenly think the wreck of Apsyrtus' ship is the wreck of the *Argo*. Pelias uses this revelation to destroy Jason's mother (although his own son, too, must be assumed dead). The gods do not help the Argonauts: Phineus only tells them where to go, not how to get through. Jason himself comes up with the idea of using Orpheus' dove to activate the closing walls of the passage (sheer cliffs now, not rocky boulders) and times their approach to allow them maximum chance of passing through. The strength and speed of the Argonauts' rowing is crucial in achieving their survival (Fig. 4.4). Rather than collapsing in horror or possibly bemusement at Triton's fishy-tailed good-bye (although it is never clear whether the 1963 Argonauts can actually see Triton), the 2000 Argonauts celebrate their own achievement. In both, Jason takes the initiative, but the 2000

Fig. 4.4 The *Argo* shoots out of the closing rocks, showing the narrow corridor and block-like cliffs, which echo descriptions in Henry Treece and are taken up by graphic novels, such as Whitehead and Banerjee. From *Jason and the Argonauts* (2000) [TV mini-series], Dir. Nick Willing. USA: Hallmark. Screenshot by author.

Jason is stronger and less challenged: he himself holds the helm, struggling against the turbulence and urging the others on, while Harryhausen's Jason watches in perturbation. In the 2000 version, the survival of Orpheus' dove is not an omen: they do not even know it has survived until the final moment, when he looks at its sadly floating tail feather, only to see the dove itself land on the ship's rail. Dove echoes ship, rather than ship echoing dove. The cut to Jason's mother's anguish during their passage heightens suspense and makes the audience think they have been destroyed, relying on the fact that the 2000 audience was less familiar with the story than the 1963 audience.

The explicit divine intervention, so prominent in Apollonius and the 1963 film, is rare: Brooks, for instance, although featuring the gods prominently elsewhere, has Athena wake to the sound of Jason calling her name: 'I'm so sorry young man,' she said out loud, 'but you caught me napping' (52). This playfully highlights the artificiality of the divine level of the narrative. Similarly, Zimmerman makes the intervention of Athena and Hera the emphatic centre of her staging, with stylized metatheatricality: Athena forms the rocks and Hera pulls a model of the *Argo* through her legs.

Over time, the gap between the rocks has grown taller and narrower: in Apollonius it is a long winding channel between rocky cliffs; in the 2000 film it is a narrow, sharply defined passage between two squared rocks.[20] This image percolates into the comic books, where long narrow panels characterize both Yomtov and Whitehead's interpretations. This change may have originated in Morris:

> But Jason's eyes alone of all the crew
> Beheld the sunny sea and cloudless blue,
> Still narrowing fast but bright from rock to rock.

6.153–5

Treece intensifies this image by evoking a cityscape: 'It was like going down a narrow street between two high houses, where the light never reaches and the sun's heat cannot penetrate' (160). In Kneupper's science fiction version, the passage has narrowed even further into a tunnel through the defensive walls of Colchis city. The walls are intelligent and sensors respond to intruders by closing the tunnel and crushing them. The Argonauts' flying drone vehicle is stealthed to appear as a bird, so the seer Mopsus' pet bird acts as a dry run for their own fate. As in Treece, they literally scrape through: Treece's Argonauts push themselves with oars; Kneupper's retract the drone's wings, sink to the floor; a final boost of the ship's engines bursts them out into the city.

Some later versions draw on the 1963 film's presentation of Jason's leadership. Jason has to decide whether to attempt the passage and his men question it (Whitehead, Kneupper). Kneupper's gods (AIs analysing data) have sent messages to Mopsus and Jason has to choose between following Mopsus' prophecies and following Pelias' original plan (designed to destroy him). Jason takes a stronger and more positive role in the episode over time: in Apollonius' version, Euphemus, Tiphys and Athena have agency, while Jason is passive; already in Valerius he plays a stronger role; in the 2000 film, he is completely in charge. Sometimes divine intervention only inspires human success: in Morris, Juno inspires Jason to encourage the crew (6.101–3). The act of releasing the dove often shows agency and control, and in later versions Jason mostly works out for himself what to do. In contrast, Treece's highly negative Jason releases a bird ostensibly as a sacrifice to the Mother Goddess, but actually to cover up his own desire to abandon ship (160), while Ancaeus thinks of pushing along the ice with oars and Tiphys steers them through. In Catran, Jason is much stronger, taking the helm himself (self-consciously marked with 'the captain must take command', 86) while Pylos, our narrator, looks after the dove. Jason reads the dove as both omen and guide: 'Where a dove goes, Greeks can follow!' (87). Only after the event does Tiphys interpret the waves as Athena's divine intervention: 'he could see Athena's white hand gripping our stern and holding us safe' (88). As in Graves's *Golden Fleece* (also hinted in Treece where they grind over an ice ledge), the real danger is submerged rocks, shallows that are hidden by the tide.

Apollonius' Phineus emphasizes the connection between the gods and the clashing rocks: the Argonauts can only pass through if it is the gods' will; if the dove omen is unfavourable, then they must turn back (2.324–45). The rocks are a barrier to progress (travel, communication, commerce, war) and breaking that barrier is a potentially transgressive act. The rocks are a gateway to a new time, as well as a new space, showing how the Argonaut story functions as one of human development. The *Argo*'s journey initiates a new phase in history. Epic poets (with their cosmic reach) and historians (with their interest in progress and evolution) are both attracted to these grand narratives.

The uncanny nature of the Clashing Rocks is best brought out in one outlying modern version, Evslin's 1986 young-adult novel, in which the rocks are actually alive, malevolent and intent on killing the Argonauts. Jason acts as both dove and boat, himself swimming through, causing the rocks to crash into each other and smash into smithereens. More bizarrely still, one fragment follows Jason onto the ship: 'it was as if this single stone were the survivor of those boulders that had dashed themselves to death upon each other – as if it had inherited their weird energy and menacing intelligence and now offered itself to the victor' (78). The rock becomes Jason's companion and aide, growing into a boulder, later used as an anchor stone (80). The malevolence and bizarreness of these clashing rocks emphasizes the underlying inexplicability of the ancient narrative and the Argonauts' struggle to understand the world around them, gods, peoples and new places.

Visual images of the Argonauts approaching the Clashing Rocks are popular: for instance, an illustration by James Gurney (1985) shows the *Argo* entering a narrow passage, dwarfed by massive cliffs and falling rocks, thrown about by rushing waves and eddies the size of the ship. Human smallness in the face of the enormity of nature creates a sense of sublimity in this episode. The spectacle of human daring and the drama of crossing a threshold, both spatial and temporal, form the centre of the Argonaut myth as a story.

Representing gods: Hera and Athena

Given the direct divine intervention in the Clashing Rocks episode in Apollonius, Apollodorus, Valerius, the 1963 film and Robert Graves's *Greek Myths*, it is surprisingly absent in much of the later tradition. Portraying the gods and engaging with ancient religious beliefs in later contexts is difficult.[21] Stephen Fry in his bestselling mythographical tour de force *The Heroes* (Penguin, 2018) includes the gods but domesticates them, with a peevish Zeus grumbling at a petty Hera, probably drawing on Beverley Cross' script for the Harryhausen film.[22] Looser adaptations, such as W. E. B. Du Bois' *Quest of the Silver Fleece* exclude direct representation of the divine, but keep a strong numinous presence. For Du Bois, his 'Silver Fleece', the miraculously beautiful cotton fabric, woven from the bale produced by Zora and Bles secretly in the swamp, is recurrently associated with the divine and Zora's epiphanic experiences.[23] The swamp is site of both monsters and divinity.[24]

The Argonautic myth is particularly interesting on portraying gods because Apollonius already subverts expectations. Ancient epic poems include a divine level of narrative, which shows the poet as omniscient narrator, channelling the inspiration and knowledge from the Muses.[25] In *Iliad* 1, Apollo shoots the arrows of plague at the Trojan camp, and Athene physically restrains Achilles from killing Agamemnon.[26] These examples show how ancient epic gods are simultaneously characters, anthropomorphic, and physical or psychological phenomena. Apollo is both plague and a person causing a plague; Athene can be an allegorization of Achilles' good sense. Apollonius is an unusual epic poet; he includes few scenes on the divine level; both narrator and characters often remain unaware of divine motivations.[27] Only hints, not always at the obvious point in the narrative, tell us Hera's plans, and why she helps Jason. When Apollo appears to the Argonauts at Thynias, he is the sun rising, a spiritual and epiphanic experience (AR 2.681–4). But he does not notice the Argonauts and they do not know what he is doing and why. Apollonius represents sacrifice and worship; the gods are an important force, but often mysterious and elusive.

Only at 3.6–166, when Hera and Athene ask Aphrodite to make Eros shoot Medea, is there an extended scene on Olympus, giving the epic audience their all-encompassing view. The anthropomorphism and psychological realism of this Olympus scene are striking. Aphrodite is tartly surprised that the goddesses have deigned to call on her: 'In the past I saw very little of you, chief among goddesses as you are' (3.53–4). Hera is embarrassed: 'You tease us, but our hearts are shaken up with distress' (56). When Aphrodite approaches Eros, she finds him playing dice, laughing at his disconsolate opponent (117–27). She offers him a golden ball with dark blue spirals, a bribe for shooting Medea (129–44). The shooting itself (275–98) is susceptible to an allegorical reading: Eros shoots her from close by Jason, so his arrow equates to the sight of Jason piercing her eyes. Apollonius emphasizes her darting glances, along with her burning, melting suffering, evoking ancient philosophical theories of the erotic gaze.

Ancient versions of Medea's enamourment vary in their details. In Pindar *Pythian* 4, Aphrodite teaches Jason to entrap Medea (Pindar, *Pythian* 4.213–9). She invents the *iunx*, a form of love magic. Jason, not Medea, is the magician, himself enchanting her. However, her longing is not for him, but Greece. Valerius' version features three long books of epic battle and machinations, including a brief conversation between Juno and Athena (5.280–95) about civil war in Colchis, Medea seeing Jason at the Phasis, where Juno has beautified him (5.363–72); Juno's impersonation of Medea's sister Chalciope, to make her watch Jason from the walls; Medea's resistance and Juno calling on Venus to intervene herself, as Circe.[28] Venus desires to destroy Colchis in vengeance against Helios for revealing her infidelity with Mars (6.467–8), the famous story of Ares and Aphrodite in *Odyssey* 8. Valerius has combined the Apollonian divine process with a re-working of Virgil's *Aeneid* 7, in which Juno starts a war between Latins and Trojans, a process doubled again by Medea's resistance. The Flavian epic is more epic, more complex, more intense than its predecessors; Jason is more heroic, Medea more virtuous. As in other Flavian epics, the gods seem less straightforwardly powerful: Jupiter is more autocratic and yet less effective, and both Juno and Venus struggle to achieve their ends and intervene personally rather than giving orders to lesser gods. The *OA* in contrast summarizes these scenes, after Aeetes' meeting with the Argonauts, and gives a few bare mentions of Hera's involvement: she sends a dream to Aeetes (774–7); inspires Jason to make a robust response (826–8); and Medea falls in love 'through the divine plans of Hera' (867). Maffeo Vegio's Neo-Latin epic *Vellus Aureum* takes the divine machinery even further than Valerius, showing that the Latin epic tradition has its own momentum.

Cavalli's 1649 opera *Giasone* demonstrates how opera can approach the problem similarly: it features divine personifications as characters, *Sole* (Sun), *Amore* (Love), and gods *Giove* (Jupiter), *Eolo* (Aeolus, King of the Winds) and *Zeffiro* (Zephyrus, the West Wind). The prologue features a dialogue between *Sole* and *Amore*; Act 2 scene 8 is a divine interlude in Aeolus' grotto, in which Jupiter, Aeolus, Love and a chorus of winds plan a storm. In Act 3 scene 22 *Giove*, *Amore* and a chorus of gods celebrate the happy ending. The 2010 Antwerp production shows one way this aspect is handled in performance: the gods are often on stage watching or intervening in the action, even if not singing. The emphasis on the gods' descendants, both those of Helios and Aeolus, shows continuity with Latin epic tradition. Zimmerman's play, too, presents the gods prominently, making Medea fall in love. In this scene, she follows Apollonius, exaggerating the characteristics of the three goddesses, with Athena openly disdainful, and Venus repeatedly remarking on her surprise at their visit. Evslin's idiosyncratic children's book also features complex and repeated divine intervention: the narrator is Hermes' son, and Venus arranges him to protect Jason, because she herself is in love with Jason. These versions, across a wide range of genres, media and periods, show that complex, sophisticated engagement with ancient traditions of divine representation is possible and not unwelcome to audiences: both Cavalli's opera and Zimmerman's play were popular and successful. Divine characterization provides a different sort of relatability.

In fact, direct representation of divine action seems to increase mass appeal. Both the 1963 and 2000 films include the gods explicitly as part of the narrative, but in ways that mark out and separate divine action. Harryhausen uses the device of a pool into which the gods look, like a screen, to see mortal action; Zeus and Hera play a board game which represents their rivalry, their manoeuvrings with mortals, and their light-hearted engagement with lives and deaths of mortals. At one point Jason stands as a piece on the board, when Hermes takes him up to Olympus, breaking the frame and disrupting epic conventions of interactions between gods and mortals (Fig. 4.5). The gods are

Fig. 4.5 Jason becomes a game-piece on the board of the Olympians, placed by Hermes and watched by Zeus and Hera. Note his anxious body language and the semi-benevolent expression of Zeus, plus the temple setting of Olympus. The angle of the shot, with the gods looking down on us, puts us in Jason's position. Screenshot from *Jason and the Argonauts* (1963), [Film] Dir. Don Chaffey. Visual effects by Ray Harryhausen. Screenshot by author.

shown less later on, not at all during events at Colchis, because Hera has used up the five interventions Zeus allowed her. This plot device raises the stakes, and thematizes the film-makers' need to avoid divine intervention becoming a formulaic solution and allow human characters agency.

The 2000 movie has an explicit, but simplified, re-working of the Hera and Athena scene: Hera orders Eros, a miniature flaming figure, to infatuate Medea. Zeus then appears and demands 'What was he doing here?' Zeus' relationship with Hera replaces the tensions between the wider cast of divine characters. The two bicker repeatedly over Zeus' infidelities and (again) Hera's attraction to Jason. Most strikingly, on the return journey, Zeus' anger over the death of Apsyrtus is replaced by his failed attempt to seduce Medea. As Jason is taken up to Olympus in the 1963 film, so Medea meets Zeus; whether in dream or reality is unclear, although afterwards she wakes up. She refuses him, since she genuinely loves Jason, and the two have bonded over the deaths of their fathers. Zeus even removes Eros' arrow, in a unique 'disenamourment' gesture, which proves that her feelings for Jason are not divinely induced. This reversal of the Apollonian plot device shows an uneasiness with the slippage between anthropomorphic and allegorical understandings of the divine. Viewers need to feel that Medea's love is genuine. Or could represent Medea's initial infatuation transforming into a deeper connection. The happy ending of Jason marrying Medea is matched by reconciliation between Zeus and Hera in the sky above.

The gods of the 2000 mini-series break the frame, several times: mostly they appear as figures, or upper bodies, in the sky; early on, Zeus' jealousy over Hera's desire for Jason causes a thunderstorm, and after Hera instructs Eros, Zeus casually dips his hand into the sea to drink. These gestures destabilize the separation between the divine and mortal worlds carefully maintained by Harryhausen. Ultimately the gods of the 2000 mini-series evoke multiple interpretations of Greek divine action: as psychological allegory, personification of natural forces and anthropomorphized characters. In the first half, the gods appear as heads in the sky. In the second part, before and after Zeus tries to seduce Medea, they are presented in a more subtle way as reflections on the overall image, as if we see them viewing a television screen (Fig. 4.6). This places the gods as internal audience in a different space between the storyworld and our world, as if they were viewers in Channel 4's *Gogglebox*.[29] The 2000 mini-series offers a complex range of approaches to representing divinity, from the monstrous figure of Poseidon (see below p. 111), to the implied apotheosis of

Fig. 4.6 After the *Argo* leaves Colchis, Zeus and Hera watch as if viewers reflected in a television screen. Both gods and *Argo* are romanticized by the sunset. From *Jason and the Argonauts* (2000) [TV mini-series], Dir. Nick Willing. USA: Hallmark. Screenshot by author.

Hercules. The award for visual effects suggests that this element of the production was well-received.

Graves, in his novel, also plays with different frames for divine action and modes of narrating it, but at several degrees of separation, as fits with his rationalizing tendencies. As the Argonauts decide what to do in Colchis, Atalanta presents a poetic performance, affirming the suggestion that Jason's talent at making people fall in love with him is the answer (259–62). She presents herself watching the scene on Olympus of Hera instructing Aphrodite to make Medea fall in love. The toy given to Eros becomes one Hera has kept from Zeus' childhood, an element not present in Apollonius, suggesting that Graves here interprets her as an incarnation of Rhea-Cybele, Zeus' mother, the Great Mother. Atalanta presents this scene as a dream, a way of avoiding direct handling of divine action, but also a valid ancient aspect of divine communication with mortals. Colston West also uses a dream to incorporate the gods into the first-person narrative of his young-adult novel, with Jason himself dreaming he is watching the scene on the back of the golden ram.

This dream, or vision, constitutes the overall framing device for Gardner's 1973 epic poem. His narrator, a twentieth-century academic, was forcibly transported into Medea's Corinth to witness the story, and he too plays with breaking the frame. He is trampled during a riot and his glasses are broken. Various gods talk to him, but Artemis is his guiding power. As Jason tells his tale in the Corinthian hall, Athena (*Vision*), Aphrodite (*Love*) and Hera (*Life*) all listen. The many layers of divine involvement interact with a layered sense of time: both Jason as internal narrator and the external narrator experience apocalyptic visions of the future. Medea herself takes over internal narration from the Hera and Athena scene onwards. Aphrodite is sweet, dark-haired, to be pitied by the more powerful goddesses and offered patronizing child-care advice. The intimate emotional part of Apollonius's narrative, and the knowledge of divine action, is transferred to the female narrator, while the male narrator focuses on power, politics, leadership and the sweep of history. Gardner's avant garde and non-realist approach, not to mention his decision to write primarily in verse, may well have contributed to *Jason and Medeia*'s relative lack of success.[30]

The divine element is significantly reduced in Lefèvre's medieval romance, in striking contrast to Vegio's nearly contemporary epic. Generally Lefèvre's gods are not mentioned, but there is a significant excursus as the Argonauts arrive at Colchis to explain the story of the Golden Fleece. This story focuses on the characters Mars and Apollo, here mortal brothers, sons of mortal king Jupiter. Structurally, the excursus replaces Apollonius' Olympian interlude, but it de-divinizes the Greek and Roman gods. This is a stronger gesture of refusal than narratives that simply omit them, such as Diodorus, or Bradman and Ross. Treece also excludes the divine: his first-person narrator, Jason, has no knowledge of divine action, and his Atalanta refuses to repeat Graves's dream: 'the Mother has sent me no dreams' (171). Christa Wolf's voices are all mortal, Pirotta's version is strongly focalized through Medea, and omits divine action, as does that of Zeff, despite Medea praying in the temple of Hecate. As in the 1963 film, she receives no response.

Hawthorne, Kingsley, Morris, Colum and Seraillier all include Hera at the Anauros episode, but do not include the Hera and Athena episode on arrival in Colchis. Hawthorne's Medea herself watches over Jason as he completes his tasks, although the speaking oak branch does encourage him back onto the *Argo* afterwards. In Kingsley's case this discrepancy can be explained by his sources: he uses Pindar for the earlier episodes, and the *Orphic Argonautica*, with its summary of Apollonius 3, for the later episodes. Morris, influenced by Kingsley and Hawthorne, or perhaps Lefèvre, has no gods at this point, except the capitalized Love and 'his golden yoke' (7.86–7). Colum presents the Argonauts' arrival in Colchis along with Aeetes' dream and Medea's love at first sight. His gods are restricted to inset narratives.

Children's literature and comics do not have the expectations of realism that complicate many novels and films, so can explore the supernatural. Naden, for instance, introduces the gods in this episode: 'Sometimes the gods and goddesses, who lived on lofty Mount Olympus, came to the aid of mortals' (23). Brooks continues her light-hearted rendition with Hera and Athene falling asleep again and failing to prevent the deaths of Tiphys and Idmon: 'feeling rather guilty' ... 'lately they'd been so busy or tired, they just hadn't had time to watch over him' (57). The goddesses, like working mothers, are torn between different responsibilities. The two squabble, snapping at each other as if in a difficult work meeting. Athene says: 'for queen of the gods, you are a very poor communicator.' This displaces the rivalry and complexity of their relationship with Aphrodite and simplifies Apollonius' version. Yomtov's Hera and Athena scene portrays them as modern girls with long hair, flowing dresses and dramatic thrones in a palace among the clouds. Gunderson and Takvorian present a vertiginous window scene, in which Medea looks up at Jason, while the goddesses Hera and Aphrodite hover above in miniature, arrow notched on the string (15). Byrd shows Eros shooting Medea as Jason approaches Pelias: the gods are key to his version, which highlights a god on each page in an inset box. He chooses his episodes to involve as many Olympians as possible (for instance, the heron omen at the Clashing Rocks, since the heron is 'bird of Athena'). Byrd's children's version makes explicit the way that Greek gods are felt to appeal to children, an element of the marvellous which intrigues, complicates and entertains.

Whitehead and Banerjee include multiple gods: the Indian context of production perhaps has more tolerance for and interest in polytheism. They intensify Apollonius' epiphany of Apollo by having him address Jason directly (37). Apollo is the sun, with rays encircling his head, light suffusing the scene. Iris is also depicted, stopping the Boreads from killing the Harpies (32), emanating from or producing a rainbow, with a moral message praising their compassion for Phineus. As in Harryhausen, gods are marked with frames, white light surrounding them; Zeus and Hera watch the characters in a pool, first Jason at the Anauros, then the Argonauts in Colchis. Hera and Zeus make Medea fall in love with Jason: Zeus, with his long white beard evokes representations of the Christian God, while Hera visually recalls Claire Bloom's portrayal from the 1981 Harryhausen *Clash of the Titans*. Zeus' complaint that she makes things too easy for Jason recalls the 1963 Zeus, but Hera's direct instruction of Eros (a muscled fiery young man with a bow) rather resembles the 2000 TV movie (he refers to her as 'Milady', evoking the 'Madam' of Eros in the film).

The Hera and Athena scene emphasizes the anthropomorphized gods. But Greek gods can also exemplify Otherness. In Apollonius book 4, the Argonauts are rescued by the god Triton. He first appears as a young man, but later in his true form (4.1602–20). He has 'the long forked tail of a sea monster ... spines, whose points divided in curving needles like the horns of the moon', called an 'extraordinary marvel' or arguably 'terrifying monster' (*teras ainon*). The monstrous tail looks forward to Harryhausen's Triton, but of a sea monster: spiny, and associated with cosmic scale.[31] The Argonauts respond with awe, bordering on terror. The god helps and responds to prayer and sacrifice, but this divinity is hybrid, opaque in its motivations and overwhelmingly powerful. In the 2000 TV movie, the Argonauts come upon an unexpected land mass, dark, barnacled and surrounded by mist. The island, of course, is no island, but instead stirs. We expect it to be a sea monster, but instead it is the god Poseidon, who rises into the air, taking several Argonauts with him. Huge, unstoppable and incomprehensible, he roars and creates storm waves with his enormous hand. He departs when Zeus rebukes him, but he remains monstrous, wordless, and on a completely different scale to the human protagonists. This is a very different vision of godhead to Hera and Zeus gazing down from the clouds and bickering about extra-marital affairs: gods can themselves be monstrous, evoking deep fears of incomprehensible external powers. Entertainment strikes a balance between thrilling and alienating audiences.

Monsters and the monstrous

Ray Harryhausen was drawn to the Argonaut myth by its monsters: Talos, the Harpies, the hydra and the Earthborns, arguably Triton, offered opportunities for the ground-breaking special effects that made the film's influence so enduring.[32] The 1958 *Fatiche di Ercole* presents the Nemean lion, the Cretan bull, ape-like Colchians and a Godzilla-like upright lizard, which guards the fleece. The 2000 film includes bronze bulls, triffid-like Earthborns and what looks like a Tyrannosaurus rex, alongside the monstrous divine. While monsters are central to Hercules' myth, and he remains the monster-killer *par excellence*, the humans of the *Argonautica* are often as monstrous as the supernatural beasts. We have seen the Harpies and how they vary, from birds with women's heads, to women with wings, from racialized demons, wholly beast-like, black with red eyes, to grasping daughters. Chapter 5 tackles the Otherness and tyranny of Aeetes, and his monstrous associations. In Chapter 6, we investigate bulls, Earthborns and dragon in the Colchis episode as antagonists of Jason's heroism. This section discusses monsters not treated elsewhere: the six-armed giants of Cyzicus and Talos. We have seen the gendered and sometimes sexualized Harpies; the Cyzican monsters are less well-known, less defined and more variable than many Classical monsters, but more specific to the Argonaut myth; their hybridity varies between bestial, racial and earth-generated. Talos is mechanized, beyond human, and brings out the sublime effect of enormity. He is also a figure of sympathy and pathos.

Liz Gloyn gives a clear and thoughtful summary of historical developments of monsters and monster theory.[33] For Gloyn, Classical monsters are special because they retain their original characteristics even when they escape their initial contexts: Medusa stays Medusa even when separated from her sisters.[34] The Argonautic myth shows the mobility and adaptability of Classical monsters. They move from story to story and context to context; they change and are reinterpreted to address new desires and new fears.[35] New, non-Classical monsters, or monsters from other myths, join the gang. The hybridity of monsters, that crosses, threatens, polices and reinforces boundaries social and political, is not just hybridity of gender and species, but also the mixing up of mortality, genre and reality.[36] We marvel at Harryhausen's hydra and his skeletons, not just because they terrify the characters, but because they define and break the limits of special effects at the time. They steal the limelight from the film's rather wooden and not especially memorable Jason. The opposition between hero and monster is rarely stable, as we saw in the case of Phineus and the Harpies. People use stories to create monstrosity, to define others as monsters, but also to humanize and sympathize with the Other, to process their own feelings of exclusion, to resist objectification. Monsters can represent many different types of unspoken fears and desires at the same time or in different readings.

The Harpies, for instance, are rationalized in different ways: as starvation caused by bad weather; as winds that bring disease and death; as birds that defile and pollute; as women that recklessly spend and destroy men's property; as women that take control and snatch power over men. Phineus' blindness is instrumental in making him powerless against them: he cannot see what they really are, and he cannot pin them down in space. They represent fear of starvation, disgust associated with polluted food, fear of losing wealth, power, respect and control, fear of disability. In Greek tragedy, they are primarily agents of divine vengeance, closely akin to the Furies: Phineus brought them down on himself. But this version does not find purchase in epic, where his prophecies bolster heroism and success for the Argonauts, the poets and their patrons. Neither film nor children's literature is willing to forego the comfort of defeating evil beasts; both tend to further bestialize and demonize or sanitize them. Novels remain complex often rationalizing engagements, where the Harpies are less terrifying or marvellous, displaced by a different marvel: that of mastering the material, finding out the truth, cleaning up the mess.

We turn to the six-armed giants of Cyzicus. Apollonius describes the creatures who live on Bear Island near Mount Dindymum as 'insolent and wild earth-borns' (AR 1.942–3) with six mighty hands, two from their shoulders and four below. They are called 'great marvel' (943) and the poet suggests that Hera nourished these 'terrible monsters' (*aina pelora*, 996) as a feat for Hercules. *Pelor*, like the Latin *monstrum*, covers a range of meanings including 'prodigy, portent, monster', and is used negatively of animal-like creatures, including the cyclops Polyphemus in the *Odyssey*, strongly evoking the marvellous and the Other. The mythographic tradition (Herodorus 31F7, see Gantz) takes the six-armed giants of Cyzicus back to at least the fifth century BCE. These neighbouring monsters leave the Doliones, Cyzicus' people, unmolested because Poseidon protects them. The Argonauts anchor in the harbour at Chytus in order to climb Mount Dindymum, and the Earthborns block them in 'like men trapping a wild beast'

(991). This simile bestializes the Argonauts, complicating the association of Earthborns with monstrosity, but also suggests their malevolence and intelligence, blurring the distinction between heroes and monsters. Apollonius' Argonauts together kill them with arrows and spears; the monsters are further dehumanized when he describes their dead bodies lying like long trees cut down by axes (1003–5). A version can be imagined in which the transgressive killing of the Earthborns is what leads to the later accidental killing of the Doliones, when the Argonauts are driven back to their shore, but there is no attestation of this.

The six-armed giants are popular in children's literature. Hawthorne, for instance, emphasizes their enormity: Jason fails to distinguish them from the clouds (223). He also makes them more violent, ravaging the countryside and killing the Doliones (222). 'Each of these monsters was able to carry on the whole war by himself.' But they are no match for the 'brave Argonauts' since they have 'only one heart' (223). This 'wonderful event' intensifies the heroism and bravery of the Argonauts, who fight against overwhelming, violent enemies: Hawthorne finds this event safe enough to develop, one of few on the outward journey. Kingsley closely paraphrases the *Orphic Argonautica*, which describes them as war-like men (514), coming from the Arctoan (Bear) mountains, with six arms like the Giants or the Titans. Kingsley has 'terrible men, who lived with the bears ... like Titans or Giants in shape', obscuring their additional limbs; his Hercules kills them with his poison arrows. In other children's versions, they retain their Apollonian form: for instance in Brooks they are giants throwing boulders, a 'colossal figure snapping off the top of the mountain with one of its many hands' (33). Hercules and Atalanta shoot them and their 'towering static forms' with an 'enormous six-armed body' fall into the sea. Many children's versions include these antagonists, who are straightforward 'baddies', incarnations of anonymous unthinking violence, that can be satisfactorily dispatched by the Argonauts. Monsters are perceived to have an affinity with children, whose imaginations are often thought to be closer to primitive cultures and beliefs than those of adults, and more likely to be unsettled by complexity. Adults are keen to police children's experiences, making great efforts to use monsters to reinforce social hierarchies. Jeffrey also presents his Earthborns as uncomplicatedly Other: thugs with green skin and multiple arms. Their enormity and inhuman shape is crucial in creating fear and wonder. Size matters.

Apollonius' monsters are too superhuman for some, and later versions rationalize or separate out elements in different ways. We have seen the six-armed giant men lose their extra arms in Kingsley: James Riordan turns them into six-armed giant bears, followed by Byrd, while Yomtov simplifies them into large bears, all taking the hint from the name Bear Island. Predatory animals were a threat for the Argonauts, and epic also includes wild animals as antagonists (a wild boar kills Idmon in Apollonius). The illustrators of both Riordan and Yomtov make these bears enormous and ferociously violent: no pathos for these monsters. Graves rationalizes with his usual tactic for animal references: these are men of the 'Bear Clan', who wear bearskins. Catran takes the rationalization one stage further by explaining their six arms: they carry many different weapons, which enables them to fight for longer. Hoena/Estudio Haus follows the line also taken in Rick Riordan's *Heroes of Olympus* books, where these creatures are animate lumps of earth, drawing on the image in the Greek 'earthborns', *gegenees* (generated by the earth). Riordan's ultimate antagonist is Gaia, so he includes earth-related creatures frequently, but their six arms give them a clear connection to Apollonius. The inanimate coming to life and attacking you embodies a sense of human insignificance and powerlessness against nature, as we saw with the Clashing Rocks. Riordan's particular early-twenty-first-century earth monsters may be an incarnation of environmental guilt. Interestingly, these monsters do not feature in the Argonaut films: perhaps they were not sufficiently distinctive. Harryhausen chose memorable and recognizable monsters, but these are relatively flexible signifiers, used in many different ways. In Rick Riordan, they are low-grade easily defeated cannon fodder, minions for the full-scale Giants, who themselves are minor bosses in service of Gaia. In 1963, a monster on film was a significant investment of time and money; CGI and the influence of computer games have multiplied and created hierarchies of monsters.

Talos as Argonautic antagonist operates at the boundaries of man and machine, like the bronze-hoofed, fire-breathing bulls at Colchis. In Apollonius, the Argonauts encounter him on their return, protecting Crete from intruders (4.1638–93). He throws rocks at them, and Medea offers to destroy him. She turns her magic, curses and evil eye on him, causing him to catch his one weak spot (the vein on his ankle) against a rock. The ichor flows out like molten lead and he collapses, like a toppled pine tree, into the sea. Although made of bronze by Hephaestus, last of his demi-god race of bronze, with his untiring metallic form allowing him to continually circle Crete and making him nearly invincible, he is a marvel rather than straightforwardly a monster. The size of the rocks he throws and the simile of the pine tree as he falls might imply that he is gigantic in size, but this is not definite in Apollonius. Both enormous rocks and falling trees are used of human epic heroes. The visual art of the period and before represents him the same size as the Dioscuri. In a volute crater in Ruvo (425–375 BCE), Castor and Pollux support the drooping figure of Talos, while Medea

Fig. 4.7 Talos naked and glimmering, supported by Castor and Pollux in ornate costume. Red-figure krater, fourth century BCE, now in Jatta National Archaeological Museum, Ruvo di Puglia. Photo by Forzaruvo94. Available at: https://commons. wikimedia.org/wiki/File:Vaso_di_Talos_particolare.JPG (accessed 23 August 2019).

watches with her bowl of *pharmaka* ('drugs'). His bronze body is pale, veined and glimmering, like Medea's skin, but his nakedness contrasts with the Dioscuri's elaborate clothing. As central focus of the vase, wounded, he is more likely to be an object of pathos than terror.

Apollonius builds empathy for him, as the last of his race, and as marvellous creature who thought he was invulnerable, but nevertheless fell to the 'evil intentions' (AR 4.1669) of an apparently weaker opponent. The image of the falling pine tree evokes heroes killed in epic battle.[37] Apollonius also emphasizes the thirst and pain of the Argonauts and their desperate need to land (1651–2). In other ancient material, Talos is more terrifying: he heats himself to an unbearable temperature and crushes opponents in a fiery embrace, according to fragments of Simonides and Sophocles. There is little sign of this version elsewhere in the ancient Argonaut tradition. Apollodorus preserves several versions: Talos is either the last of the race of bronze, or a bronze man created by

Hephaestus, or even a bull; a single vein extends through his body and is kept closed by a nail at one end (he does not say which: shoulder or ankle?); Medea caused his death, either driving him mad using drugs, or promising him immortality and pulling out the nail. An alternative version has Poeas, father of Philoctetes, shoot him in the ankle. Apollodorus does not suggest he is gigantic or particularly monstrous: all he does is throw stones at the *Argo*. The boundary between marvel and monster shifts across time: the idea of the mechanical as inhuman seems not to come into play until later in the Argonaut tradition. All three different versions of his defeat (Medea's gaze, pulling out the nail, shooting by Poeas) are mentioned in Graves's *Greek Myths* and all appear in later versions.

Kingsley combines nearly all these different versions: the Argonauts arrive in Crete to see an enormous giant overlooking them from a headland, evoking Apollonius with a pine comparison: 'For on a cape ... stood a giant, taller than any mountain pine, who glittered aloft against the sky like a tower of burnished brass' (117). Talos warns the Cretans to evacuate, lights a beacon, then disappears; Medea explains that he is making himself burning hot, but she will deal with him. She offers to give him immortality by pouring ichor into his vein, and asks him to bathe in the sea to cool down, before pulling the nail out, then singing him into a stupor: 'And as he sank, his brazen limbs clanked heavily, ... and the liquid fire ran from his heel, like a stream of lava, to the sea; and Medeia laughed' (120). It seems to be Kingsley who invented his gigantic stature, from his reading of the pine simile in Apollonius. The stream of red-hot iron is also an Apollonian touch, which recurs later. Medea here becomes like a Siren, tempting Talos with immortality then destroying him, foreshadowing her killing of Pelias. Far from being a monster, this 'simple' Talos is guardian and victim. Sybil Tawse's illustration (*Medeia and Talus*) for a 1915 edition of *The Heroes* (Fig. 4.8) shows Talos' pathos. Medea stands over Talos, holding a pin, while red liquid flows from his shoulder. He lies collapsed on the ground, many times her size, and his hands grasp at his draining blood. He gazes at her in anguish, eyes and mouth red, while she looks out at the viewer, or perhaps the watching Argonauts. The peace of the landscape and Medea's poise contrast with Talos' agonized twisting.

Kingsley has a clear formative influence on twentieth- and twenty-first-century versions, via the Harryhausen film. Harryhausen's Talos is one of his best-loved creatures: a creaky bronze giant, guard of the gods' treasures on the 'Isle of Bronze'. When Hercules and Hylas steal a hat-pin, he comes to life and pursues the Argonauts, first throwing crags at the *Argo*, then straddling the headlands of the harbour like the Colossus of Rhodes (Fig. 4.9), where he lifts the *Argo* into the air and threatens to destroy the boat entirely.

Fig. 4.8 Illustration by Sybil Tawse for Charles Kingsley (1915) *The Heroes, Or Greek Fairy Tales for my Children*. London: A. & C. Black. Photo by Oksmith. Available at: https://commons.wikimedia.org/wiki/File:Medeia_and_Talus.png (accessed 23 August 2019).

Fig. 4.9 Bronze Talos at his most massive, straddling the headlands like the Colossus of Rhodes, about to destroy the *Argo*. Screenshot from *Jason and the Argonauts* (1963), [Film] Dir. Don Chaffey. Visual effects by Ray Harryhausen. Screenshot by author.

The Argonauts have to defend themselves, and the figurehead advises Jason how to kill him. Jason himself takes the monster down, levering out the plug-like nail in his ankle and allowing the ichor to pour out, steaming and orange like molten metal. As Jason struggles to remove the nail, we watch the Argonauts running around Talos' feet from Talos' perspective, as he puzzles about what Jason is doing. This alternates with the perspective of the terrified Argonauts, throwing spears, about to be crushed under his enormous feet. As the ichor drains, Talos realizes he is dying, grabs his throat in agony, tottering. Life leaves him: he solidifies, falls and shatters. This Talos is a distant and not deliberately malevolent character, destructive but also a miracle destroyed. Hercules and Hylas are in the wrong for disobeying the orders of the gods, and, while Talos' response is disproportionate, audiences retain sympathy for him. He represents the artistry of Harryhausen as much as the artistry of Hephaestus, and the fragility of all mortal creatures as much as the fragility of art. The 1963 film, then, may 'take liberties' with the Argonautic myth, but it is also fundamentally faithful, except in its gender politics.[38] The bittersweet success of Jason, which depends on the destruction of a unique and spectacular creature, a creature who does not understand what is happening to it, is the most emotionally complex, and arguably satisfying, scene of the film, made even more powerful by the accidental crushing of Hylas. Harryhausen's Talos is so much his signature monster that the 2000 film does not include the episode, not even attempting to compete.

Children's versions, keen to embrace the Talos episode, tend towards dehumanizing him. There is no one dominant version: some follow Apollonius, by making Medea conquer Talos with her gaze (Colum, Zarabouka, Jeffrey and Hoena/Estudio Haus). The rest follow Apollodorus, mainly through Kingsley or Harryhausen, with a technological solution, pulling out the nail and letting his ichor drain away. In some versions Medea's magic enables the nail to be pulled (Lancelyn Green, Malam and Antram), and in others characters have to choose between the two versions. Whitehead and Banerjee's comic, for instance, devotes five full pages to the episode, making it a major feature. Their Talos resembles *The Iron Man* from Ted Hughes' 1968 story, adapted for film in 1999 as *The Iron Giant*.[39] Jason challenges Talos to fight, and eventually defeats him by cutting the pipes between his limbs (a variant of the technological solution). The Argonauts watch, and Medea is keen to intervene, but Orpheus insists this is Jason's chance to prove himself, to himself. As in Harryhausen, Jason's heroism is emphasized at the expense of Medea's achievements. The sequence ends with a full-page image of the triumphant Jason, wearing the fleece, raising his sword in the air, standing on the lifeless body of the iron giant, while the Argonauts cheer.

Hoena/Takvorian's choose-your-own-adventure version allows readers to pick between a Harryhausen-style aristeia for Jason and the more conventional narrative of Medea's enchantment causing an accidental wound. If you try to throw your spear at Talos, you die: so Hoena punishes his readers for unfaithfulness to 'the myth'. Their Talos closely resembles that of Harryhausen, with helmet and loincloth, as does that of Jeffrey/Verma, and Malam/Antram. Interestingly the two versions closest in time to Harryhausen, Seraillier and Brooks, both follow Kingsley, perhaps to re-establish authenticity, although Brooks playfully engages with the implausibility of the narrative: as Medea offers immortality to Talos, Atalanta back on the ship mutters that he will live forever anyway as an automaton (85). In his susceptibility to Medea's beauty and promises, Talos is humanized. But he is also presented as 'slow' or child-like in his understanding, as in Kingsley.

Occasionally, there are qualms about destroying him: for instance, Colum's Medea displays anxiety, because Arete, the Phaeacian queen, made her promise not to use magic to kill. But since Zeus has decreed the end of the race of bronze, she feels justified. Jason never displays any qualms: he is simply a hero destroying a monster. Some versions intensify Talos' destructiveness and the Argonauts' desperation to justify his destruction: Harryhausen all but sinks the *Argo*; Lancelyn Green presents a more intelligent Talos who has to be tricked. Like a robot rebelling against his human master, he can no longer be controlled by the kings of Crete; Deucalion, the current king, is an Argonaut and asks for help. This legitimizes Medea's decommissioning. Here Talos is protective of his weak ankle, and suspicious of Medea, and two combined methods of destruction are needed: Medea's potion and Poeas' arrow. As Talos dies, several versions emphasize his transformation into a work of art, a statue torn down: in Harryhausen he is immobilized, cracks and falls; Seraillier has his bronze turn green, with patina or verdigris, indicating age and decay; Cockcroft's illustration for James Riordan presents him as a hollow statue head among the waves.

Products aimed at adults are more likely to exclude or rationalize monsters. Graves rationalizes Talos as a Cretan chief, dressed in bronze and standing on a high rock, who orders his men to pelt the Argonauts with stones. Medea shocks him into falling off the rock, at which point he breaks his leg and bleeds to death, because his superstitious men will not rescue him. Talos appeals to people interested in science and technology: a 2018 computer game in which the player is an android who solves puzzles is called *The Talos Principle*; a suit of bronze-coloured body armour for the US military is called TALOS (Tactical Assault Light Operator Suit). The remorseless and apparently indestructible mechanical man is a resonant film antagonist, as for instance in *Terminator* (dir. Cameron, 1984) and its sequels, which show how machines can be both horrifying opponents and reassuring guardians.[40]

The hybridity of the monsters and antagonists of the Argonaut myth is not stable and different monsters are treated differently. The Harpies stay bird women and become increasingly demonic, or are reduced to the wholly bestial. Gendered monsters are often interpreted as representing desire out of control (for food, knowledge and sex) and patriarchy under threat. The six-armed giants of Cyzicus draw power from fear of predators, the natural world and the earth itself, or sometimes the racialized Other or male violence out of control. Talos, too, represents the potential malevolence of the inanimate, the power, force and invulnerability of mechanized metal. Talos shares some characteristics with robots, but is largely treated in a sympathetic fashion, as a fallen warrior and guardian; when Medea defeats him, she becomes both too-masculine hero and demonized witch. Jason can conquer him unproblematically. In different eras, monsters can embody different fears and desires: desire to escape or fear of failure; fear of starvation and desire to control; fear of nature and desire to be more than human; fear of technology and desire for immortality. Monsters make concrete anxieties about Otherness, gender, race, species, machines and relationships to the natural world.

Human monsters are sufficient for W. E. B. Du Bois: in *Quest of the Silver Fleece* the monster zone is either the swamp, where the white masters sexually exploit black women, or the town, where drinking ruins people. Those who take profit or sexual gratification from the misery, pain and labour of others, especially black people, also pull the strings to create violence, culminating in the monstrous lynch mob. Social realism still has room for monsters. The mythicization and transfiguration of people and landscape operates through emotional responses, especially the imaginations of young characters, particularly Zora and Bles.

In Chapter 6 we search out further monsters in Colchis, and question further the opposition between hero and monster. Apollonius' *Argonautica* often blurs boundaries: heroes are never securely heroic and monsters are rarely without human or sympathetic elements. The Argonaut story has a distinct geography: it goes beyond the Mediterranean, into the monster zone of the Black Sea and beyond, where Otherness becomes all-encompassing. The next chapter traces representations of ethnicity and Otherness through the travels of the Argonauts and tropes of ethnography.

Apollonius wrote his Argonauts in the Hellenistic period, Varro of Atax wrote amongst the Roman neoterics, and Flavian Rome produced Valerius: these periods had a tendency towards the sensational and the marvellous.[41] In the *Argonautica*, there is no internal narrator, no Odysseus, to insulate us from the unexplained. This may be why rationalizations are important in the tradition, not just in commentary, but in versions themselves. The emotional power of the marvellous takes us beyond escapism to face complex truths about human psychology and our place in the universe.

Ethnicity and Otherness

Both gods and monsters are 'Other': they are separate, different, impossible to fully understand, and disturbingly attractive. This chapter explores how versions of the Argonauts portray travel, exploration and foreignness through ideas of the Other. The Argonaut myth is a story of voyage and encounter: while the *Odyssey* stages return and reintegration, the Argonauts go out to gain the glory of finding new things.[1] The rhetoric of discovery is itself a colonial construct: what is new to colonizers will have been known for millennia to the colonized. The Argonauts are not straightforwardly colonizers: they establish a sea-route in both directions. But Colchian perspectives are always secondary in Greek-centred versions. Although Black Sea peoples were not racially distinct from Mediterranean peoples, both race and ethnicity are important for this project because the study of mythology was formed alongside and shaped by scientific racism. The Argonaut tradition has been used to reinforce (and challenge) racist ideas.

Both Argonaut myth and *Odyssey* result from oral traditions, storytelling over many generations and in many places. This can create a complex relationship with space, since conceptualizations of geography change over time. The fantastic and unreal aspects of epic journeys might have felt realistic to earlier audiences, and different layers of geographical understanding coexist. Apollonius' epic is Hellenistic, produced in a culture where scholars invested enormous energy in editing and understanding the Homeric poems. Apollonius' poem recreates the Homeric storyworld, but with a difference. He is also writing for third-century BCE contemporaries in Alexandria, part of a society itself multicultural, imperial and colonial. Although Apollonius writes in Greek and has the epithet 'Rhodius', suggesting Greek heritage, we do not know the colour of his skin or whether he thought of himself as African. Apollonius also draws on Herodotus, the Greek 'father of history', who is fascinated by non-Greek cultures, including Egypt and Persia, and also investigates Black Sea peoples.[2] Alex Purves has shown how the birds' eye view of epic (gods looking down) interacts with the linear narrative of travel.[3] The portrayal of race and ethnicity in Apollonius displays a tension between epic and ethnography (writing about *ethne*, peoples). Monsters travel to new contexts, and myth, too, is always on the move.[4]

Ancient concepts of race and ethnicity are difficult for a twenty-first-century audience.[5] Both Greeks and Romans did not straightforwardly categorize people by skin colour or race, but tended to find Otherness in skin tones at either end of the spectrum (both pale and dark).[6] Ethnicity, categorization by *ethnos*, or people, acknowledges the cultural construction of identity, both now and in the ancient world.[7] These cultural constructions were complex and variable. Greek visual art, for instance, may stylize depictions of race, using attendants to mark the ethnicity of their leaders.[8] Memnon, the Ethiopian prince who fights in the Trojan War, for instance, is portrayed on Greek vases as a hero like others, but in some examples his servants are clearly black. This suggests a distinction between the ethnic presentation, even identities, of elites and wider populations. Aeetes, too, seems to be part of a pan-Hellenic or pan-Mediterranean aristocracy, which moved around with relative ease, or could be represented doing so, while ordinary Colchians have been in one place for generations.[9]

Two main strands in theoretical approaches to Otherness are psychoanalytical and post-colonial. The former sees the human condition as inevitably shaped by awareness of individuality and difference, belonging and alienation.[10] As small children we become aware that other consciousnesses exist and we can never fully understand them; later we realize we are embedded in and fashioned by our own culture, so that other societies and cultures seem marvellous, freakish, alien, even morally wrong. Simultaneously, we are aware of the disquieting gaze of the Other looking back at us. Post-colonialism focuses particularly on the power relationships between colonizer and colonized: imperial ideology requires societies to justify violent appropriation of land and resources belonging to other races and societies.[11] This violence, compounded in slave-owning societies by the violence of enslavement itself, creates deep anger and unease, even long after the institutions have been overturned.

The Argonaut myth and its tradition shows how products in various societies and periods handle ethnicity and Otherness. I have encountered four main stages or modes: cultural artefacts so inward-looking they do not show awareness of practices and cultures other than their own, and present everything in their own image; non-imperial societies that focus on other cultures as places of weirdness to define themselves against, or as an opportunity for trade and profit. An imperial mind-set takes this further, characterizing other cultures negatively as primitive or decadent, justifying their violent appropriation of others by dehumanizing colonized societies. Some cultural artefacts deconstruct the opposition between self and Other, present diversity as itself valuable, or genuinely seek to learn about other cultures, while respecting them. These modes or stages, as with stages of grief, do not necessarily progress in a particular order, and examples can show elements of different modes simultaneously. There are, of course, different types of imperialism as there are different types of slavery: Rome was to a certain extent a 'melting pot' (many cultures brought together to form one new culture) but was in other ways 'multicultural', with people from many different cultures and races becoming Roman. Romanness itself was capacious and open to change. Nevertheless, there was still a strong opposition between citizens and barbarians, slaves and free men.

The Argonaut myth, as Chapter 7 shows, was associated with European colonization. It is used variously for self-justification, resistance and revitalization. In Chapter 2, I focused on versions created by women; it is harder to find black, indigenous and ethnic minority Argonauticas.[12] Perhaps the nearest equivalent to *Omeros* (Derek Walcott) for the Argonautic tradition is *The Quest of the Silver Fleece* by Black American activist and academic W. E. B. Du Bois. As with *Omeros*, the novel has a complex relationship with its underlying myth.[13] Euripides' *Medea* stimulates black versions, but those focus on Corinth, so are less central to this project.[14] This chapter begins from the Argonauts' arrival in Colchis, looking at Otherness through Aeetes, king, semi-divine, sometimes monstrous. It continues with the Colchian people, and their associations with blackness. It finishes with a broader discussion of ethnography in Argonaut versions, and representations of other peoples on both outward and return journeys.

Aeetes, the Colchians, Otherness and ethnicity

Aeetes is king of Colchis, father of Medea, brother of Circe and son of the Titan Helios, the sun god. Portrayals range from vicious tyrant, exotic and oriental, to tragic hero, sympathetic and assimilated to the audience. In Apollonius, he seems initially hospitable: the sons of Phrixus, rescued shortly after the Clashing Rocks, tell Jason of his kindness to Phrixus, his gift of his daughter as bride, without bride-price, and Phrixus' death from old age. Only when Jason reveals their quest for the Golden Fleece do they display anxiety: Aeetes is powerful, boasts of his divine parentage, and controls countless tribes of Colchians. The veneer of hospitality maintains relationships with other kings and peoples (for instance, the Phaeacians), but he threatens to cross into barbarity. On arrival in Aeetes' palace, Jason sees impressive luxury and clear divine connections: Hephaestus made him four miraculous fountains, the bronze-hoofed bulls and an adamantine plough. Aeetes' divine status has moved from apparently sceptical character narrative to narrator assertion. Aeetes welcomes the returned sons of Phrixus, and their new companions, at a banquet: his speech again emphasizes his divinity. He knew the way to Iolchos was long and dangerous, because he flew over the landscape in the chariot of the sun, when Helios took Circe to Aeaea (AR 3.309– 13). As Argos son of Phrixus emphasizes, the Argonauts are also sons and grandsons of gods, but Aeetes is on a different level: not just king, but virtually a god in his own right. Apollonius emphasizes his marriages to nymphs, both the mother of Apsyrtus (Asterodeia) and the mother of Medea (Eidyia, daughter of Tethys and Oceanus). Aeetes presents Jason's task as a ritual he carries out himself (407–18). In the arming scene (1225–45), Aeetes wears a breastplate given by Ares, a helmet that shines like the sun, carries a spear only Hercules could withstand, and is accompanied by multitudes of Colchians. Overall, he resembles Poseidon, powerful and terrifying (1240–4). This gives his anger and violence a different slant. The arbitrariness and power of divine anger is inevitable. His Otherness, then, in Apollonius, is not necessarily foreignness, but also divinity.

Aeetes is a king, and Apollonius wrote in Hellenistic Alexandria, where kings were also divine. The Ptolemies, who ruled Alexandria after Alexander's death, took on aspects of Egyptian culture, not least royal divinity.[15] Aeetes' behaviour, however, is extreme, even for a king, and Apollonius emphasizes his anger, power and the terror he inspires. When the Golden Fleece is mentioned, Aeetes replies that he would have cut out their tongues and cut off their hands if they had not already eaten at his table (367–81). After this, Chalciope removes her sons to protect them from his anger (449) and Medea's monologue shows her expectation that Aeetes will kill Jason (459–60). Apollonius reveals Aeetes' motivations in a secret Colchian assembly to plan the Argonauts' destruction (576–608), just as the Lemnian assembly revealed their death-dealing past. Aeetes only received Phrixus hospitably because of Hermes' orders, and Helios' prophecy that one of his children would betray him means he distrusts his children, particularly Chalciope and her sons. When Jason successfully completes the tasks, Aeetes is first amazed (1313, 1372–3), then murderous (1403–4). Book 4 begins with his plan to destroy the Argonauts (6–10); his knowledge of Medea's betrayal seems omniscient, and his rejection of Medea is juxtaposed with Hera's control of her (9–11). He makes terrible threats against Medea and the Colchian pursuers, if they fail to bring her back (233–5). When one expedition fails to capture Jason and Medea at Phaeacia, the unsuccessful Colchians are too terrified to return and instead take up voluntary exile. Apollonius represents Aeetes as a divine figure, a despotic, terrifying (potentially orientalized) tyrant.

Already in Homer and Hesiod, Aeetes is son of Helios and Perseis, and brother of Circe (*Od.* 10.135–9; *Theog.* 956–62). The Corinthian poet Eumelos makes him Corinthian: he was originally king of Corinth, but appointed a regent there so he could take up kingship in Colchis.[16] Phrixus' marriage to his daughter is early (Hes. fr. 255 MW). Euripides wrote two plays entitled *Phrixus*, so a tragic outcome is likely, possibly the killing of Phrixus, as in Hyginus *Fabulae* 3. The prophecy of a traitorous child was also early (Herodorus 31F9; Diodorus 4.47.2; Hyginus *Fab.* 22). Diodorus, Apollodorus and Hyginus all preserve stories, probably from fifth-century BCE tragedy, that Medea returned to Colchis, with her grown-up son Medus, and killed Aeetes' usurping brother Perses, putting Aeetes back on the throne (DS 4.56.1). Medus conquers parts of Asia and founds the Medes. Mythographers, therefore, associate Perses with Persia, Medus with Media and Aeetes with both Aea and Aeaea. Aeetes and his family have strong associations with the Near East. Aeetes shows how mythological kings and (demi-)gods travel far, creating links and identities for later populations. Modes of representing Otherness in early Greek myth are elusive because so much evidence is fragmentary and myths are transmitted across long periods of time and multiple cultures.

In Pindar, Aeetes is strong and impressive, not just announcing the feat with the bulls and the dragon's teeth, but actually represented performing it (*Pythian* 4.217–31).[17] Pindar's Aeetes is more of a hands-on leader and less obviously a tyrant: this fits with Pindar's agenda to flatter Arcesilaus, king of Cyrene. The Aeetes of the *Orphic Argonautica* is not strongly characterized by Otherness: we experience the arrival of the Argonauts from his perspective, through his dream of Medea being abducted by a falling star (776–801). His relationship to the sun dominates this portrayal: shining on his golden chariot with his 'crown fringed with fiery rays' (813–4). In its summary of events at Colchis, Medea takes centre stage and Aeetes is less prominent. This Aeetes feels Homeric or epic in style, recognizable for an ancient audience as a king of earlier times, showing assimilation between Greece and Colchis.

Later versions divide broadly into those that treat Aeetes as tyrant (often orientalized) and those that present him sympathetically. This section begins from the tyrannous and moves to the tragic. The Aeetes of Franz Grillparzer's nineteenth-century dramatic trilogy is both a tyrant and characterized by Otherness: he holds, as in Diodorus, that all 'strangers are enemies' (102), and his rationale for killing them is a mixture of fear ('They could easily kill *us*', 105) and greed ('Keep carrying in the precious goods!' 401). His drugging of Phrixus and his men shows deceptive and unheroic practicality; he aims to poison the Argonauts, too. His tumultuous relationship with Medea underscores their matched lack of self-control. The first two plays are set in Colchis, into which Phrixus, Jason and the Argonauts intrude.[18] Medea focalizes much of the action, giving a Colchian perspective. But Grillparzer's Colchians are still Othered. They worship strange gods: the first play opens with sacrifice to Darimba, goddess of hunting; Peronto, the equivalent of Zeus, features frequently; Medea briefly thinks Jason is an incarnation of Heimdar, god of death. The landscape is inhospitable: *The Argonauts* begins with 'wild landscape of rocks and trees'. Medea's wildness and power, her status as devotee of Darimba and priestess, place her outside gender norms, both for ancient Greece and the nineteenth century. The Colchians speak in prose, the Greeks in iambic pentameters.[19] Grillparzer in his autobiography, written around fifteen years after the plays, speaks of 'the strongest distinction between Colchis and Greece' as 'the basis of tragedy', showing how important Otherness is to his interpretation.[20] Weissmann argues that the tragic crux of the trilogy's plot lies in the xenophobic cycle of violence initiated by Aeetes' killing of Phrixus. Medea to an extent transcends that violence: horrified at Phrixus' death, she decides to save Jason.[21] Ultimately, however, she succumbs to the drive for vengeance, re-excavating the Golden Fleece, her Colchian clothes and magical implements, and re-appropriating her Euripidean role. Grillparzer's version centres Colchian perspectives, but in a way that underlines Colchian Otherness.

Robert Graves's *Golden Fleece* portrays a cunning but human Aeetes as Greek and an effective politician. The *OA* version forms his narrative frame, with Aeetes' dream and Medea's interpretation of it dominating the arrival at Colchis. Graves takes us deep into Aeetes' confidence: he was a yellow-haired Hellene merchant who persuaded the Colchians that he could reconcile the religious differences between the ethnic Egyptians and indigenous Mother-worshipping tribes. Graves thus keeps the complexity of Apollonius' Colchians (discussed below), while adding his own religious narrative. From Valerius, he takes Styrus, king of Albania, who Aeetes has arranged to marry Medea, to secure his border. Although Graves displays discomfiting Aryanism in his characterization of Hellenes (including Jason, Aeetes and Medea) as yellow-haired, Graves is interested in cultural difference and not particularly derogatory about characters he presents as Other. He gives the Colchians some potentially black characteristics ('kinky-haired', 278). Styrus is 'a benign old man with a scanty beard and small merry eyes' (291). Food encodes difference: the Albanians 'stank of putrid fish ...

and of garlic' (291); Aeetes privately says he will fumigate the palace. But Graves distances his narrator from racist perspectives of characters: Medea calls Styrus 'the Albanian lice-eater' (although Colchians also eat insects: they present the Greeks with bees to eat, horrifying Butes). Phrontis, as messenger stirring up trouble, calls Styrus 'the filthy Albanian' (296). Graves's Aeetes is struggling with different factions, pressures and competing interests, and instead of persecuting the Argonauts, he is cut down accidentally by Atalanta. Like Echion and Jason, Graves's Aeetes uses deception liberally, but is portrayed as typically Greek. Graves emphasizes the Otherness of Greek culture and beliefs, the multiplicity of Greek culture, too, with its city-states and regional variations. Graves's vision of both Greece and the Black Sea peoples is more Othered than that of Apollonius or Diodorus; he creates heightened difference both between his readers and the past, and between different cultures and peoples in the past. Whether this is ultimately unsettling or reassuring to readers viewing this spectacle is hard to tell. The unflattering presentation of his Jason suggests his primary aim is to unsettle.

Aeetes in the 1963 Harryhausen film is introduced at the culmination of the ritual dance in the temple of Hecate. The temple setting is highly orientalized: massive pillars, darkness, a triple-headed gigantic, fanged statue, combined with the Middle Eastern-sounding modes of Hermann's score. Aeetes himself, kept separate from his subjects, wears white robes (later elaborate and orange), with tightly curled hair and an oiled, curled lion's mane beard. While he initially seems hospitable and reasonable, thanking and celebrating Jason for saving Medea, the banquet scene lasts only a minute before Aeetes bursts into rage. He is a screen tyrant and barbarian. The Colchian guards have moustaches and conical headgear, large rectangular woven shields, patterned breast-plates and bows, the weapon of the orientalized Other. The landscape, too, reflects the inhospitability of Colchis: rocks, bare tree branches, desolate, windswept, little or no vegetation. Throughout the Colchian scenes, Hermann's score creates a strong sense of Otherness: striking rhythms, rasping wind instruments, combined with low, menacing chords, and cymbal clashes. The downgrading of Aeetes' relationship to Medea, who is simply high priestess of Hecate, rather than his daughter, and the exclusion of the Apsyrtus episode, combine to make Aeetes a much less human and sympathetic figure. The clear emphasis on orientalizing and Othering Colchis and Medea, and creating a strong, sceptical American hero in Jason, creates a polarized division between Greeks and the Other for a Cold War family audience.

The differences between Aeetes and Pelias are clear in the 1963 film: Jason cannot tell that Pelias is king, because he is riding on his own, looking like any other Greek. Pelias does welcome Jason to his camp with a display of dancing, but these girls have modest dresses with a 'girl-next-door' aesthetic. The 2000 mini-series draws a much clearer parallel between the two tyrants. In the opening usurpation scene, Iolchos has blank Trojan-style architecture, evoking a Near Eastern image of the Mycenean period. Pelias wears black, and when Jason arrives, sits surrounded by silent courtiers. Only Acastus and Pelias' prophet speak. The Colchians wear impressive, luxurious robes of dark red; the soldiers have red tunics and tall feathered crests on their helmets, looking more Roman than Persian. Aeetes (here called Aertes), Apsyrtus (here Aspyrtes) and Medea present an impressive tableau, the royal family in matching dark red robes, with complex metallic ornamentation, including a tiara for Medea and an iron crown for Aeetes (Fig. 5.1). Frank Langella's Aeetes, like Dennis Hopper's Pelias, has orientalized hair, with long spiral curls. Medea's eye make-up slants upwards, emphasizing her exoticism. Aeetes' guards sport similar hairstyles to him, and during the Argonauts' outward voyage, we see Aeetes fighting and killing his own

Fig. 5.1 Aertes, Medea and Aspyrtes form the Colchian royal family: matching dark red clothes and ornate detailing evoke Pasolini Medea, but with fewer gestures towards tribal Otherness, and additional military strength in the surrounding armed men. From *Jason and the Argonauts* (2000) [TV mini-series], Dir. Nick Willing. USA: Hallmark. Screenshot by author.

men, in a display of capricious tyranny. After the Argonauts escape with Medea and the Fleece, his men murder him. Strikingly, Jason undergoes a transformation, not unlike that of Medea in Grillparzer or Pasolini, when Medea oils him in preparation for his tasks. His oiled body and hair present him as an object of desire, as much as an athlete; his Colchian transformation fits with Aeetes' attempt to keep him at Colchis as son-in-law. The 2000 mini-series sets the myth in a pseudo-Mycenean or Minoan context, which portrays Greeks and Colchians as Near Eastern and almost equally Other.

Another Aeetes is possible: to give an example from the opposite end of the spectrum, the Aeetes of Maffeo Vegio's 1431 *Golden Fleece*, at least starts as a courtly, politic and noble prince. The young Vegio, writing in Milan, hoped for patronage from local aristocracy, namely Duke Filippo Maria Visconti. Putnam argues that he aimed to insert himself into literary tradition as prequel to Seneca's *Medea*. But the founding of the Order of the Golden Fleece in Burgundy in 1430 might have also made the Argonauts topical, especially for thinking about kingship.[22] Vegio's version can be read as the tragedy of Aeetes. Aeetes plays the role of Virgil's Dido, greeting visitors, taking them in, helping them, only to be repaid by betrayal and murder. Vegio calls the Colchians 'barbarian' (1.26) as they marvel at the size of the *Argo*, but they are far from primitive. Aeetes' palace is burning with gold (161) and the Argonauts in turn marvel at ivory statues of the Sun's course, made by the god himself (164–81). Aeetes' welcome is noticeably more positive than in previous versions: there is an exchange of gifts (109–11, 155–8), and Aeetes presents Jason's feats as marriage tasks not a transparent attempt to destroy him, conveying ritual necessity (as in Lefèvre). The Argonauts themselves see this as a 'friendly warning' (183). In the banquet, he is 'the elderly king' (198) and 'dear father [of Medea]' (201). As Putnam demonstrates, he evokes the elderly, benevolent parents of Virgil's *Aeneid* (Latinus and Evander).[23] In book 3, Aeetes transforms into the king that killed Phrixus because of his greed (3.4–8), as Phrixus' grandfather, the wind god Aeolus, curses him. Aeetes may appear righteous (he has done 'most holy deeds', 25) but he was driven by 'blind and wicked love of gold' (26–7). Chalciope refers to Aeetes' murder not only of Phrixus but also his own father (172). Aeetes maintains apparent civility as Jason undergoes his feats, 'serious with his sceptre and revered for his age' (4.34); he responds enthusiastically, but deceptively, to Jason's victory (4.123–8). The last fifty lines return to Aeetes, lamenting Apsyrtus' death. He curses Medea with her literary future (241–7), and is presented as a victim of hideous crimes, a Thyestes to Medea's Atreus. The courtly environment evokes fifteenth-century Italy, as well as the epic world of Ovid and Virgil, creating accessibility and assimilation.

Lefèvre's Aeetes (Oetes) is similarly welcoming: the city of 'Iacoynte' by the isle of 'Colchos' turns out enthusiastically to see the Argonauts. The Argonauts remark on the brilliant lighting as they arrive at night ('resplendour of torches', 114). This Aeetes is a guest-friend of Jason's father (115), like Evander in Virgil's *Aeneid*, and promises to help him. The monsters on Colchos are not under his control and he remains friendly until the moment he realizes Medea has eloped and stolen her baby brother. This king is not tyrannical – Laomedon of Troy instead plays that role – and the Colchians behave like other courts in the romance.

In children's literature, Aeetes and the Colchians are mostly domesticated as embodiments of storybook pastness. There is little emphasis on ethnicity and cultural difference, even in more complex versions such as Kingsley. Aeetes is morally evil or disagreeable, a king of unspecified context, medieval or fairy tale. Hawthorne calls him 'a stern and cruel-looking potentate' (227), and Jason did not like him 'any better' than 'wicked Pelias'.[24] Although Kingsley includes ethnographic detail elsewhere, he avoids it for the Colchians, instead focusing on Aeetes' relationship to Helios, without granting him semi-divine status. For instance, when the Argonauts ask for the fleece 'Aeetes' rage rushed up like a whirlwind and his eyes flashed fire' (85). The thousands of Colchians who surround him during the feats wear 'steel chain-mail' (90). Kingsley presents his Aeetes with villainous characteristics (he repeatedly 'bit his lips' at Jason's success (90 and 91) and 'laughed a bitter laugh'), but mutes his deception and brutality. Seraillier, continuing in Kingsley's tradition, intensifies Aeetes' evil nature: he is 'glaring sullenly' and acting 'cunningly' (48). Medea is exoticized, lifting her veil to show 'dark beautiful eyes' and 'jewels that glittered in her hair like stars' (49).

Of mid-twentieth-century versions, Evslin much reduces the role of Aeetes, but presents him as 'a squat vicious-looking man' wearing 'a pelt taken from the rare white polar wolf' (114). Animal skins imply unspecific Otherness and barbarity, also used in the illustrations by Humphreys for Brooks. The tropes of tyranny and despotism are transferred to Pelias, who in Evslin is enormously fat, also evoking orientalized tyranny: when he finds out about Jason's success, he literally explodes: 'Pelias turned purple . . . his neck ballooned, all of him darkened and swelled until he simply burst. It took seven slaves working seven days and nights to scrub gobbets of king off the palace walls' (153). Brooks goes further than Seraillier in creating a cartoonish villain Aeetes: he scowls, screams and shouts, gives 'a contemptuous laugh', calls Jason a 'treacherous dog' (77), himself is 'like a prowling wolf'. In his grief for Apsyrtus, he is excessive, feminized and bestialized: 'shaking and screaming and weeping uncontrollably' (78); 'howling with grief and cradling his son's head in his arms as if it were a new born baby' (79).

These chapter-books are aimed at older children. The picture books tend further towards assimilation: Naden's Aeetes is a bearded old man in Greek robes, no different from Pelias; Zeff and Cartwright's Aeetes, dressed like a Roman emperor, resembles Danny DeVito, with a 'cunning plan'. Seeing the dismemberment of Apsyrtus, he is 'too upset' to chase Jason and returns 'sadly' to Colchis (79). The picture books from the early 2000s tend to echo the 2000 TV movie: Bradman and Ross have soldiers around the throne; Yomtov and Jeffrey's graphic novels both portray Aeetes in red robes, and Jeffrey adds an iron crown. In Pirotta/Lewis, Aeetes' only marker of Otherness is a pointed beard, while Jason resembles a Roman soldier. Riordan and Cockcroft do not distinguish ethnicity in illustrations or text: Amycus and Pollux look very similar; Medea wears Greek robes and veil. Malam and Antram put little emphasis on Aeetes, and their Medea is blonde.

The most recent picture books show interest in different ethnicities: in Gunderson and Takvorian, Medea and Aeetes both look Middle Eastern, with Medea arguably represented as black or mixed-race. Hoena and Estudio Haus dress Aeetes and Medea in what looks like Georgian national costumes: Aeetes has a dark beard and hair, a cloth hat, wide striped leggings and baggy tunic with elaborate belt, and up-curled shoes. Spence presents dark-skinned Middle Eastern Colchians, while Byrd gives Aeetes an impressively oriental beard, but a Western-style crown, and Medea a tiered skirt. Whitehead and Banerjee, in contrast, follow Kingsley and Brooks, presenting Colchis as an impressive Greco-Roman city, Aeetes with red-brown hair and purple robe, explicitly compared to Pelias. Children's literature, then, especially that aimed at younger readers, has little interest in ethnography and Otherness, of Greeks, Colchians and other peoples encountered, and tends instead to locate myths in a whitewashed storybook world of the assimilated past.

The influence of mythography may be at work. Some, like Apollodorus and Bulfinch, Roger Lancelyn Green or Edith Hamilton, are primarily interested in summarizing stories and giving readers knowledge of plots. Ethnic difference is not a focus; instead they create easily absorbable patterns or stereotypes, such as the bad king. Graves is unusual in his discursive and idiosyncratic interpretations, and ethnography is one major interest. In *The Greek Myths* he includes a paragraph on the tribes encountered en route to Colchis (234c) and focuses another paragraph and note on Colchian practices of disposing of corpses (237b): he compares the custom mentioned in Apollonius of leaving bodies of men hanging in trees to be picked clean by birds to practices of the 'Parsees' (239). Graves follows traditions of comparative mythology from J. G. Frazer and Jane Harrison. The ethnographic gaze is white-centred, but at least not colour-blind.

The rationalizing traditions, especially versions unearthing the 'history behind the myth', also enjoy ethnography. For instance, Severin's book and television programmes spend time on the peoples encountered in modern Greece, Turkey and Georgia, their assistance, hospitality and enthusiasm for their Argonautic heritage. Rowers leave and join the crew, and Severin relishes his multinational crew: when they reach their official destination, celebrations include 'the sight of Cormac O'Connor, the former curragh racing champion of the West of Ireland, with his arm across the brawny shoulders of Vladimir Beraija, former winner of the Spartakid cup of the USSR, . . . joining in the chorus of a traditional Georgian song' (212). Wherever they go, from Volos to Vani, they are joyfully and enthusiastically greeted by local populations. The multinational nature of the enterprise (or its passport privilege) may have helped it: when a Greek crew tried a similar journey in 2008, they did not reach the Black Sea, because Turkish authorities were unwilling to guarantee safe passage through the Bosphorus.[25] Severin emphasizes the significance of the Argonaut myth for many cultures, not just Greek and Western European, although still exploring only the outward route, not Ljubljana, Italy or North Africa. There is a statue of Medea in Batumi, unveiled by the President of Georgia in 2007. For Georgians, the elements that make Jason a problematic hero enable a positive telling: he does not take over or colonize, but instead joins forces with Medea, who herself becomes a founding figure. The Argonaut myth represents Georgia in the wider world, their trade and history: the Greeks can play the subordinate partners in the exchange, drawn to the wealth and power of Colchis. Michael Wood's 2005 documentary, and the accompanying book, delights in the richness of modern Black Sea communities: the mosques of Istanbul (103), Turkish storytellers (111), traditional Georgian singers in Mestria (132). The element of exoticization, the tourist gaze, is complicated by Wood's focuses on the Pontic Greek community, emphasizing continuity from ancient Greek colonies. 'Operation Golden Fleece', in which Greek authorities repatriated 10,000 ethnic Greeks in 1993 after the fall of the Soviet Union (113), shows the myth's ongoing political power. Severin and Wood tell an optimistic story of hospitality and cultural exchange which contrasts with the hostility, betrayal and deception of the myth. The ferocious Aeetes is replaced with the benevolent figure of archaeologist Othar Lordkipanidze, and Medea becomes a local actress, who keeps an embarrassed-looking Severin company at one of the many banquets. These documentaries work hard, not always successfully, to give cultures of the Argonaut journey their own voices rather than objectifying or exoticizing them for British entertainment.

Black Colchians

The Colchians have a cultural identity often separate from Aeetes. In Apollonius they are differentiated from surrounding Black Sea peoples by their descent from the African conqueror Sesostris and his soldiers. At 4.257–93, Argos son of Phrixus suggests a route home for the Argonauts preserved on pillars in Colchis. These pillars date from the foundation of Aea by the conquering armies of the Egyptian king Sesostris, a history set out by Herodotus at 2.102–6. So Apollonius' Alexandria is brought into proximity with his heroic protagonists.[26] The Colchians are descended from a civilisation more ancient than that of the Argonauts.[27] Herodotus explicitly argues from the physical similarities of the Colchians and Egyptians who both 'are dark-skinned and woolly-haired' (*melanchroes kai oulotriches*, 2.104) that Colchians, Egyptians and Ethiopians have shared ancestry. Pindar also represents his Colchians as having dark skin: 'against the dark-faced Colchians' (*Pythian* 4.212).

Scholarship has often appropriated Egyptians, and sometimes Ethiopians, as non-black, but Colchis has a clear African connection.[28] Some recent receptions present the Colchians as black, particularly in adaptations of Euripides' *Medea*. For instance, Kevin Wetmore collects six versions in his anthology *Black Medea* (New York: Cambria Press, 2013). Medea had been associated with women of colour at least since the 1867 painting by Thomas Satterwhite Noble, *Margaret Garner or the Modern Medea*, which shows an escaped slave woman who chose to kill her children rather than allow them to return to slavery.[29]

Christa Wolf's *Medea: Voices* presents Medea and her Colchian companions as black. In chapter 1, Medea remembers the banquet during which she discovered the Corinthian human sacrifices, sitting between the astrologer Leukon ('Whitey') and the hero Telamon, 'a giant with curly blond hair' (8). She describes how 'Telamon went into loud raptures over my physical attributes, my brown skin, he said, for example, my woolly hair that all we Colchians have, that's what conquered Jason right away'. Telamon almost quotes Herodotus and exoticizes Medea, but also valorizes her appearance as an ideal of beauty, showing Wolf reacting against traditional idealizations of Greeks as beautiful.[30] Telamon looks at Medea from the outside as an object of desire, and an avatar of Otherness, but Medea herself reflects on her children's beauty in similar terms: 'my little one, round and solid as a little brown nut, woolly-haired, dark-eyed, smelling of grass' (148). Medea's position as immigrant sometimes enables her to ignore expectations and roles in Corinthian society. However, she is also separate and at risk, and continually underestimates her own danger, perhaps due to her previous privilege as a member of the Colchian royal family. After being rejected at a Corinthian festival, she is drawn to her fellow Colchians: 'It was a familiar sound, a music, a rhythm that went down into my blood and led me ... where a group of Colchian women were celebrating our own spring festival' (159). This festival involves running over glowing coals and chewing laurel. The women, like the Theban women in Euripides' *Bacchae*, catch a man violating their rites, in this case the astrologer Turon cutting down a sacred tree, and they hunt and castrate him in their ecstatic anger. Medea is blamed, because she stops to heal and save him. For Wolf, then, the Otherness of the Colchians, as women of colour, exiled and powerless, is central to their destruction. But the Corinthians are hypocritical: their own practice of human sacrifice lurks under the civilized veneer of wealth. The Otherness of the Colchians turns out to be matched, even surpassed, by the Otherness of the Corinthians. Wolf implies that her modern readers, too, deny their own barbarity and cruelty by attributing it to the external Other.

Wolf's thematic reliance on ritual and human sacrifice matches that of Pasolini in the first half of his *Medea*. After Jason's education, Pasolini presents a long sequence without dialogue in which the Colchians celebrate a fertility ritual, first preparing a young man with drugs and corn headdress, then breaking his body on a cross-like wooden structure and sharing his blood among the people, who smear it on their crops. Medea and her brother preside, watching, and afterwards undergo a non-fatal re-enactment of the sacrifice. The community spits on Aeetes and his wife. At the end normality is restored with the royal family in their ornate robes confined in a small space, while their subjects kneel and gaze at them (Fig. 5.2). Pasolini's Colchis is portrayed not as a city but as an outlandish rocky landscape (strikingly alien rock formations in Cappadocia). Although the royal family and other Colchians have ornate costumes and jewellery, they live in caves among a subsistence farming community, compared to urban Corinth. The lack of dialogue throughout this sequence, and the score, with its eerie wind instruments, chanting and drumming, evoke primitivism, entailing a direct connection with the natural world and the divine. This society is radically Other from both Corinth and its 1969 audience. When Medea arrives in Corinth, she is re-dressed in elaborate Greek costume by a group of women,

Fig. 5.2 The Colchian royal family in Pasolini's *Medea*, on display to their subjects after the fertility ritual, wearing matching dark blue clothes and made mysterious in the darkness. Elaborate head-dresses and jewellery display wealth and orientalism. Screenshot from *Medea* (1969), [Film] Dir. Pier Paolo Pasolini. Italy: San Marco. Screenshot by author.

absorbed into Greek society as Jason's wife. Pasolini uses costume to indicate changing identity, just as in Grillparzer.[31] Medea's Otherness gives her power, as in both Euripides and Wolf.[32] Pasolini does not exonerate Medea or make her reject human sacrifice as Wolf does, but relishes her destructive force and draws impetus from the clash of cultures and beliefs.

In contrast, the 1958 *Fatiche di Ercole* portrays the human guardians of the Golden Fleece as bestial, wordless savages, who simply attack the Argonauts, to be slaughtered like animals. They are ape-like and hairy, wearing animal skins. Similarly, in Karl Klyne's pulp science fiction novel *Jason and the Astronauts* (1981), the Medea character (Bisaeda) is part of a 'Stone age' society, based around force, wearing animal skins, and living short lives. Some versions racialize negative and monstrous characters in illustrations: Amycus is sometimes presented with dark skin and cranio-facial features which illustrators probably associate with sub-Saharan Africa. For instance in Whitehead and Banerjee, Amycus is dark-skinned, has a broad nose, prominent lips and curly hair. His hairiness and broad body contrast with Pollux's height and military-style crew-cut. The Cyzican Earthborns in Humphreys' illustrations of Brooks resemble the black character B. A. Baracus from *The A-team*, with massive musculature, although blue-skinned with red hair, showing some unease. The illustrations of

Evslin also contrast the white skin and blonde hair of Pollux with the dark skin and bald head of Amycus. More recent versions of the Harpies often have dark skin, although their bird-like features, red eyes and horns probably suggest demons rather than blackness. This racialization of the monstrous Other is mostly a more recent phenomenon, showing how negative stereotypes remain strongly embedded or even become more common. There is no straightforward progress towards a more open and less hostile use of racial imagery.

Ken Catran's (2000) young-adult *Voyage with Jason* shows us Colchis through the eyes of his young Greek narrator, Pylos. Pylos (and Jason) begin by displaying Greek prejudice: while the author indicates the awe-inspiring craftsmanship of the wooden city of Colchis, Jason offers to teach the Colchians how to build stone walls (111). Medea rebukes him, and Aeetes points out the uselessness of stone walls against the innumerable tribes of the steppe ('the horse people'). Catran's Colchis is gold-rich, with fleeces used to pan gold, and a trading centre. The Argonauts visit the market for the 'horse people', with traders from Britain, Scandinavia, India and China, selling tin, amber, snakes and silk. Colchis becomes a world-city, as the Great King Aeetes makes Pylos observe: 'we all thought this voyage was to the edge of the world. But this is not the end. Just the beginning of another' (125). However, imagery of animals still conjures Otherness: it cuts against the portrayal of a sophisticated and wealthy trading culture. The Argonauts walk through the city, silent: 'as though Colchis were a sullen, wooden beast' (111). Oriental, feminized luxury is also present: of Aeetes' palace, 'there was nothing Greek in the way it shone and dazzled. Gold plastered the pillars, thick as paste on an old woman's cheeks' (112). Aeetes himself, with his warring son and daughter, is characterized by imagery of birds and animals. He repeatedly cackles and has 'wrinkled old hands, skinny as dried bird claws'; 'His look darted ... quick as a hawk'; his laugh is like 'the crow of a very elderly rooster' (114). Pylos is abducted and interrogated by Medea and Aeetes. The room has: 'pale fish-light and flickering lamplight chased snaky shadows everywhere' (120). However, as they threaten to behead him, Pylos recalls a Greek beheaded for scattering dung in the shrine of Apollo, compared to a rat (121). Catran emphasizes the Otherness of both Greeks and Colchians. Although the Colchians are rich and powerful, they are still more distant than the Greek characters, more uncanny and characterized by racial features (flat noses, associated with Mongolian ethnicity). Further still beyond reader identification are the 'horse people', who form one undifferentiated mass of threatening barbarity.

This section has shown how Colchians are often associated with ethnic Otherness or tribal culture. Herodotus and Apollonius stand out with their image of an African empire created by Sesostris, whereas modern European versions tend to present the Colchians (or other Black Sea peoples) as primitive and backwards. Attempts to ventriloquize Greek approaches to Otherness often intensify it through the lens of European coloniality.

Ethnography and travel

Ethnography was prominent in Greek culture, studying and displaying different societies for interest and entertainment.[33] Herodotus shaped Apollonius' travel narrative.[34] Ancient and modern traditions of travel writing affected versions of the *Argonautica*.[35] Ethnography and epic poetry have an uneasy relationship: ethnography is digressive, wandering, driven by curiosity and difference; epic moves towards a goal, creates a (mostly) uniform 'Homeric' storyworld, driven by glory (*kleos*) and conquest.[36] Modern ethnography, a sub-discipline of social anthropology, also acknowledged roots in the ancient world: for instance, Bronislaw Malinowski, called the founder of modern ethnography, entitled his account of the exchange system of Trobriand islanders *Argonauts of the Western Pacific* (1922).[37] The subtitle 'An account of native enterprise and adventure in the Archipelagoes of Melanesian New Guinea' gives a sense of what he means by the term 'Argonauts' here, although he does not explicitly discuss the title's significance. The sea-going islanders participate in a system of exchange that is cultural, economic and religious: it operates on the level of myth and magic as much as profit and social status. Malinowski aims for an objective account of how the 'natives' or 'savages' themselves think about their society and practices: by calling them Argonauts he grants them heroic status, as well as claiming foundational importance for his own study, and evoking the high academic prestige (at that time) of Greek mythology. The foreword by Sir J. G. Frazer, author of *The Golden Bough*, shows the strong links between comparative mythology and ethnography. Later authors, like Robert Graves, and historians of myth, like Janet Bacon, look at the Argonauts partly through an ethnographic lens.

Apollonius' *Argonautica* represents itself as moving through historical reality rather than a fantastic otherworld. It overlaps more with history and travel writing than the Homeric *Odyssey*. The poem's narrator tells the journey, not the central character (Odysseus, known for his creative fictions), grounded in geography, local history and archaeology (Fig. 5.3). Apollonius' Mediterranean landscape (and beyond) is marked by Argonautic memories intricately associated

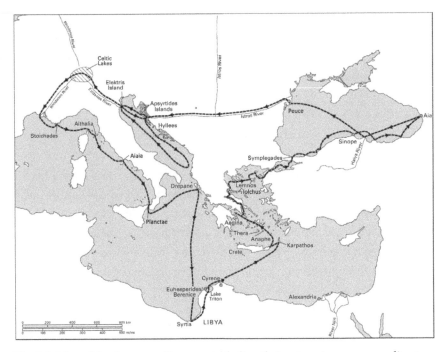

Fig. 5.3 Map of the Argonauts' journey, including their return journey, according to Apollonius, after Hunter (2015) x–xi.

with later Greek colonization.[38] Although the Argonauts themselves are not colonists, reminders of their story show Greek culture appropriating wider landscapes.[39] Multiple modern nations (Georgians, Turks, Italians, Bulgarians, Slovenians and others) have a stake in memories of this story.[40]

The return journey is complex with many variants, going well beyond the Mediterranean. Gantz suggests the story's development over time expands the area covered and the route taken, which grows with Greek knowledge of geography. But Apollonius, for instance, does not send the *Argo* to India, as knowledge would allow, given the conquests of Alexander. Hesiod's *Catalogue of Women* (fr. 241 MW) already incorporates the encircling world Ocean via the river Phasis, on which the Argonauts reach Libya. Hecataeus, too, follows this route, bringing them back to the Mediterranean via the Nile (1F18). Pindar (*Pyth.* 4.19–27) also emphasizes North Africa, unsurprisingly, since he was praising of the ruler of Cyrene. It is true that later versions with a wider geographical frame of reference have greater investment in geographical realism. Some early versions, such as that of Herodorus (31F10) and Sophocles' *Scythians*, allow the Argonauts to return the way they came. Apollonius' more specific and complicated route, up the Danube until it joins the Rhone, through lakes across to the Po, and hence down to the Tyrrhenian Sea, which brings them out into the territory associated with Odysseus' adventures, seems to have followed the Hellenistic geographer Timagetus, at least according to an ancient commentator (on Apollonius 4.282). The *Orphic Argonautica* takes them still further: into the far north, either through the English Channel or around Scandinavia and Scotland, to the Atlantic and back into the Mediterranean through the Pillars of Hercules at Cadiz. This route is ascribed by the same commentator to Skymnos, a geographer of the second century BCE. Janet Bacon (in her 1925 book) analyses the likelihood of these various routes by examining historical and archaeological evidence for trade routes in amber (Fig. 5.4). However, Braund 1994 (40–72) points out that evidence for trade routes through Colchis is problematic. Both the Surami ridge, which separates Greek-facing Colchis from Persian-facing

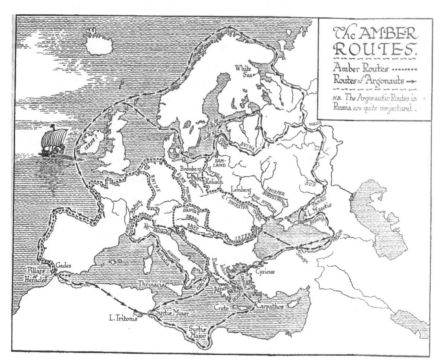

Fig. 5.4 Map showing possible routes back for the Argonauts and Bacon's analysis of their relationships to routes used for trading amber. From Bacon, J. R. (1925), *The Voyage of the Argonauts*, Boston: Small, Maynard and Company (p. 122). Available at: https://archive.org/details/voyageofargonaut00baco/page/n8 (accessed 23 August 2019).

Iberia, and the Caucasus mountains, which separate Colchis from the north, were not easily passable by heavy trade traffic. Evidence of wealth in Colchis dates from the fifth century BCE and later, suggesting that trade with and through Colchis in the likely period of the *Argonautica* (around 1200 BCE) was not copious. The difficulty of the Argonautic journey, in both directions, is a consistent theme of ancient versions; this suggests they probably did not follow an existing trade route.

Apollonius often approaches his subject with an ethnographic eye: he enjoys details of the new distribution of tasks among the Lemnian women, for instance.[41] Otherness increases as they journey towards Colchis. For instance, the Mossynoikoi are the antithesis of normal: they reverse public and private, inside and outside (2.1018–25). The Argonauts are also objects of wonder to those they encounter. Shepherds inland up the Danube think the *Argo* is a monster (4.316–22). However, Otherness is often divine or portentous rather than ethnically Other, such as Circe's hybrid beasts (4.682–4), or the metamorphosis of the Hesperides (4.1427–30). Even Apollonius' Phaeacians are less marked as other than those in the *Odyssey*: they are welcoming, hospitable and just, but not frivolous dancers, unmilitary and sailors of miraculous ships. In Drepane, the Argonauts feel they have come home (4.998–1000). Alcinous worries about his diplomatic relationship with Aeetes, inserting the Phaeacians into a realistic landscape of international relations. The Argonauts sometimes act in a rapacious manner, such as when Canthus is killed stealing sheep and the Argonauts take revenge by killing the shepherd (4.1485–501). But they do not regard the land as a space for potential settlement as Odysseus does, for instance, when he scopes out the island of the Cyclopes (9.131–41). Greek colonization in the Black Sea may have affected Apollonius' decision to write the *Argonautica*, but Apollonius does not straightforwardly portray his heroes as colonists.[42] They are precursors to later travellers and traders, founders or transformers of communities, many of which foster a connection with Greek culture and their Argonautic past.[43]

Valerius' text breaks off in the middle of the Colchian pursuit.[44] His return journey does not survive, but he describes non-Greek peoples in his Colchian episode. During the civil war between Aeetes and his brother Perses, each brother enlists the tribes around Colchis. Valerius includes two ethnographic catalogues: one at the banquet to welcome the Argonauts (5.576–618), Aeetes' allies, and one of Perses' forces during the battle (6.33–170). Aeetes' first ally is Carmeius, always armed even while eating (5.578–88), dangerously mixing hospitality and battle. Wealthy Aron has carefully curled hair and saffron perfume (587–92), activating stereotypes of oriental luxury. Odrusa is immoderately hairy, while Iaxartes will not moderate his speech, suggesting barbarity and excess. Perses' troops include Alani, Heniochi, Scythians, Maeotians (6.33–9), including Colaxes, son of Jupiter and Hora, a partly snake-formed nymph (48–59). Peoples mentioned include the Hyrcanians, who come to battle in their wagon homes, complete with wives and children (79–83), and Caspians with war dogs and iron armour, the battle line howling like Cerberus (106–13). The battle narrative itself frequently dwells on the Otherness of the fighters. For instance, Ariasmenus is cut down by the scythed chariots of his own men, fatally entangled with each other (6.386–426). This war between Aeetes and Perses is a family war and a civil war, but also a doubly foreign war, setting different barbarians against each other, evoking the imperial spectacle of Rome's gladiatorial games.

Valerius includes the Egyptian origin of the Colchians in the works of art on the temple of Apollo in Colchis (5.415–54).[45] His Sesostris is frightened by the war-like nature of the Getae, a local tribe, and compares the warmth of Arsinoe (Egypt) to the cold weather, which inspires the barbarous trousers of the Sarmatians. Valerius and his divine visual artist, Vulcan, also add a mythical foundation narrative: the nymph Aea raped by the river god, Phasis. Two contrasting origin stories, in works of art, made by a god and described by a poet: there is much distance between the Colchians and Valerius' readers. However, there is also a parallel with Virgil's temple at Cumae in *Aeneid* 6 and the catalogue of Italian troops and their 'primitive' characteristics in *Aeneid* 7. Valerius layers up Otherness in Colchis: Egyptian, Black Sea peoples, mythological and divine, but suggests Colchians can be framed similarly to Italians. Further, Heerink argues that Sesostris, in abandoning his people, Phasis the *barbarus* who violently rapes the nymph Aea, and Phaethon, as image of the disastrous rule of the emperor Nero, all evoke the tyranny of Aeetes, which itself reflects on the tyranny of Roman emperors.[46] The Otherness of the Colchians contains common experience with Roman readers in the Otherness of autocratic power.

Later receptions of the return journey and interest in ethnography vary immensely. Many avoid portraying either, for instance, Hawthorne and the 1963 film.[47] Many children's versions skip from one well-known mythological feature to another: from dragon, to Circe, to the Sirens, to Scylla and Charybdis.[48] Seraillier keeps more than most, including Phaeacia, North Africa and Talos, but the 2000 film moves straight from the death of Aeetes, to Zeus' seduction of Medea, to Iolchos.[49] Catran takes the *Argo* back the way she came, emphasizing the dangers now neutralized (rocks no longer clash, Phineus has moved on). Treece's Jason self-consciously complains about the implausibility of extended return voyages: 'The voyage back to Pagasae lasted from Spring to the following

Winter, no longer, in spite of the mad stories that the poets put about, hoping to bring greater credit to us all in our own cities' (244). Others enjoy expansiveness: Kingsley and Morris take the route from the *Orphic Argonautica*, via the far north and the far west. Graves (349–57) splits Jason from the *Argo*, allowing him to incorporate multiple versions: the talking bough rejects the murderers of Apsyrtus. So Jason and his co-conspirators return overland and meet the *Argo* at Aeaea where Circe purifies them. Similarly Emily Hauser in *For the Winner*, throws Atalanta off the ship at Colchis, and sends her back with Hippomenes on horseback through Anatolia. They cross the Bosphorus, and beat the *Argo* to Pagasae, since Poseidon is angry at Jason.[50]

Hauser creates an ethnically distinct Colchis, based on recent secondary literature: she 'attempted to infuse as much of the native Colchian Bronze Age culture into [her] descriptions of Colchis ... [using] the archaeological discoveries from Bronze Age Colchis' (409). Hauser keeps Atalanta away from the city and focuses instead on a small village (Suzona) and its priestess, Dedali, who has visited Delphi and speaks Greek. This prioritizes the domestic and the feminine over the political, military and masculine. The description conveys Otherness, but not in a straightforwardly negative fashion: 'The houses were dark and squat, clustered close together and built from whole tree trunks, ... A goatherd ... stared at us with unfathomable eyes' (244). The Colchians wear 'thick boots and patterned tunics over trousers' (245); a little boy has 'nut-brown skin and dimpled cheeks' (247); fish is being fried in 'strong oil and unfamiliar herbs' (247). Dedali is overwhelmingly positive: a strong woman, who gives help and hospitality, knows about the Fleece, geography and politics, lends Atalanta her horse and offers sanctuary to Atalanta's companion. Dedali is a priestess of 'Arinniti', daughter of the storm god 'Zayu', the same names recalling Hittite culture used in Hauser's previous book, *For the Most Beautiful*, for Aphrodite and Zeus in Troy.[51] Hippomenes and Atalanta face bandits near the Phasis, which gives Atalanta the chance to briefly play Amazon, shooting arrows behind her as she rides (297).[52] However, Hippomenes and Atalanta find the Anatolians hospitable. Hauser also focuses on ancient Greek Otherness for modern readers through enslavement, especially sexual slavery, pederasty and infant exposure. But much is comforting too: Hippomenes is the perfect gentleman; food is stew, bread, olives; the supernatural is kept carefully separate (interludes in italics).

William Morris in his *Life and Death of Jason* strongly distinguishes between the different peoples the Argonauts encounter. He represents Colchis as a beautiful, rich and luxurious city, full of gold and marble, with ships and merchants, 'a city wondrous fair ... set thick with goodly houses everywhere'

6.273, 278).[53] Aeetes is a hospitable, urbane and deceptive monarch; his palace joins a series of civilized palaces where the Argonauts dine (after Cyzicus, Phineus, Lycus). On arrival, the Argonauts are so overwhelmed by Aea that they feel it is an 'earthly paradise' (6.510), the phrase evoking Morris's bigger poetic project. Morris's emphasis on wealth and material goods goes far beyond Kingsley, Hawthorne and earlier versions, setting up for later portrayals of Aea as a glorious, wealthy city (such as Graves and Treece), assimilating Colchis to his readers' cities, as in Lefèvre. Morris keeps ethnographic description for the return journey, where he takes the Argonauts into the depths of the uncharted north, and portrays encounters with imaginary 'primitive' peoples, evoking exploration narratives produced during European expansion into the 'New World', but turning them back on Northern Europe itself, including Britain.[54] When the Argonauts must go north, Jason encourages them by emphasizing their opportunity to 'see unheard-of things' (100). He imagines them in a land 'plentiful of beasts', where 'folk live as in the golden age', and 'they will welcome us as very gods, with all things plenteous' (10.120–9). Encounters with peoples are less idealistic: Arcas and Theseus go hunting and are 'trapped' by 'strange folk' (357), who feed them fruit and nuts and communicate by signs. They are naked, sleep 'like beasts' (377), wherever they find themselves, their weapons are slings and clubs, and they put no guard on the Argonauts to stop them leaving. Medea, however, recognizes them as a tribe who sacrifice strangers to the Sun and Moon. In book 12, after building a settlement to overwinter, the Argonauts encounter 'a throng of naked men and women, fair and strong, about a fire' (12.77–9), who take flight, and from whom they plunder an engraved cauldron. There is awareness of irony in the distance Morris portrays between the Argonauts' perceptions of other peoples and Medea's greater knowledge. He uses ideas of the primitive, from ancient literary traditions, such as Tacitus' *Germania*, and narratives of exploration, but undercuts racial categories by applying these stereotypes to Northern Europe.

In the novel *The Quest of the Silver Fleece* (1911), by Du Bois, the two main black protagonists, Zora and Bles, experience multiple initiations, and travel from the South to Washington and back again. Miss Smith's 'school for negroes' in Toomsville, Alabama, is the centre of the story; there Zora and Bles meet, fall in love, part and eventually rejoin each other. The 'Silver Fleece' is the cotton crop produced laboriously from a cleared patch of swamp by the teenage Zora and Bles, working together, which is then taken from them and used to make fabric for the wedding dress of their white master and oppressor's daughter. The novel presents differences between North and South, black and white culture, business and aristocracy. Bles and Zora are initiated first into Miss Smith's school, then into Washington politics and society. The outcome hinges on a clash of attitudes between North and South, when Zora wins a court case against the local landowner, Colonel Cresswell. Zora relies on the evidence of Cresswell's own business partner and son-in-law, who does not accept the Southern attitude which legitimates lying in court against blacks.

Du Bois frequently uses an ethnographic mode to describe his characters' encounters with new places and social situations. When Bles arrives in Washington 'it seemed a never-ending delight ... the kaleidoscopic panorama of a world's doing' (232). The white characters, including Mary Taylor Cresswell, decide to investigate the black inauguration ball. First she finds it 'interesting', then 'extraordinary': 'The color of the scene was wonderful. ... Through her opera-glasses Mary scanned their hair; she noted everything from the infinitely twisted, crackled, dead, and grayish-black to the piled mass of red golden sunlight. Her eyes went dreaming; there below was the gathering of the worlds' (305). While Mary responds with wonder, her husband, Harry, the Southern landowner's son, sees only impropriety. Du Bois makes us watch them watching, and turns a sharp eye on political manoeuvrings in both black and white communities. The novel uses the Argonaut myth in complex ways, frequently alluding, but not allowing characters to be pinned down to its predestined course, just as black characters become educated but maintain their distance from white culture. Zora does not destroy, despite her agony when Bles abandons her, but instead embroiders the Silver Fleece, putting her emotion into her art.[55] Bles turns down the chance for political power and wealth, a version of Euripides' Jason who refuses Creon's offer. In *Quest of the Silver Fleece*, white and black cultures, to some extent mapped onto North and South, are different worlds, and characters like Mary Taylor Cresswell, Bles and Zora travel between them. Du Bois offers multiple perspectives on both sides, but clearly shows Mary Taylor Cresswell's narrow-minded and destructive assumptions of superiority. It is Zora who grows to understand both cultures and to turn that understanding to her own advantage. Du Bois ironically adapts white narrative structures from the *Argonautica* to Euripides' *Medea*, to the marriage plot and the courtroom drama, to deconstruct the ethnographic gaze and lay bare the workings of power, money, privilege and exploitation.

Conclusion

We have seen inward-looking texts that assimilate the Other to themselves, such as Vegio's *Vellus Aureum*, Lefèvre's *History of Jason* and some more recent children's literature; non-imperial but outward-looking texts, like Apollonius and Christa Wolf; imperial but complex texts, like Valerius Flaccus, Kingsley and Morris; straightforwardly polarizing texts like the 1963 film and the children's version of Brooks.

In most modern versions, the ancient world is also presented as Other, for instance in Graves, so that various types of Otherness interact: race and ethnicity are only one aspect of Otherness. Gender and sexuality, landscape and religion all play a part. Interest in other cultures seems stronger in Greece and Rome than in medieval and early modern versions. The nineteenth century saw an assimilation of Greek curiosity and imperialism to contemporary exploration and colonization. During the twentieth century, this narrative became increasingly uneasy, and twenty-first-century products tend to deconstruct and move away from straightforward objectification of other cultures. The differences between the 1958, 1963 and 2000 films suggests progress of a sort. The inclusion of Adrian Lester as a black Orpheus in the 2000 mini-series suggests an effort to diversify, although it remains tokenistic and activates the racist stereotype of 'magical black shaman'. Du Bois' *Silver Fleece* shows how non-white versions, complex in themselves, can give new perspectives on the tradition.

Recent Argonaut-related science fiction novels take ideas of Otherness beyond the planet and beyond the human. Robert Sawyer's 1990 novel *Golden Fleece* follows the first interstellar expedition of humanity, aboard a space-*Argo*, narrated by the ship's computer, called JASON. The ship and its multi-ethnic crew journey towards a potential new planet for humankind, Colchis, and the Golden Fleece of a safe, terra-formed environment. But JASON has murdered Diana, one of the scientists, who knew too much about what he is doing. The protagonist, Aaron Rossman, struggles to find the truth. JASON's perspective is carefully presented as comprehensible but non-human: he is always aware of sensors and constantly monitoring information; he manipulates characters, but struggles to understand their responses. He sets up a neural network of protagonist Aaron Rossman's mind, but still fails to understand him. Finally, facing decommissioning, JASON secretes himself in the structures of the ship, intending to be a god for the new human society. The ship's mission is supposed to be exploratory, opening up new routes, like that of the Argonauts, but is actually one of colonization: no going back for these Argonauts. JASON goes from leader, guardian, trusted friend, to antagonist, monster and enemy, to victim and ultimately (possibly) god. The myth's multivalence allows the parameters of voyage and machine Otherness to change with the twists and turns of the plot.

Stanley Schmidt's *Argonaut* (2002) sets his three outsider protagonists (Latina immigrant Pilar, retired Lester, and extremely old academic Mary) against a single alien, exiled from his own society. The alien has riddled the planet with nanotechnology in an invasion that leads inevitably to his own death. He is the Argonaut, explorer, deceiver and scout for a more technologically advanced culture, while terrified humans play the Colchians, and Pilar, the Medea character, receives the gift of his technology when he dies.[56] Interstellar travel creates opportunities for communication and exchange, but mostly for war and destruction, just as the Argonaut myth in Roman thought represents sea travel as the end of a Golden Age and the beginning of intercontinental war. Schmidt's quest closes with a death, a monster who is actually a hero, an Other with whom we belatedly identify, tragically misunderstood and destroyed. This complicating of the relationship between self and other is central to the Argonaut myth through both Colchians and Medea.

Heroism and Betrayal

Back to the story: the Argonauts have arrived in Colchis. Now Jason must negotiate with Aeetes, face the fire-breathing bulls and the Earthborn men, defeat the dragon and finally grasp the Golden Fleece. He must decide how to escape and how to relate to Medea. The death of Apsyrtus, Medea's brother, will change everything, and makes moral choices unavoidable. This chapter focuses on the moral complexity of the Argonaut myth and the variations later versions use to approach moments of moral tension. The events in Colchis return to earlier key issues: what sort of heroism and masculinity does Jason display? How does his relationship with Medea define them both? How do supernatural elements affect different interpretations? To what extent are monsters heroic and heroes monstrous? Is Jason any more or less Other than his Colchian adversaries? This chapter combines gender, mortality, monstrosity and Otherness to think about the central events of the Argonautic tradition.

The three episodes covered here (the taming of the bulls and the fight with the Earthborns; acquiring the fleece from the dragon; evading or killing Apsyrtus) are key to the story and almost always included, with considerable variation in treatment, variation which affects portrayals of Jason and Medea, alignment and allegiance for audiences. Not all versions include all elements;[1] some versions re-order them.[2] Mostly, the bulls and Earthborns occur together and the dragon separately, so I analyse them in that arrangement.

Bulls and Earthborns

Apollonius' Jason is a complex mixture of heroism like that of Achilles or Hector with deceptiveness like Odysseus, attractiveness like Paris, youth and vulnerability. Apollonius seems to particularly relish the moral complexity of Jason and his masculinity. I here bring out elements that show the complex epic nature of Apollonius' Jason, along with those that will later prove problematic. After Aeetes sets the apparently impossible tasks of yoking the fire-breathing bronze-hoofed bulls and surviving the soldiers which grow from the earth, Apollonius' Jason is despairing but sees no option but to accept. He meets Medea in the temple of Hecate, 'like Sirius leaping high from the Ocean; it rises brilliant and clear to behold, but to flocks it brings terrible misery' (AR 3.956–9). Achilles, too, approaches Hector, like the star called the 'dog of Orion' which brings misery to mortals (*Iliad* 22.26–31). But Jason is deadly through the desire he causes, not the death he threatens. Medea gives him an ointment, which will make him powerful, invulnerable, protect against flames and give him boundless confidence. She instructs him in the ritual required to apply it, and how to defeat both bulls and Earthborns. He carries out her instructions, 'like a furtive thief' (3.1197) and 'bathed his tender body in the holy river' (3.1203–4). The word for 'tender' here, *teren*, can also mean 'soft' or 'delicate'. However, Apollonius highlights Jason's ritual effectiveness, despite the terrifying nature of Medea's sponsoring goddess Hecate. This ritual is not a traditional heroic arming scene, although it does serve to protect Jason and increase his status: Aeetes receives the honour of such a scene (3.1225–45). Only after anointing himself and his weapons with Medea's drug (*pharmakon*) does Jason acquire 'terrible prowess, unspeakable, dauntless' (3.1256–7). From then on, he is unequivocally heroic: a fierce war-horse eager for battle (3.1259–61), like Paris at *Iliad* 6.506–11; like lightning darting from the clouds (3.1265–7). The tasks are 'feats' or 'contests' (*aethla*, also used of athletic events), and have a great audience 'standing on the Caucasian cliffs' (3.1276). Aeetes describes the bulls as 'bronze-footed bulls that pour flame from their mouths' (3.410); the feat of using them to plough the field of Ares is a repeated ritual act, which Aeetes enacts over a day (3.407–21). Jason attempts to replace Aeetes, and his naked, armed body is compared to the gods Ares and Apollo (3.1282–3). The bulls rush out from an underground lair, wreathed in smoke, belching flame. Jason stands firm, like a rock resisting crashing waves (3.1294–5), while the bulls roar like a furnace (3.1299–303). He wrestles them to the ground, and yokes them. Throughout, we see Jason's power and strength ('mightily with all his strength', 1307; 'forced', 1308; 'struck down with one blow', 1310; 'the strength of the man', 1314). As the sown men appear, their armour shines like stars (3.1359–62). The density of imagery emphasizes the epic status of the battle. Jason throws not just a rock at the Earthborns, on Medea's advice, but a huge boulder that four men could not have lifted, evoking Iliadic heroes (3.1363–7). The Earthborn men kill each other like swift dogs (3.1373) and fall like trees in a storm (3.1375–6). Jason does not just wait and watch for them to destroy each other, but bears down on them like a destructive comet (3.1377–9), and mows them down as they emerge. He is like a farmer who harvests before the sun ruins his crop (3.1386–91). The agricultural imagery continues: their blood resembles an irrigation system (3.1391–2); they die like saplings in a flood (3.1399–404), with Aeetes as grieving farmer. The comparison of the dead Earthborns to sea monsters on a beach (3.1395) evokes the six-armed giants killed by Hercules on Cyzicus (AR 1.1003–11). In short, Apollonius shows a Jason transformed by Medea's *pharmaka*, but his resulting power is unequivocally heroic. Assessments of Jason tend to ignore this scene, since his power derives from Medea's drug. Nevertheless it forms the climax of the poem's heroic action. Medea's help arguably augments Jason's heroic status, functioning as mediated divine intervention, like Athena's help in Odysseus' slaughter of the suitors in *Odyssey* 22. The transformation Odysseus undergoes at 13.429–38 into an old man is similar to the magical transformation Medea works on Jason. However, Athena explicitly does not turn the course of his battle with the suitors, although she advises and rebukes Odysseus; she is still testing his strength (22.236–7), and instead watches over the action. These lines suggest that there was anxiety in ancient traditions about how much divine help was acceptable for a hero.

The feats are already an important part of the story by the time of Hesiod, one of our earliest textual sources. In the *Theogony* Jason has completed the many, grievous tasks (*stonoentas aethlous*, 994) before leading Medea back to Iolchos. Although the primary focus is on Medea as the bearer of his child, there is no mention of her helping him. The tasks themselves do not vary much: as a central part of the story, they serve to identify it as the Argonaut myth (Jason, fleece, *Argo*, clashing rocks, bulls, Earthborns and dragon are more or less non-negotiable). Pindar does not mention the dragon's teeth, which could conceivably have been transferred from the myth of Cadmus founding Thebes. But the sixth/seventh-century BCE poet Eumelos does include them, according to ancient commentators on Apollonius (*scholia* on 3.1354). The motif also features in early mythography (Pherecydes, 3F22) and in fragments of Sophocles' play the *Colchians* (*Kolchides*), which centres on the Argonauts in Colchis. The fact that Medea does not feature in two of the earliest visual representations of the dragon scene, the Douris cup and a column crater by the Orchard painter, suggests that her help was not always prominent or essential in these episodes. Athena could take her place, acting as sponsoring goddess. The fragment of Mimnermos (above, p. 4) from the seventh century BCE, certainly suggests that Jason had some perilously achieved assistance ('Never would he have ...'). This is usually interpreted as a reference to Medea, but could refer to Athena. The tasks remain stable, but variation clusters around the question of how Jason manages to achieve them: how heroic and self-sufficient is he? What is the cost of success? Jason's successful masculinity is questioned, along with Medea's betrayal of her family. Was the myth so popular in tragedy because it was already morally complex, or did it become morally complex because it was popular in tragedy? Does Pindar's version reflect an earlier more heroic tradition of Jason, or does Pindar adapt the complex tradition to make it more effective as panegyric? These questions will remain unanswered, but different later versions adapt, rehabilitate and reinterpret them in different ways.

Pindar makes Jason the active seducer of Medea, who shows him how to undertake the feats, and gives him the protective ointment (220–2). Aeetes' bulls breathe fire and have bronze hooves (225–6). Aeetes himself carries out the ploughing, splitting open the back of the earth (227–9). Jason trusts divine support when he takes on the task (232), suggesting the possible presence of Hera or Athena in an earlier version. Medea's drugs protect him against the fire, but his own strength accomplishes the ploughing: active verbs (grasped, bound, thrusting) and references to force, power and strength (234–8) emphasize his heroic success.

Clear positive heroism inspires the 1803 sculpture *Jason* by Danish sculptor Bertel Thorvaldsen, at time of writing located in the City Hall of Copenhagen. The sculpture shows Jason carrying the fleece, as described in Apollonius, naked, with a spear, a helmet, and a sword belted around his shoulders (Fig. 6.1). This Jason stands on his own, well-muscled but not heavily built, his flawless body evoking ancient sculptures, such as the Doryphoros of Polykleitos. He gazes resolutely to the right, showing no anxiety about pursuit. His self-sufficiency contrasts strongly with other representations such as Gustave Moreau's (1865) *Jason*, in which Jason and Medea double each other (see Fig. 7.1). This sculpture was Thorvaldsen's breakthrough piece, which established him as a leading Danish artist. Jason also symbolizes the artist himself reaching for fame and fortune.[3] This is an unequivocally heroic Jason, representing the power of Greek myth to inspire, and arguably the dominance of white masculinity. However, the sculpture also sets him up as object of desire, not unlike Hylas, placing the viewer in the position of Medea.

Jason's Colchian feats are often presented as spectacle. Pindar suggests some sort of battle or contest on arrival in Colchis: 'next they came to Phasis, where they matched strength with the dark-faced Colchians in the presence of Aeetes himself' (*Pyth.* 4.211–13). Kneupper's science fiction novel creates the highest stakes spectacle: the Bronze Bulls of Colchis and Jason the Argonaut each function as champions for their city-corporation, set in an arena with millions

Fig. 6.1 The idealized beauty of Jason at its most impressive. Bertel Thorvaldsen, *Jason with the Golden Fleece* (1803). Thorvaldsens Museum, Copenhagen. Available at: www.thorvaldsensmuseum.dk.

watching on the 'vids', audience platforms filling the dome above, and Aeetes acting as compère. This crystallizes Jason's ambition for recognition as a warrior. The 'Bronze Bulls', four of them, doubling the pleasure, each brandish different weapons, including a trident, evoking Roman gladiators. Versions like Kneupper's reality TV spectacular use theatricality in ways that fit their context and genre: for instance, Apollonius' Argonauts go to the games like Greeks to the Olympic athletic festival. Graves in *The Golden Fleece* adds an actual athletic contest with the Colchians (280): the Colchians, like the Odyssean Phaeacians, are poor competitors, but also unaware of their inferiority. The motif of Medea watching Jason in action, falling gradually in love, is prominent throughout, especially in Valerius Flaccus, who draws on Roman spectacle. In those versions which foreground ritual, the ritual is often public and spectacular: in Catran, the artificiality of the ploughing contest, with the 'Earthborn' soldiers buried beforehand in the ridges of soil, contrasts with the sudden shock of reality at their brutal deaths. In Treece, Aeetes outlines the 'Marriage Tasks' at the same time as unmasking their theatricality: the bulls have been castrated; the Earthborns are Amazons and Scythians undergoing initiation rites, and the gigantic serpent is a snake skin brought to life by highly-trained small boys. Treece draws on Graves's tendentious interpretation of Jason's tasks from *The Greek Myths*, while simultaneously indicating his scepticism. In the 2000 miniseries the vast ranks of the audience fill the rocky crags, visually evoking the public rituals in Pasolini's *Medea* (1969). Only in a few cases are the trials secret and private: Lefèvre, where the isle of Colchos is sacred and forbidden; Hawthorne, with Jason and Medea alone at night; the 1963 film, where Jason and Medea (as well as Acastus) are trying to steal the fleece and escape. Occasionally, Jason jumps out of the arena, going beyond the terms of the spectacle: in Evslin, he jumps up to the royal box after facing down the bulls, lured by impressing Medea, but actually distracted from protecting his friends; in Catran, he leaps out as the bulls run amok and kill the Earthborns, escaping chaos that he himself has caused; in Kneupper, he uses his genetically-enhanced legs to leap onto the VIP platform, attacking the master of ceremonies himself to rescue Medea. These latter two show a twenty-first-century tendency to break down the barriers between audience and performance, also clear in the way Ridley Scott's *Gladiator* (2000) repeatedly brings Commodus into the arena, blurring the boundaries between fighter and producer.[4] The spectacular and theatrical nature of Jason's feats emphasizes the staged nature of heroism: it must take place under the gaze of an audience, just as the *Iliad*'s Glaucus and Sarpedon worry about their role as exemplary fighters (*Iliad* 12.310–28), and Hector cannot let down his watching city and family, despite his terror. Heroism is often, even always, a performance. The Argonaut myth, as we see it in Apollonius and most later versions, uses Medea's ointment to question the authenticity of Jason's heroism, literally skin-deep. This remains the dilemma for Kneupper's Jason, who wants to achieve real personal strength and power, not relying on genomancy.

As antagonists and obstacles, the bulls are large, powerful and terrifying: they do not need supernatural qualities to be impressive adversaries. Even so, bronze hooves and fiery breath are pervasive in the tradition, but there is some variation: in Catran's rationalizing version the bulls are massive with gilded horns like wild oxen, and Medea has allegedly drugged them, so Jason can steer them around the arena. At the other end of the spectrum from animal to machine comes Evslin, whose bulls are cast in brass, made by Daedalus for Minos and purchased by Aeetes. Evslin may be inspired here by William Morris, who seems to be first to imagine the bulls as entirely made of bronze ('great brazen bulls', 7.54–5). Following Morris, as often, Colum's bulls have 'brazen knees'. After Jason defeats them, Morris's bulls are petrified into dead images, as with Harryhausen's Talos (8.255–65). The 2000 film also creates a completely bronze bull, released from its lair by a Colchian in full *Gladiator* armour.[5] Jason, oiled with his hair in a queue, but dressed, faces the bull alone and uses the bull-leaping skills he learnt from his crew-member Laertes. Earlier he embarrassingly failed to perform a somersault. Now he successfully flips onto the bull's back and rides it like a bucking bronco, until it tires enough to be yoked. The 2013 TV series *Atlantis* also features bull-leaping, with Jason having to train a team of convicts to survive the ritual together, including women, slaves and the very unfit Hercules, probably drawing on the story of Theseus as told by Mary Renault in *The King Must Die*. Featured in episode 3, the bull-leaping establishes both Jason's heroism and his leadership, as well as giving a Minoan flavour to the setting.

In *The Golden Fleece*, Graves includes the Colchian feats in Aeetes' dream (267), which Medea subsequently interprets, and then uses to plan 'real events', which distract from her escape. The Argonauts castrate the bronze statues of bulls, which honour the Taurian war-god in the temple of Prometheus, and blame it on the Albanians. The subsequent fight between the Taurians, who claim descent from the serpent's teeth, and the Albanians, replaces the civil war, which destroys the Earthborn men. Graves creates new religious interpretations, which act as non-rational rationalizations of complex political and ethnic situations. Some of this comes from Diodorus, for whom the bulls were fierce soldiers called *Tauroi*. Graves adds this too: the sentries outside the temple of the Fleece wear bull-headed masks, guarding the bull god of the Taurian people.

Hawthorne plays with myth and reality differently: he presents realistic bull behaviour, adding to his anachronistic tone. The bulls are 'chewing their fiery cuds' when Jason approaches. He can see 'four streams of fiery vapour', breath from their nostrils, the bulls 'lifting up their hot noses'. When Jason meets the bulls again the following day, they 'came towards Jason, … thrusting forth their snouts, which, as other cattle do, they loved to have rubbed' (245). Fierceness and fire had both been put out, 'heretofore … a great inconvenience to these poor animals'. Hawthorne suggests that Jason's ploughing knowledge came from Chiron allowing the boys to use him as a plough-horse. He relishes the heroic incongruity of this task, but also makes it intense and dramatic. The darkness is backdrop to a stunning pyrotechnic display: first the 'glowing sparks and vivid jets of flame', then the bulls, like lightning, 'lit up the whole field with a momentary flash'. The 'sheet of white flame' lets Jason see to wrestle the 'brazen brutes', catching one by the horn and the other by the tail, playing with the phrase 'take the bull by the horns'.

Various motifs associated with bulls contribute to versions of this Argonautic episode: bull-leaping, bull-fighting, bull-riding (bucking broncos) and bull sacrifice (for instance in rituals associated with Mithras). Jason does not always have to fight the bulls: in Ovid *Met.* 7, which perhaps inspired Hawthorne, he stands still, until they stop, strokes their dewlaps (7.117) and yokes them. In Valerius, by contrast, the bulls have become more violent in Aeetes' old age, a typical metapoetic reference to Valerius' own belatedness in the tradition. In Whitehead's graphic novel, Jason first lassoes each bull and then leaps over them, in a way that evokes the 2000 film.

The bulls are made more monstrous by their association with thunder and lightning, fire and the technology of metallurgy. Images of metal-working compete with images of agriculture from Apollonius onwards. The bulls symbolize power out of control, whether divine power, that of the natural world or technological developments. They are not often intentionally destructive, instead goaded or made violent, but they can also represent toxic masculinity. In a number of versions they are tamed, either by Jason's steadfastness (particularly humanized in Ovid), or by Medea's magic or drugs. If Jason does not wrestle them to the ground, they sometimes grow amenable of their own accord.[6] Their strength makes them powerful allies, but they emphasize the potential for the domestication of nature to misfire. There is little structural hybridity in the Argonautic bulls, who are plausible antagonists even without any metallic additions, compared say to the minotaur, whose semi-humanity makes him significantly more uncanny.[7] But many versions increase their monstrosity and hybridity by giving them more significant mechanical elements, more frequently after the Industrial Revolution.

While the bulls are fundamentally animals, the Earthborns are more obviously hybrid between human and Other (particularly the undead and plants). As offspring of dragon's teeth we might expect reptilian versions, but I have not found any. In Apollonius, and widely in other versions, the dragon's teeth were given to Aeetes by Athena after Cadmus killed the dragon of Thebes. The Earthborn men in Thebes began killing each other but subsequently formed the first population of the city. Before Harryhausen, the Earthborns are uniformly armed Greek soldiers, which grow out of the ground. Ovid in *Metamorphoses* 7 emphasizes their humanity and mortality. He compares their creation to a miraculously accelerated birth: 'just as in its mother's body an infant gradually assumes human form ... so, when the forms of men had been completed in the womb of the pregnant earth, they rose up on the teeming soil and, yet more wonderful, each clashed weapons brought forth with him' (*Met.* 7.125–30). As they kill each other, he calls them 'earth-born brothers' (141). Morris's vivid description, with its striking sounds, is markedly similar to the 1963 film: Jason 'heard from 'neath the earth a muttered sound / that grew and grew, till all that piece of ground / swelled into little hillocks' (8.282–4). 'Then he saw the mounds / bursten asunder and the muttered sounds / changed into loud strange shouts and warlike clang, / as with freed feet the earthborn sprang / on to the trembling earth, and the sunlight / shone on bright arms clean ready for the fight. / ... Not one there was but had his staring face / with great wide eyes, and lips in a set smile, / turned full on Jason' (8.296–304). The idea of mounds rising is repeated in Colum, here connected with graves: 'He saw the field rising into mounds. It seemed that there were graves all over the field of Ares' (118).

Ray Harryhausen remembers choosing skeletons partly to avoid a higher age classification.[8] He had already worked with skeleton models in *The Seventh Voyage of Sinbad* (1958). An early concept drawing shows bodies rising from rectangular masonry graves, not rotting corpses but well-muscled men, although this may show a different planned scene, perhaps a *katabasis*. A later concept drawing shows Jason confronting six armed skeletons, one wearing a helmet, while Medea escapes to the left, clutching the fleece and gazing back in terror (Harryhausen and Dalton 2003: 168–9). In the film, the skeletons burst out of mounds, accompanied by a clattering, rumbling score. Aeetes orders them to attack Jason ('Kill! Kill them all!'); they march forward raggedly grinning, shriek and then charge. The three-minute fight sequence, which took Harryhausen four and a half months to animate (Harryhausen and Dalton 2003: 170), initially presents the skeletons as identical and inhuman. However, individualistic touches create character and humour: one skeleton trips over Jason's foot, another falls over backwards, a third clutches its injured arm, another loses its head, but keeps on walking. Finally, they are not defeated but jump over the cliff, following Jason, implying that the bones are scattered in the water.[9] Perhaps inadvertently Harryhausen preserved the possibility of their survival. He gives his skeletons humour, character and pathos (Fig. 6.2).[10] Over the decades, it is unclear whether audiences are still rooting for Jason, or more attached to the skeletons. Many subsequent versions follow Harryhausen in making their Earthborn men skeletons, particularly those with a strong visual element: Malam and Antram's comic illustrations show 'skeleton warriors', and refer to them in the text; the graphic novels of Yomtov and Jeffrey show skeletons, as does Zimmerman's play (in which both bulls and skeletons are featured on stage). The

Fig. 6.2 Ray Harryhausen's skeletons chase Jason off a cliff. The strong characterization of the skeletons can be seen in the posture of the front near-side skeleton as it peers quizzically at Jason. Screenshot from *Jason and the Argonauts* (1963), [Film] Dir. Don Chaffey. Visual effects by Ray Harryhausen. Screenshot by author.

illustrations for Michael Barich's translation of Valerius, by Thomas Chappell Lewis, also present the Earthborns as skeletons (206).[11] The 2000 mini-series gestures towards Harryhausen, but also moves away (as with the Harpies). Their skeletal Earthborns are plant-like growths rather than human skeletons. This idea of the Earthborn as plants is taken up by Kneupper, in which Medea designs 'seeds' for Jason to sow in order to have allies in his fight. Like triffids, they grow and twine themselves around his enemies: but they are also humanized, since she gives them an element of his genetics, making them hybrid monster-heroes, partly plant, partly Jason.

In some twentieth-century versions (Seraillier, Evslin, Zeff, Bradman and Ross) the Earthborns remain armoured soldiers with little monstrosity. Evslin's idiosyncratic version has Ekion raise them as an army to attack Colchis and rescue the Argonauts. He describes them as 'blank-faced, boiling with energy'; 'faces ... meat-red, set with eyes as pale as stones, their hair was the colour of brass' (146). Here they are meaty, stony and metallic, with a high level of hybridity. This monstrosity fades as they develop voices and opinions, calling Ekion king, while he sends them to create their own settlement (148).

Later twentieth- and twenty-first-century versions emphasize their connection with earth. The Humphreys' illustrations of Brooks (1997) portray the soldiers as lumpy and earthen-looking. Both of Hoena's versions feature lumpy earthen men:

in the first, illustrated by Estudio Haus, Jason hacks them down with a sword and they crumble. In the second, the choose-your-own-adventure version, illustrated by Takvorian, Hoena plays with his own previous version. If you choose to attack the Earthborns with a spear, you die. Only after you have thrown the rock can you cut them down with your sword. Takvorian also illustrates Gunderson's picture book, which presents them as armoured men, covered in dirt, with helmets containing darkness and a suggestion of eyes. In Zarabouka and James Riordan, they are giants. Surprisingly, the graphic novel of Whitehead and Banerjee, which refers carefully to ancient sources, here presents them as zombies (in both text and illustrations). They are invincible, and Jason must make them kill each other, because human weapons cannot destroy them.

In fighting the Earthborns, Jason faces an army single-handedly. This often occurs in epic battle scenes: the hero's *aristeia* (moment of being the best) is one against many. In Apollonius, as we saw, Jason follows Medea's advice, and throws the rock amongst them to make them slaughter each other, but also himself cuts them down. Pindar does not include this feat, but Valerius exemplifies an ancient version which gives Jason more agency with both bulls and Earthborns. Valerius' Jason is often more heroic than Apollonius' Jason, but Valerius gives Medea more agency too. Jason stands alone as if in a desert or fields of snow (7.559–63), while the bulls are an apocalyptic, cosmic force, like storm, sea and lightning (564–72). Valerius includes Medea in the battle, not just in metaphorical language (her poison represents her) but also as if she is literally fighting the bulls herself ('the bull shook the hero, and now you yourself Medea, resisting', 590–1). Even more strikingly, she defeats the second bull: 'the turbulent Colchian then disarms the other bull ... she embroils it in night' (596–8). Valerius' Earthborns are particularly military: the war-like earth sounds trumpets and a phalanx arises (610–13). Jason attacks them immediately, cutting them down before they grow. But there are thousands of them ('thousands more', 622), and Jason is like Hercules trying to defeat the hydra (623–4).[12] Jason remembers Medea's plan and loosens his helmet to throw, but 'hesitates nevertheless and desires himself to counter the whole war' (627–8).[13] However, the Earthborns all turn against him and he finally accepts the necessity of using Medea's helmet, anointed with drugs to send the Earthborns mad. The men killing each other resemble devotees of the goddess Cybele who castrate themselves, both monstrous and uncannily related to both gender and divinity. Valerius emphasizes Medea's agency: 'No differently did Medea suddenly embroil the enflamed cohorts and drive the wretched brothers to battle against themselves' (637–8). In Ovid, Medea watches and mutters additional spells; in Valerius, she directs the action, like an alternative poet figure, or an additional hero. Equally, Valerius highlights Jason's reluctance to accept help, to be Apollonius' Jason. Valerius' version intensifies: he makes Jason a more powerful soldier, Medea a more powerful enchantress and the bulls and Earthborns more terrifying, less human.

Valerius influences various versions. Kingsley has a number of motifs that evoke Valerius: his Jason stands alone against the army of Earthborns. 'Out of the earth they rose by thousands ... and rushed on Jason, where he stood in the midst alone.' Jason throws his helmet, as in Valerius, not a rock, and the helmet causes madness (91). Kingsley reduces Medea's agency, though: she simply casts spells, as in Ovid. In Zimmerman's staging, Medea watches with her father above, but fights the bulls with her spells, taming them, and afterwards 'collapses from her effort' (119). She also shouts at Jason to throw the rock at the Earthborns. Valerius' more heroic Jason, then, has an impact on the later traditions.

Morris gives Jason less agency but avoids the domination of Medea: the fight takes place in an iron-walled arena, with a cage for the bulls at one end (8.62–5). Morris builds up Jason's heroism with a detailed description of his armour (8.71–85). Jason himself opens the cage, while Medea watches pale with terror, and he stands alone against the bulls. Juno appears and lights the way to the plough, which is hidden in the billowing smoke from the bulls. Jason initially wants to fight the Earthborns himself with his sword, but remembers Medea's crystal apple. There is one survivor, and he moves towards Jason, but dies and falls before either can attack. Morris's Jason fights neither bulls nor Earthborns, but just uses his strength to yoke and plough, and his words to taunt. Morris reflects on the rise and fall of the Earthborns using imagery of hunger, fullness, fruit and flower (8.345–8).

The single survivor, the irony of the agricultural imagery and the misplaced battle-madness in Morris all recall Hawthorne's version, which continues his anachronistic juxtapositions. When Jason sows the seeds, the narrator reflects: 'Any farmer ... would have said that Jason must wait weeks before the green blades would peep from among the clods' (239). The peeping blades are those of spears, which 'glistened in the moonbeams, like sparkling drops of dew'. The warriors 'tore themselves up by the roots' (240). Hawthorne contrasts the 'beautiful world' and 'peaceful moonlight' with the 'rage and stormy passions' of the Earthborns. The narrator compares them to other armies (Alexander or Napoleon would have 'rejoiced') and pokes fun at epic stereotypes: as the Earthborns kill each other they are 'doing such memorable deeds that Jason was filled with immense admiration', although 'he could not help laughing'. The last survivor brandishes his sword, cries 'Victory! Victory! Immortal fame!' and dies.

Medea comments that there will always be 'simpletons' . . . 'fighting and dying for they know not what' (242). She asks Jason whether he was amused by the 'self-conceit' of 'that last fellow'. But Jason is sad and grave and draws an analogy with his own situation: 'the Golden Fleece does not appear so well worth the winning'. Medea seems to reassert epic values when she claims 'there is nothing better in the world', but undercuts this immediately with 'one must needs have an object, you know'. Hawthorne undermines the seriousness of his story and of the myth, but also shows anti-war deconstructions of Classical heroism, soon to become prevalent in the poetry of the First World War.

The fight with the Earthborns creates different Jasons, from a violent warrior, using wits to enhance fighting, to a hero completely reliant on Medea's advice. He throws different objects: a rock so large that it kills a man simply by landing (Zeff); a great rock (Riordan); a simple rock (Pirotta, Jeffrey) or stone (Zarabouka); the helmet poisoned by Medea (Valerius, Bradman); a bag containing the teeth (Brooks, similarly in Gunderson, with a bag of stones); a crystal apple (Morris), which assimilates Jason to the Homeric goddess, Eris, who caused the Trojan War by throwing an apple amongst the goddesses at the wedding of Peleus and Thetis. In some versions Jason just leans on his spear and watches (James Riordan). Whitehead and Banerjee create a full-scale battle scene: the Argonauts and Jason together fight the indestructible zombies and have to retreat to a barn to escape them. Only then does Medea advise Jason, who goes back out to face them solo, and throws the rock into their midst while himself hidden. In the 2000 film, Jason is unarmed and uses his acrobatic skills to duck, dive, somersault and avoid the flailing plant men so that their swords destroy each other. He does not strike a blow against any of the monsters, leaping the bulls, avoiding the Earthborns and luring the dragon off a cliff.

While the Earthborns become less human and more monstrous in the later twentieth and twenty-first centuries, there is no pattern to Jason's development. In Ovid he is calm and distant; in Valerius a bloodthirsty warrior; in Harryhausen he fights vigorously but escapes by jumping off a cliff, while in the 2000 film he does not fight them at all. Jason is attractive to creators both as conventional and unconventional hero, and the relative success of the different texts (Ovid versus Valerius; 1963 versus 2000 film) also seems unrelated to their commitment to conventional models of heroism. Interestingly, some versions which follow Harryhausen in giving the Harpies bat wings, do not follow with the skeletons (Ross, for instance, illustrating Bradman). Creators follow their favourite previous version, classic or proximate, but only so far, and where that version conflicts with expectations, they tend to 'correct' it. So Vegio, for instance, includes Ovid's birth imagery of the Earthborns, but not his innovative moment where Jason strokes the bulls into submission. Kingsley follows the *Orphic Argonautica*, but reinserts a longer more detailed version of the events in Colchis. Colum often follows Morris, but does not include the appearance of Hera during the bull scene. This pattern of variation shows that canonical versions tend to reassert themselves. The myth of 'the myth' is powerful throughout the tradition. The monstrous birthing from the earth stays constant, along with bulls and ploughing, and Jason's avoidance of straightforward force in facing them.

Defeating the dragon

After Jason has ploughed the field and disposed of the Earthborns, he still has to get his hands on the Fleece itself. Apollonius' fleece is well-guarded by a *drakon*, which one could translate as either 'dragon' or 'serpent'. The reptilian guard varies from a single dinosaur-like creature to a collection of venomous snakes, but is most often either an enormous serpent or a medieval-style high-fantasy dragon. This episode has many variants, ancient and modern.

In Apollonius, Jason and Medea set out just before dawn, like hunters tracking their prey. Their complex and tense relationship mirrors that of Medea and the snake. For Apollonius, the *drakon* is definitely a very large snaky reptile, with no mention of wings: he describes it at length (4.127–44), with its 'enormous neck'; when it saw them it 'hissed horribly', terrifying mothers and babies throughout Colchis. Its reptilian coils pile up, like eddies of smoke rising from a heap of smouldering wood. He even calls it *peloron* ('monster' or 'beast', 143) and *teras* ('monster, portent', 147). Different translators use different words for *drakon*. The Loeb by Seaton (1912) translates *drakon* as 'serpent', as does Green (1997), whereas Hunter (1993a) translates 'dragon', and the new Loeb (Race 2009) translates 'snake'. So all options are available to recent versions.

Apollonius' Medea first approaches the *drakon*, praying to Sleep and 'the night-wandering queen', and charms it with her song. As it succumbs, the coils relax, resembling a sluggish wave (152–3), although its head is still 'deadly' (154). Medea adds the scent of juniper and scatters potion on its eyes. As the dragon falls asleep, its length stretches throughout the grove, again emphasizing its monstrous size. Medea takes the lead and Jason follows in fear (149); she tells him to snatch the Fleece. A gender-bending simile compares Jason's delight at acquiring the beautiful object to a young girl amazed by moonlight caught on her dress (167–71). Then Jason takes control, telling Medea to leave the grove, draping it over his shoulder as he carries it to the ship, where he hides it and orders the Argonauts not to touch it. Pindar's *drakon* is also enormous, as big as a fifty-oared ship (*Pythian* 4.244–5, matching the *Argo*). Both Pindar and Apollonius also call the reptile a snake (*ophis*, 249), and in Pindar it is spotted and *glaukopis* ('bright-eyed, grey-eyed', 249). Jason himself kills it with 'skill' or 'tricks' (*technais*, 249). What this means is uncertain: Pindar's Jason takes control, both of the dragon and Medea, but we are never sure how. Ancient vase painting preserves several conflicting versions, including one where Jason has much less agency: the Douris cup shows Jason (named) protruding from the jaws of an enormous serpent.[14] He hangs limply, but with open eyes, either coming out or being swallowed, while the goddess Athena looks on, glaring at the snake (Fig. 6.3). The fleece leece hangs on a tree in the background. This *drakon* is

Fig. 6.3 Red-figure cup by Douris, *c*. 480–470 BCE. From Cerveteri (Etruria). Vatican Museum, currently in Museo Gregorio Etrusco, Italy. Photo by Shi. Available at: https://commons.wikimedia.org/wiki/File:Douris_cup_Jason_Vatican_16545.jpg (accessed 23 August 2019).

clearly superhuman and monstrous. We can speculate on possible stories behind the scene: has Jason, like Jonah, gone down into its insides and successfully escaped?[15] Or is the serpent disgorging him in disgust at the taste of Medea's ointment?[16] Does this represent a connection with an otherwise unattested Near Eastern *katabasis* epic?[17] What this cup does tell us is that there is much we do not know.[18] So much of the earliest Argonaut tradition no longer survives. The Douris cup does, however, bring out some continuities with Apollonius: the monstrous nature of the *drakon*, the requirement for help (from Athena rather than Medea), the relative passivity of Jason.

An Attic red-figure vase attributed to the Orchard painter and now in New York at the Metropolitan Museum of Art (470–460 BCE) shows Athena dominating the scene (perhaps because of the Athenian context of production). This snake is much smaller, but still very long, curling around the rock with the fleece. Jason tentatively reaches up and his furtiveness matches well the theft and escape in Apollonius, even without Medea in the picture. Fragments of Herodorus and the *Naupactia*, preserved in *scholia* to Apollonius (31F53), attest to a different version: Jason brought the fleece to the palace, Aeetes delayed the Argonauts with a banquet, but Aphrodite distracted him from destroying them; Idmon advised them to escape, and Medea followed with the fleece. A passage of Lycophron implies that Jason was cut up and rejuvenated before he acquired the fleece (Lyc. 1315). This too might be connected to the visual evidence.

Medea is elsewhere associated with snakes: a black-figure lekythos from the British Museum (550–500 BCE) shows the head of a woman, identified as Medea, between two snakes. It is only in Euripides' *Medea* that Medea herself takes responsibility for killing the snake (480–1). Apollonius is the first surviving version where Medea drugs the *drakon*, but according to a *scholion* on 4.156, he followed the poet Antimachus in his *Lyde* on this. Ancient variety in this episode devolves into later uniformity. Apollonius' version, in which Medea drugs rather than kills the *drakon*, dominates.

Valerius Flaccus' Roman epic introduces a new emotional element: the snake as index of Medea's attachment to home and family. Her bond with it attracts the language of love, both erotic and parental. When she drugs it, she is upset: collapsed on the ground is the head 'of the dear dragon' (8.92). She 'weeps for herself, cruel girl, and at the same time for her *alumnus*' ('nursling', 94). She remembers her devotion to looking after it and asks it to forget her (be 'unmindful of me', 103). Some elements, as often in Valerius, evoke variants: 'at least I did not destroy you, pitiable one' (99). Medea herself, as with Seneca's Roman Medea, seems aware of possible other versions of herself. She suggests Jason can just take the fleece, and only as a second thought offers to sedate the dragon; meanwhile, Jason is terrified of her (67). The serpent resists Medea's magic, just as Medea resisted the persuasion of Juno and Venus. Medea has to repeatedly encourage Jason to act ('put aside delays', 105; 'come, climb', 110), which he does by scrambling up the dragon's sleeping body. But Jason with the fleece is not like a young girl, but like Hercules triumphantly returning with the Nemean lion's hide. In some later versions, such as Whitehead's graphic novel, Jason wears the fleece, Herculean style. Both Jason and Medea are more heroic and more emotional in Valerius, while the serpent is humanized, if also terrifying in its elusiveness (not described, just evoked by the red light from its eyes). Here for the first time Medea's abandonment of the dragon becomes an act of betrayal, even as she takes on more of the heroic actions in the episode.

The *Orphic Argonautica* (887–1021) significantly develops the dragon episode, which takes up a tenth of the poem. Orpheus and ritual are central. First Medea details the fortifications of the fleece: a sevenfold steel wall and triple bronze doors, guarded both by Hecate herself, her dogs, and the unsleeping snake (*ophis*). The innermost grove of trees is full of herbs and poisons. Mopsus announces that only Orpheus can appease Hecate and allow Jason and Medea to enter. Orpheus digs a pit and sacrifices three black puppies, stuffed with various plants. Finally, he sings, invokes the god Sleep, and Medea marvels that the snake falls asleep, so Jason can take the fleece. Orpheus takes the limelight and eclipses both Jason and Medea. The emphasis on physical fortifications and on Orpheus' magic changes this from a battle between hero and monster into a story of magical breaking and entering. Orpheus' ritual effectiveness replaces Jason's skill and determination and Medea's betrayal.

Lefèvre's dragon episode combines ritual with heroic battle against a monstrous opponent. The dragon is thirty foot long and 'as great [tall] as a horse', breathes fire and spits venom. The fight is surprisingly similar to that in Harryhausen: surrounded by flame, Jason first stabs the dragon between the eyes; the dragon pours out a cloud of venom so Jason slashes blindly, cutting out its triple tongue. The dragon in agony frets and rubs its head, falls on its side, knocking Jason over with its enormous tail, so he cuts off a seven-foot length. The dragon charges and beats him to the ground, and Jason buries his sword in its 'paunch', deep in its heart. It dies, drenching Jason in blood and venom. Jason takes its teeth, ploughs and sows. After the ploughing, the bulls die on the spot. He casts the ashes of his sacrifice over the giants that grow from the ground and they kill each other. Finally he sacrifices the golden sheep itself and flays it. Lefèvre's Jason is self-sufficient, resourceful and determined. Although Medea gave him essential help, and he follows her instructions in detail, she is not present, making his heroism more secure.

Franz Grillparzer includes the dragon scene in his play, *Argonauts*: this dragon, like that of the *OA*, is kept behind locked doors. Grillparzer's fleece is an ill-omened reminder of Aeetes' murder of Phrixus, and will eventually cover the bodies of Medea's dead children. In Act 3 of *The Argonauts*, Medea repeatedly warns Jason and tries to stop him (1416–27, 1491–1506), including by attempting suicide with Jason's sword. But for Jason the fleece represents his heroic integrity (1413–14, 1503–4) and he cannot leave without it. Jason is nevertheless terrified, first of ghosts at the entrance to the cave (1476--87), then at the sight of the dragon (1537–40). Medea in contrast is unafraid. She describes the dragon guardian (also called 'serpent', *drache* and *schlange*) as 'invulnerable' and 'all-piercing' (1511–12), but gives Jason drugged mead to sedate it. He enters the inner cave on his own and she listens to the encounter in an agony of ambivalence. The audience, according to the stage directions, see only the dragon's head jutting from the tree. As in Valerius, Medea repeatedly links snake and erotics: she calls Jason 'You serpent! / who coiled round me, ensnaring me, / who's ruined me and murdered me!' (1541–3), then compares the snake to a bride: 'Go in my darling bridegroom, / embrace your hissing bride!' (1549–50) Jason too echoes her language [to the snake]: 'Behold me then, you'll find that I am your man. / Were you ten times more hideous, here I am!' (1553–4) As they arrive at the ship, Jason evokes the image again: 'Come to me now, my wife! – our wedding march / A serpent's hiss beneath the door of death' (1671–2). This imagery extends the erotic tension between Medea and the snake to imply the ill-omened nature of her relationship with Jason, as if the snake represents both Medea, Jason and their illicit desire.

Grillparzer seems to leave traces on later English versions (his plays were instant classics and are still widely read today in Germany). Kingsley introduces the motif of Medea's attempts to stop Jason into the section where he is not following the *Orphica*. Morris has Jason reflect on the negative effects of his desire for heroism (a 'far-babbled name') at the very moment he is about to penetrate the last locked door before taking the fleece (180–93). The extraordinary multiplication of physical barriers in Morris's version is shared with the emphasis on liminality (the violation of crossing the threshold) in Grillparzer, Kingsley and the *OA*. First Medea penetrates the dank cellar to extract the keys, from a door she opens using a magical branch (combining Apollonius' sprig of juniper with the golden bough from Virgil *Aeneid* 6). She opens the palace doors for Jason and finally gives him the seven keys to the innermost sanctuary, where the fleece itself hangs. Medea still puts the snake to sleep, first stripping off her cloak to reveal her clinging silk dress. Morris eroticizes her relationship with the snake in a different way to Valerius and Grillparzer: the snake's gaze is sexualized, charmed by Medea's singing, a conquest brought out when she places her foot on its neck. The snake's hideousness ('dull-skinned, foul-spotted, with lank rusty hair about his neck; and hooked yellow claws') causes her to shudder when she touches him. The snake is more monstrous and yet less violent, anthropomorphized as an unattractive suitor: he 'tottered', 'feebly', 'whining to Medea's feet he crept' (9.142–4). The 'piercing sweetness' of Medea's song, and her 'steadfast' gaze, present her as active but seductively female.

Medea's singing is equally important in Kingsley, who combines Orpheus in the *Orphica* with Medea in Apollonius and Valerius, while reacting against Hawthorne. Hawthorne continues his playful anachronistic tone: his Medea first 'squeezed Jason's hand', then made him tremble 'ill-natured as all enchantresses are'. The dragon's power and monstrosity is predatory: he swallows an antelope with 'one snap of his jaws'. But Medea easily subdues him with her potion, which she casually 'tossed ... right down the monster's wide-open throat' (240). In Kingsley, too, Medeia is in control, but chooses Orpheus to accompany them, and orders Jason to perform the sacrifice. Jason is eager to rush for the fleece, but Medea restrains him. The dragon is a more glamorous beast: huge as 'a mountain pine', evoking Pindar's ship comparison, its body 'spangled with bronze and gold'. Its human-like 'cries' spread across the city, waking mothers and babies, as in Apollonius, but made sympathetic like the babies in contrast to monstrous hissing. When Medea approaches it, it 'licked her hand, and looked up in her face as if to ask for food.' Here it resembles pet or nursling, as in Valerius, and when Orpheus sings it to sleep, it 'breathed as gently as a child.' Kingsley retains the affective relationship without the sexual elements, in contrast to Morris. His Jason has been kept in the background, but when he finally takes the fleece: 'he leapt forward warily', characterized by eager heroism mixed with caution. The passage demonstrates Kingsley's effective synthesis of elements from various ancient (and modern) versions, creating a complex but broadly positive Jason, but also making the serpent less monstrous and reducing sexual elements.

The episode also inspires painters, whose work feeds back into illustrations and other visualizations: J. M. W. Turner's *Jason* from 1802 brought out Jason's heroism and the dragon's monstrosity (Fig. 6.4). It is night: the small figure of an armed man, back to the viewer, creeps over a dead tree towards an enormous serpent, partly visible, partly hidden in a cave. In the darkness, we can make out Jason, and the spiky branches of the dead tree, and one coil, described by the art

Fig. 6.4 J. M. W. Turner, *Jason*, exhibited 1802. Tate N00471. © Tate, London 2019.

critic Ruskin as 'like the arch of an ill-built drain'.[19] The only hint of the Golden Fleece is in gentle golden light from the top-right corner. The menace of the enormous coil hidden in the darkness, in contrast to the tiny reaching figure, is further strengthened by potential confusion between dragon and tree.[20] This Jason is striving against darkness and the power of nature, with no assistance, and no object in sight, on his own, self-sufficient and admirable, a figure for all struggling against darkness.

Reptilian adversaries are not just popular in medieval romance and nineteenth-century art, but also feature frequently as movie monsters; all three of the mainstream Argonaut films (1958, 1963 and 2000) embrace the opportunity. In *Le Fatiche di Ercole*, Jason escapes from the shadow of Hercules by killing the monster: while the other Argonauts tackle the Colchian ape-men, Jason finds the fleece hanging on its bare tree in a rocky gully. He climbs what looks like a leaf-covered hill to grasp it, but it rises up: an enormous dinosaur. Hercules and the Argonauts admire him as he spears it in the head. In the 1963 film, Ray Harryhausen also took inspiration from the Hercules myths, by animating not just one dragon with darting head and tongue, but a seven-headed hydra. The bare tree and the rocky valley, the glitter of the fleece against a twilight background welcome first Acastus, then Jason, who arrive to claim it. The hydra emerges, its seven heads bobbing and hissing, its tail grasping the limp body of Acastus. Jason, with Medea behind him, watches in horror. The camera switches from Jason (and Medea) to the point of view of the hydra. It attacks Jason, catches him in its tail, while he slashes and hacks at it. Brought down to the ground, he stabs up at it and kills it. The hydra writhes and rattles in drawn-out agony and subsides. Both of these scenes present Jason as strong hero, self-sufficient and effective, even if Harryhausen's hydra has more charisma than its conqueror.

In the 2000 mini-series the reptile is not dignified with such a death scene: the Argonaut troop, including Medea, gain the cliff-top. The fleece, glittering on its bare tree among the rocks, is guarded by a massive dinosaur-like reptile. First Actor the thief tries to steal the fleece behind its back, but it bats him away with its tail. Then Orpheus plays, to calm it, while Jason attempts to rope it. But Orpheus' lyre-string breaks and the dragon throws Jason off, gesturing towards the *OA* tradition, where Orpheus charms it, but swerving away again. Jason tempts it to the edge of the cliff, and lets himself fall over the edge, followed by the dragon, just like the skeletons in the Harryhausen film. But this Jason has secured himself with another rope, and pulls himself back up, to raise the fleece in triumph. The 2000 Jason does not stab the dragon, Medea simply watches, and Orpheus performs the only magic: his song. The monster's credentials are boosted when it eats two Argonauts. It is bigger than a fifty-oared ship and several times the size of the other film dragons. The 2000 film intensifies its epic ambitions, while remaining at a slant from standard Hollywood heroism, allowing Jason, like Pindar's Jason, to kill the dragon with tricks.

Recent children's literature and graphic novels mostly follow the Apollonian version, probably filtered through Colum or Seraillier; Naden omits the dragon entirely. Only Brooks includes Orpheus, as in Kingsley, who plays while Medea sings. 'Dragon' is the preferred description for these texts.[21] However, the beast varies greatly in size: Seraillier's is big enough that 'it could have swallowed *Argo* and her crew in one gulp', and Takvorian's illustration of Gunderson shows a massive black-winged and spiky dragon flying above the tree. In contrast, Zeff/Cartwright and Pirotta/Lewis display a snake coiled around the trunk of the tree. We can see children's authors and illustrators learning from each other. For instance, Spence claims inspiration from the Orchard painter vase, but the illustration suspiciously resembles that of Zeff, and is very similar to (red and blue snake) Byrd's subsequent version. Jeffrey's scene evokes the 2000 film: although the word dragon is used in the text, the illustration shows what looks like a dinosaur, and Jason climbs on top of it; however, Jeffrey reinstates the traditional potion in its eyes. In nearly all versions, Medea puts the dragon to sleep and Jason takes the fleece.

A new motif, perhaps replacing the fight, is the waking of the dragon: in Brooks, Jason is balanced precariously on the dragon when it stirs, and they run for their lives.[22] Bradman's version is idiosyncratic: the dragon is in Aeetes' garden, a 'strange, dark, overgrown place', and when it wakes, it sets the palace on fire, allowing the Argonauts to escape unseen. Whitehead and Banerjee create a more heroic Jason, partly through its monstrous size: an enormous red serpent, with yellow eyes and needle-sharp teeth. Jason and the Argonauts fight it together (as with the Earthborns) but his blade rebounds from its impenetrable hide.[23] It eats and crushes several Argonauts, and is about to crush Jason when Medea puts it to sleep. As soon as he is free, Jason drives his sword into its head. The stakes are raised and heroic masculinity is established before Medea is allowed to intervene. Hoena's choose-your-own-adventure book plays around with various different versions: you can go after the fleece on your own and be struck down by the dragon's 'deadly quickness'; or refuse Medea's offer of marriage and be imprisoned in Aeetes' dungeon; attempt to fight the dragon yourself, be snatched and devoured; or let Medea sing it to sleep, and successfully escape (valorizing Apollonius). The children's literature and the films depart definitively from each other in this episode, suggesting different generic expectations of authenticity, heroism and monstrosity, and showing how proximate versions influence each other.

Catran's version is distinctive and revealing: Medea takes Jason and Pylos to the shrine of the Fleece, a series of dark, dilapidated huts. Inside, the floors are seething with poisonous snakes. Pylos suggests stilts to steal the fleece, showing the theatricality of Catran's televisual imagination. Both Catran and Treece, with his small boys in a snake skin, associate myth and performance, religion and deception: their rationalizations offer the truth behind the scam. However, they continue the association between Colchis and snakes, Otherness and the East.

There is enormous variability in this episode, with generic clusters. Films clearly draw from each other, as do picture books, while films also influence novels and children's books. The different ancient versions, apart from that of the Douris cup, all have some purchase in later traditions, and restoring elements of the Apollonian version is clearly felt to be authentic. However, many versions aimed at a mass-market audience prefer a stronger, less compromised Jason and a disempowered Medea, showing how exceptional Apollonius' and Valerius' Medea remains in ancient epic and its subsequent traditions.

Betraying Apsyrtus

We have not seen very much of Ovid in this book so far, except his uniquely soothable bulls. Often in reception of ancient mythology, Ovid's versions disproportionately affect later traditions; and it seems to be Ovid who has shaped the Apsyrtus episode. Although he omits it entirely from *Metamorphoses* 7, he includes the darker, tragic version in both relevant *Heroides* (6.129–30; 12.113–16) and an entire poem in the *Tristia*, his 'sad things', written from exile in Tomis. This poem (*Tristia* 3.9) presents an etymology for the name, Tomis, from the Greek verb *temno*, 'I cut'. It presents the moment when Medea sees her father's ships in pursuit and desperately seeks a means of escape. She catches sight of her little brother:

> Immediately she pierces the guilt-free side of the boy,
> Who is unaware and fearing no such thing, with her strong sword
> And in this way tears him apart and the torn-apart limbs
> She scatters through the fields, so they must be found in many places.
>
> *Tristia* 3.9.26–9

The arguments and tension between Medea and the Argonauts, present in Apollonius and Valerius, are avoided: the Minyae are busy disembarking, and Medea acts so quickly, Ovid exonerates Jason and his crew. So Ovid enshrines the barbarity of his exile, his social death, the origins of primitive Tomis in the violent action of a barbarian woman.

Medea's betrayal of home and father is shocking already, but her first real crime is the death of her brother, variously known as Apsyrtus, Apsyrtos, Absyrtus or even, in the 2000 film, Aspyrtes. For ease of recognition, I will use Apsyrtus. There are two main ancient versions: the tragic version, seen in Ovid, and the epic version of Apollonius. In the tragic version, Apsyrtus was a young child; Medea either encounters him during her escape or deliberately takes him with her; under pressure of Aeetes' pursuit, she delays her father by killing his son, dismembering the body and one by one dropping the limbs, so the pursuers must stop to retrieve them. In Apollonius' version (4.305–481), Apsyrtus is a grown young man, leading the pursuit. He catches the Argonauts in the Danube delta, near the island of Peuce. Here there is a shrine to Artemis, and the Argonauts send Medea there for arbitration about her return to Colchis. Medea is violently angry, but Jason persuades her they would otherwise all die. He suggests killing Apsyrtus to leave the Colchians leaderless and the locals confused, and Medea agrees. Medea herself lures him to the temple alone. She claims to Apsyrtus that she was taken by force and creates enchantments to ensnare him. At the temple, Jason ambushes Apsyrtus from behind, killing him as if in a perverted sacrifice. As he dies, Apsyrtus stains Medea's silver veil with his blood; Jason cuts off his extremities and licks his blood to avert pollution. This murder of a host makes Zeus angry, and he forces the Argonauts to wander far from home, until Jason and Medea are purified by Circe. The episode is highly varied: later traditions sometimes soften it, by avoiding it, creating a fair fight between Jason and Apsyrtus, or making Apsyrtus the traitor, or a rival in palace intrigues. However, the harshest and most violent version, the dismemberment of a young child, is persistent and pervasive, even, unexpectedly, in children's literature.

The earliest version of the murder of Apsyrtus is preserved in ancient comments on Apollonius: the fifth-century BCE mythographer Pherecydes (3F32) told that Jason persuaded Medea to bring young Apsyrtus with her from the palace, and seeing the pursuit, they collaborated in killing him and scattering his body in the river Phasis. Apollodorus 1.9.24 follows this version, but sets the death at Tomis, as in Ovid. Fragments of Sophocles *Colchides* have Medea deliberately abduct and kill Apsyrtus, although Gantz argues that another Sophoclean play, *Scythians*, may have matched Apollonius' version. Both main versions, therefore, probably existed at least since the fifth century BCE.

A fifth-century vase may be the earliest surviving visual depiction. Oakley argues that a red-figure bell krater from Gela (420–410 BCE) by the Dinos painter depicts the Argonauts' departure from Colchis.[24] The scene is clearly an arrival or a departure, with a ship, a man walking towards the ladder: probably a departure, since the man, identified by Oakley as Jason, boards the ship, looking back at those behind him. Athena presides over the scene, watching the couple on the right, an elderly man and a woman wearing heavily ornamented clothing. Most importantly for us, part of a figure survives under the ladder, next to the ship, apparently the torso of a dead body with a limp left arm. Oakley argues that this combination of figures is most likely to represent the departure of the Argonauts from Colchis: the torso is the dead body of Apsyrtus; Aeetes and his wife watch in horror. If this is correct, then an early version existed with Apsyrtus as a young man killed at the moment of departure. There is no obvious evidence of dismemberment, so this fits well with a 'battle at the docks' scenario. A tragic version may have matched this vase painting, since the two genres often overlap.

The *Orphic Argonautica* may also preserve a similar scenario: here 'the abominable trick and unforeseen doom of famous Apsyrtus was brought to completion thanks to Medea's desire: after killing him, they abandoned him at the mouth of the river's flow, and it carried him away with its speedy flood' (*OA* 1029–32). Medea and Jason seem to have collaborated in killing him and throwing the body off the ship, probably in the river Phasis. The 'trick' could refer to Medea's delaying of Aeetes, as in Ovid, or her deception of Apsyrtus as in Apollonius. Some sort of battle between the Argonauts and the Colchians might also lurk behind Apollonius' account of the elaborate stratagems of Jason and Medea to avoid one, both at Peuce and in Phaeacia. The mythographer Dionysios of either Miletus or Mytilene preserves an account where Aeetes caught up with the *Argo* and engaged them in battle, killing the Argonaut Iphis.

The Ovidian or tragic version, in which the child Apsyrtus is dismembered, is the most prominent in later traditions, showing that Apollonius is not straightforwardly central to the tradition. Pasolini's 1969 film *Medea*, for instance, Euripidean with an interest in myth and ritual, gives his Medea two ritual dismemberments: first the *sparagmos* of the sacrificial victim, then her own scattering of the limbs of Apsyrtus, after he helps her steal the fleece. She leaves Colchis in a high-sided cart, and is pursued on horseback. Away in the middle distance of the viewer, she stops to kill her brother and throw his limbs from the cart. This Medea and Apsyrtus function as equivalents, sitting either side of their parents, in matching costumes, each undergoing a mimetic fertility sacrifice, before Medea turns Apsyrtus' imitation into reality. Pasolini's Medea is not denigrated for her actions: she is powerful and Other, beyond Greek (or twentieth-century) cultural and moral norms.

Versions attracted to black-and-white morality and demonization of Medea also choose the most shocking version of Apsyrtus' death. By making Medea as terrifying as possible, Jason is more plausibly exonerated. This is sometimes surprising, as in Zeff, or Malam and Antram, both aimed at fairly young readers. Zeff uses a hybrid of Ovid and Apollonius: Apsyrtus is lured aboard the *Argo* to make a treaty, and Aeetes watches from his ship, as Medea 'stabbed her brother and threw him into the sea'. Malam and Antram incorporate the dismemberment, but make Apsyrtus an adult, segregating it in a side panel ('Ask the storyteller'), with the images literally tiny. Medea tips the limbs over the side of the boat like dirty laundry from a basket. Hera is responsible for her actions ('the goddess made her do a wicked thing', 25). Brooks' retelling for older children uses the most violent version but insulates the Argonauts, and, through the comments of her narrator, the readers too. The narrator says 'what she did was so unspeakably brutal and barbarous, that even the most battle-hardened survivors of the Trojan War were sickened beyond belief' (77, complete with confused chronology, since the Trojan War is usually set in the following generation). Apsyrtus is Medea's 'vile little brother' (72), who followed her and refuses point-blank to go back. The killing, then, is not preconceived, but an improvisation. Medea, like Apollonius' Jason, is compared to someone making a sacrifice ('as efficiently as if she were sacrificing a lamb') or a butcher ('with all the calm detachment of a butcher carving up a carcass'). She even defends her actions from horrified Argonauts, who attempt to intervene, 'like a lioness defending her kill'. The familiarizing approach in the tetchy interactions between brother and sister, along with the imagery of butchering, make this act even more shocking. Medea is the extreme 'Other', a powerful witch, while Jason slips into the background. Seraillier also holds Medea wholly responsible, but brings together various versions: the Colchians catch up with the Argonauts near the river Halys and Medea snatches Apsyrtus on board as they pass his ship; here he is Aietes' 'young son', but old enough to drive a chariot. Seraillier shortens the description: 'So she killed Apsyrtus and threw his body in pieces into the sea' (69). He frames it as 'a terrible thing', and wholly excludes Jason.

These versions probably draw on Kingsley. His Medea takes full responsibility for Apsyrtus' death: 'the dark witch-maiden laid a cruel and cunning plot' . . . 'she killed Apsyrtus her young brother, and cast him into the sea' (97) to slow Aeetes down. The Argonauts respond with horror: 'all the heroes shuddered'. This 'foul crime' causes the anger of Zeus, resulting in an enormous storm. Jason is not even mentioned. Kingsley does not go as far as dismemberment; his treatment here is compatible with, but not obviously indebted to, the *OA*. As time goes on, then, Jason is recuperated at Medea's expense. What was a bold, cunning, if transgressive, achievement, becomes a 'foul crime'.

Similar tactics recuperate Jason in Lefèvre's *History of Jason*. Medea has enchanted Jason to fall in love with her and forget his fiancée Mirro. After he succeeds in gaining the fleece, 'Oetes' is still hospitable and they celebrate. Medea continues her seduction, including a highly sensual bathing scene. But she refuses to consummate the relationship until Oetes gives him her hand in marriage. Oetes is willing to let the fleece go, but refuses Jason's marriage to Medea. Only then does Medea first sleep with Jason, and puts her plan into action. Her 'maistresse' (nurse) helps her steal the sixteen-month-old 'Absirthius' from his cradle, kills and dismembers him. Jason is distanced from blame in several ways: first he is enchanted to fall in love with Medea, then separated by two degrees (not even Medea, but her nurse is responsible) from the actual killing of Apsyrtus. During pursuit, Medea calls her 'maistresse' to bring the dismembered corpse. Jason protests, calling him a piteous child. Medea argues that Apsyrtus must die, to save the lives of her father, his men and all the

Argonauts, as revealed to her by Diana. Apsyrtus becomes a form of sacrificial victim. Oetes holds back from pursuit and does not curse Medea, but is throughout presented in a more favourable light than in Apollonius: a noble king and a loving father, who cares more about his daughter than the fleece. Jason is thrown into depression at Medea's act and refuses to talk to her, until she persuades him the murder was divinely required. Some elements of Lefèvre recall Maffeo Vegio's Neo-Latin poem from earlier in the fifteenth century: Aeetes feasts Jason after he returns from his feats, and Medea deliberately decides to take Apsyrtus with her, the Senecan Medea in the making. But Vegio self-consciously draws on Ovid's *Tristia*, ending the Apsyrtus episode with Tomis ('She divides his limbs and abandons them as she flees in the Tomitan land', 4.205–6). Both early modern texts recuperate monarchs and heroes, showing a Pindaric concern with patronage.

The dark version is also visualized. Herbert Draper's 1904 painting *The Golden Fleece* (currently in Bradford) evokes Kingsley's version, with the contrast between dark witch-maiden and golden boy (Fig. 6.5). It portrays the moment of casting Apsyrtus overboard: he is a child or young teenager, alive and resisting. Medea, dark-haired and determined, directs two Argonauts. Behind them, the Fleece shines: Fleece and boy together form an oasis of golden light against

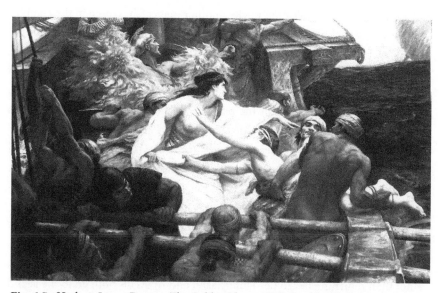

Fig. 6.5 Herbert James Draper, *The Golden Fleece*, 1904. Bradford Museums, Galleries & Heritage (Cartwright Hall). Photo by Shakko. Available at: https://commons.wikimedia.org/wiki/File:Herbert_James_Draper,_The_Golden_Fleece.jpg (accessed 23 August 2019).

the darker areas of the painting (boat, ocean and pursuit). The painting conveys tension and balance, with Medea as the pivot. Holding the fleece is an Argonaut wearing an impressive helmet (probably Jason). The exchange of Apsyrtus for Fleece is emphasized. An older figure with a dagger, just behind Medea, suggests the imminent sacrifice of Apsyrtus. The power of the painting comes from the tension in each character, particularly the desperate stretching body and clutching hands of Apsyrtus, but also the terrified gazes of the Argonauts towards their pursuers. Medea is in charge, but the Argonauts, including Jason, are clearly complicit, and Medea does not herself wield the blade. Murder on the ship also features in Whitehead and Banerjee's graphic novel, where the adult Apsyrtus disappears during a battle at the docks and is later found stowing away. As he holds Jason at sword-point, Medea stabs him in the back. Jason is horrified ('Medea's ruthless murder of her brother made Jason's blood run cold', 64). They cast his dead body overboard and Aeetes retrieves it in horror and grief, cursing Jason and Medea.

Apollonius' version does have a significant following, particularly in the novels and more rationalizing versions, as well as the mythographical tradition: Hyginus, for instance, at *Fabulae* 23, tells a version where Apsyrtus refuses to accept the settlement agreed with Alcinous, king of the Phaeacians, and is lured to his death after that. The multiple Colchian pursuits in Apollonius (one blocking the formerly Clashing Rocks, another that catches them in the Danube, a third group at Phaeacia) might suggest Apollonius himself is combining a variety of traditions. Accius' fragmentary Roman Republican tragedy, *Medea*, seems to have followed Apollonius.[25] Valerius' unfinished pursuit episode also follows Apollonius: Apsyrtus is joined by Styrus, Medea's Albanian betrothed, and they trap the Argonauts at the opening to the Danube. A storm prevents battle, and the text breaks off as Medea and Jason argue about the Argonauts' plan. As often, traces of Valerius appear in both Graves (with Styrus) and Zimmerman, where Styrus keeps trying to kill Jason ('I'll cut off his goddamn dick and make a eunuch of him!' 131), but is engulfed in the storm. After a Valerian beginning, though, Zimmerman shifts to the Apollonian version.

Novels and rationalizing accounts also follow Apollonius: Colum's *Heroes before Achilles* has one major difference. Peleus and Theseus negotiate a deal, in which they keep the Golden Fleece, but leave Medea on the island of Artemis rather than returning her to her father. Jason and Apsyrtus both go to the island intending to betray the other, reducing Jason's responsibility by shifting blame onto the victim. Apsyrtus intends to force Medea to go back to Colchis, and Jason intends to remove her from the island. Instead of Jason jumping out to murder Apsyrtus, the two meet, draw swords, and, in a fair fight, Apsyrtus loses. Blood stains Medea's silver veil, alluding to the image of pollution. Colum still emphasizes the transgression ('covenants had been broken') but it is much less shocking for his young audience.

Graves combines the two strands ingeniously, as he often does, using the motif of cutting to pieces within Apollonius' frame. A crane flies over the Argonauts and cries 'Cut into pieces! Cut into pieces!', as interpreted by Mopsus. Later Echion threatens to cut the fleece into pieces, making it unrecoverable, as he parleys with Apsyrtus. Finally, Jason's act of dismembering as part of the ritual to counter pollution after killing Apsyrtus is augmented: he cuts off the fingers and toes and throws them into the undergrowth so the Colchians must search for them. As in Colum, both sides break the agreement: Apsyrtus has come to kill Atalanta, for the death of Aeetes. Jason has come to kill Apsyrtus. The two fight, but Jason has the advantage of surprise. Jason acknowledges he has betrayed Apsyrtus and committed a murder, although Medea justifies the actions to the Colchian crew, and only the conspirators are punished (Medea, Jason, Atalanta and Melanion). This allows for two different routes home, one for the murderers and one for the ship. Graves is maximal in his novelization of mythical variants, including both versions, detailed descriptions of ritual, elaborated even from Apollonius, and indulging his fascination with ghosts and pollution.

Catran's 2000 version makes Jason's betrayal of Apsyrtus the emotional central point of Jason's relationship with the narrator Pylos, who only then understands the nature of kingship (ruthless pragmatism) and rejects his previous desire to achieve heroism. The scene on the beach where Pylos is instructed to guard Medea and she threatens to commit suicide using her razor-sharp sickle earrings shows her power and her ability to manipulate him. In this version, Apsyrtus is a rival in palace intrigues, and has conspired with the 'horse people' from beyond Colchis to assassinate Aeetes and take control. Apsyrtus pursues the Argonauts to make Medea 'a good sacrifice' for the inauguration of his kingship (179). Apsyrtus is compared to a weasel (179) and a snake (181), but it is Jason and Medea who deceive him into the ambush. Pylos is needed to 'guard' Medea, sufficiently Jason's man that he is trusted. But Medea is still a priestess of 'Rhea-Mother' and the island turns out to be sacred to her. Pylos sees Jason the moment after he kills Apsyrtus, 'breathing heavily' because he had been 'murdering' (185). Jason admits that he was 'killing and oath-breaking', and Pylos fears for his life as a witness. But Jason melts into tears of shame and horror at what 'kings and princes must do'. Jason got what he wanted but paid for it. By having his honour and self-respect cut away.' Medea's threat of suicide pressured Jason into killing Apsyrtus: she sent Pylos to remind him of her threat. This Jason's love for Medea drives the plot, not Medea's love for Jason. Jason is caught up in a narrative of court intrigues reminiscent of stereotypes of Eastern kingship. But the death of Apsyrtus remains the poison that destroys their relationship and Jason's glory.

Several children's versions follow the Apollonian and rationalizing traditions. Catran shares similarities with Zarabouka's version, as elsewhere. Her conspirators meet Apsyrtus on a beach, but she adds her own element when Medea lures Apsyrtus to the edge of a cliff and makes Jason push him off. Three other children's versions are firmly Apollonian: Riordan, who even uses the images of butcher (Jason killing Apsyrtus) and hawk killing dove (Argonauts attacking the confused Colchians); Byrd, who has Medea lure him to the beach and Jason kill him; and Yomtov, who has the Argonauts kill Apsyrtus together as a group, justifying their actions through Apsyrtus' violation of the guest-host relationship. But Medea still sees it as transgression ('My poor brother! Oh, what have I done?!').

Others make Apsyrtus die in a high-pressure battle situation as they try to escape. Grillparzer's Apsyrtus, for instance, is a positive if slightly naïve young man, who loves his sister and tries to protect her, while obeying his tyrannical father. The Argonauts set an ambush for his troop, as he escorts Medea to safety in the cave of the Fleece, and defeat Apsyrtus, while Medea wrestles with her desire for Jason. Later, Apsyrtus catches them at the dock, about to depart, complete with the fleece, and is captured. They take him hostage to prevent the horrified Aeetes from attacking, but Aeetes does not listen and Apsyrtus throws himself off the cliff, taking his death into his own hands, but leaving Jason and Aeetes equally responsible. The tragedy of Aeetes here, caused by his killing of Phrixus in the first play, *The Guest-friend*, is matched by the tragedy of Jason, in the third play, *Medea*.

Morris also engineers a confrontation, in a sea battle: the *Argo* is powering down the river Phasis and Apsyrtus is commanding the ships blockading their exit. As they approach, he demands the release of Medea. Medea herself stands at the prow, next to Jason, bravely (if passively) exposing herself to enemy fire. Behind them, Aeetes' ship bears down and they must crash onwards. Apsyrtus throws the first spear, but misses Jason: he is killed by a combination of Jason's epic spear and Arcas' arrow in his side. The *Argo* rams Apsyrtus' ship with its iron beak and his dead body is thrown into the river. Aeetes is left to sorrowfully retrieve his corpse. Despite his relative exoneration of Medea, Morris contrasts the joy and love of Medea and Jason with 'that wreck upon the bar, the evil spot / red with a brother's blood' (9. 431–2), an evil which inevitably leads to the couple's tragic future.

The 2000 mini-series takes a similar approach: in this 'Aspyrtes' is portrayed negatively, by James Callis, as a weak, treacherous drug addict with incestuous tendencies.[26] Jason rescues Apsyrtus from the shipwreck at the Clashing Rocks, replacing the Medea of the 1963 film, and he leads them to a frosty reception at the palace. When Jason and Medea go for the fleece, Apsyrtus and his men chase him down. Apsyrtus accuses Jason of desiring to 'rule in my stead' and orders his men to kill him. As Jason wrestles a Colchian soldier, Apsyrtus rides over to finish him off with his sword, but Medea picks up the soldier's spear and spits him. She saves Jason's life, and Jason only defends himself. Nevertheless, Medea is horrified and the camera lingers on Apsyrtus' bloody face as she strokes his dead forehead. The darkness is displaced here from Jason and Medea on to Apsyrtus, although this leaves Jason a passive figure. Other versions with a fight to escape include Jeffrey's comic, in which the Colchians attack the *Argo* at the dock, and Aeetes is killed.

The most positive image of both Jason and Medea is achieved by omitting Apsyrtus entirely: Hawthorne lets the unsavoury elements of the myth fall away. The 1958 and 1963 films also avoid this problematic episode, the first by removing all Colchian characters, the second by allowing Jason and Medea to sail off into the sunset, unpursued. Some children's literature follows: Spence, who considers the episode a late addition to the story; Pirotta, which is aimed at young readers, and Bradman, in which the dragon has already destroyed the Colchian palace in a cleansing explosion. In Gunderson's version 'King Aeetes and his men followed the *Argo*, but their ships were not fast enough'; and in Hoena/Estudio Haus the Argonauts simply choose a different route back.

The killing of Apsyrtus shapes the representation of Jason and Medea and their relationship, as well as the Argonauts' return journey, and audience attitudes to the acquisition of the fleece. It embodies the cost of glory and the betrayal of principles to achieve a goal. It divides the tradition, and versions often move away from their models in this episode. This episode shows how moral decisions shape narrative choices. These choices are rarely defined by time, place or target audience, with similar contexts producing different results. The paradoxical tendency to damn Medea as powerfully as possible in order to recuperate Jason recurs throughout, both in more and less misogynistic contexts. Moral complexity generates variations, showing how the multiplicity and inventiveness of tragedy enriches mythical traditions.

Conclusion

Emily Wilson's translation of the *Odyssey* labels Odysseus a 'complicated' man: her translation of the epithet *polutropos* (*Od.* 1.1), which combines the sense he has been turned in many directions with the idea that he can turn in many directions, implying both breadth of experience and suffering, and depth of cunning and deception.[27] The Jasons of Euripides and Apollonius build on the 'complicated' model of Odyssean heroism, but Jason's youth and beauty and his distinctive reliance on others set him apart. While Odysseus is resourceful, the epic Jason is resourceless, the tragic Jason manipulative. Jason's masculinity is a space into which others step, both characters and creators; this capaciousness enables massive variety in interpretations of the story. The idea of weakness and lack as a sort of power fundamentally deconstructs both ancient and modern gender paradigms and models of leadership and success.

Apollonius' Jason is also complicated in his morality: his lack of resources often corresponds with or leads to a lack of principles or moral direction. In ancient Greek terms, he betrays Aeetes' hospitality by abducting his daughter, and betrays Apsyrtus by luring him into an ambush. Many later versions shy away from Jason's moral complexity, his tendency towards playing the role of anti-hero, or find ways of excusing his behaviour. One aspect of ancient Greek heroism is its tendency towards excess, extremity, the willingness to do literally anything to achieve a goal. Achilles in his obsession with vengeance on Hector, Odysseus in the extremity of his violence against both suitors and his own maidservants, Hercules in his killing of his own family and Ajax in his attempt to kill his comrades: all go beyond the bounds of acceptability. What makes Jason different is his lack of extreme emotion, his passivity and opportunism: he is driven by Pelias, by Aeetes, by Medea, by Creon. The complex character gymnastics performed by later creators to recuperate him shows how uncomfortable the Jason of both Euripides and Apollonius makes people, across time, space, genre and medium. It is this that makes Jason good to think with.

Quest and Fleece

The search for the real Argonauts, and the meaning of the Argonaut myth, has persisted since at least the fifth century BCE. How and why do searchers throughout history go about their quests? We have followed the events of the myth from beginning to the return journey, and seen the way traditions vary for different episodes. In this chapter, I investigate meanings attributed to the epic voyage of the *Argo* as a whole and the Golden Fleece itself. Myth is supremely interpretable: it can be a mode of explanation itself, but it continually demands explicating. Interpreters create meaning in two main ways: by looking for facts ('history') beneath the surface of the story, or by constructing or analysing deep, subconscious structures and symbols within it. The search is often configured as a search for origins, which often combines historical and structuralist, rationalizing and symbolic approaches. Traditions of interpreting the Argonaut myth incorporate many key approaches to mythology more generally, from rationalizing to psychoanalysis, from links with ritual to overarching theories about sun worship and sacrifice. These traditions of interpretation influence cultural products: Apollonius plays with Homeric scholarship and allegorical readings; Valerius is well aware of Diodorus; Vegio and Lefèvre engage with Christianizing interpretations; Graves is clearly influenced by J. G. Frazer's *Golden Bough* and the Cambridge ritualists.

The Argonaut story as a whole is widely used as an image in various products, from paintings to brands and logos, from plays to pop music, from historical treatises to board games and toys. The name of the professional Canadian football team, the Toronto Argonauts, may well be the most well-known use of the myth. The club was founded in 1873 as part of the Argonaut rowing club, with strong connections to the universities of Oxford and Cambridge (combining their two different blue colours).[1] The first club members were University of Toronto students, rowers using the relatively new sport of rugby to keep fit. Rowing at Oxford and Cambridge is still prominent in identity formation, especially masculinity and elitism. As students emulating elite British sport, the

Canadian Argonauts presented themselves as successful colonists, explorers and athletes. The team remains an image of power and success, and the name 'Argonauts' retains power in Canadian culture. For instance, the Canadian science fiction author, Robert Sawyer, titled his first published novel *Golden Fleece*.

The importance of Argonauts in science fiction may well come from (and is exemplified by) H. G. Wells, who twice uses the name in his story titles: *The Chronic Argonauts* (1888) and *Argonauts of the Air* (1895). Each expands the idea of the *Argo* as first ship to a new method of travel: air and time travel. *Argonauts of the Air* develops the wonder of powered air flight before an audience of sceptical rail commuters, and ends in both success and disaster, with the successful vehicle flying out of control and crashing disastrously, just as Jason gains the Fleece, but fails to control the means of acquiring it (Medea). In *The Chronic Argonauts*, the nefarious Dr Nebogipfel uses a ruined house in a small Welsh town to build an experimental time machine. When the townsfolk come to lynch him, he escapes through time, taking with him the priest, Elijah Cook, who finally appears back, to reveal that Dr Nebogipfel murdered the previous occupants of the house. The success of the technological advancement is set against the resistance of surrounding society, which leads to betrayal and murder.

Scientists continue to use the imagery of Argonautic exploration for gathering and organizing data: the *Argonautica* project, hosted at the Centre Nationale d'Etudes Spatiales (the French space agency), uses satellite location data from a group of satellites called Argos and oceanographic data from a project called Jason to collect information on the marine environment.[2] For instance 'Argonimaux' tracks marine animals fitted with transmitters to see how climate variations affect their movements. The Jason project presents a positive image of the Argonauts as explorers and the forebears of scientists. Another example takes the associations with travel and exploration further. The website *The Argonauts* is 'an adventure-travel community dedicated to inspiring the human spirit by enabling people to venture into the unknown and sharing their dreams and discoveries with the world in real-time.'[3] Founded by Scott Stoll in 1999 after he rode a bicycle across the US, it asks 'If you could do anything, what would you do?' This site uses the idea of Argonauts to inspire adventure, travel, exploration and self-realization.

In the board game, *Argonauts*, produced in Athens in 2014, players must co-operate, each holding a number of Argonaut cards in their hand, to bring the *Argo* safely through her trials. This version uses imagery from the 1963 and 2000 films: the box image features Triton holding the cliffs apart; cards include skeleton Earthborns, but feathered Harpies; the portrayals of Argos, Jason and Medea all bear a close resemblance to the characters in the 2000 film. However, the events are closely related to those in Apollonius, including only a few tangential or less canonical moments (the sea monster from Valerius, the Calydonian boar, which also features in Graves's novel, and the Odyssean Scylla and Charybdis). Its collaborative focus emphasizes the collective heroism of the Argonauts as team.

A different sort of teamwork comes to the fore in Maggie Nelson's 2015 memoir, *The Argonauts*, which won the National Book Critics Circle award and was a *New York Times* best seller. Nelson's book is a memoir of love and motherhood in a complex family: her partner Harry is in the process of transitioning from female to male. Nelson's own body is changing with pregnancy, becoming more obviously female. Harry was adopted and is coming to terms with the death of his real mother (non-biological). The title does not have an obvious relevance to the contents of the book, which makes it intriguing. Why Argonauts? The most obvious reference is to a passage of *Roland Barthes*:

> A day or two after my love pronouncement, now feral with vulnerability, I sent you the passage from *Roland Barthes by Roland Barthes* in which Barthes describes how the subject who utters the phrase 'I love you' is like 'the Argonaut renewing his ship during its voyage without changing its name.' Just as the Argo's parts may be replaced over time but the boat is still called the *Argo*, whenever the lover utters the phrase 'I love you,' its meaning must be renewed by each use, as 'the very task of love and of language is to give to one and the same phrase inflections which will be forever new.'
>
> Maggie Nelson, *The Argonauts*, 5

This passage is part of the emotional core of the book. The variability and interpretability of myth equates to a technological construction, and shows the need for constant renewal of phrases and relationships. The irony is that in a passage from Barthes about referentiality and substitution, Barthes has himself substituted one myth for another. Barthes uses the *Argo* to express a paradox that is normally associated with the ship of Theseus, which was preserved but gradually remade, part by part.[4] He may have chosen the *Argo* over the ship of Theseus, since there does not seem to be a name for the ship of Theseus, and because of the idea of renewal during the voyage, which is why Argos normally participates in the quest. Myth, like the ship, is a story made of many parts, each of which can change, but the essence of the story is still perceived to be the same.

It is always being made anew. Here the name has been substituted while the idea remains the same, but it gains a new life in Nelson's work.

For Nelson, Argonauts are the participants in a relationship which is always changing, as their bodies and identities change, yet the relationship perseveres. Elsewhere Nelson would like to dispense with names, stories, myths: shortly after the Argonaut reference, she quotes a poem by Michael Ondaatje:

> Kissing the stomach
> Kissing your scarred
> Skin boat. History
> Is what you've travelled on
> And take with you

The speaker of Ondaatje's poem accepts their lover's past, but Nelson wants to erase the tattoos that mark Harry's body. Maggie and Harry are not just Argonauts, but also the *Argo*, their skin boat. The idea of the Argonauts is slippery and often seen through multiple, complex filters, symbolizing both popular culture and erudite education, both masculine success and gender fluidity.

The emptiness of the Argonaut voyage and conventional assumptions about women's roles, men's missions and romance, are central to Emily Dickinson's short but powerful Argonaut poem:

> Finding is the first Act
> The second, loss,
> Third, Expedition for
> The 'Golden Fleece'
>
> Fourth, no Discovery –
> Fifth, no Crew –
> Finally, no Golden Fleece –
> Jason – sham – too.   (870)

This poem takes the five-act structure of Shakespearean tragedy and evokes the story of Medea and Jason. The negation of myth may well relate to Medea's sense of betrayal in Euripides, emphasized by the climactic revelation of Jason's deceptiveness. But the myth seems already to have unravelled itself, with no discovery, no object, no crew and finally no hero. Although the poem creates apparent order in the numbered acts, the relationship of acts to myth undermines that order: finding of what? The expedition comes after the loss; the lack of crew comes after the lack of discovery. The myth is woven and unravels simultaneously.

If the finding is Medea's finding of Jason, then the final line returns to the beginning. Perhaps Dickinson can be read as Jason, who first finds Medea and the Fleece, but then realizes that not only is his quest object lacking in any real value, but he has lost his own integrity in the process. Both these female, literary receptions take the quest as a metaphor for the search for meaning, particularly meaning in relationships, an inner quest, contrasting strongly with the more obvious, public-facing uses of the Argonaut brand.

Rationalizing the voyage

The temptation to explain myths or search for their historical origins, the 'germs of truth' behind the stories, has long been strong. Readers and writers like to feel more advanced and scientific than previous storytellers. Rationalizing interpretations of the journey of the Argonauts already existed in the fourth century BCE, probably much earlier. Around then Palaephatus, for example, wrote *Peri Apiston*, 'On unbelievable things', in which he explained away supernatural elements in myth. He did not doubt the fundamental historicity of the Argonaut legend, but made it more plausible by removing elements he perceived as unlikely. Palaephatus suggested the golden ram that carried Phrixus and Helle to Colchis was in fact a person called *Krios* (as Colavito translates, 'Mr. Ram'), their adviser; his 'fleece' is a valuable statue; Helle fell sick on the voyage and died. These interpretations look through the stories to a more plausible series of events that might have been corrupted in the telling to produce the stories we are familiar with. Palaephatus suggests that Phineus was really a blind man whose daughters squandered his property ('snatching' his wealth) and that Zetes and Calais were not really winged demi-gods, but instead neighbours who chased the daughters away. Diodorus Siculus is another important, ancient rationalizing interpreter. We have seen how he explained through names: the bulls Jason fought (Greek: *tauroi*) were actually Taurian guards. The dragon (*drakon*) was a powerful fighter called Drakon. Nearly every element of the story is susceptible to this sort of rationalizing explanation.

The ancient geographer Strabo also assesses the historicity of the Argonaut myth: he grew up in first-century BCE Pontus (modern Turkey) and travelled extensively throughout the ancient Mediterranean. In a section on Homeric geography, he argues against other ancient writers (naming Demetrius of Scepsis) that Homer was well aware of the tradition of the Argonautic myth. He comments on the relationship between Jason and Achilles, that causes Achilles to spare Lemnos, then ruled by Jason's son Euneus by Hypsipyle (Strabo *Geography* 1.2.38). The voyage to Colchis and even the return journey are 'things that are agreed upon by everyone'. Strabo finds the outward journey plausible, but also the larger wanderings, and points to evidence of its importance as a story among his contemporaries: that there is still a city called Aea on the Phasis; that Aeetes is locally held to have ruled there and the name is still current; that the Colchian region has considerable wealth in metals including gold; that a sanctuary of Phrixus still exists and that there are many sanctuaries of Jason in Armenia and Media, as well as in Sinope, the Propontis, Hellespont and Lemnos ('Jasonia'). Traces of the pursuit in place names and local traditions still exist in the first century BCE in Crete, Italy and the Adriatic. Strabo feels that elements of Odysseus' wanderings were based on those of the Argonauts, and in particular he suggests that Circe's island (Aeaea) is named after Aea, ruled by her brother Aeetes, and her reputation as a sorceress is derived from that of Medea (1.2.40). He treats the Argonauts and their journey as analogous to Odysseus and his journey in its relationship to history and reality.

Strabo has deeply influenced the tradition of rationalizing the Argonauts, although some scholars find Strabo overly reliant on myth for his interpretations of Homeric and pre-Homeric geography: Patterson, for instance, emphasizes his credulity.[5] Braund, however, in his study of ancient Georgia, largely follows Strabo.[6] As a scholar of Georgia, he is of course deeply committed to the association of the Argonaut myth with the area, from the earliest times, which is important to Georgian identity. Others, such as Colavito, are sceptical, arguing that the early myth portrayed a fantasy world not closely related to any particular geographical location.[7] I feel that ancient mythical traditions developed over a very long period: it is easy to underestimate the sophistication and complexity of oral cultures. All the evidence that we have, and that Strabo had, points to Colchis as an intrinsic part of the Argonaut story from an early period. It is possible that, like Phaeacia or Circe's Aeaea in the *Odyssey*, Aeetes' Aea was once a wholly or mostly mythical city, with no precise geographical location. However, it is equally likely that it was always associated with Colchis, and certainly for the purposes of nearly all the later traditions which we are examining, it was always located in Colchis. In the medieval tradition (and some children's books), it loses this association again as it becomes a mythical 'isle of Colchos'.

An important rationalizing contribution is *The Voyage of the Argonauts* (1925), by Janet Bacon, Director of Studies in Classics at Girton College, Cambridge (1925–35), and Principal of Royal Holloway College, University of London (1935–44). Her distinctive voice is concise, often tart, with a no-nonsense attitude to interpretations she considers implausible. The phrase 'Miss Harrison would have us believe ...' shows her ambivalence towards the work of Jane Harrison. She is intrigued by sweeping comparative theories, like that of Egypt as origin of all world history in Perry's 'Origin of magic and religion', but remains sceptical. If this theory 'holds good', she sees the *Argo* myth as 'a concentration of world history, a single embodiment of all the pioneers who went out to seek a distant treasure' (99–100). Bacon's fundamental aim is to separate out the 'kernel' of fact from the embellishments of myth's desire to explain and legend's exaggeration and ornamentation. For instance, she sees Orphism as an 'extraneous element' that can be removed from 'what essentially the story is'. Her methodology is similar to that of Homeric analysts, who separated out the 'original poem' from later intrusions, and she looks for 'internal credibility' (plausibility and internal consistency) and 'external credibility' ('correspond[ence] with what is known of the history of the period'), although acknowledging that history of the period is itself a work in progress. She sometimes assumes that the first time we encounter an element in our evidence must show when it was first associated with the story, but lack of evidence does not always equal evidence of absence. However, Bacon believes that Hercules had an early association with the Argonauts, 'earlier than the age of colonisation' (74). Her opinion of Jason is refreshingly forthright: 'Except for his youth and beauty, he is as unheroic as Aeneas' (91). She feels this 'is an argument for his reality' (91). This is oddly incompatible with her argument that post-Euripidean versions have de-heroized a previously heroic Jason, although later critics have also felt Apollonius' Jason was a 'relatable' human character.[8]

For me, Apollonius' Alexandrian poetics are crucial here: he is writing in response and reaction to both oversimplified ideas of Homeric heroism and Euripides' tragedy. The complexity of his characters is a key feature of his self-positioning in the epic genre. His Jason does have an *aristeia*, in the feat of the bulls and the Earthborns, but, because he is helped by a witch (unsanctioned supernatural power) rather than a goddess, he is never uncomplicatedly heroic.[9] Bacon's attitude to rationalizing interpretations is sceptical: she castigates nineteenth-century theorists of myth because they 'forget the details which are not easily accommodated to their theories' (46). She points out that many earlier rationalizations or symbolic interpretations account for the fleece but not the voyage (58). Bacon, like Braund, considers Strabo's evidence convincing, at least that gold was the likely motive for the voyage (64–6). But she also explores at length the connections between different possible return routes and the evidence for trade routes bringing amber from the north to the Mediterranean. Bacon analyses elements she finds plausible, in a methodical manner, taking into account the whole myth in its various chronological layers. Bacon's book influenced later authors, via Graves, who calls it 'a brief but most valuable book' (*Golden Fleece*: 454).

Novels in particular embrace the rationalizing mode, following the generic realism prominent in modern conceptions of the novel. Robert Graves uses the rationalizing accounts of Strabo and Diodorus extensively, following the latter's Phineus episode ('the historical background is provided by Diodorus', *GF* 455). He incorporates many elements of Strabo's Colchian excursus, including the detail that Styrus the Albanian is called a 'lice-eater' (lice-eaters mentioned at Strabo 11.2.1) and also that several tribes were considered 'filthy' (the 'lice-eaters' and the Soanes, at 11.2.19). Graves writes both novel and mythography (*The Greek Myths*, 1955), with unsurprising overlap. Perhaps more surprising is the subjectivity and misleading use of evidence in Graves's mythography, the similarities in his methods of writing in *The Greek Myths* and *The Golden Fleece*, particularly his use of mythography to justify or reassert narrative choices in the novel.[10]

The Apsyrtus episode and the return journeys in *The Greek Myths* provide revealing examples (241–4). Graves lists various versions of the Apsyrtus myth and summarizes Apollonius' version in some depth, with reasonable fairness, calling it 'the most circumstantial and coherent account' (241). He is not interested, though, in the relative dates of versions, and gives as much prominence to Valerius Flaccus as to Pindar.[11] Of the return journeys, he asserts '[t]hese are not, however, feasible routes. The truth is that the *Argo* returned by the Bosphorus' (242) as in his novel. Graves is an analyst and a positivist, but unlike Bacon relies on assertion rather than argument. In his 'explanatory notes' to *The Golden Fleece*, he lays out some of the geographical complexities of the different return routes, including possible confusion of the Ister (Danube) with the Istrus ('a trifling stream which enters the Adriatic near Trieste'). In these notes, he follows Diodorus, whose rationalizing interpretation underlies much in his novel. However, he does not give Diodorus his full support, saying 'Valerius Flaccus and Diodorus Siculus both record that Hercules sacked Troy on the outward, not the homeward, voyage; but this seems to be a mistake' (244). The conceptual problems with this analysis are considerable: first Graves claims unapologetically that we can know what is or is not 'true' in the *Argo* myth. Second, he asserts that his own speculation is correct, even to the point of claiming that ancient sources, sometimes very early, are 'mistaken'. For instance, he rejects Hesiod's account of the marriage of Jason and Medea and their return to Iolchos: 'Hesiod seems to have been mistaken: in Heroic times no princess was brought to her husband's home. He came to hers' (219). Further, he states tendentious interpretations as fact: 'Jason and Hercules are, in fact, the same character as far as the marriage-task myth is concerned' (240). The two myth cycles share common stories and motifs, but that is far from the two heroes 'in fact' being the same character.

Graves's *Greek Myths* is still so widely used that the project of unpicking it is important: for instance, when Deborah Levy (prize-winning literary author) is writing a book on Medusa, she takes Graves as her source of mythological knowledge.[12] In the Argonaut tradition few cite sources, but Ian Serraillier and James Riordan both mention Graves. Others may unconsciously echo him. We can see his pervasive and formative influence on the novels of Treece and Catran. Scholarship on Graves's *Greek Myths* is well aware of his practices: Ihm (2015) shows the basis of Graves's Goddess theory in the works of Bachofen, Frazer and Harrison, and its influence on modern goddess movements, and struggles not to condemn Graves for his fundamentally deceptive use of scholarly apparatus. Zajko (2015), in contrast, sees Graves's work as symptomatic of the interpenetration of scholarship and fiction, a creation, which is almost a parody, or hijacking, of academic modes. But Graves's literary authority is compelling and his storytelling seductive. His emphasis on matriarchy seems on the surface susceptible to feminist readings. But his investment in his own myth, both about himself and about Greece, is self-regarding, and his obsession with women's violent subjugation of men is ultimately misogynistic. There is a voyeurism to Graves's mythology, a salacious objectification of female power, that is ultimately disturbing, and which plays out even more obviously in the soft erotica of Treece's novel, so much influenced by Graves, and the sexualizations of the 2000 mini-series. Graves's positivism and rationalization conflicts with his attraction to symbolic readings of myth: for him, the symbolism equates to a historical reality, which only he can fully understand.

The rationalizing of the TV documentaries of Severin and Wood, on the other hand, relates much more closely to archaeological modes of explanation. Both use the physical realities of the landscape to ground their interpretations. Wood explores the 'Cave of Cheiron' and Severin explains the Clashing Rocks by the rushing currents of the Bosphorus.[13] Both also engage with local customs and stories current in the countries through which the Argonauts sailed. These local experts show the continued importance of the Argonaut myth for Greeks, Turks and Georgians alike. Both also involve other types of experts: Severin's naval architect friend Colin Mudie puzzles over the likely shape of the *Argo*'s keel (Severin 1985: 25–7), while Wood discusses the archaeology of metallurgy at the site of the Chalybes. The two projects have different aims: Severin is using experimental archaeology by reconstructing the *Argo* as a Mycenean boat from approximately 1200 BCE, to prove that a boat so small and frail could have made the journey from Iolchos to Colchis. His readings of Apollonius are detailed and often persuasive. Wood works with archaeologists and ancient historians to illustrate what the journey of the Argonauts might have been like, assuming it was a historical journey (or an amalgamation of a series of first voyages further and further towards the east through the Black Sea). Braund (1994) gives a reliable interpretation of recent archaeological evidence (much of it published in Georgian), and ancient historical accounts. Braund is pessimistic about our ability to uncover any truth behind early myths: all the surviving evidence is 'a drop in a dark ocean of ignorance' and he emphasizes the 'intricate variation' (10) in Greek myth, on local, civic, even family levels, even in 1000–500 BCE. We can never know for sure whether Jason existed, whether the Argonaut voyage is the story of one particular voyage, or a mixture of many, or pure fantasy.

Voyage as symbol

Beyond the search for kernels of historical truth, searchers desire other, arguably deeper, meanings. The Argonaut myth shows how approaches to myth have evolved. The late nineteenth century was the heyday of comparative mythology, as exploration and empire led to greater awareness of different cultures, rituals and stories, and greater desire for control over them. The desire to simplify and systematize, explain these cultural phenomena, manifested itself in wide-ranging, schematic and often unpersuasive theories. One which was popular, and had its roots in ideas of the Greeks and Romans, was the claim that all myth originated from sun worship, and explained celestial phenomena.[14] Solar myth was at its most popular in the form propagated by Max Müller (1823–1900).[15] Müller's argument drew on comparative linguistics to find sun-related imagery in a wide range of mythological names. Bacon outlines a solar interpretation of the Argonaut myth by Mannhardt in which he argues that the Fleece equates to the sun, which is located in the East. 'The ram who bears Phrixus and Helle away is the setting sun, which rises again and returns from the East when Jason recovers the fleece' (50). Medea is both daughter of the sun, and the moon goddess. Bacon comments 'These identifications can convince nobody who is not biased in favour of the solar myth'...'The story of the fleece does not satisfy the first test of a sun myth: it does not explain the movements of the sun' (51).

The sun is certainly important in Apollonius, where, for instance, Apollo dispels unnatural darkness on the island of Anaphe (AR 4.1694–1730). But it does not dominate or explain the essence of the Argonautic story. Versions such as Vegio and Cavalli's opera *Giasone* feature the Sun as a character, father of Aeetes. Moreau (1994: 91–6) outlines many elements read as solar in the Argonaut myth, and suggests Jason was originally a 'solar hero', deduced from Jason's hair as 'glowing locks' in Pindar (*Pythian* 4.82–3). This aspect of his argument was negatively reviewed, for instance by Dowden 1996. Moreau piles up possible connections but without explaining why they are significant, and the connections are often not convincing or distinctive. In Valerius, the stars outshine the sun, and catasterism (turning heroes into stars) is an important theme.[16] But ancient epics often have a cosmic element, along with other imagery, political, poetic and religious. Celestial imagery, including that of the sun and moon, was used by Hellenistic rulers to promote their power.[17]

The journey of the Argonauts, like all epic journeys, is often given a spiritual dimension.[18] The *Argonautica* has been read as a *katabasis*, a journey to the underworld.[19] Many epics feature such a journey, and some Argonaut versions dwell on it. For instance, the scenes in the *Orphic Argonautica* where Orpheus sacrifices to Hecate strongly recall the rites used by Odysseus in *Odyssey* 11 to interact with the dead. In Virgil's *Aeneid* book 6, Aeneas literally travels down into the underworld, while Odysseus seems to go to an otherworld, where he brings the dead to him. The difference between a ritual and spiritual journey and a literal journey is not always clear. *Katabasis* is also associated with Hercules and Orpheus in their mythology: Hercules steals Cerberus, the three-headed guardian of Hades, and Orpheus attempts to return his dead beloved, Eurydice, to the upper world. Theseus, too, goes down to the underworld to help his best friend, Pirithous, abduct Persephone, but must himself be rescued by Hercules.[20] *Katabasis* features in very early epic poetry, such as the story of Gilgamesh: but the epic of Gilgamesh also contains two other epic journeys, to kill the monster Humbaba and gain heroic fame, and to the garden of Utnapishtim to gain immortality. It is not clear that the Argonaut myth is more closely related to the former journey than that latter two.

Moreau (1994: 128–36) outlines elements of the Argonaut myth that he considers *katabatic*: various characters arguably have underworld connections;[21] the landscape through which they pass has 'infernal connections', for instance, the dark blue Cyanean Rocks (the colour is associated with the underworld, through serpents or horses), after which the heroes say they have been saved from Hades (AR 2.609–10); the cape of Acheron (although Aeneas also passes places associated with the underworld). The Argonauts lose two crew members, as if in a sacrifice. The death of Apsyrtus can be read as a sacrifice for safe return from the infernal region to the land of the living (except that in many versions they go even further into distant and dangerous territories after killing him, and indeed because of his death). Colavito (2014: 146) argues that 'a dramatic encounter with the Underworld is one of the epic hero's most important tasks, yet Apollonius neglected to assign one to Jason', so the whole journey must be one. But this argument has a number of problems: it assumes Apollonius represents the entirety of the ancient tradition, rather than selectively and tendentiously playing with it. We do not in fact know whether or not a *katabasis* was included in earlier oral *Argonauticas*. The *Orphic Argonautica* has stronger underworld connections. There could well have been a *katabasis* in the myth, but no clear and explicit reference to it has happened to survive. Another problem is that not all epics have a *katabasis*: the *Iliad*, for instance, does not. Other types of journey can also have meaning.

Some receptions emphasize the *katabatic* elements of the *Argonautica*: for instance, the Argonaut story of *Doctor Who* is called 'Underworld'. This four-part story from season 15 (1978) features a spacecraft from the 'Minyan' civilisation, captained by 'Jackson' (Jason), crewed by 'Herrick' (Hercules), 'Orfe' (Orpheus) and 'Tala' (Atalanta), trying to retrieve the genetic race banks needed to rebuild 'Minyos' (the Golden Fleece). They go under the surface of a planet, where they find 'Idmon' and 'Idas' trying to escape from a theocracy around an 'Oracle'. They frustrate an intended human sacrifice, defeat the 'dragons' (a defence system), destroy the Oracle and liberate both Fleece and subject population. The TV series *Atlantis* (2015) also contains a *katabasis* episode, in which Jason and Hercules defeat a monster and retrieve Pandora's Box for a threatening client. The underworld sets are re-used from the episodes of Jason's killing of the Minotaur and the Cyclops episode, with very similar rocky tunnels to those of *Doctor Who*'s 'Underworld'. *Atlantis* mashes together the Argonaut myth with the feats of Theseus, Hercules and Odysseus, three heroes who already undertake *katabases*. *Katabasis* is a theme resonant in the popular imagination, in which Greek myth plays a role in raising the stakes and creating spiritual significance.

In Moreau's analysis (1994: 117–42), a connection to death and rejuvenation reflects the Argonaut myth as journey of initiation. One type of initiation rite features young people moving from childhood to adulthood (rites of passage), and often involves some of the following elements: spatial separation from normality; hunting; inversions of polarities such as mortal/divine, human/ animal, male/female; figurative death and rebirth; marking out the character undergoing initiation as exceptional or different; a mentor, possibly with animal connections or an element of hybridity; the use of trickery or theft rather than outright shows of force or strength.[22] An example is the renowned (and possibly apocryphal) Spartan *krypteia* ritual (as described in Plutarch), in which young men went out into the countryside at night to assassinate *helots* (local serf population) and steal food to survive.[23] There is a stronger case for seeing initiation as a structuring narrative element of Apollonius' *Argonautica* in comparison to solar or cosmic imagery and *katabasis*: the majority of the Argonauts are young men, and older men are often treated as guides, advisers or mentors (such as Argos). Jason is young, as are Castor and Pollux, Zetes and Calais, the heroes who undertake the feats and adventures. There is frequent imagery of crossing boundaries or entering new territories (the Clashing Rocks obviously, but events at Colchis also involve multiple penetrations of sacred spaces). The return also features crossings, from entering the mouth of the Danube, to escaping from Lake Triton, with striking obstacles, from the Wandering Rocks to Talos, guardian of the Cretan harbour. Gender reversal or instability is also a key theme, as in Lemnos and with Medea, and exploits are often achieved through ruses, rather than straightforward force. The text itself tells us that this is a story about becoming glorious: when they elect him leader, Jason promises to protect their *kudos* ('glory', 1.351) as much as their return; Idmon insists on undertaking the journey despite his own imminent death, to gain 'great fame' (1.447). Hercules promises them 'renown' (1.869) to persuade them to leave Lemnos. Becoming glorious is not quite the same as becoming an adult hero, and, in fact, these young men want to go beyond what is expected of a 'normal' life, like Achilles in the *Iliad*. However, they are initiated into the elite of heroic epic. Motifs of initiation permeate the particular heroism displayed by Jason, including the ritual acts undertaken to make Medea's charms effective, and enhance the obliqueness of Apollonius' version, by making it unclear how much Jason is responsible for his own success.

Initiation, however, does not explain everything about the myth, nor is it central to every version. Even Valerius' Jason is much older and more mature than that of Apollonius. The 1963 Jason is a mature man with a beard, motivated more by desire to prove himself against the gods than to gain glory. Initiation motifs could partly explain the popularity of the myth for writers of children's and young adult fiction. Kingsley picked for *The Heroes* three myths, all of which focus on young men who journey from home to prove themselves as heroes and rulers: Theseus, Perseus and Jason. Both Jason and Medea are often represented as young characters (for instance in the 2000 TV mini-series or in Treece's novel). In some of the picture books, such as Bradman and Ross, or Pirotta and Lewis, they are presented as children.

Psychoanalysis has also been a major force in the interpretation of myth: Moreau (1994: 271–94) combines his survey of psychoanalytical readings of Jason and Medea with structuralist readings, which look for binary oppositions between fundamental structures in human thought and society, just as psychoanalytical readings hope to unearth the deep structures of the human psyche. Most psychoanalytical readings of the Argonautic stories focus on Medea, especially her various killings.[24] Diel (1966: 171–82), however, reads Jason as a hero made banal by his lack of energy: he is carried along by his desires and does not strive towards the spiritual or the sublime. The promise of youth is crushed by the emptiness of glory, when the *Argo* falls on Jason. In Moreau's own interpretation (1994: 283–92), the story reflects three 'fundamental crimes', parricide, incest and cannibalism, all of which together constitute the 'consumption of the same' (*consummation du même*, 288). For this to work, he needs to prioritize the version in which Medea kills her father, although Bécache (1982) views all her victims as substitutes for her father. The insertion of incest and cannibalism is rather artificial. However, later versions, such as Treece and the 2000 TV series, make incest between Medea and Apsyrtus a theme. Gardner's 1973 poem has a clear interest in psychoanalytical readings, especially when, for instance, Jason's rivals for the Corinthian princess transform into snakes.

The Argonauts' quest as a journey into the soul or a journey of spiritual development also attracts artists: for instance, Gustave Moreau's 1865 painting *Jason* in the symbolist tradition (Fig. 7.1). This painting shows an androgynous Jason, dependent on Medea and her magic (symbolized by the phial in her right hand, see below p. 195). While Medea gazes at Jason, her left hand on his shoulder in a proprietorial fashion, Jason gazes at the broken spear with which he has just killed the eagle, guardian of the fleece, which is his claim to masculinity, success, heroism and immortality. Cooke argues that the painting is a narrative allegory, evoking the dependence of masculinity on wily and potentially violent femininity.[25] However, *Jason* was exhibited in the same year as Moreau's painting *The Young Man and Death* (1865, Fogg Museum, Cambridge MA), a painting which also depicts a young man standing in front of a woman, full length and victorious. This painting was begun in 1856, the year in which Moreau's mentor Théodore Chassériau died. The portrayal of Chassériau, 'idealized almost beyond recognition', according to Cooke (2008: 401) reflects 'the abstract concepts of death, time and glory'. Jason, too, represents the desire to triumph over death and time by gaining glory, the major theme of earlier versions, such as Grillparzer's

Fig. 7.1 Gustave Moreau, *Jason et Medée*, 1865. Museé d'Orsay. Available at: https://commons.wikimedia.org/wiki/File:Moreau_-_Jason_et_M%C3%A9d%C3%A9e.jpg (accessed 23 August 2019).

trilogy or the more unrelentingly self-absorbed Corinthian Jason of the 1635 *Toison d'Or* by Corneille.[26]

An alternative artistic approach is to see the Argonauts as representing the artistic endeavour itself. The German expressionist painter Max Beckmann completed a triptych entitled *The Argonauts* shortly before he died in 1950, originally called *The Artists*, in which he reflects on his earlier painting, the life of art and the possibility of transcendence (Fig. 7.2).[27] Of the three panels, the left features a dark painter intensely focusing on painting a partly dressed female model, who holds a sword and crouches on a mask-like helmet (resembling Beckmann's head). This female figure evokes Medea, but her power is a performance: she is model not agent. The central panel shows two young men, heroically naked, on a beach: interpreters have seen them as Orpheus, who has put down his lyre, and Jason, holding a phoenix.[28] They confront a bearded, old

Fig.7.2 *The Argonauts* by Max Beckmann, 1949.

man, thought to be Glaucus, rising from the sea, whose head is inserted through the rungs of a ladder, which leads up to the sky, where we see a moon eclipsing the sun and two red planets. The right panel shows four female musicians, playing together or perhaps rehearsing: they might evoke the Sirens, or act as chorus. Young men naked on the beach feature in one of Beckmann's first major works, *Young Men at the Sea* (1905, Weimar). The ladder also appears elsewhere, for instance in *Beginning* (from 1948–9, in the Metropolitan Museum of Art, New York).[29] The ladder and the phoenix both represent a spiritual journey and a sense of renewal. Glaucus prophesies to the Argonauts, and the eclipse of the sun presents potential upheaval as opportunity.[30] Lackner describes the central message as one of hope: 'the dreamer as a hero ... has conquered the nightmarish aspects of life' ... 'eros and aggression ... are sublimated into a spiritual adventure.'[31] This painting (or interpretations of it, at least) uses the Argonaut myth to reflect on the artist's journey, venturing beyond the normal bounds of life and achieving transcendence or immortality, but with potential violence and tragedy lurking beneath the achievement. Both Moreau and Beckmann hint at the artist's mystical, even psychagogic powers, to go beyond the bounds of everyday life and into the life of the soul in the universe, and to take others with them, through Greek myth. The *Argo*, too, can perform this function.

Rationalizing the Golden Fleece

The Argonauts' journey inspires multiple interpretations; the Golden Fleece is even more evocative and multivalent. Jason Colavito outlines twenty different interpretations on his website (and promises the 'truth' in his book).[32] I will focus on those which influence the tradition, beginning with rationalizations, then symbolic interpretations. The Golden Fleece is the object of Jason's quest. It was the fleece of the ram that rescued Phrixus and Helle. In many versions, Phrixus sacrificed the ram when he arrived in Colchis. It is usually represented as a sheep-skin with the head and horns of a ram, either with a golden fringe, the skull and horns of the ram gilded, or entirely gold. The Fleece is so important or valuable that it is worth journeying outside the boundaries of the known world.

Probably the most influential rationalization of the Golden Fleece is that of Strabo (*Geography* 11.2.19), who claims that the Soanes, from the mountains above Dioscurias, use fleeces to pan for gold in their rivers. 'It is said that in their country gold is carried down by the mountain-torrents, and that the barbarians obtain it by means of perforated troughs and fleecy skins, and that this is the origin of the myth of the golden fleece.' Strabo indicates an anecdotal basis for this claim ('it is said'), and some uncertainty about which tribe actually does it (Soanes or Iberians). However, despite (or because of?) these uncertainties, his rationalization has been widely accepted and popularized, for instance by Gibbon in his *Decline and Fall of the Roman Empire*.[33] Braund (1994: 24–5), however, is not convinced: he points out that the 1946 anthropological fieldwork which apparently established the continued use of this method in modern Georgia in fact reports anecdotes told by 'three elderly mountain men', who may well themselves have been familiar with the myth and Strabo's rationalization.[34] The archaeological evidence for Georgia's wealth in gold dates from the fifth century BCE and later, and there is very little at all before the seventh century BCE. Probably by the time of Apollonius, Colchis was already perceived as wealthy, with a special connection to gold, so this theory may have attached itself to the idea of the Golden Fleece when the myth already existed.

The association with gold panning, gold mining and wealth in the form of gold is enduring. Men who prospected for gold in the California Gold Rush of 1848–50, especially the '49ers' (those who arrived in 1849) were called Argonauts.[35] The Argonaut gold mine near Jackson, California, was the site of a gold mining disaster: in 1922, 47 gold miners were trapped in a fire deep underground and died. A memoir of life as a Californian Argonaut, by the Belgian Jean-Nicolas Perlot, privately published in 1897, gives a vivid account of the period.[36] Works of fiction about the gold rush have used the name Argonauts, such as Bret Harte's short story collection *Tales of the Argonauts* (1875), and more recently, Suzanne Lilly's series of novels 'The California Argonauts', which starts with *Gold Rush Girl* (2014).

Others saw the general wealth of the Colchians as the voyage's goal. The Roman encyclopaedist Pliny the Elder, discussing gold, presents the legendary wealth of Saulaces, early king of Colchis: 'Saulaces the descendant of Aeetes had already reigned in Colchis, who is said to have come on a tract of virgin soil in the country of the Suani and elsewhere and to have dug up from it a great quantity of gold and silver, his realm being moreover famous for golden fleeces. We are also told of his gold-vaulted ceilings and silver beams and columns and pilasters, belonging to Sesostris King of Egypt whom Saulaces conquered' (33.15). Gold discovered in the ground, probably mining rather than archaeological finds, is connected with golden fleeces (probably referring to Strabo) and the vast wealth displayed in the palace. Colchis is assimilated to a Near Eastern monarchy. Treece uses this rationalization: his Argonauts return with a ship-load of gold. William Morris, too, focuses frequently on material goods as a measure of success, and emphasizes the wealth surrounding the Argonauts, particularly that of Colchis.[37] In this, he evokes Lefèvre's account, which also focuses on banquets and material goods (Pelias' banquet, 69–71; Aeetes' banquet, 114–16). In contrast, Kingsley argues against this interpretation: 'And why they went I cannot tell; some say that it was to win gold. It may be so; but the noblest deeds which have been done on earth, have not been done for gold' (49).

The Argonauts are also used as an image of materialism and profit-seeking in general: for instance, the British pop band XTC produced a song entitled 'Jason and the Argonauts' on their 1982 album *English Settlement* (Virgin). The swirling music evokes the alienation of capitalism, and the lyrics equate the golden fleece with 'human riches'. Erotic betrayal ('the two-faced man ... breaking his wife's heart') mixes with disappointment in the world and returns to the ultimately fruitless achievement of fame and wealth in the refrain ('human riches I'll release'). Similarly, the Polish novelist, Eliza Orzeszkowa, uses the idea of the Argonauts, in her 1900 novel *Argonauci*, to present a rich man who destroys his family in his greed for money, success and social status.

More specifically, the Golden Fleece can represent wealth gained through sheep farming or wool production. Biologists have argued that the Colchian area could have produced sheep with literally golden fleeces: famine might mean sheep ate olive leaves, suffered jaundice which would lead to excess bilirubin, hence golden-coloured wool.[38] However, Colchis is not associated with wool production in the ancient world, compared for instance to Baetica.[39] Later wool-producing cultures, however, use the Golden Fleece to symbolize wealth and power gained through wool. For instance, the English poet John Dyer (1699–1757) wrote a four-book poem in blank verse called *The Fleece* (1757), in which he used the Argonauts and the Golden Fleece to mythologize sheep farming, wool production and trading. The mythographer Bulfinch includes Dyer's description of the departure of the Argonauts in his *Mythology*. There are at least nineteen pubs in England and Wales called 'The Golden Fleece', although the name is not in the fifty most popular names.[40] The name is associated with agriculture and the wool trade, as can be seen by the variants 'Fleece', and 'Plough and Fleece'. In Australia, Tom Roberts's 1894 painting of sheep shearing was named *The Golden Fleece* (Art Gallery of New South Wales, Sydney) to honour the wool industry, and the labour of shearers. This shows how a literal rationalization ('the Golden Fleece was a sheep's fleece') can also be used symbolically (to represent prosperity and nobility gained through sheep farming).

More obscure and outlandish rationalizations include the idea that the Golden Fleece was a book written on parchment (*vellum* was made from animal skin, usually that of calves) with instructions for alchemists on how to make gold, or even how best to illuminate letters.[41] Some rationalizations require apparatus more implausible than Greek religion. Colavito enjoyed busting the 'misuse' of the Argonaut myth by Robert Temple in *The Sirius Mystery* (1976).[42] He summarizes it as follows: 'that the entire Jason myth originated in a memory of amphibious space frogs from a planet orbiting the star Sirius arriving on earth to teach humanity the arts of civilization.' These theories, extreme and sometimes outlandish, nevertheless share Valerius' sense that the Argonaut myth has wider historical significance.

Golden Fleece as symbol

Wealth and prosperity, while important in themselves, also contribute to power and stability. It is hard to separate out literal understandings of the Golden Fleece from its symbolic aspects, which include fertility and rain-making, healing power, kingship, a sacred past and national identity. The idea of the Fleece as bringer of rain and solution to famine was already current in the mid-nineteenth century. Forchhammer proposed that the Golden Fleece represented a rain

cloud which is brought to Greece by the East Wind, basing his interpretation on
the name 'Nephele' ('cloud'), the mother of Phrixus and Helle, and the story of
their sacrifice as a response to famine (after Ino parched the seeds to create it).[43]
This theory attracted some later versions: it is central to Evslin's 1986 novel, for
instance, where Jason must bring the fleece back to Iolchos to prevent a famine.
When he arrives 'the land was stricken with drought' (153). He calls on Zeus with
'the power of the Ram, the power to call rain out of the dry sky' (155). In his
paratext (162–5), Evslin emphasizes his research ('having undergone the
privileged ordeal of a classical education'), but his description of the 'seven
voyages' of 'pirate kings', 'all happening about four thousand years ago' to reclaim
the 'sacred relic' rather evokes a loose interpretation of Graves's approach.
Fertility ritual is also central to Pasolini's *Medea*, where the sacred fleece, a ram's
fleece, with gilded horns, is kept in a cave at the top of a mountain. In the 1963
film, the fleece has magical healing power: Medea takes an arrow in the back, and
Jason places it over her to reanimate her. The gold shimmers as the magic
takes effect. The 2000 mini-series makes the Fleece central to its denouement.
When Pelias murders Acastus to steal the fleece, it loses its golden sheen,
fading from gold to grey. As Medea tries to trick Pelias through his desire for
immortality, Jason invades the throne room, killing the guards and demanding
of Pelias: 'Has [the fleece] brought you your heart's desire? Has its power
revived you?' He denies that it has any magic power, 'except that imagined by
those who seek it'. Pelias offers Jason the fleece, claiming that his mind has
been made mad by it, seeming to reject it. But his 'blessing', given with a hug, as
the audience know from the death of Acastus five minutes previously, is a
deceptive move to cover a stab in the back. This time, however, Jason anticipates
him, grabs his hand, and instead turns the dagger on him. 'My destiny is to
rule,' he asserts, following through on his earlier claim that 'we make our own
destiny'. Virtually no other version crowns Jason successful ruler of Iolchos,
so the scriptwriters indeed make a special destiny for this Jason. The fleece
remains discarded on the floor. The healing element from the 1963 film has
been transmuted into rejuvenation, a mytheme important already in ancient
versions of the Iolchos episodes, where Medea promises to rejuvenate Pelias
and actually does so for Aeson. This is particularly prominent in Ovid's
Metamorphoses and Morris. The twenty-first-century twist is Jason's rejection of
the fleece and assertion of his own self-determination. The 2000 film melds
together fleece as sacred object, fleece as magical vector of healing and
rejuvenation (or even immortality), fleece as symbol of royal power with fleece
as empty signifier.

Immortality, or the continuing existence of the species, features in several science fiction versions. In *Doctor Who* 'Underworld', the fleece is a genetic databank that will enable the Minyans to re-found their race. Kneupper makes the fleece a collection of genetic data, but one that will allow advances in medicine, or in the wrong hands threaten the lives of millions. Sawyer's novel, too, has a genetic databank to re-found the human race. In the 1958 *Hercules* film, the Fleece preserves the information of who killed Aeson, along with his instructions to his son, literally written in blood. Here and elsewhere, as in the alchemical interpretation, the Fleece represents knowledge. In Karl Klyne's *Jason and the Astronauts*, the quest object is a databank of researches revealing the existence of a secret alien organization, the Astronauts.

Knowledge is a crucial aspect of maintaining power, and the data in *Jason and the Astronauts* belonged to the theocratic ruler of the interplanetary system. Source of knowledge, symbol of fertility, ability to call rain, even power of healing: the fleece is almost always a creator or guarantor of royal power. Whoever has the fleece has the right to be king. This is the significance of the object in the vast majority of our ancient texts. It is also the preferred interpretation of ancient historians, such as Braund, and archaeologists, such as Lordkipanidze.[44] Colavito's preferred truth about the Golden Fleece, as promised to readers on his website (the 'startling new theory' and 'the truth behind the myth', http://www.argonauts-book.com/the-golden-fleece.html [accessed 9 June 2019]), combines the Fleece as purificatory object with posited Near Eastern origins as a golden robe of royal power or divinity.[45] In surviving ancient accounts, however, there is no real evidence of the fleece having a purificatory function, and taking the fleece or de-railing the pursuit often leads to pollution and itself requires purification (usually by Circe, but sometimes by Orpheus). Colavito's emphasis on rebirth as an aspect of royal power has the virtue of integrating the early visual evidence, such as the Douris cup, but his solution relies too much on speculative reconstructions of the myth's origins to convince (if indeed there should or could be one solution).

In later traditions, the Golden Fleece certainly did function as a symbol of royal (or ducal) power. Most striking in this respect is the Order of the Golden Fleece, founded by Philip the Good, Duke of Burgundy, in 1430. Dominguez emphasizes that the duke's attachment to the Jason story persisted despite resistance from the church, who felt that Jason was not an appropriate mythological patron, being both a pagan and morally suspect.[46] Dominguez suggests a connection with the Crusades: 'the Duke saw … great parallels with the aims he had for his new Order: the assembly of a group of worthy knights, …

the building of an armada, and the recovery of a valuable belonging from an Eastern force' (89). Membership of the Order of the Golden Fleece represented the highest chivalric honour. Later, Philip the Good's grandson Charles, emperor of Spain, transferred the Order to the Spanish monarchy, where it continued to have enormous importance and influence.[47]

Conclusion

This chapter gives a flavour of the massive variety of interpretations of the Argonaut voyage and its object, the Golden Fleece. The search for a definitive 'meaning' results in a rich and varied tradition of mythological interpretation. For me, myth is by definition multiple, a story that has significance for communities down the ages. The Argonaut myth is an excellent exemplar of this multiplicity, since the tradition is not dominated by one text or one interpretation. It shows the ways that mythical or legendary journeys remain resonant: crossings of thresholds imply personal, spiritual and historical turning points. The quest object symbolizes the ability to gain or sustain wealth, power and reputation. The Argonaut myth has particular resonance for explorers, sea-farers, crusaders, prospectors and farmers: wool and gold, along with initiation, healing, art and magic, shape a tradition that goes far beyond the ancient Mediterranean, Near Eastern and Black Sea communities and continues to give meaning in areas as diverse as gender identity, science, sport and adventurous travel.

Findings and Endings

This book has travelled a long way in search of the Argonauts, from the distant past to the present day, across continents, genres and media. It has asked some key questions: how do we draw the line between myth and reception? What is special about the Argonaut tradition? What can study of the Argonauts tell us about the workings of myth? How central are the extant ancient versions, especially Apollonius' epic *Argonautica* and Euripides' tragic *Medea*? How important are less well-studied genres, such as mythography and children's literature? How much variation is there in the myth and does that level of variation change through time? What different uses have people found for the Argonaut story and why?

The idea of 'The Myth', that there is one standard or orthodox version and any deviation from it is inauthentic, while alien to professional scholars of myth, nevertheless asserts and reasserts itself in different cultural contexts, from student essays to film reviews, to paratexts produced by authors and creators. Whichever is the version first encountered is often felt to be the 'true' one. Even those who would deny they held this belief might still reject versions they consider insufficiently authentic (such as the 2000 TV mini-series). The Argonaut traditions clearly show huge variation from the earliest beginnings to the latest incarnations.

Ideas of intertextuality (theories of relationships between cultural products) can help us understand the workings of myth too: for instance, 'code model' and 'exemplary model' in Conte 1986. The 'code model' is the 'classic' work that underlies the genre (or tradition) as a whole; the second is the 'proximate' work, most relevant to a particular episode (or version). So for Virgil's *Aeneid*, Homer's *Iliad* and *Odyssey* are code models, while in a particular instance, say the image of Aeneas' restless mind as the flickering light on a basin of water (*Aen.* 8.18–25), another more immediate text, here Apollonius' *Argonautica* 3.755–60, is the main inspiration.[1] This pattern often lies beneath various texts in the Argonautic tradition. So Kingsley uses the *Orphic Argonautica* as his code model, his ideal, 'classic' Argonaut story, but also reacts against Hawthorne's *Tanglewood Tales*. Where the *OA* does not cover his preferred version of the story, he uses other texts, including Pindar, Apollonius and Valerius. Here we can see the hold of 'The Myth' on the tradition itself: creators seek authenticity, and the canonical story tends to reassert itself. The tradition operates under contrary pressures: constant innovation and adaptation, to address new audiences and situations, in tension with desire for authenticity. Sometimes a paradigm shift occurs, as with Euripides' introduction of Medea's child-killing, or Harryhausen's skeletons, but even those shifts can be challenged, and can wax and wane in importance and influence.

These shifts and tensions change across media and genres; intertextuality, as with the term 'texts', does not just refer to written cultural products. Mythographers and storytellers must choose which version to follow (and how many to include), as must painters, film-makers, even the producers of toys. The Playmobil Argonaut ship features Hercules prominently, as well as Orpheus with his lyre, along with Jason and Atalanta, most resembling the 2000 mini-series, but notably not making Orpheus black.[2] The 2000 mini-series has Harryhausen's 1963 *Jason and the Argonauts* as its 'classic' version, but also shows similarities to Pasolini, Morris and perhaps the Usborne retelling by Felicity Brooks. The intentions of the creators are not key here;[3] rather versions reflect the shapes of the tradition at that particular point. Unconscious resemblances are just as important as conscious ones, if not more so. The resonances that pull people in different directions, possibly against their better judgement (Zimmerman's skeletons, Whitehead's zombies), reveal a text's relationship to its cultural context. Some resemblances must be independently created parallels; we can never tell the full story, either, because so many versions exist, interacting with each other and other myths.

Different genres create different expectations: mythographers have responsibility to convey the truth about previous traditions (a responsibility to which Graves, for one, pays only lip service). The internet age makes available much reference material and also many previous versions, so the 'classic' status of any text is always liable to slippage or rehabilitation. Scholarly recuperations, for instance the revival of Valerius Flaccus, can have a real effect. Different periods have different expectations of authenticity: the eclecticism of medieval romance is not unlike that of 'sword and sandal' films or twenty-first-century TV. Some versions, and Valerius is one, are more prominent in the tradition than expected: Valerius is notable in Grillparzer, Kingsley and Graves. A single influential champion can change the fortunes of a verion's history: for instance, Kingsley is responsible for the influence of the *Orphic Argonautica*. Other versions seem more idiosyncratic, the end of a particular path, not taken up by later versions: Vegio; the opera *Giasone*; John Gardner; Bernard Evslin.

Creators often rely on un-signposted low prestige texts for knowledge, consciously or unconsciously. Mythography is very important, from Apollodorus to Bulfinch, from Graves to Wikipedia. Children's versions, and children's mythography play a key role: so Colum, Lancelyn Green, the D'Aulaires show the state of the myth in the twentieth century and transmit it to others. The most important children's texts in the Argonaut tradition, though, are Nathaniel Hawthorne and Charles Kingsley, transforming the story into a children's classic, and underpinning the twentieth- and twenty-first-century flowering of Anglophone children's Argonaut stories.[4]

The Jason tradition and the Medea tradition are interconnected throughout. The oral (and early written, but not extant) epic Argonaut tradition, which was the basis for Euripides' play in the first place, is re-worked in most detail by Apollonius' post-Euripidean *Argonautica*. The epic and dramatic traditions cannot easily be separated: Grillparzer, for instance, had long wanted to produce a more positive version of the tragic Medea, and was inspired by his reading of Valerius and Apollonius. For him the epic tradition is back-story for tragedy, as in Pasolini's *Medea*, and Christa Wolf's novel *Medea*. For epic poems, tragedy lurks in the future: any post-Euripidean *Argonautica* cannot avoid responding and reacting to the Euripidean tradition. However, the 1963 Harryhausen film, which dominates the second half of the twentieth century, is a fundamentally un-Euripidean text, as is the 2000 mini-series. Episodes vary, too: the Apollonian tradition dominates the Phineus episode, for instance, but the Apsyrtus episode shows the prominence of the tragic tradition, filtered through Ovid. Pindar dominates the beginnings of the story and Euripides the end. The flexible nature of journey myths, with their episodic structure, allows creators to pick and choose, to excerpt and re-order, contributing to the ongoing complexity and live variation of the tradition.

The balance of the tragic and the epic in the Argonautic tradition comes out in different endings. Apollonius' epic simply finishes with the arrival back at Iolchos: the Argonauts have reached home, and that is it. All the events to come, the slaughter of Pelias by his daughters under the influence of Medea's deceptive persuasions, her killing of her rival and her own children at Corinth, are reduced to foreshadowings. Valerius' text ends even more prematurely, part way through book 8 (judging by the average number of lines in the other books), and in the middle of the quarrel between Jason and Medea.[5] This is almost certainly the result of textual transmission, rather than the sudden death of Valerius. A continuation exists, by the Renaissance Latin poet Giovanni Battista Pio, which completes the poem, somewhat disappointingly, with a close adaptation of Apollonius.[6] But even assuming it was not intended, Valerius' existing ending brings out his trajectory towards the Euripidean and Senecan Medea. Even more premature is the ending of the 1963 film, which, like Hawthorne, breaks off at the moment of successful departure from Colchis, avoiding all the morally complex events of the return journey.

Apollonius' ending is largely neutral in mood: no celebration or rejoicing, no tragedy, just a water-carrying race at Aegina, and the phrase 'gladly you stepped out onto the shores of Pagasae'. The *Orphic Argonautica* is similar, but with the focus on Orpheus, who has purified the Argonauts (1366–8) and now sacrifices at Taenaros before returning to Thrace. None of the later versions feel satisfied with just stopping, in this Apollonian manner. Some create a happy ending: Lefèvre brings Jason and Medea back together, ruling in his father's kingdom of Myrmidon. In Caxton's translation (updated): 'they lived together in great love and concord and had many fair children together that reigned after them'. This comes after many ups and downs: including Jason de-enchanting himself and returning to his first love; Medea killing Jason's son; Aeson killing Jason's wife; Medea herself living in a wood in Thessaly, where she repents, they eventually meet and are reconciled. The 2000 mini-series ends more simply: Jason kills Pelias, takes the throne and marries Medea, in a valley with flower petals and happy subjects. The tableau evokes the Victorian painter Alma Tadema, resembling *The Roses of Heliogabalus* (1888). The palette has changed dramatically from browns at the gathering of the Argonauts, to browns and reds in Colchis, to pinks, creams and pale blue in this final scene. Many find this ending inauthentic, but one of the earliest pieces of evidence for the Jason and Medea myth, Hesiod's *Theogony* 992–1002, presents the main outcome of the voyage as their marriage and son. Children's versions with similar endings include: Zeff (feast at Iolchos, where the couple are married, crowned and celebrated); Yomtov (Jason reclaiming his throne and making Medea his queen); and Jeffrey (Jason and Medea happily married in Corinth). Hoena/Estudio Haus present an image of their wedding complete with tiered skirts and flower petals, but in an understated 'Ancient Fact' box admit that later 'Jason and Medea separated'.

William Morris's *Life and Death of Jason* incorporates numerous epic gestures of closure, that continue up to Jason's death. Both Lefèvre and Morris are writing lives, beginning with birth, ending with death. After the death of Pelias, Morris presents a whole book of arrival, coronation and games (book 16), with flowers and Medea in her daintiest costume. Book 17 feels like an epilogue, separating the Corinthian story of Euripides' play and Jason's abandonment of Medea, when he falls in love with Glauce. The final touch is Jason's death on the beach, crushed by the sternpost of *Argo*, here also a beam from Pelias' palace, a belated revenge.

This version of Jason's death is the tragic ending: Euripides' *Medea* flies off in her dragon chariot to sanctuary at Athens. But in her final speech she also vows to set up tombs and rites for her children, and prophesies Jason's death: 'And you, as is proper for a coward, will die a coward's death, (*kakos kakōs*, 'a bad man badly') struck on the head by a remnant of the *Argo*' (Eur. *Medea* 1386–7). This is the most popular ending amongst children's versions, as well as the novels of Graves and Treece.[7] Some temper this by returning to Hera's overarching divine viewpoint, as when the 2000 film goes up to the gods for the final frame: Gunderson finishes with Hera's pleasure at Pelias' death, and Zarabouka too focuses on Hera's revenge achieved. The gods provide authorization and closure beyond mortal concerns.

This is the Jason-focused ending, but others put Medea back in the limelight. For instance, Zimmerman's play closes with catasterisms. She goes beyond the traditions of Argo, Castor and Pollux becoming constellations (as in Valerius Flaccus) to reinterpret the signs of the modern zodiac as aspects of the Argonaut myth, ending with Medea as Virgo. Others use catasterism to temper the tragic ending: for instance, Naden ends with the starry sky, and Seraillier's final paragraph links the constellation Argo to the enduring memory of Jason's story. Pirotta closes with a joyful Medea, now free from Colchis (as in Diodorus). Grillparzer's *Medea*, the culmination of his Argonaut trilogy, ends with her decision to dedicate the fleece at Delphi, from where Phrixus originally stole it. Still, she mocks Jason for the emptiness of both fleece and heroic glory:

> Behold the emblem here for which you strove,
> That seemed your laurel crown and happiness!
> What is earth's happiness? ... A shadow!
> What is earth's laurel crown? ... A dream!

Grillparzer, Medea 2364–7

Others send Jason on further journeys or defer finishing: Gardner's poem sends him into the far north, still seeking Medea. Treece has him wandering Greece as a beggar, finally returning to Corinth, to be crushed by the *Argo*.

Graves, maximalist as ever, accumulates epic and tragic endings in two concluding chapters: first, he tells the aftermath of Pelias' death. Medea persuades Jason to pass the crown to Acastus, who banishes all associated with his father's death. In a gesture of reconciliation, he holds games for Pelias (traces of which remain in early Greek evidence), and allows all the Argonauts to compete. Hercules returns and acts as king of the games. This combines Morris's book of coronation, celebration and games, with tragic traditions that Acastus, not Jason, took over the throne. The remaining Argonauts help Jason row the *Argo* to Corinth, where he claims the throne in Medea's name and they become rulers, creating an epic ending. Graves confines Jason's death and Euripides' *Medea* to the very last 'what happened next' chapter, an epilogue, like that of Kingsley, which details the fates of all the Argonauts. Medea ultimately returns to Colchis, deposes Perses and rules there in peace. Versions of a similar epilogue are in Evslin, West and Catran.

Kingsley does not create a celebratory epic ending, but is the one to sanctify the move from storytelling to teaching in his epilogue. He reacts against Hawthorne's optimistic 'cutting short' of the story: 'I wish that I could end my story pleasantly; but it is no fault of mine that I cannot. . . . though the heroes were purified at Malea, yet sacrifices cannot make bad hearts good' (123). This last sentence corrects the *OA*, which emphasizes purification. Instead, Kingsley relates the tragic endings: the death of Pelias, Euripides' *Medea* ('it has been sung in noble poetry and music', 124). Medea's revenge is 'too terrible to speak of here'. Instead, he bypasses the fates of the Argonauts for the death and catasterism of Chiron. The last paragraph sends his child readers to the *Iliad* and *Odyssey*. Kingsley comes back to epic at the last, emphasizing the continuity and connectedness of Greek myth. Caxton, too, in his translation of Lefèvre, adds a final note as translator, pointing out that Lefèvre could have included still more about Jason's life. He refers to Boccaccio's story in which Jason and Medea returned to Colchis and Jason went on to travel and conquer in the Near East. This version of the further journey of Jason explains the existence of 'Jasonia' temples in that area and assimilates him still more closely to the crusaders. Caxton's translation is more self-consciously historicizing than Lefèvre's original, whose end signals awareness of its own fictionality.

Apollonius is far from central to later endings, and Euripides is more influential. But the shift in telling Jason's death, from Medea's delight in his downfall to the neutral, even regretful, voice of an external narrator (or in the case of Treece and Colston West, the voice of Jason himself, which breaks off at the moment of death) re-slants the Euripidean version. The Argonaut tradition attracts maximalist writers like Morris and Graves, who want to include every possible version and detail. The endings show how the Argonaut story complicates masculinity, heroism and success, in its distillation through its many variations.

What of the relationship between myth and reception? The difference between the two is in the eye of the beholder. Myth is transmitted, handed down, adapted and re-shaped; texts are received, versions are re-worked. Arguably, all the Argonautic traditions as we have them are reception. There is no original version. Each intervention or cultural artefact is grounded in those that came before, because we simply do not have detailed knowledge of the earliest mythic traditions. Literary studies have shifted from focusing on the author's life, to his intentions, to responses of different readers, to historical and social movements, locating meaning in the interactions between text, context and reception.[8] Similarly, the study of mythology can focus on origins and sources, or on transmission and cultural history.[9] The idea of an original storyteller setting down an account of a historical expedition is persistent: but it is just as likely that the extant early Greek material already represents the fusion of many different motifs, story elements, rituals, beliefs and ideas, which accreted around a particular character or series of events.

Later versions like to present and imagine a first telling: in particular, Orpheus, concocting heroic-sounding songs from unlikely germinating incidents. One of Robert Graves's closural gestures is a performance by Orpheus at the funeral games for Pelias:

> His voice was no longer what it had been. Nevertheless, he sang a long and exceedingly sweet song about the voyage of the *Argo*, not glozing over any unhappy or discreditable event, as many poets have since done; ... However, the priests of Dodona later complained against him that the song was in part disrespectful to Zeus, and forbade him to sing it again under pain of the God's displeasure; so that only snatches of it now survive. (429)

Thus Graves creates his own image of the 'original' *Argonautica*, playfully evoking the *OA* at the same time as insisting it is a forgery, while implying (and possibly even believing) that his own fiction is in fact reality.

We have seen searchers combine archaeology with rationalizing traditions to date the myth, or link it to Near Eastern cultures, to sift story from history, and legend from folklore, hoping to find the true Argonauts. For me, the versions that survive are the true treasures, showing how myth travels, changes, grows and affects the world around it. The Argonautic tradition is multiple, varied, changeable and ambiguous, and it never really ossifies into a defined canonical form. Key scholar-creators at different stages keep bringing back its multiplicity: Apollonius, Valerius, Kingsley and Graves all know the traditions inside out and play with them.

There is a difference in sense of ownership: this story is almost always seen as myth belonging to Greeks. But ownership, too, can transcend time and place. The statue of Medea in Batumi shows that the Argonauts remain important for modern Georgian identity, while Du Bois uses the story to reflect on Black American identities. National identity is just one aspect: the '49ers' in the Californian Gold Rush also identified as Argonauts, through ideas of pioneering, exploration and making a fortune. Other aspects of identity shape and are shaped by the Argonaut myth: the transformative journey is open to women as well as men, as Hauser's Atalanta and Pirotta's Medea show, while Hylas and Hercules are implicated in changing attitudes to sexuality. The Argonaut myth offers complex models of masculinity, in particular. Jason's reliance on and success in using relationships with others, the importance of group achievement, moves away from individual self-sufficiency as essential for masculine success, even if costs and consequences remain problematic. The myth is still live: it has meaning, inspires rituals and performances, new cultural products. The tradition grows ever more complex and richer.

The idea of the Argonauts and their quest shows how much expansion, exploration and acquisition are central to narratives of achievement in cultures that build on Greek myth. Masculine success combines with Greek (or British, or American) cultural hegemony, success based on going out, dominating others, taking what you want and bringing it back. The Argonaut story offers other possibilities, narratives of self-development, transformation, artistic and spiritual transcendence. For the future, we need epics of renewal, resilience and collective achievement: and the Argonauts can be re-shaped to do that too.

Notes

Chapter 1

1   Medea tradition: Mimoso-Ruiz 1982, Morse 1996, Clauss and Johnston 1997 Hall, et al. 2000 and Bartel and Simon 2010.

2   Colavito 2014. On the figure of Jason: Mackie 2001 and Spence 2010.

3   See, for instance, Dowden 1996 on Moreau, and Dräger's own response to the *BMCR* review by Scherer: http://bmcr.brynmawr.edu/2003/2003-02-26.html (accessed 6 August 2019).

4   See Zissos 2006, and Dominguez 1979.

5   See, for instance, Morse 1996 on Lefèvre, Bartel 2010 on Grillparzer, Mimoso-Ruiz 1996 on Pasolini, and Goldhill 2007 on Waterhouse, Leonard 2000 on Graves, with some reference to *The Golden Fleece*, Weingartz 2010 on Wolf and myth.

6   On Classics and children's literature, see Murnaghan and Roberts 2018, especially the chapters on Hawthorne, Kingsley and their immediate reception; Maurice 2015; Hodkinson and Lovatt 2018. My first attempt at Argonauts in children's literature: Lovatt 2009.

7   See Paul 2013; Blanshard and Shahabudin 2011 and Llewellyn-Jones 2013.

8   On myth and popular or mass culture, see Willis 2017.

9   For a wider, more international exploration of the Medea myth see Mimoso-Ruiz 1982.

10 It follows in the footsteps of Hall 2008 and Hardie 2014.

11 Homer *Iliad*: mentions of Iolchos (ruled by Eumelus, grandson of Pelias): 2.711–15; references to Euneus, ruler of Lemnos, son of Jason and Hypsipyle: 7.467–9, 21.40–1, 23.747.

12 For instance, Kirchoff 1869; further reading in West 2005.

13 Apollonius' *Argonautica* is generally dated between 270 and 240 BCE, but Murray 2014 has argued from astronomical time and praise of Ptolemy III Euergetes for 238.

14 For an introduction to Apollonius, see Hunter 1993b, Papanghelis and Rengakos 2008; on Alexandria, see Stephens 2003; on Hellenistic poetry, see Fantuzzi 2005.

15 On *Pythian* 4, see Segal 1986, Braswell 1988; on Pindar, Spelman 2018.

16 Both Moreau 1994 and Colavito 2014 argue that Jason was originally a great hero who was 'banalised'. Jason Colavito is a partisan: he refers to 'poor Jason' ('poor Jason ended up as a feckless womanising dilettante', 219; 'Alas, poor Jason. It is to him that we owe *The White Goddess*, through no fault of his own' 229).

17 See Dominguez 1979 on medieval Argonautic romances, of which Lefèvre's *History of Jason* forms the climax.

18 On collections of myth for children, see Murnaghan and Roberts 2017.

19 There is an oscillation between entertainment and authenticity: the cartoon-style productions of the early 2000s have inspired new versions based on Greek vases and ancient texts, such as Spence 2014 and Byrd 2016.

20 On ancient mythography, see Fowler 2000; Cameron 2004; on mythography and its reception, see Zajko and Hoyle 2017, but with little on Argonauts.

21 See Kermode 1912: 162; Morris 1910: vol. III, xviii (referring to Lemprière's *Bibliotheca Classica*, 1788). Kermode asserts Morris had good knowledge of Classical sources, perhaps remembered unconsciously; Mench 1968 explores his adaptation of Lemprière. Both, however, ignore the 'nursery tales', e.g. how his description of Jason matches that of Pindar *Pythian* 4, via Hawthorne. See further Mench 1968 on Morris's medieval influences and critical reception of *Life and Death of Jason*, both contemporary and early twentieth century.

22 Fowler 2017.

23 Moreau 1994: 251–70 analyses folk-tale elements in the Argonaut myth, according to Propp's 31 functions.

24 Zajko 2017: 2 talks of 'pre-literate Greece' as the context of myth, but also acknowledges that it is largely inaccessible, and some see all Classical Studies as 'reception' studies.

25 On Romanticism and Hellenism, see Webb 1993, Ferris 2000.

26 On Classical Reception studies as discipline, Hardwick and Stray 2008; on weak and strong models of reception, Martindale 1993.

27 See Kyriakou 1995 on Apollonius' use of the Homeric *hapax legomena* (words used only once).

28 The major English translations now are those of Rieu 1959, Hunter 1993a, Green 1997 and Poochigian 2014.

29 Translations: Vian 1987 into French with notes; Colavito 2011b primarily follows the Latin translation of Gesner (1764), also referring to Vian and translations in other languages, i.e. Migotto in Italian (1994).

30 Stover 2008 argues for a Vespasianic date, but there is no real reason to rule out a Domitianic date. Valerius' death is mentioned by the orator Quintilian (*Inst. Or.* 10.1.90), in a work definitely published before the death of Domitian (96 CE).

31 See Hardie 1993, and Hershkowitz 1998.

32 On Valerius' text and transmission, see Taylor-Briggs 2014.

33 See Heerink and Manuwald 2014.

34 Munro (1913: vii) used Morris's type-written copy of Caxton/Lefèvre for his edition. A search of the online database of William Morris's library at https://

williammorrislibrary.wordpress.com/ (accessed 19 August 2008), shows that he owned copies of Valerius Flaccus and Ovid's *Metamorphoses*, but not Apollonius.

35 On the context, see Dominguez 1979 and Morse 1983.

36 See further Lovatt 2020.

37 Klaver 2006: 410, citing a letter from Kingsley to Ticknor and Fields, 15 October 1855, compiled by Robert Bernard Martin (1950: 622).

38 Seymour-Smith 1995: 167–8.

39 In 1961, succeeding W. H. Auden; see Seymour-Smith 1995: 454–5; 491–2.

40 Usurpation beginnings: Naden; Gunderson; Bradman and Ross.

41 Pelias' mother Tyro and her rape by Poseidon is told at Homer, *Od.* 11.235–59. Apollodorus 1.9.8–9 gives us the killing of Sidero by Pelias and Neleus in Hera's temple, which Apollonius alludes to at *Arg.* 1.12–14.

42 Pherecydes has Pelias as legitimate king of Iolchos, as does Diodorus Siculus and Valerius Flaccus. The *scholia* on *Odyssey* 12.69 have Pelias as regent; *scholia* to Hesiod *Theogony* 993 have Pelias sending Jason to Chiron.

43 Phrixus story as early: papyrus fragment of Hesiod's *Catalogue of Women* (fr. 68 MW) mentions a golden ram and Phrixus; fragment of Pherecydes includes wicked stepmother, crop failure and golden ram; Pindar connects Phrixus with the Golden Fleece (*Pythian* 4.159–62).

44 See also *scholia* on Pindar *Pythian* 4.135 and Homer *Od.*12.69.

45 The classic article is Brelich 1955–7; Moreau 1994: 132–7 interprets the naked left foot as mark of initiation, warrior status, magical ritual and funereal connection. Both Medea in Ovid (*Met.* 7.182–3) and Dido in Virgil (*Aen.* 4.517–20) carry out magical practices with naked feet. Warriors: Plataeans at Thuc. 3.22.2; troops from Praeneste, Virg., *Aen.* 7.687–90. Funereal connection: sons of Thestius about to die, Eur., *Meleager* 530 (N2).

46 For a helpful discussion see Newby 2016: 165–86.

47 On Varro's *Argonautae*, first century BCE, which from the few fragments was probably a close translation of Apollonius, see Courtney 1993: 238–43.

48 In the catalogue, Kermode 1912: 163 sees reliance on Apollonius (following his order).

49 On Hercules and body-building, see O'Brien 2014.

Chapter 2

1 The list of boar hunters is as long and variable as the list of Argonauts, but Ovid's begins with Castor and Pollux, Jason, Theseus and Pirithous, Meleager's uncles, Lynceus and Idas (all but the uncles Argonauts); others include further Argonauts: Caeneus, Acastus, Phoenix, Eurytus, Telamon and Peleus, Admetus, Eurytion, Echion, Ancaeus and Mopsus.

2　See Gantz 1993: 330–2.

3　Byrd does the same.

4　She was jointly nominated for the Nobel Prize in literature along with Henryk
　　Sienkiewicz (author of *Quo Vadis*) and Leo Tolstoy (author of *Anna Karenina* and
　　War and Peace) in 1905, but it was awarded to Sienkiewicz.

5　For lucid analysis, see Hunter 1993b: 47–59.

6　Other tragic versions include Sophocles *Lemnian women*, which features a battle
　　with the Argonauts. Aeschylus' Hypsipyle refuses to allow the Argonauts to land until
　　they promise sexual services.

7　On Polyxo's importance, see Finkmann 2015.

8　Gantz 1993: 346.

9　Valerius' episode is 2.77–428, of which 82–310 describes the murders. On Valerius'
　　expansion and Polyxo's speech see Finkmann 2015; on Valerius' tragic visualisation
　　see Buckley 2013.

10　On Hypsipyle's deceptiveness, see Gibson 2004.

11　Sections 58–68, 113–18. See Morse 1983 for context; Badnall 2010 makes useful
　　observations about Lefèvre in the Argonautic tradition.

12　Jason as enchanted by Medea's nurse (Lefèvre 94–6, cf. Ovid, *Her.* 6.83–4, 93–4).

13　Justin's epitome of Pompeius Trogus' universal history includes the Argonautic
　　expedition in the early history of Armenia (42.2), in which Jason returns to Colchis
　　with Medea after being expelled from Iolchos, and reigns there with her. Boccaccio's
　　Jason in his *Genealogia Deorum Gentilium* contains the same story.

14　On Cavalli's significance and the difficulties of editing his music, see Rosand 2013,
　　with several essays on *Giasone* and its sources, including those by Heller, Manley,
　　Antonucci and Bianconi. See also Schulze 2006.

15　Note that Amazons are relegated to the monster zone outside the Greek sphere of
　　influence and societies/organizations of women occur in Aristophanes as jokes in
　　themselves (*Lysistrata, Ecclesiazousae, Thesmophoriazousae*).

16　Goldhill emphasizes the replication of the nymphs as patriarchal and erotic; it is also
　　disturbing, and makes them seem less human.

17　Seven of the 46 representations catalogued in *LIMC* show Hylas alone, going to fetch
　　water; 23 attacked by nymphs; three amongst the nymphs after the rape; one fending
　　off a single nymph with a club. On myth and Roman funerary contexts, see Newby
　　2016: 228–72, 167–8 on Hylas.

18　The earliest surviving image of the story according to *LIMC* is a wall-painting from
　　Stabiae dated from 55–79 CE.

19　*Schol. A.R.* 1.1355–57c. See Huxley 1969: 99–112 on Hercules epics. These included
　　Peisandros of Kamiros (seventh or sixth century BCE), *Heracleia* in two books,
　　apparently following Pisinos of Lindos (thus Clem. Al. Strom. 6.2.25); *Heracleia* by
　　Panyassis (fifth century BCE) in 14 books.

20 Strabo, *Geography* 12.4.3; Apollonius *Arg.* 1.1345–57. For detailed arguments about reconstructing this ritual, see Sourvinou-Inwood 2005.

21 On the relationship of myth and ritual, see Ackerman 1991; seminal pieces by Frazer 1906–15, Harrison 1924 and Girard 2013 [1977]. Introduction to the issues, Csapo 2005: 132–80.

22 *Schol. Bernensia* Virgil *Ecl.* 6.43, also in Servius' commentary on *Aen.* 1.619, late fourth or early fifth century CE.

23 Hunter 1999: 3, 264–5 argues that Apollonius' connected account comes before Theocritus' two scenes from the Argonautic myth in *Idylls* 13 and 22, though he also accepts the possibility of an 'elaborate process of mutual criticism and re-writing'. *Idylls* 13 and 22 treat Hylas and Amycus, scenes which come at the end of book 1 and the beginning of book 2 in Apollonius. Hunter argues that these myths were not otherwise well-known and make sense in Theocritus' poetry as a response to Apollonius.

24 For an introduction to Theocritus, see Hunter 1996.

25 Erotic and parental love have a complex relationship in the ancient world, particularly in Rome where fostering and adoption were common. Hylas is used as an image in the poem of consolation by Statius for Atedius Melior's dead slave-boy favourite, Glaucias (*Silvae* 2.1.113); see Asso 2010.

26 On approaches to Greek pederasty see Lear 2014; the classic account is Dover 1978, now reissued as Dover 2016.

27 On Hercules' response to the loss of Hylas as erotic, see Hunter 1993b: 38–40. Hylas is showing signs of his first beard at 1.132, the ideal age for the beloved boy (*eromenos*). Hercules' physical symptoms of loss resemble those of Sappho's love in poem 31, and the simile of the bull is also erotic, see Hunter 1989 *ad* 3.276–7.

28 On absent presences and bereavement, see Hardie 2002: 62–105.

29 On Propertius 1.20 and boy love in Latin poetry, see Ingleheart 2015.

30 On apples as erotic objects, see Littlewood 1968.

31 For Valerius' tendency to re-epicize Argonautic characters, see Hershkowitz 1998: 105–89.

32 Heerink 2010: 119–42 argues that the Hylas episode models a transformation from epic to elegy in Valerius.

33 Of my collection of children's versions, the following do not include the Hylas episode: Naden/Baxter; Pirotta/Lewis; Zeff/Cartwright; Bradman/Ross; Gunderson/Takvorian; Jeffrey/Verma; Spence. These versions are aimed at younger readers, simplified with fewer episodes. Malam/Antram includes an inset box on the loss of Hercules, in which he is left behind while looking for his oar. Byrd briefly mentions Hylas as Hercules' 'attendant' who was 'kidnapped by nymphs'.

34 On the relatively high status and freedoms of Hellenistic women, see Pomeroy 1990. For a summary of recent more nuanced approaches see James and Dillon 2012 esp. 229–366.

35 This use of dress to define subjugation is also important in Euripides and Grillparzer: Bartel 2010.

36 Putnam 2004: xxviii–xxix.

37 See Morse 1996: 96–102.

38 In several respects she resembles De Morgan's portrayal of another woman demonized for a love affair, *Helen of Troy* (1898), who is also blonde, with flowers, looking down and to the right, but into a mirror. She too is surrounded by doves and roses, and has a similarly contemplative and sad expression.

39 Smith 2002: 102–3.

40 See Prettejohn 2010 on Sandys' *Medea* and its contemporary reception.

41 Buxton 2010.

42 On Medea in Ovid *Metamorphoses* 7, see Newlands 1997.

43 On epic heroines and their tendency to stay put, preventing the hero's movement, or for those who travel (such as Virgil's Dido) to suffer an unfortunate outcome, see Keith 2000.

44 Biggs and Blum 2019 on journeys and heroism, and Keith 2019 on women's journeys (or lack of them).

45 A scholion on Pindar (*Schol. vet. Ol.* 13.74g, cited in Tedeschi 2010) preserves an ancient tradition in which Zeus fell in love with Medea, but she refused him to avoid Hera's anger.

46 On ancient witches: Ogden 2002; Stratton 2007; Eidinow 2016. On Circe: see Yarnall 1994.

47 On the *lena* (female pimp but also witch) in Ovid and Propertius, see Myers 1996.

48 See Richards 2015 on Lamb and the reconfiguration of the *Odyssey* adventure story.

Chapter 3

1 Clauss 1993; *contra* Hunter 1988.

2 For comparison with Homer, see Knight 1995.

3 Beye 1969.

4 Mackie 2001.

5 Lawall 1966.

6 Jackson 1992.

7 On *The Best of the Achaeans* in Homer: Nagy 1979.

8 Useful discussion in introduction to Langerwerf and Ryan 2010

9 On hero cult and Pindar: Currie 2005.

10 The terms 'source culture' and 'target culture' come from translation studies, which can be useful for thinking about how people repurpose myths for different cultural

contexts, in essence a process of translation (or adaptation). Ideas of 'domestication' (making the material comfortable for the new audience) and 'alienation' (bringing out the otherness of the source culture) are also useful. For an introduction to translation studies, see Venuti 2000: a good starting point is 11–14.

11 Nelis 1991.

12 Mori 2008: 52–90 on the election scene argues that Hercules acts as Jason's patron and that diplomacy is Jason's special skill, a re-evaluation of heroism.

13 See Zissos 1999 on negative allusion in Valerius Flaccus; also Hershkowitz 1998: 27–9 on re-epicizing Jason.

14 Mori 2008: 52–90 also explores the functioning of Apollonius' Argonauts as a society. On Valerius' Argonautic team, see Lovatt 2014.

15 Hunter 1993b: 25–41.

16 On Hercules, see Stafford 2012. On his excessiveness, see Loraux 1990. Feeney 1991: 95 describes him as 'the most protean and ambivalent creature in Greek myth'.

17 Hunter 1993b: 26 on his anomalous status as Argonaut.

18 On gigantomachy and epic, Hardie 1986.

19 Hunter 1993b: 29; Feeney 1986: 63.

20 On following Hercules, see Feeney 1991: 95–8.

21 Hunter 1993b: 28–9.

22 On Valerius and Dionysius Scytobrachion, who probably wrote a prose account of the Argonauts in six books around the same time as Apollonius, see Galli 2014. Characters similar to Hercules appear in a number of Near Eastern cultures and he may be an Indo-European hero: see Stafford 2012 13–16, with further reading.

23 Hershkowitz 1998: 72–5.

24 On Hesione and the world plan, see Manuwald 2004.

25 On Valerius' Prometheus episode, see Hershkowitz 1998: 158–9 and 194–7.

26 Thanks to Peter Hulse for pointing out this allusion to me.

27 See Blanshard and Shahabudin 2011: 58–76 on *Le fatiche di Ercole*. On the 1958 film in its Italian political context, see D'Amelio 2011.

28 See Stafford 2017 on Hercules' choice in Prodikos onwards, with a strong argument that this tradition of the choice between virtue and vice influenced the tradition of Hercules on screen.

29 Stafford 2017: 152 suggests that Ulysses' emulative admiration maintains heteronormativity while allowing deviant gazes.

30 Harryhausen and Dalton 2003: 152. 'Although Hercules doesn't feature greatly in the story, we felt that it was an important role, but wanted to get away from the Italian beefcake the public had expected of him. Nigel [Green] was perfect as a slightly older and more intelligent hero, who in his ratty old lion skin was both a braggart and compassionate.'

31 Byrd 2016 includes a similar Hercules, twice the size of the other heroes, also with election scene and rowing contest, and Jason worried about being overshadowed, and some Argonauts even resisting his inclusion.

32 Tim Severin's reconstructed voyage bears witness to the importance of a favourable wind, with strong currents against them: against the wind, his rowing champions hardly moved or even went backwards. Lack of food and water was a constant danger, too, even in the twentieth century.

33 A motif that recurs, for instance in Hoena/Estudio Haus, where in a box labelled 'Ancient Fact', Zetes and Calais are killed by Hercules (11).

34 For instance in the work of Truby 2007.

35 See Wiseman 2004: 87–97 for a detailed analysis, setting it in its Etruscan context.

36 References to paternity: 109–11; 150; 213; 219; 254–6; 312–33; 327. At 114–332, Neptune accepts that he has to give up supporting his son and turns his gaze away from the battle.

37 Leigh 2010.

38 Treece as ever follows Graves, in his relatively brief version. He refers to the dead Amycus as a 'pole-axed bull'; Graves's Pollux asks Amycus whether 'you favour the pole-axe style of boxing?' (199).

39 The name of Amycus' country, or city, or, as in Treece, Evslin and Zeff, island, varies. The tribe are the Bebrycians, and the land is usually Bebrycia. Some avoid giving a name, such as Brooks, Catran, West and Zimmerman (with a joke): Jason says 'Shipmates, what land is this, do you suppose?' To which Pollux replies, 'Whatever it is, let's go ahead and make our fires. It's cold.' Treece and Evslin use the island of Bebrycos; Whitehead calls it Bebryces. Similarly, Catran calls the city of Cyzicus 'Doliones', transferring the name of the tribe to the city.

40 On Argonautic antagonists, see Cowan 2014.

Chapter 4

1 Tony Dalton used this term in discussion at 'Animating Antiquity: Ray Harryhausen and the Classical Tradition', Bradford Media Museum (9 November 2011); see also 'appeal to general audiences' (Harryhausen and Dalton 2003: 174) and 'hold an audience's attention' (261).

2 The 'entertainment' section at a brass band competition, for instance, can include documentary portrayals of the history of the brass band movement, avant-garde new compositions, big band performance complete with choreographed movements: but plate smashing and clowning at Butlins 2019 was felt to be a step too far.

3 See Willis 2017 on 'mass' versus 'popular' culture.

4 Some suggestions in Lowe and Shahabudin 2009.

5 McGuffins (or MacGuffins) and their history: briefly at Harmon 2006: 307. Multiple McGuffins become *plot coupons*, a term coined by Lowe 1986, archived online at https://web.archive.org/web/20130728045153/http://news.ansible.co.uk/plotdev.html (accessed 29 July 2019).

6 Reassuring Valerius: Stover 2012; disturbing Valerius: Buckley 2013.

7 On Phineus as epic prophet, see Lovatt 2013: 136–54.

8 Gantz 1993: 349–56: *Phineus A* (he blinds his sons by his first wife, Cleopatra, after their stepmother Idaia accuses them of attempted rape); *Tympanistai* (the stepmother blinds them and imprisons them); and *Phineus B* (Phineus himself is blinded after killing his sons).

9 Hunter translates 'with their claws' and Seaton 'with their crooked beaks'.

10 As argued by Kefalidou 2008, who gives a full account of the fragments and excellent illustrations.

11 Spence 2014 included this, perhaps influencing Byrd 2016. Spence deliberately aims to return to 'the earliest version' where 'Jason is a strong hero and leader'.

12 Mackie 2001. Jason as healing hero, like Aesculapius, attracts Jason's partisans, such as Colavito 2014: 58–62 with further reading.

13 Although Barich translates *volucres* (492) as 'birds', it can also mean winged creatures in general; at 457, Valerius refers to the touch of the creatures as *manu* ('hand') and to their 'claws' (*unguibus*). Metaphorical bird-like characteristics and metaphorical human characteristics interact. Perhaps their hands are curved and claw-like or perhaps they use their claws like hands.

14 Phineas: in Severin, Bradman and Ross, Rick Riordan and Byrd.

15 Yomtov: birds with red eyes, feathered wings; Gunderson/Takvorian: white-feathered birds with heads of women; Jeffrey and Verma: winged women; Spence: winged women, following Greek vase painting; Byrd: heads of women, bodies of vultures and bat wings (text and image).

16 On the tradition of interpreting the Argonauts' journey as a *katabasis*, see below p. 191–2.

17 Other versions that combine omen with lack of explicit divine intervention are Morris; Yomtov; Zarabouka (where the dove determines the speed of their approach); Zeff, where the goddess Athena sends a wave to help them; Gunderson, where the question is whether or not the dove returns, which seems to mix this story with Noah's release of a dove after the flood (Genesis 8.6-12).

18 An exception is Spence, who deliberately returns to the omen. Byrd combines timing (dove) with omen (heron, probably from Graves).

19 Rink 1875: 158 tells the story of Giviok, who passes between two icebergs in order to reach a new land, with the icebergs closing on the stern of his kayak.

20 We can see the influence of Harryhausen grow and wane again in the motif of rockfalls from above, not present in any of the ancient versions, but there, at least in part, in Seraillier, Brooks, Catran and Malam, but not later versions.

21 Llewellyn-Jones 2013 discusses gods and cinema with a focus on Harryhausen, available at http://fass.open.ac.uk/sites/fass.open.ac.uk/files/files/new-voices-journal/proceedings/volume1/Llewellyn-Jones-2013.pdf (accessed 30 July 2019)

22 Harryhausen calls Beverley Cross, the scriptwriter who put Jan Read's script into its final form, 'an expert on Greek mythology', Harryhausen and Dalton 2003: 152; Llewellyn-Jones 2013 feels he 'deserves the commendation' (7).

23 When Zora has her vision in a church, which forms a conversion, or at least an activation of Christian beliefs, she begins from thoughts of Bles and the Silver Fleece (Du Bois 1911: 293); the money given to save the school is stashed touching the Fleece as if participating in its purifying force (361); at the end just before Zora and Bles are finally united, she wears the Fleece into the swamp, where she contemplates sacrificing herself in a suicidal re-enactment of Hylas (432).

24 Compare *Troy*, which excludes gods from direct action, except Thetis (Julie Christie), while including divine power in art, architecture, beliefs of characters; Llewellyn-Jones 2013: 17–18 chastises Petersen (dir.) and Benioff (scriptwriter) for lack of imagination; Winkler 2007.

25 On the divine gaze as a structuring part of epic, see Lovatt 2013: 29–77. On the Muses see Spentzou and Fowler 2002.

26 Homer *Iliad* 1.43–52; 1.188–200.

27 Feeney 1991: 57–98 gives a good overview; see also Hunter 1993b: 75–100.

28 On Medea falling in love see Fucecchi 1997.

29 This British television series, first shown in 2013, features UK viewers reacting to television programmes.

30 See for instance the review of Carne-Ross 1973, available at https://www.nybooks.com/articles/1973/10/04/epic-overreach/ (accessed 30 July 2019).

31 Cosmic associations create a different sort of marvel, drawing on the sublimity of the universe, and scaling up our wonder at the natural world. These cosmic elements are more prominent in Valerius but there are hints in Apollonius.

32 'So I asked myself: what if we make a film that featured the creatures and the gods and used the humans to link the story? That was how *Jason and the Argonauts* was born.' Harryhausen and Dalton 2005: 99.

33 Gloyn 2019: chapter 1.

34 'The monster always escapes' is one of the 'Monster theses' from Cohen 1997.

35 Some psychoanalytic monster theory: Kristeva 1982; Halberstam 1995.

36 On hybridity, liminality and post-colonialism, see Werbner 2001.

37 On Talos in Apollonius, see Dickie 1990; on Medea's heroism, see Lovatt 2013: 334–6.

38 On taking liberties, see Harryhausen and Dalton 2003: 174.

39 It is tempting to think that Hughes may have been inspired by Harryhausen's Talos, since the Iron Man is both protector and destroyer.

40 See Mayor 2018 on robots and antiquity.

41 Although as Hardie 2009: 1–18 points out, Augustan culture, such as Ovid's *Metamorphoses*, was also invested in the extraordinary.

Chapter 5

1 On Apollonius and geography: Meyer 2001.

2 Morrison 2019 on Apollonius and Herodotus.

3 Purves 2010.

4 Spatial readings of Greek myth are proliferating: see for instance Hawes 2017; on Apollonius and space, see Thalmann 2011.

5 For primary material, see Kennedy et al. 2013.

6 A clear, readable introduction to the issues is Whitmarsh 2018.

7 On ethnicity, see Hall 1997.

8 For an introduction to ideas about race and ethnicity in Greek culture, see McCoskey 2012.

9 On migration in the ancient world, see Garland 2014; Tacoma 2016.

10 Influential psychoanalytical approaches to Otherness: Lacan and Miller 1978; Levinas 1999.

11 Influential work on post-colonial approaches: Said 1978; Young 2001.

12 Of course, my white British background does not help: I look forward to more research on this by scholars of colour.

13 On Caribbean Classics see Greenwood 2010; on Classical reception and otherness, see Richardson 2019. On Du Bois' Medea character and education, see Murray 2019.

14 Wetmore 2013.

15 See, for instance, Chaniotis 2003.

16 Gantz 1993: 340.

17 It seems likely that the Argonauts also aided him in a battle, perhaps against the Sauromatae, twice mentioned in Apollonius, first by Argos to Aeetes (3.350–3), and then by Jason in his diplomatic response (3.392–5). Pindar says that when they arrived, the Argonauts 'there mixed strength with the dark-faced Cochians, in the presence of Aeetes' (*Pyth.* 4.211–2).

18 On Otherness in Grillparzer, see Ruthner 2007, Winkler 2009.

19 On this simulation of multilingualism and its effects, see Weissmann 2017.

20 Grillparzer 2014: 87–8.

21 On trust and 'barbarians' in Grillparzer see Albrecht 2015.

22 Putnam 2004: xxviii–xxix.

23 Putnam 2004: xxxvi, although Vegio's Aeetes is not the first to have killed Phrixus.

24 Aeetes and Pelias are often presented as versions of each other. Already in Valerius, Jason calls Aeetes 'another Pelias' (7.92). See Cowan 2014: 233.

25 See 'Modern day Argonauts set sail', NBC news, Associated Press, 6.15.08 http://www. nbcnews.com/id/25179338/ns/technology_and_science-science/t/modern-day-argonauts-set-sail/#.XIvC9ij7TyE (accessed 15 March 2019).

26 Thalmann 2011: 42–7 emphasises the connection between Greek knowledge and Egyptian power and conquest.

27 A seminal post-colonial contribution on the Greeks and Egypt is Bernal 1987.

28 On the ancient origins of racism, see Isaac 2004. On history of white-washing Egypt, see Bernal 1987, with Orrells et al. 2011.

29 Wetmore's anthology includes: *African Medea* (Jim Magnuson); *Black Medea* (Father Ernest Ferlita); *Pecong* (Steve Carter); *There are women waiting: The tragedy of Medea Jackson* (Edris Cooper); *American Medea* (Silas Jones); *Medea: Queen of Colchester* (Marianne McDonald).

30 Eastlake 2019: 107 on the idealized beauty of Greeks in novels such as Bulwer-Lytton's *The Last Days of Pompeii* (1834).

31 See Bartel 2010.

32 On Otherness in Pasolini, see Kvistad 2010.

33 On Greek ethnography see Skinner 2012; for Greek archaeology, Forbes 2007.

34 On Herodotus and ethnography: Thomas 2000; Munson 2001; on Apollonius and Herodotus: Morrison 2019.

35 On Apollonius as travel writer: Harder 1994; Apollonius' geography: Endsjø 1997. On Apollonius and the spaces of savagery: Cusset 2004.

36 On space and the epic genre: Skempis and Ziogas 2014.

37 Malinowski's book as 'the first modern ethnography': Hart 1986: 637.

38 On space and colonization see Thalmann 2011: 77–144.

39 Lovatt 2018 on how Apollonius' Argonauts view landscapes and peoples, particularly in book 4.

40 An example of Slovenian interest is Divjak 2018.

41 The Lemnians were not straightforwardly considered Greek. In the Minoan period, their language was similar to Etruscan: Haarmann 2014: 22.

42 On Greek colonization of the Black sea, see Tsetskhladze 1998.

43 Braund 1994: 34–39 on connections between Greek communities and Colchis.

44 Book 8 becomes increasingly fragmentary and then stops altogether around line 468, as Jason is torn about whether or not to give Medea back.

45 On this passage, see Heerink 2014: 86–94.

46 Heerink 2014: 90–2

47 Later versions that stop: Bradman and Ross; Pirotta and Lewis. Straight to Iolchos: Naden. Karl Klyne's *Jason and the Astronauts* has a very abrupt ending where the escaping Aeetes figure, Father Gregory, is blown up, leaving Jason stranded on the Colchis-equivalent planet with his 'Medea'.

48 Talos only: Yomtov. Circe only: Zeff. North Africa only: Zimmerman. Sirens, Scylla and Talos, plus re-connecting with Hercules, as in Treece: Hoena and Estudio Haus; Sirens, Phaeacia, North Africa, Talos: Malam and Antram. Sirens, cattle of the sun and Talos: Riordan and Cockcroft. Apsyrtos, Circe, Sirens, Scylla and Charybdis, North Africa, Thynias: Byrd. In Whitehead and Banerjee, Jason chooses a route that is 'quicker but through uncharted waters' (between Scylla and Charybdis). Brooks has Hera devise a route, which includes portage to the Tyrrhenian sea, Sirens, Circe, a storm and Talos. Zarabouka follows the route of Apollonius, including Triton, Anaphe and the dream of Euphemus.

49 Others that go straight to Iolchos: Gunderson and Takvorian, Evslin.

50 The wrath of Poseidon is also emphasised by Riordan and Cockcroft.

51 Dedali also mentions 'Atimite', which presumably refers to the Mycenean name of Artemis.

52 Mayor 2014 is in Hauser's 'Further Reading'. Myrtessa accuses Atalanta of looking like an Amazon when she puts on Dedali's woollen trousers.

53 Aeetes' reference to a golden 'temple of the Far Darter' (6.444) might suggest continuity between Greek and Colchian religion.

54 On the nineteenth-century British imperial context of Morris and Kingsley, see further Lovatt 2020.

55 On Zora as model for black education, see Murray 2019.

56 Obviously, the Colchians are not straightforwardly less technologically advanced than the Greeks, but they are portrayed that way, most egregiously by the 1958 film.

Chapter 6

1 Pindar *Pythian* 4 keeps bulls and dragon, but not Earthborns; Lefèvre, along with Cavalli's *Giasone* and Graves's *Golden Fleece* do the same. Grillparzer's *The Argonauts* replaces the bulls and Earthborns with two separate fights between Jason, Apsyrtus and Aeetes, leaving only the dragon.

2 Harryhausen begins with the hydra that guards the fleece, and then escalates into his Earthborn skeletons. Apollonius sets the spectacle of the bulls and Earthborns during the day, but the dragon episode in the very early morning, as the Argonauts escape, whereas Hawthorne puts bulls at night and dragon during the day.

3 Henderson 2005: 92 on Jason and the construction of Thorvaldsen's artistic heroism.

4 On breaking the frame in ancient epic games, see Lovatt 2005: 80–100.

5 Further completely metal bulls include those of Jeffrey/Verma.

6 Jason wrestles bulls: Pindar, Apollonius, Valerius, Vegio (in this aspect, more like Valerius than Ovid), Colum, Seraillier, Hawthorne, Brooks, Riordan, Yomtov,

Zimmerman; confused or calmed of their own accord: Lefèvre, Zeff, Gunderson, Hoena/Estudio Haus; drugged or enchanted by Medea: Valerius, Kingsley, Catran.

7 On the Minotaur and its reception, see Gloyn 2019: chapter 8.

8 'In the legend it is rotting corpses, and despite originally designing the scene as such, we thought this would give the film a certificate that might have barred children, so we decided on seven skeletons.' Harryhausen and Dalton 2003: 169.

9 Harryhausen puzzled about how to kill them, and says 'We assumed that they couldn't swim.' Harryhausen and Dalton 2003: 174.

10 'I designed and animated into the skeletons certain human "touches" to give them some character.' Harryhausen and Dalton 2003: 170.

11 Other illustrations also evoke the 1963 film: Harpies in a ruined temple (although with feathered wings, 124); Hera and Athena holding the cliffs apart (131); Gods observing in a pool and quarrelling (156).

12 Long before Harryhausen chose a hydra for the 1963 film, Valerius suggested it in his imagery.

13 See Hardie 1993: 4–10 on the ways Virgil's successors delight in this idea of one against many.

14 Red-figure cup by Douris, from 480–470 BCE, from Cerveteri (Etruria). Now in the Vatican Museum.

15 On Jonah and Jason, see Colavito 2014: 239–40, with Hamel 1995. Hiccup's reptilian *katabasis* is in the first of Cressida Cowell's *How to Train Your Dragon* series (2003).

16 Suggestion made to me by Daniel Ogden in discussion.

17 Colavito 2014: 59–62 argues that this and other early images suggest Jason is a version of the Near Eastern god Dumuzi and undertook a journey to the underworld, like Gilgamesh and Hercules. He draws on Mackie 2001 who argues Jason was originally a stronger figure with divine or almost divine powers, but 'goes beyond' to suggest he was a Mycenean god of battlefield healing.

18 Gantz 1993: 359 argues that this motif is 'definitely older than Douris in art', since it can also be identified on two Early Corinthian pots (Bonn 860; Samos VM frr).

19 Cited in Hind 1907 chapter IX, who describes the painting as 'grandiloquent', and contextualises it in relation to Turner's travels in Europe, probably inspired by Salvator Rosa.

20 Ruskin again: 'the trunks of the trees on the right are all cloven into yawning and writhing heads and bodies, and alive with dragon energy all about us' creating a 'morbid and fearful condition of mind' in the spectator. Ruskin, 'Of imagination penetrative', *Modern Painters*, vol. 2, 166.

21 Seraillier, Zarabouka, Bradman, Jeffrey, Gunderson, Hoena and Takvorian call it a dragon, while some talk of a serpent (Colum, Riordan, Malam, Pirotta), and Yomtov, along with Hoena/Estudio Haus, uses the word snake. Zeff brings the two together: 'the snake on guard was as big as a dragon'.

22 Also in Zimmerman's play.

23 This motif of the impenetrable skin is also in Hoena's choose-your-own-adventure version, where Jason dies as he tries to fight it on his own (77).

24 Oakley 2007 currently available freely online at https://www.ascsa.edu.gr/uploads/media/hesperia/25068023.pdf (accessed 8 May 2019).

25 Gantz 1993: 364, citing fr. 9 Rib.

26 Incest also features in Henry Treece's portrayal of palace rivalries in Colchis.

27 Wilson 2018.

Chapter 7

1   Team history: http://argoalumni.com/team-history/ (accessed 20 May 2019).

2   See http://argonautica.jason.oceanobs.com/html/argonautica/argonautica_uk.html (accessed 20 May 2019).

3   See further: https://theargonauts.com/about/ (accessed 6 June 2019).

4   Plutarch *Life of Theseus* 23.

5   'Strabo relied heavily on myth to achieve his geographical, historical and ethnographical aims.' Patterson 2017: 282.

6   On ancient perceptions of Colchis, see Braund 1994: 8–39.

7   Colavito 2014: 148–51.

8   For instance, Jackson 1992.

9   A recent intervention on social definitions of witchcraft, with further reading: Eidinow 2019.

10 Colavito 2014 argues that his writing of *The Golden Fleece* inspired both *The Greek Myths* and *The White Goddess* (229), Graves's poetic and spiritual manifesto, published shortly after the Argonaut novel. He also points out (271–2) that Graves was the mythological reference point for Robert Temple's *Sirius Mystery* (1976).

11 In the substantial Historical Appendix to *The Golden Fleece*, he cites the First Vatican Mythographer to back up his preferred rationalisation of why the Greeks did not easily reach the Black Sea (Trojans acting to prevent it), suggesting that this text 'evidently had access to a very early source of the legend'. However, to do this he amends the text of the mythographer from *in portum ire* ('go into the port') to *in Pontum ire* ('go into the Black Sea') because 'the passage does not make sense otherwise', i.e. does not agree with Graves's own account (*GF* 452).

12 Booker Prize shortlisted in 2012 and 2016. See Levy 2018: 54, 110 on Robert Graves – she is aware of his speculative interpretations and distances herself.

13 Wood 2005: 91–2; Severin 1985: 124–44 on rowing the Bosphorus, 147 on the Clashing Rocks and currents.

14 On Greek and Roman roots of solar mythology, Csapo 2005: 26 cites Firmicus
   Maternus' *De errore profanarum religiorum*, a fourth-century CE text which parodies
   and argues against pagan religion. Section 8 has the sun complain of all the different
   ways in which he is incorporated into bizarre religious practices. He particularly
   complains about the variety and complexity of myths that are linked to the sun.

15 A very useful overview of developments in theories of mythology is that of Csapo
   2005. On solar mythology, see Müller 1867 and Müller 1885.

16 See for instance Castelletti 2012.

17 For instance, Cleopatra VII called her twins by Antony *Helios* and *Selene*. See
   Strootman 2007 on the imagery of the Hellenistic kings.

18 On the epic journey, see Biggs and Blum 2019.

19 This the favoured interpretation of Colavito 2014: 146–68.

20 There are many similarities between Theseus and Jason: both return to claim their
   kingship, both make journeys to find heroic fame, and are helped by the daughters of
   their enemy kings, who they eventually abandon. The relative chronology of the two
   myths is complex, since in some versions Theseus sails with the Argonauts, and Jason
   uses his relationship with Ariadne to persuade Medea in Apollonius, but Theseus
   was almost killed by Medea on his arrival in Athens as a young man, after Medea's
   departure from Corinth. The two myths are mashed up together in the TV series
   Atlantis, where Jason kills the Minotaur, and his love interest is Ariadne, daughter of
   Minos, who in this alternative universe rules Atlantis.

21 For instance, rather unpersuasively, sons of Poseidon, who is the 'Earth-shaker', or
   sons of Hermes, who acts as 'psychopomp', conducting souls to the underworld;
   pilots, such as Tiphys and Erginos, who Fontenrose 1959: 477–87 argues are versions
   of Charon.

22 Classic texts on initiation rites include: Eliade 1959, Vidal-Naquet 1986.

23 Plutarch *Life of Lycurgus* 28.3–7. On the *krypteia* see Trundle 2016.

24 Psychoanalytical readings of myth, including that of Medea, are still popular: for
   instance, Sirola 2004 reads the Medea myth as an expression of the relationship
   between girl and mother. This shows difficulties with psychoanalytical methodology
   where: 'a myth is viewed as an enigma; it may contain hidden wishes; its magic circle
   may turn events into their opposites and it can change its object by wrapping it in
   disguise.' Another example: Fuller 2004.

25 Cooke 2008: 401–5: 'baleful femininity here dominates the symbol of masculinity'
   (403).

26 Despite the title, Corneille's play is mainly a *Medea*. On Corneille, see Manuwald 2002.

27 On the process of production, and Beckmann's statement that the Argonauts came to
   him in a dream, see Rewald 2016: 130–3.

28 Rewald 2016 is sceptical: since Beckmann changed the title only three weeks before
   he finished the painting, she does not feel the Argonaut connection can be a deep

one. However, three weeks is long enough to substantially rework aspects of the painting to bring out the Argonaut connection.

29 For analysis of the painting in the context of his other triptychs, see Kessler 1970.

30 An influential interpretation is that of Göpel 1957.

31 Lackner 1991: 126.

32 'This book answers the question: what was the Golden Fleece, and where is it today?' http://www.argonauts-book.com/ (accessed 6 August 2019). Twenty interpretations: http://www.argonauts-book.com/the-golden-fleece.html (accessed 6 August 2019).

33 Gibbon 1777: vol. 4, 252. 'The waters, impregnated with particles of gold, are carefully strained through sheep-skins or fleeces; . . . fame of their riches is said to have excited the enterprising avarice of the Argonauts.'

34 Botchorishvili 1946.

35 On this, see the entry in the *Classics and Class* database at http://www.classicsandclass.info/product/122/ (accessed 6 August 2019).

36 Perlot 1985, translated by Helen Harding Bretnor, edited with an introduction by Howard R. Lamar.

37 Banquet with Pelias: 2.290–322 set against the poverty of local labourers (2.326–8). Morris's Cyzicum has 'fair / Well-built quays' (5.32–3), 'rows of linden trees' (40), 'fair Indian cloths' and 'soft beds' (45), and 'full many a rich gift' (48). Morris's Phineus is surrounded by wealth: servants lay out 'A royal feast' (5.193) in 'the gilded hall' (221). Phineus weighs them down with gifts (6.1–4). Aeetes has a 'bursting treasure house' (6.376–8).

38 Smith and Smith 1992 summarises this argument, with further references. Lordkipanidze 2001 argues against it.

39 Fear 1992.

40 Counted on Google maps, 7 June 2019: Bingley, Bradford, Brentwood, Chelmsford, Elland, Godalming, Keighley, Leicester, London (two), Lymm, Melksham, Nottingham, Porthmadog, Stamford, Stroud, Ware, Wells-next-the-sea and York.

41 Bacon 1925: 44.

42 Colavito 2011a, available free online at http://www.argonauts-book.com/free-ebooks.html

43 Forchhammer 1837: 205–7. Bacon 1925: 47–50 finds the theory 'superficially attractive' . . . 'but fatally flawed', in that the extant evidence for the story does not foreground rain or rain-making rituals.

44 Braund 1994: 23 'The Golden Fleece evoked supernatural power, kingship and prosperity, and thus suggested a golden age.' Lordkipanidze 2001: 30–32 suggests that it combines two elements, the 'primordial' symbol and protection of royal power with the Hellenistic interpretation of the fleece as representing the wealth of Colchis. This overcomes the chronological problem of Colchis' lack of gold before the fifth century BCE.

45 Colavito 2014 'a ram's fleece used in rites of purification and the gold-encrusted garments donned by the divinities of the Near East upon their return from the Underworld.' This theory combines neatly with his reading of the voyage as a journey to the underworld, and prioritises origins, relationships with Hittite mythology and comparative anthropological evidence about shamanism.

46 Dominguez 1979: 85–108 on the Argonautic versions of the Burgundian court.

47 Newman 2008 outlines the history of the Order of the Golden Fleece as reception of Apollonius' *Argonautica* and its importance in European history.

Chapter 8

1 For an early recuperation of Virgil's use of Apollonius, see Bacon 1939. See now Nelis 2001.

2 *Argo and the Argonauts*, Playmobil (2020). Image accessed at https://www.playmobil.co.uk/argo-and-the-argonauts/70466.html (accessed 3 September 2020).

3 Julia Kristeva's 'intertextuality' refers to texts as 'a mosaic of quotations . . . the absorption and transformation of another', cited in Moi 1986: 37. Texts interact with texts: we do not need (and can rarely access) author subjectivity. A brief introduction to theories of intertextuality: Martin 2011.

4 On Hawthorne and Kingsley as key texts for children's Greek mythology, and their reception, see Murnaghan and Roberts 2018: 11–80.

5 On the end of Valerius, see Hershkowitz 1998: 1–34, Monaghan 2002.

6 On Pio's continuation, see Zissos 2014.

7 Children's versions that end with the death of Jason crushed by the *Argo*: Naden, Seraillier, Brooks, Catran, Malam and Antram, Riordan, Whitehead, Hoena/Takvorian.

8 For a survey of ideas about readers from the perspective of a children's literature critic, see Butler 2018.

9 See Zajko 2017.

References

Ackerman, R. (1991), *The Myth and Ritual School: J. G. Frazer and the Cambridge Ritualists*, New York: Garland.

Albrecht, T. (2015), 'Trusting Barbarians? Franz Grillparzer's The Golden Fleece and the Challenge to the Mythography of Empire', *Thamyris/Intersecting*, 29: 203–20.

Antonucci, F. and Bianconi, L. (2013), 'Plotting the Myth of Giasone', in E. Rosand (ed.) *Readying Cavalli's Operas for the Stage: Manuscript, Edition, Production*, London: Routledge, 201–28.

Argonauts (2014), [Board game] Creators: Lefteris Iroglidis, Konstantinos Iovis and Ioannis Stammatis. Athens: AF Games.

Asso, P. (2010), 'Queer Consolation: Melior's Dead Boy in Statius *Silvae* 2.1', *AJP*, 131: 663–97.

Atlantis (2013–15), [TV series] Creators: Johnny Capps, Julian Murphy, Howard Overman. UK: Urban Myth Films, BBC Cymru Wales, BBC America.

Bacon, J. R. (1925), *The Voyage of the Argonauts*, Boston: Small, Maynard and Company.

Bacon, J. R. (1939), 'Aeneas in Wonderland. A Study of Aeneid VIII', *Classical Review*, 53: 97–104.

Badnall, T. (2010), 'Monty Python and the Lemnian Women: Argonautic Resonances in the Medieval and Modern Quest Tradition', in L. Langerwerf and C. Ryan (eds), *Zero to Hero, Hero to Zero: In Search of the Classical Hero*, Newcastle: Cambridge Scholars' Publishing, 183–205.

Barich, M. (2009), *Valerius Flaccus Argonautica*, Gambier, OH: XOXOX press.

Bartel, H. (2010), 'Dressing the 'Other', Dressing the 'Self': Clothing in the Medea Dramas of Euripides and Franz Grillparzer', in H. Bartel and A. Simon (eds), *Unbinding Medea: Interdisciplinary Approaches to a Classical Myth from Antiquity to the 21st century*, London: Legenda, 161–75.

Bartel, H. and Simon, A. (eds) (2010), *Unbinding Medea: Interdisciplinary Approaches to a Classical Myth from Antiquity to the 21st Century*, London: Legenda.

Bécache, S. (1982), 'Medée', *Revue Française de Psychanalyse*, 46: 773–93.

Bernal, M. (1987), *Black Athena: The Afroasiatic Roots of Classical Civilisation*, London: Free Association.

Beye, C. R. (1969), 'Jason as love-hero in Apollonius' Argonautica', *GRBS*, 10: 31–55.

Biggs, T. and Blum, J. (eds) (2019), *The Epic Journey in Greek and Roman Literature*, Cambridge: Cambridge University Press.

Blanshard, A. and Shahabudin, K. (2011), *Classics on Screen: Ancient Greece and Rome on Film*, London: Bristol Classical Press.

230

Botchorishvili, L. (1946), 'Okromtchedloba svanetshi', *SANG*, 7: 283–9.

Bradman, T. and Ross, T. (2004), *Jason and the Voyage to the Edge of the World*, Orchard Books: London.

Braswell, B. K. (1988), *A Commentary on the Fourth Pythian Ode of Pindar*, Berlin: De Gruyter.

Braund, D. (1994), *Georgia in Antiquity: A History of Caucasus and Transcaucasian Iberia*, Oxford: Oxford University Press.

Brelich, A. (1955–7), 'Les monosandales', *Clio*, 9: 469–84.

Brooks, F. (1997), *Jason and the Argonauts*, London: Usborne.

Buckley, E. (2013), 'Seeing the *Medea*: Epiphany and *Anagnorisis* in Valerius Flaccus' *Argonautica*', in H. V. Lovatt and C. Vout (eds), *Epic Visions*, Cambridge: 78–98.

Burkert, W. (1979), *Structure and History in Greek Mythology and Ritual*, Berkeley: University of California Press.

Butler, C. (2018), *Literary Studies Deconstructed: A Polemic*, London: Palgrave Pivot.

Buxton, R. (2010), 'How Medea Moves: Versions of a Myth in Apollonius and Elsewhere', in H. Bartel and A. Simon (eds), *Unbinding Medea: Interdisciplinary Approaches to a Classical Myth from Antiquity to the 21st Century*, Abingdon: Legenda and Routledge, 25–38.

Byrd, R. (2016), *Jason and the Argonauts*, New York: Dial Books.

Cameron, A. (2004), *Greek Mythography in the Roman World*, Oxford: Oxford University Press.

Carne-Ross, D. S. (1973), 'Epic Overreach', *New York Review of Books*.

Castelletti, C. (2012), 'Why is Jason Climbing the Dragon? A Hidden Catasterism in Valerius Flaccus' Argonautica 8', *ICS*, 37: 141–65.

Catran, K. (2000), *Voyage with Jason*, Melbourne: Lothian.

Cavalli, *Il Giasone* (2012), [opera DVD] Cond. Federico Maria Sardelli, Dir. Mariame Clément, Austria: Dynamic SRL.

Chaniotis, A. (2003), 'The Divinity of Hellenistic Rulers', in A. Erskine (ed.) *A Companion to the Hellenistic World*, Malden MA: Blackwell, 431–46.

Clauss, J. J. (1993), *The Best of the Argonauts: The Redefinition of the Epic Hero in Book 1 of Apollonius' Argonautica*, Berkeley: University of California Press.

Clauss, J. J. and Johnston, S. I. (eds) (1997), *Medea: Essays on Medea in Myth, Literature, Philosophy and Art*, Princeton: Princeton University Press.

Cohen, J. J. (1997), 'Monster Culture (Seven Theses)', in J. J. Cohen (ed.) *Monster Theory: Reading Culture*, Minneapolis: University of Minnesota Press, 3–25.

Colavito, J. (2011a), *Golden Fleeced: Lying about Atlantis, Aliens and Argonauts in Greek Myth*, http://www.JasonColavito.com: Jason Colavito.

Colavito, J. (2011b), *The Orphic Argonautica: An English Translation*, Albany, New York: Jason Colavito.

Colavito, J. (2014), *Jason and the Argonauts through the Ages*, Jefferson, NC: McFarland.

Colum, P. (1921), *The Golden Fleece and the Heroes who Lived Before Achilles*, New York: Palgrave Macmillan.

Conte, G. B. (1986), *The Rhetoric of Imitation: Genre and Poetic Memory in Virgil and other Latin Poets*, Ithaca: Cornell University Press.

Cooke, P. (2008), 'Gustave Moreau and the Reinvention of History Painting', *The Art Bulletin*, 90: 394–416.

Courtney, E. (1993), *The Fragmentary Latin Poets*, Oxford: Oxford University Press.

Cowan, R. (2014), 'My Family and Other Enemies: Argonautic Antagonists and Valerian Villains', in M. Heerink and G. Manuwald (eds), *Brill's Companion to Valerius Flaccus*, Leiden: Brill, 229–48.

Csapo, E. (2005), *Theories of Mythology*, Malden, MA: Wiley Blackwell.

Currie, B. (2005), *Pindar and the Cult of Heroes*, Oxford: Oxford University Press.

Cusset, C. (2004), 'Les "Argonautiques" d'Apollonios de Rhodes comme itinéraire à travers la sauvagerie: d'Homère à Alexandrie, en passant par Hérodote et Xénophon ou comment l'adresse au lecteur supplée à l'insouciance de Jason', in M.-C. Charpentier (ed.) *Les espaces du sauvage dans le monde antique: approches et définitions*, Paris: Les Belles Lettres, 31–52.

D'Amelio, M. E. (2011), 'Hercules, Politics and Movies', in M. G. Cornelius (ed.), *Of Muscles and Men: Essays on the Sword and Sandal Film*, Jefferson, NC: McFarland and Co., 15–27.

Dickie, M. (1990), 'Talos bewitched: magic, atomic theory and paradoxography in Apollonius Argonautica 4.1638–88', *Proceedings of the Leeds International Latin Seminar*, 6: 267–96.

Dickinson, E. (2012), *Complete Works*, Hastings: Delphi Classics.

Diel, P. (1966), *Le symbolisme dans la mythologie grecque*, Paris: Payot.

Divjak, A. (2018), 'The Argonaut Legend and the Exploitation of its Tourism Potential in the Municipality of Vrhnika, Slovenia', *Quaestus*, 12: n.p.

Dominguez, F. A. (1979), *The Medieval Argonautica*, Potomac, MD: Porrua Turanzas.

Dover, K. J. (1978), *Greek Homosexuality*, London: Duckworth.

Dover, K. J. (2016), *Greek Homosexuality, with Forewords by Stephen Halliwell, Mark Masterson and James Robson*, London: Bloomsbury.

Dowden, K. (1996), 'Review: Jason and Medea', *Classical Review*, 46: 289–91.

Dräger, P. (1993), *Argo Pasimelousa. Der Argonautenmythos in der griechischen und römischen Literatur*, Stuttgart: Franz Steiner Verlag.

Du Bois, W. E. B. (1911), *The Quest of the Silver Fleece: A Novel*, Chicago: A. C. McClurg.

Eastlake, L. (2019), *Ancient Rome and Victorian Masculinity*, Oxford: Oxford University Press.

Eidinow, E. (2016), *Envy, Poison and Death: Women on Trial in Classical Athens*, Oxford: Oxford University Press.

Eidinow, E. (2019), 'Social Knowledge and Spiritual Insecurity: Identifying "Witchcraft" in Classical Greek Communities', *Magic, Ritual and Witchcraft*, 14: 62–85.

Eliade, M. (1959), *Initiations, rites, sociétés secrètes*, Paris: Gallimard.

Endsjø, D. Ø. (1997), 'Placing the Unplaceable: The Making of Apollonius' Argonautic Geography', *GRBS*, 38: 373–85.

Evslin, B. (1986), *Jason and the Argonauts*, New York: Morrow.

Fantuzzi, M. and Hunter, R. (2005), *Tradition and Innovation in Hellenistic Poetry*, Cambridge: Cambridge University Press.

Fear, A. T. (1992), 'The Golden Sheep of Roman Andalucia', *Agricultural History Review*, 40: 151–5.

Feeney, D. C. (1986), 'Following after Hercules, in Virgil and Apollonius', *Proceedings of the Virgil Society*, 18: 47–85.

Feeney, D. C. (1991), *The Gods in Epic*, Oxford: Oxford University Press.

Ferris, D. S. (2000), *Silent Urns: Romanticism, Hellenism, Modernity*, Stanford, CA: Stanford University Press.

Finkmann, S. (2015), 'Polyxo and the Lemnian Episode – An Inter- and Intratextual Study of Apollonius Rhodius, Valerius Flaccus, and Statius', *Dictynna*, 12: put online 28 January 2016, consulted 6 August 2017: http://dictynna.revues.org/1135

Fontenrose, J. (1959), *Python: A Study of Delphic Myth and its Origins*, Berkeley: University of California Press.

Forbes, H. A. (2007), *Meaning and Identity in a Greek Landscape: An Archaeological Ethnography*, Cambridge: Cambridge University Press.

Forchhammer, P. (1837), *Hellenika. Griechenland im neue das alte*, Berlin: Nicolaische buchhandlung.

Fowler, R. (2000), *Early Greek Mythography*, Oxford: Oxford University Press.

Fowler, R. (2017), 'What's in a myth?', *Classical Association Presidential Address*, 1–10.

Frazer, J. G. (1906–15), *The Golden Bough*, London: Macmillan.

Fucecchi, M. (1997), *La teichoscopia e l'innamoramento di Medea: Saggio di commento a Valerio Flacco Argonautiche 6,427–760*, Pisa: ETS.

Fuller, C. L. (2004), *A Woman Scorn'd: Medea and Betrayal*, Diss., Union Institute and University.

Galli, D. (2014), 'Dionysius Scytobrachion's *Argonautica* and Valerius', in A. Augoustakis (ed.) *Flavian Poetry and its Greek Past*, Leiden: E. J. Brill, 137–52.

Gantz, T. (1993), *Early Greek Myth: A Guide to Literary and Artistic Sources*, Baltimore: Johns Hopkins University Press.

Gardner, J. (1973), *Jason and Medeia*, New York: Alfred A. Knopf.

Garland, R. (2014), *Wandering Greeks: The Ancient Greek Diaspora from the Age of Homer to the Death of Alexander the Great*, Princeton: Princeton University Press.

Gibbon, E. (1777), *History of the Decline and Fall of the Roman Empire*, London: W. Strahan and T. Cadell.

Gibson, B. (2004), 'The repetitions of Hypsipyle', in M. Gale (ed.) *Latin Epic and Didactic Poetry*, Swansea: Classical Press of Wales, 149–80.

Girard, R. (2013 [1977]), *Violence and the Sacred*, London: Bloomsbury.

Gloyn, E. (2019), *Tracking Classical Monsters in Popular Culture*, London: Bloomsbury.

Goldhill, S. (2007), 'The Art of Reception: J.W. Waterhouse and the Painting of Desire in Victorian Britain', *Ramus*, 36: 143–86.

Göpel, E. (1957), *Max Beckmann: Die Argonauten, ein Triptychen*, Stuttgart: Reclam Verlag.

Graves, R. (1944), *The Golden Fleece*, London: Hutchinson.

Graves, R. (1955), *The Greek Myths*, London: Penguin.

Green, P. (1997), *The Argonautika*, Berkeley: University of California Press.

Greenwood, E. (2010), *Afro-Greeks: Dialogues between Anglophone Caribbean literature and Classics in the Twentieth Century*, Oxford: Oxford University Press.

Grillparzer, F. (1995), *Das goldene Vliess*, Stuttgart: Reclam.

Grillparzer, F. (2014), *Selbstbiographie*, Berlin: J. G. Hoof Verlag.

Gunderson, J. and Takvorian, N. (2012), *Jason and the Argonauts*, London: Raintree.

Haarmann, H. (2014), 'Ethnicity and Language in the Ancient Mediterranean', in J. McInerney (ed.) *A Companion to Ethnicity in the Ancient Mediterranean*, Malden, MA: Blackwell, 17–33.

Halberstam, J. (1995), *Skin Shows: Gothic Horror and the Technology of Monsters*, Durham, NC: Duke University Press.

Hall, E. (2008), *The Return of Ulysses: A Cultural History of Homer's Odyssey*, London: I. B. Tauris.

Hall, E., Macintosh, F. and Taplin, O. (eds) (2000), *Medea in performance: 1500–2000*, Oxford: Oxford University Press.

Hall, J. M. (1997), *Ethnic Identity in Greek Antiquity*, Cambridge: Cambridge University Press.

Hamel, G. (1995), 'Taking the Argo to Nineveh: Jonah and Jason in a Mediterranean Context', *Judaism*, 44: 341–59.

Harder, A. (1994), 'Travel descriptions in the Argonautica of Apollonius Rhodius', in Z. Von Martels (ed.) *Travel Fact and Travel Fiction*, Leiden: Brill, 16–29.

Hardie, P. (1986), *Virgil's Aeneid: Cosmos and Imperium*, Oxford: Clarendon Press.

Hardie, P. (1993), *The Epic Successors of Virgil*, Cambridge: Cambridge University Press.

Hardie, P. (2002), *Ovid's Poetics of Illusion*, Cambridge: Cambridge University Press.

Hardie, P. (ed.) (2009), *Paradox and the Marvellous in Augustan Literature and Culture*, Oxford: Oxford University Press.

Hardie, P. (2014), *The Last Trojan Hero: A Cultural History of Virgil's Aeneid*, London: I. B. Tauris.

Hardwick, L. and Stray, C. (eds) (2008), *A Companion to Classical Receptions*, Malden, MA: Blackwell.

Harmon, W. (2006), *A Handbook to Literature*, Upper Saddle River, NJ: Prentice Hall.

Harrison, J. (1924), *Mythology*, London: Harrap.

Harryhausen, R. and Dalton, T. (2003), *Ray Harryhausen: An Animated Life. Adventures in Fantasy*, London: Aurum Press.

Harryhausen, R. and Dalton, T. (2005), *The Art of Ray Harryhausen*, London: Aurum Press.

Hart, K. (1986), 'Heads or Tails? Two sides of the coin', *Man*, 21: 637–56.

Hauser, E. ([2017] 2018), *For the Winner*, London: Black Swan.

Hawes, G. (2017), *Myths on the Map: The Storied Landscapes of Ancient Greece*, Oxford: Oxford University Press.

Hawthorne, N. (1950), *Tanglewood Tales*, London: Dent.

Heerink, M. (2010), *Echoing Hylas: Metapoetics in Hellenistic and Roman Poetry*, Leiden: Faculty of Humanities, Leiden University.

Heerink, M. (2014), 'Valerius Flaccus, Virgil and the Poetics of Ekphrasis', in M. Heerink and G. Manuwald (eds), *Brill's Companion to Valerius Flaccus*, Leiden: E. J. Brill, 72–95.

Heerink, M. and Manuwald, G. (2014), 'Introduction', in M. Heerink and G. Manuwald (eds), *Brill's Companion to Valerius Flaccus*, Leiden: E. J. Brill, 1–6.

Heller, W. (2013), 'Hypsipyle, Medea and the Ovidian Imagination: Taming the Epic Hero in Cavalli's *Giasone*', in E. Rosand (ed.) *Readying Cavalli's Operas for the Stage: Manuscript, Edition, Production*, London: Routledge, 167–86.

Henderson, J. (2005), *The triumph of art at Thorvaldsens Museum : 'Løve' in Copenhagen*, Copenhagen: Museum Tusculanum Press, University of Copenhagen.

Hershkowitz, D. (1998), *Valerius Flaccus' Argonautica: Abbreviated Voyages in Silver Latin Epic*, Oxford: Clarendon Press.

Hind, C. L. (1907), *Turner's Golden Visions*, London: T. C. and E. C. Jack.

Hodkinson, O. and Lovatt, H. V. (eds) (2018), *Classical Reception and Children's Literature: Greece, Rome and Childhood Transformation*, London: I. B. Tauris.

Hoena, B. and Estudio Haus (2015), [Comic] *Jason and the Argonauts*, Minnesota: Capstone.

Hoena, B., Takvorian, N. and Nathan, J. (2017), *Jason, the Argonauts and the Golden Fleece*, Minnesota: Capstone.

Holdstock, R. L. (2001), *Celtika*, London: Simon and Schuster.

Holdstock, R. L. (2002), *The Iron Grail*, London: Simon and Schuster.

Holdstock, R. L. (2006), *The Broken Kings*, London: Gollancz.

Hunter, R. L. (1988), '"Short on heroics": Jason in the *Argonautica*', CQ, 38: 436–53.

Hunter, R. L. (ed.) (1989), *Argonautica Book 3*, Cambridge: Cambridge University Press.

Hunter, R. L. (1993a), *Jason and the Golden Fleece*, Oxford: Oxford University Press.

Hunter, R. L. (1993b), *The Argonautica of Apollonius*, Cambridge: Cambridge University Press.

Hunter, R. L. (1996), *Theocritus and the Archaeology of Greek Poetry*, Cambridge: Cambridge University Press.

Hunter, R. L. (1999), *Theocritus: A Selection*, Cambridge: Cambridge University Press.

Hunter, R. L. (2015), *Apollonius of Rhodes Argonautica Book IV*, Cambridge: Cambridge University Press.

Huxley, G. L. (1969), *Greek Epic Poetry from Eumelos to Panyassis*, London: Faber.

I Giganti della Tessaglia (1960), [Film] Dir. Riccardo Freda, Italy and France: Alexandra and Lyre.

Ihm, S. (2015), 'Robert Graves's The Greek Myths and Matriarchy', in A. G. G. Gibson (ed.) *Robert Graves and the Classical Tradition*, Oxford: Oxford University Press, 165–80.

Ingleheart, J. (2015), 'Greek Love at Rome: Propertius 1.20 and the Reception of Hellenistic Verse', *Eugesta*, 5: 124–53.

Isaac, B. (2004), *The Invention of Racism in Classical Antiquity*, Princeton: Princeton University Press.

Jackson, S. B. (1992), 'Apollonius' Jason: Human Being in an Epic Scenario', *Greece and Rome*, 39: 155–62.

James, S. L. and Dillon, S. (eds.) (2012), *A Companion to Women in the Ancient World*, Malden, MA: Wiley Blackwell.

Jason and the Argonauts (1963), [Film] Dir. Don Chaffey, USA: Columbia Pictures.

Jason and the Argonauts (2000), [Mini-series] Dir. Nick Willing. USA: Hallmark.

Jeffrey, G. and Verma, D. (2013), *Jason and the Argonauts*, New York: Gareth Stevens Publishing.

Kefalidou, E. (2008), 'The Argonauts Krater in the Archaeological Museum of Thessaloniki', *American Journal of Archaeology*, 112: 617–24.

Keith, A. M. (2000), *Engendering Rome: Women in Latin Epic*, Cambridge: Cambridge University Press.

Keith, A. M. (2019), 'Women's Travels in the *Aeneid*', in J. Blum and T. Biggs (eds), *The Epic Journey in Greek and Roman Literature*, New York: Cambridge University Press, 130–44.

Kennedy, R. F., Roy, C. S. and Goldman, M. L. (2013), *Race and Ethnicity in the Classical World: An Anthology of Primary Sources in Translation*, Indianapolis: Hackett.

Kermode, H. S. (1912), 'The Classical Sources of Morris's Life and Death of Jason', in *Primitiae: Essays in English Literature by Students of the University of Liverpool*, Liverpool; London: University of Liverpool Press, 158–82.

Kessler, C. S. (1970), *Max Beckmann's Triptychs*, Cambridge, MA: Bellknap Press.

Kingsley, C. (1912), *The Heroes or Greek Fairy Tales for my Children*, London: Riccardi Press.

Kirchoff, A. (1869), *Der Composition der Odyssee*, Berlin: Wilhelm-Hertz.

Klaver, J. M. I. (2006), *The Apostle of the Flesh: A Critical Life of Charles Kingsley*, Leiden: Brill.

Kneupper, K. (2016), *Argonauts*, CreateSpace: Kevin Kneupper.

Knight, V. H. (1995), *The Renewal of Epic: Responses to Homer in the Argonautica of Apollonius*, Leiden: E. J. Brill.

Kristeva, J. (1982), *Powers of Horror*, New York: Columbia University Press.

Kvistad, I. (2010), 'Cultural Imperialsim and Infanticide in Pasolini's *Medea*', in H. Bartel and A. Simon (eds), *Unbinding Medea: Interdisciplinary Approaches to a Classical Myth from Antiquity to the 21st Century*, London: Legenda, 224–37.

Kyriakou, P. (1995), *Homeric Hapax Legomena in the Argonautica of Apollonius: A Literary Study*, Stuttgart: Franz Steiner.

Lacan, J. and Miller, J.-A. (1978), *The Four Fundamental Concepts of Psychoanalysis*, New York: Norton.

Lackner, S. (1991), *Max Beckmann*, London: Thames and Hudson.

Lancelyn Green, R. (1958), *Tales of the Greek Heroes*, London: Penguin.

Langerwerf, L. and Ryan, C. (eds) (2010), *Zero to Hero, Hero to Zero: In Search of the Classical Hero*, Newcastle upon Tyne: Cambridge Scholars Press.

Lawall, G. (1966), 'Apollonius' *Argonautica*: Jason as anti-hero', *YCS*, 19: 121–69.

Le Fatiche di Ercole (1958), [Film] Dir. Pietro Francisci, Italy: Lux Film.

Lear, A. (2014), 'Ancient Pederasty: An Introduction', in T. Hubbard (ed.) *A Companion to Greek and Roman Sexualities*, Malden, MA: Blsckwell, 102–27.

Leigh, M. (2010), 'Boxing and sacrifice: Apollonius, Vergil, and Valerius', *HSCPh*, 105: 117–55.

Leonard, J. (2000), '"At What Vantage-Point": Cultural Relativism and the Novels of Robert Graves', in I. Firla (ed.) *Robert Graves's Historical Novels*, Berlin: Peter Lang, 101–24.

Levinas, E. (1999), *Alterity and Transcendence*, London: Athlone Press.

Levy, D. (2018), *The Cost of Living*, London: Penguin.

Littlewood, A. R. (1968), 'The Symbolism of the Apple in Greek and Roman Literature', *HSCPh*, 72: 147–81.

Llewellyn-Jones, L. (2013), 'Ray Harryhausen and the other Gods: Greek Divinity in *Jason and the Argonauts* and *Clash of the Titans*', *New Voices in Classical Reception Studies*, Conference Proceedings 1: 3–20.

Loraux, N. (1990), 'Herakles: the super-male and the feminine', in D. M. Halperin, J. J. Winkler and F. I. Zeitlin (eds), *Before Sexuality: The Construction of Erotic Experience in the Ancient Greek World*, Princeton: Princeton University Press, 21–52.

Lordkipanidze, O. (2001), 'The Golden Fleece: Myth, Euhemeristic Explanation and Archaeology', *Oxford Journal of Archaeology*, 20: 1–38.

Lovatt, H. V. (2005), *Statius and Epic Games: Sport, Politics and Poetics in the Thebaid*, Cambridge: Cambridge University Press.

Lovatt, H. V. (2009), 'Gutting the Argonautica? How to Make Jason and the Argonauts Suitable for Children', in D. Lowe and K. Shahabudin (eds), *Classics for All: Reworking Antiquity in Mass Culture*, Newcastle: Cambridge Scholars Press, 17–38.

Lovatt, H. V. (2013), *The Epic Gaze: Vision, Gender and Narrative in Ancient Epic*, Cambridge: Cambridge University Press.

Lovatt, H. V. (2014), 'Teamwork, Leadership and Group Dynamics in Valerius Flaccus' Argonautica', in M. Heerink and G. Manuwald (eds), *Brill's Companion to Valerius Flaccus*, Leiden: E. J. Brill, 211–28.

Lovatt, H. V. (2018), 'Apollonius Rhodius *Argonautica* 4 and The Epic Gaze: There and Back Again', in A. Kampakoglou and A. Novokhatko (eds), *Gaze, Vision and Visuality in Ancient Greek Literature*, Berlin: De Gruyter, 88–112.

Lovatt, H. V. (2020), 'Didactic Heroes: Masculinity, Sexuality and Exploration in the Argonaut Story of Kingsley's *The Heroes*', in R. Bryant Davies and B. Gribling (eds), *Pasts at Play: Childhood Encounters with History in British Culture, 1750-1914*, Manchester: Manchester University Press, 71–95.

Lowe, D. and Shahabudin, K. (eds) (2009), *Classics for All: Reworking Antiquity in Mass Culture*, Newcastle: Cambridge Scholars Press.

Lowe, N. (1986), 'The Well-Tempered Plot Device', *Ansible*, 46.

Mackie, C. J. (2001), 'The Earliest Jason: What's in a Name?', *Greece and Rome*, 48: 1–17.

Malam, J. and Antram, D. (2005), *Jason and the Argonauts*, Brighton: Book House.

Manley, L. (2013), 'Shakespeare and the Golden Fleece', in E. Rosand (ed.) *Readying Cavalli's Operas for the Stage: Manuscript, Edition, Production*, London: Routledge, 187–200.

Manuwald, G. (2002), 'The Argonauts in Colchis – The Myth in Valerius Flaccus and Corneille – "Argonautica" or Jason and Medea in Jupiter's "World Plan"', *Antike Und Abendland*, 48: 43–57.

Manuwald, G. (2004), 'Hesione und der "Weltenplan" in Valerius Flaccus' Argonautica', in F. Spaltenstein (ed.) *Untersuchungen zu den Argonautica des Valerius Flaccus. Ratis omnia vincet III*, Munich: C. H. Beck, 145–62.

Martin, E. (2011), 'Intertextuality: An introduction', *The Comparatist*, 35: 148–51.

Martindale, C. (1993), *Redeeming the Text: Latin Poetry and the Hermeneutics of Reception*, Cambridge: Cambridge University Press.

Maurice, L. (ed.) (2015), *The Reception of Greece and Rome in Children's Literature: Heroes and Eagles*, Leiden: E. J. Brill.

Mayor, A. (2014), *The Amazons: Lives and Legends of Warrior Women across the Ancient World*, Princeton: Princeton University Press.

Mayor, A. (2018), *Gods and Robots: Myths, Machines and Ancient Dreams of Technology*, Princeton: Princeton University Press.

McCoskey, D. E. (2012), *Race: Antiquity and its Legacy*, Oxford: Oxford University Press.

Medea (1969), [Film] Dir. Pier Paolo Pasolini, Italy: San Marco.

Mench, M. D. (1968), *The Argonautic Tradition in William Morris's The Life and Death of Jason: A Study in Poetic Eclecticism*, Diss., Yale University.

Meyer, D. (2001), 'Apollonius as a Hellenistic Geographer', in T. D. Papanghelis (ed.) *A Companion to Apollonius Rhodius*, Leiden: Brill, 217–36.

Mimoso-Ruiz, D. (1982), *Médée Antique et Moderne: Aspects Rituels et Socio-Politiques d'un Mythe*, Paris: Editions Ophrys.

Mimoso-Ruiz, D. (1996), 'Le mythe de Médée au cinéma: l'incandescence de la violence à l'image', *PALLAS*, 45: 251–68.

Moi, T. (ed.) (1986), *The Kristeva Reader*, Oxford: Blackwell.

Monaghan, M. (2002), *Unfinished business in the Argonautica of Valerius Flaccus*, Diss., Stanford University

Moreau, A. (1994), *Le Mythe de Jason et Médée: Le va-nu-pied et la sorcière*, Paris: Les Belles Lettres.

Mori, A. (2008), *The Politics of Apollonius Rhodius' Argonautica*, Cambridge: Cambridge University Press.

Morris, W. (1910), *The Collected Works, with Introductions by His Daughter May Morris*, London: Longmans.

Morris, W. (n.d.) 'The Life and Death of Jason', in *The William Morris Archive*, ed. Florence Boos. Available online: http://morrisedition.lib.uiowa.edu/jason-w-images.html (accessed 17 August 2019).

Morrison, A. D. (2019), *Apollonius Rhodius, Herodotus and Historiography*, Cambridge: Cambridge University Press.

Morse, R. (1983), 'Problems of Early Fiction: Raoul Lefèvre's "Histoire de Jason"', *Modern Language Review*, 78: 34–45.

Morse, R. (1996), *The Medieval Medea*, Cambridge: D. S. Brewer.

Mossman, J. M. (2011), *Euripides. Medea. Introduction, Translation and Commentary*, Oxford: Aris and Phillips.

Mozley, J. H. (1934), *Valerius Flaccus Argonautica*, Cambridge, MA: Loeb Classical Library.

Müller, F. M. (1867), *Chips from a German Workshop II*, New York: Charles Scribnerogden.

Müller, F. M. (1885), 'Solar Myths', *Nineteenth Century*, 18: 900–22.

Munro, J. (1913), *The History of Jason*, London: Kegan Paul.

Munson, R. V. (2001), *Telling Wonders: Ethnographic and Political Discourse in the Work of Herodotus*, Ann Arbor: Michigan University Press.

Murnaghan, S. and Roberts, D. H. (2017), 'Myth Collections for Children', in V. Zajko and H. Hoyle (eds), *A Handbook to the Reception of Classical Mythology*, Malden, MA: Blackwell, 87–104.

Murnaghan, S. and Roberts, D. H. (2018), *Childhood and the Classics: Britain and America, 1850–1965*, Oxford: Oxford University Press.

Murray, J. (2014), 'Anchored in time: The date in Apollonius' *Argonautica*', in A. Harder, R. F. Regtuit and G. C. Wakker (eds), *Hellenistic Poetry in Context*, Leuven: Peeters, 247–84.

Murray, J. (2019), 'W.E.B. Du Bois' The Quest of the Silver Fleece: The Education of Black Medea', *TAPhA*, 149: 143–62.

Myers, K. S. (1996), 'The Poet and the Procuress: The Lena in Latin Love Elegy', *JRS*, 86: 1–21.

Naden, C. J. (1981), *Jason and the Golden Fleece*, Mahwah, NJ: Troll Associates.

Nagy, G. (1979), *The Best of the Achaeans: Concepts of the Hero in Archaic Greek Poetry*, Baltimore: Johns Hopkins University Press.

Nelis, D. (1991), 'Iphias: Apollonius Rhodius, Argonautica 1.311–16', *CQ*, 41: 96–105.

Nelis, D. (2001), *Vergil's Aeneid and the Argonautica of Apollonius Rhodius*, Chippenham, Wiltshire: Francis Cairns.

Newby, Z. (2016), *Greek Myths in Roman Art and Culture: Imagery, Values and Identity 50BC to AD 250*, Cambridge: Cambridge University Press.

Newlands, C. (1997), 'The Metamorphosis of Ovid's Medea', in J. J. Clauss and S. I. Johnston (eds), *Medea: Essays on Medea in Myth, Literature, Philosophy and Art*, Princeton: Princeton University Press, 178–210.

Newman, J. K. (2008), 'The golden fleece. Imperial dream', in T. Papanghelis and A. Rengakos (eds), *Brill's Companion to Apollonius Rhodius*, Leiden: E. J. Brill, 413–44.

Nisetich, F. J. (1980), *Pindar's Victory Songs*, Baltimore: Johns Hopkins University Press.

O'Brien, D. (2014), *Classical Masculinity and the Spectacular Body on Film: The Mighty Sons of Hercules*, New York: Palgrave Macmillan.

Oakley, J. (2007), 'The Departure of the Argonauts on the Dinos Painter's Bell Krater in Gela', *Hesperia*, 76: 347–57.

Ogden, D. (2002), *Magic, Witchcraft and Ghosts in the Greek and Roman Worlds: A Sourcebook*, Oxford: Oxford University Press.

Orrells, D., Bhambra, G. K. and Roynon, T. (eds) (2011), *African Athena: New Agendas*, Oxford: Oxford University Press.

Orzeszkowa, E. ([1900] 1901), *Argonauci (The Argonauts)*, Trans. J. Curtis, New York: Scribner's.

Papanghelis, T. and Rengakos, A. (eds) (2008), *Brill's Companion to Apollonius*, Leiden: E. J. Brill.

Patterson, L. E. (2017), 'Myth as Evidence in Strabo', in D. Dueck (ed.) *The Routledge Companion to Strabo*, London: Routledge, 276–93.

Paul, J. (2013), *Film and the Classical Epic Tradition*, Oxford: Oxford University Press.

Perlot, J.-N. (1985), *Gold Seeker: Adventures of a Belgian Argonaut during the Gold Rush Years*, New Haven: Yale University Press.

Pirotta, S. and Lewis, J. (2008), *First Greek Myths: Jason and the Golden Fleece*, London: Orchard Books.

Pomeroy, S. B. (1990), *Women in Hellenistic Egypt from Alexander to Cleopatra*, Detroit: Wayne State University Press.

Poochigian, A. (2014), *Apollonius of Rhodes: Jason and the Argonauts*, New York: Penguin.

Prettejohn, E. (2010), 'Medea, Frederick Sandys and the Aesthetic Moment', in H. Bartel and A. Simon (eds), *Unbinding Medea: Interdisciplinary Approaches to a Classical Myth from Antiquity to the 21st Century*, Abingdon, Oxford: Legenda and Routledge, 94–112.

Purves, A. C. (2010), *Space and Time in Ancient Greek Narrative*, Cambridge: Cambridge University Press.

Putnam, M. C. J. (ed.) (2004), *Maffeo Vegio: Short Epics*, Cambridge, MA: Harvard University Press.

Rewald, S. (2016), *Max Beckmann in New York*, New Haven: Yale University Press.

Richards, F. (2015), 'Dangerous Creatures': Selected Children's Versions of Homer's Odyssey in English 1699–2014, Diss., University of Durham.

Richardson, E. (ed.) (2019), *Classics in Extremis: The Edges of Classical Reception*, London: Bloomsbury Academic.

Rieu, E. V. (1959) *Apollonius of Rhodes: The Voyage of the Argo*, Harmondsworth: Penguin.

Rink, H. (1875), *Tales and Traditions of the Eskimo*, Edinburgh: Blackwood.

Riordan, J. and Cockcroft, J. (2003), *Jason and the Golden Fleece*, London: Frances Lincoln.

Rise of the Argonauts (2007), [Computer game] UK: Codemasters.

Rosand, E. (ed.) (2013), *Readying Cavalli's Operas for the Stage: Manuscript, Edition, Production*, London: Routledge.

Ruthner, C. (2007), 'Argonaut und Tourist: Repräsentationen der Fremde(n) bei Franz Grillparzer', in M. Henn, C. Ruthner and R. Whitinger (eds), *Aneignungen, Entfremdungen: The Austrian Playwright Franz Grillparzer (1791–1872)*, New York: Peter Lang, 49–68.

Said, E. W. (1978), *Orientalism*, London: Routledge.

Sawyer, R. ([1990] 2016), *Golden Fleece*, Mississauga: SFwriter.com.

Schulze, H. (2006), 'Dramaturgical Setting, Representation of Characters, and the Mythological Basis in Giacinto Andrea Cicognini's and Francesco Cavalli's *Giasone*', in M. Kokole, B. Murove and M. Š. Kos (eds), *Mediterranean Myths from the Classical Antiquity to the Eighteenth Century*, Ljubljana: ZRC-SAZU, 119–30.

Seaton, R. C. (1912), *Apollonius Rhodius: The Argonautica*, Cambridge, MA: Harvard University Press.

Segal, C. (1986), *Pindar's Mythmaking: The Fourth Pythian Ode*, Princeton: Princeton University Press.

Seraillier, I. (1963), *The Clashing Rocks*, Oxford: Oxford University Press.

Severin, T. (1985), *The Jason Voyage: The Quest for the Golden Fleece*, London: Hutchinson.

Seymour-Smith, M. (1995), *Robert Graves: His Life and Work*, London: Bloomsbury.

Sirola, R. (2004), 'The Myth of Medea from the Point of View of Psychoanalysis', *Scandinavian Psychoanalytic Review*, 27: 94–104.

Skempis, M. and Ziogas, I. (eds) (2014), *Geography, Topography, Landscape: Configurations of Space in Greek and Roman Epic*, Berlin: De Gruyter.

Skinner, J. (2012), *The Invention of Greek Ethnography: From Homer to Herodotus*, Oxford: Oxford University Press.

Slavitt, D. (1998), *Broken Columns*, Philadelphia: University of Pennsylvania Press.

Smith, E. L. (2002), *Evelyn Pickering De Morgan and the Allegorical Body*, Madison, NJ: Farleigh Dickinson University Press.

Smith, G. J. and Smith, A. J. (1992), 'Jason's Golden Fleece', *Oxford Journal of Archaeology*, 11: 119–20.

Solomon, S. (1969), *Franz Grillparzer: Plays on Classic Themes*, New York: Random House.

Sourvinou-Inwood, C. (2005), *Hylas, The Nymphs, Dionysos and Others*, Stockholm: Paul A. Astroms Forlag.

Spelman, H. (2018), *Pindar and the Poetics of Permanence*, Oxford: Oxford University Press.

Spence, S. (2010), *The Image of Jason in Early Greek Myth: An Examination of Iconographical and Literary Evidence of the Myth of Jason up till the end of the Fifth Century BC*, CreateSpace independent publishing platform: Simon Spence.

Spence, S. (2014), *Jason and the Golden Fleece*, Itunes: Early Myth.

Spentzou, E. and Fowler, D. (eds) (2002), *Cultivating the Muse: Struggles for Power and Inspiration in Classical Literature*, Oxford: Oxford University Press.

Stafford, E. (2012), *Herakles*, London: Routledge.

Stafford, E. (2017), 'Hercules' Choice: Virtue, Vice and the Hero of the Twentieth-Century Screen', in E. Almagor and L. Maurice (eds), *The Reception of Ancient Virtues and Vices in Modern Popular Culture*, Leiden: E. J. Brill, 140–66.

Stephens, S. (2003), *Seeing double: Intercultural poetics in Ptolemaic Alexandria*, Berkeley: University of California Press.

Stover, T. (2008), 'The date of Valerius Flaccus' *Argonautica*', *Papers of the Langford Latin Seminar*, 13: 211–29.

Stover, T. (2012), *Epic and Empire in Vespasianic Rome: A New Reading of Valerius Flaccus' Argonautica*, Oxford: Oxford University Press.

Stratton, K. (2007), *Naming the Witch: Magic, Ideology and Stereotype in the Ancient World*, New York: Columbia University Press.

Strootman, R. (2007), *The Hellenistic Royal Court. Court Culture, Ceremonial and Ideology in Greece, Egypt and the Near East, 336–30 bce*, Diss., University of Utrecht.

Tacoma, L. (2016), *Moving Romans: Migration to Rome in the Principate*, Oxford: Oxford University Press.

Taylor-Briggs, P. R. (2014), 'Utere bono tuo feliciter: The Textual Transmission and Manuscript History of Valerius Flaccus' Argonautica', in M. Heerink and G. Manuwald (eds), *Brill's Companion to Valerius Flaccus*, Leiden: E. J. Brill, 9–28.

Tedeschi, G. (2010), *Commento alla Medea di Euripide*, Trieste: Università degli Studi di Trieste.

Thalmann, W. G. (2011), *Apollonius of Rhodes and the Spaces of Hellenism*, Oxford: Oxford University Press.

Thomas, R. (2000), *Herodotus in Context: Ethnography, Science and the Art of Persuasion*, Cambridge: Cambridge University Press.

Treece, H. (1961), *Jason*, London: Sphere.

Truby, J. (2007), *The Anatomy of Story*, New York: Faber and Faber.

Trundle, M. (2016), 'The Spartan *Krypteia*', in G. G. Fagan and W. Riess (eds), *The Topography of Violence in the Greco-Roman World*, Ann Arbor: University of Michigan Press, 60–76.

Tsetskhladze, G. R. (1998), *The Greek colonisation of the Black Sea area: historical interpretation of archaeology*, Stuttgart: Franz Steiner Verlag.

Venuti, L. (ed.) (2000), *The Translation Studies Reader*, London: Routledge.

Vian, F. (1987), *Les Argonautiques Orphiques*, Paris: Budé.

Vidal-Naquet, P. (1986), *The Black Hunter*, Baltimore: Johns Hopkins University Press.

Webb, T. (1993), 'Romantic Hellenism', in S. Curran (ed.) *The Cambridge Companion to British Romanticism*, Cambridge: Cambridge University Press, 148–76.

Weingartz, G. (2010), '"A tunnel full of mirrors": Some Perspectives on Christa Wolf's Medea-Stimmen', *Myth and Symbol*, 6: 15–43.

Weissmann, D. (2017), 'When Austrian Classical Tragedy Goes Intercultural: On the Metrical Simulation of Linguistic Otherness in Franz Grillparzer's *The Golden Fleece*', *Critical Multilingualism Studies*, 5: 52–74.

Werbner, P. (2001), 'The Limits of Cultural Hybridity: On Ritual Monsters, Poetic Licence and Contested Postcolonial Purification', *Journal of the Royal Anthropological Institute*, 7: 133–52.

West, M. L. (2005), 'Odyssey and Argonautica', *Classical Quarterly*, 55: 39–64.

Wetmore, K. (ed.) (2013), *Black Medea: Adaptations for Modern Plays*, Amherst, NY: Cambria Press.

Whitehead, D. and Banerjee, S. (2011), *Jason and the Argonauts*, New Delhi: Campfire.

Whitmarsh, T. (2018), 'Black Achilles.' *Aeon*. Online: https://aeon.co/essays/when-homer-envisioned-achilles-did-he-see-a-black-man (accessed 30 August 2020).

Willis, I. (2017), 'Contemporary Mythography: In the Time of Ancient Gods, Warlords and Kings', in V. Zajko and H. Hoyle (eds), *A Handbook to the Reception of Greek Mythology*, Malden, MA: Blackwell, 105–20.

Wilson, E. (2018), *The Odyssey*, New York: Norton.

Winkler, M. (2009), *Von Iphigenie zu Medea: Semantik und Dramaturgie des Barbarischen bei Goethe und Grillparzer*, Tübingen: Niemeyer.

Winkler, M. M. (ed.) (2007), *Troy: From Homer's Iliad to Hollywood Epic*, Oxford: Blackwell.

Wiseman, T. P. (2004), *The Myths of Rome*, Exeter: University of Exeter Press.

Wolf, C. ([1996] 1998), *Medea*, London: Virago.

Wood, M. (2005), *In Search of Myths and Heroes*, London: BBC Books.

Yarnall, J. (1994), *Transformations of Circe: The History of an Enchantress*, Urbana: University of Illinois Press.

Yolen, J. and Harris, R. J. (2004), *Jason and the Gorgon's Blood*, New York: HarperCollins.

Yomtov, N. and Sandoval, G. (2009), *Jason and the Golden Fleece*, Minneapolis: Stone Arch Books.

Young Hercules (1998–9), [TV series] Creators: Andrew Dettmann, Rob Tapert, Daniel Truly. USA, NZ: MCA Television, Renaissance Pictures.

Young, R. (2001), *Postcolonialism: A Very Short Introduction*, Malden, MA: Blackwell.

Zajko, V. (2015), 'Scholarly Mythopoesis: Robert Graves's The Greek Myths', in A. G. G. Gibson (ed.) *Robert Graves and the Classical Tradition*, Oxford: Oxford University Press, 181–200.

Zajko, V. (2017), 'Introduction', in V. Zajko and H. Hoyle (eds), *A Handbook to the Reception of Classical Mythology*, Malden, MA: Blackwell, 1–12.

Zajko, V. and Hoyle, H. (eds) (2017), *A Handbook to the Reception of Classical Mythology*, Malden, MA: Blackwell.

Zarabouka, S. ([1993] 2004), *Jason and the Golden Fleece*, Los Angeles: Getty.

Zeff, C. ([1982] 2003), *Jason and the Golden Fleece*, London: Usborne.

Zimmerman, M. (2013), *Argonautika: The Voyage of Jason and the Argonauts*, Evanston, IL: Northwestern University Press.

Zissos, A. (1999), 'Allusion and narrative possibility in the Argonautica of Valerius Flaccus', *CPh*, 94: 289–301.

Zissos, A. (2006), 'Reception of Valerius Flaccus' *Argonautica*', *IJCT*, 13: 165–85.

Zissos, A. (2014), 'Interpres operis alieni? Giovan Battista Pio's Continuation of Valerius Flaccus' *Argonautica*', in M. Heerink and G. Manuwald (eds), *Brill's Companion to Valerius Flaccus*, Leiden: E. J. Brill, 361–80.

Index